Windows into
The West Wing

ALSO BY PATRICK WEBSTER

*A Wanderer by Trade:
Gender in the Songs
of Bob Dylan* (McFarland, 2019)

*Love and Death in Kubrick:
A Critical Study of the Films
from* Lolita *through* Eyes Wide Shut
(McFarland, 2011)

Windows into *The West Wing*

Theoretical Approaches to an Ideal Presidency

PATRICK WEBSTER

McFarland & Company, Inc., Publishers
Jefferson, North Carolina

LIBRARY OF CONGRESS CATALOGUING-IN-PUBLICATION DATA

Names: Webster, Patrick, 1953– author.
Title: Windows into the West Wing : theoretical approaches to an ideal presidency / Patrick Webster.
Description: Jefferson : McFarland & Company, Inc., Publishers, 2020. | Includes bibliographical references and index.
Identifiers: LCCN 2020009209 | ISBN 9781476680354 (paperback : acid free paper) ∞
ISBN 9781476639369 (ebook)
Subjects: LCSH: West Wing (Television program)
Classification: LCC PN1992.77.W44 W43 2020 | DDC 791.45/72—dc23
LC record available at https://lccn.loc.gov/2020009209

BRITISH LIBRARY CATALOGUING DATA ARE AVAILABLE

ISBN (print) 978-1-4766-8035-4
ISBN (ebook) 978-1-4766-3936-9

© 2020 Patrick Webster. All rights reserved

No part of this book may be reproduced or transmitted in any form or by any means, electronic or mechanical, including photocopying or recording, or by any information storage and retrieval system, without permission in writing from the publisher.

Front cover photograph by Jan Hanus (Shutterstock)

Printed in the United States of America

McFarland & Company, Inc., Publishers
 Box 611, Jefferson, North Carolina 28640
 www.mcfarlandpub.com

Table of Contents

Introduction	1
1. *Dramatis Personae*: The Cast and Casting	5
2. A Mosaic of Quotations: Intertextuality in *The West Wing*	13
3. Historical Fictions: A Parallel Universe	22
4. Death of the Author: Aaron Sorkin as Auteur?	31
5. On a Wing and a Prayer: Bartlet Deconstructs the Old Testament	40
6. Cinematic Television: The *Mise-en-Scène* of *The West Wing*	49
7. The Signifier and the Signified: Structuralist Readings	54
8. This "pitiful exercise": Temporal Rupture in the "Isaac and Ishmael" Episode	67
9. Bourgeois Wing: Marxist Readings	78
10. "The greatest country in the world": Misconstrued Politics	86
11. "It's turtles all the way down": *The West Wing* and Religion	92
12. Playing in the Dark: Racist Discourses	100
13. *Potus Interruptus*: Gender and Queer Theory	109
14. Hollywood MS: The Portrayal of Disabilities	121
15. The Politics of Maryland: *The Wire* and *The West Wing*	128
16. Nostalgia for the Present: Postmodern Readings	135
17. Cellmates in The Hague: Bartlet Flouts International Law	146
18. The Crackpots and These Women: Misogynist Discourses	152
19. Cultural Differences: Postcolonial Readings	162

20. "Education is the silver bullet": Pedagogy in *The West Wing* — 169
21. A Valentine to Washington: Narrative Authenticity — 176
22. "Your father was a prick": Psychoanalytical Readings — 182
23. Unearned Emotion and the "Plaintive Oboe:" W.G. Snuffy Walden's Music to *The West Wing* — 191
24. *Society Must Be Defended*: Poststructuralist Readings — 197

Conclusion — 205
Appendix A. Seasons 1–7: A Synopsis — 211
Appendix B. Episodes 1–155: Broadcast Credits — 215
Appendix C. Directors and Writers — 224
Chapter Notes — 227
Bibliography — 261
Index — 269

Introduction

I begin with a simple premise: *The West Wing* represents one of the most significant cultural texts ever to have appeared on network television, first in the United States and Canada, then in the United Kingdom, and subsequently in other parts of the world. However, there is a counter-argument to put forward: How could such an unquestionably sentimental, overly idealized and ultimately disingenuous television series have succeeded in attaining the aesthetic appeal it achieved? To put this another way, how could a television series that revealed such blatant contradictions in the way we consider America—its values, its aspirations, its behavior in the world—how could such a transparently counterfeit interrogation of the American way of life still hold sway, still manage to convince, still have the power to hold its audience?

This may appear to be a somewhat severe appraisal; but, as will be seen, there is much to criticize, much to interrogate, and even much to disparage within the discursive practices of *The West Wing*. An analysis of such practices reveals inherent contradictions at play within all seven seasons of the show. At times such contradictions seemed astutely veiled, but at times they seemed almost visibly risible, almost as if there may have been a satiric exercise deliberately in play.[1] However, a close reading of the series would intimate that this was not the case. It is perhaps a cliché to suggest Americans lack a sense of irony; but, while this is patently untrue, irony was often absent within *The West Wing*. In this context, it should be noted that this book is neither a vitriolic critique of the series nor a hagiographic eulogy to the supposed genius of Aaron Sorkin; instead it will merely attempt to present a neutral view of both the strengths and weaknesses of an extraordinary television show.

There are many self-evident reasons why the show was such a remarkable television drama and why it was such an aesthetic, critical and commercial success.[2] The primary reason may perhaps be money; in other words, the budget invested within each of the 155 episodes of the show enabled the high production values.[3] In addition, there was Aaron Sorkin's unquestionable ability to create engaging and likeable characters; and there was the rhythm and pacing of the dialogue by Sorkin and the other writers. Further, there was the astute casting, the quality of the ensemble acting, the photography (notably the work of Thomas Del Ruth and Michael Mayers), the set design, the signature use of lighting and so on. Perhaps the only weak element of the show was the soundtrack, the background music provided by W.G. Snuffy Walden; as will be discussed, the musical setting was arguably one of the least innovative aspects of the show. However, in an overall sense, *The West Wing* could reasonably be envisaged as one of *the* key television texts of recent times, and a text fully worthy of critical consideration and attention.

As to the critical response to the show, a review of the published literature has revealed the following array of secondary sources: five academically based monographs[4]; two more commercially based books (Paul Challen's entertaining if deliberately lightweight commentary on the first two seasons and Keith Topping's impressively detailed commentary on Seasons 1–3); two books of scripts from Seasons 1–4; and finally an official companion to Seasons 1–2 of the series. In addition, a search of the literature on the series has revealed a significant number of articles from academic journals, most of them American, together with a small cross-section of academic theses from American and U.K. universities. As to the newspaper and magazine responses of the time, these materials have not been considered in depth, for two practical reasons: first, the extensive and often repetitive nature of much of this material, and second, the difficulty of accessing such sources at a distance of over a decade from publication.[5]

Along with the range of published materials, one of the pleasures of researching *The West Wing* has been the availability of a wealth of information presented by its fan base. Such materials would generally be seen as lacking the credentials of an academically viable resource; however, the quality of material deriving from such sources would appear, at times at least, to negate such a view. The majority of such materials, almost all web-based, have a depth, accuracy and an overarching knowledge of the core text, so much so as to render such sources worthy of inclusion within a scholarly discourse.[6] For example, there are sites offering comprehensive archived press responses, there are sites presenting biographical information of the cast and crew, and there are sites wherein almost every episode of the series has been unofficially transcribed, such transcriptions being relatively accurate and hence valid and helpful for research purposes.[7] The internet may have helped in contributing to what Umberto Eco has referred to as "junk culture"—in other words, an excess of "chatter" that is too expansive to ever fully grasp; on the other hand, especially in the case of *The West Wing*, such materials would seem to possess a manageable, distinctive and constructive value.

In looking at the critical responses to the show, both published and web-based, it would seem that relatively few attempts have been made to view

Introduction 3

it through the prism of cultural theory. This would seem to apply as much to conventional academic publications as it does to online resources; in fact, some websites (albeit relatively difficult to locate) have, at times, gone some way to engage with a theoretical discourse. However, in an overall sense, one might argue that one of the most significant cultural texts of recent times has rarely been discussed in terms of a theoretical model; that is, *The West Wing* has yet to be fully interrogated in ways that might offer more informative and more revealing readings.[8] *The West Wing*, like any cultural text, can only be experienced, never defined; however, in employing the rich repository of theoretical approaches available, one of the most significant television productions of recent times may possibly be seen anew. One of the aspirations of this book will be to attempt to accomplish just this, to consider *The West Wing* through the prism of cultural theory.

In such a way, this present response to *The West Wing* will assess and analyze the ways in which the show dealt with such issues as sexuality, death, race and religion, via a recourse to a number of theoretical approaches: feminism, gender theory, Marxism, psychoanalytical theories, structuralism, poststructuralism, postcolonialism, postmodernist approaches and so on. There is an interesting sense of synchronicity in that *The West Wing* began in 1999, just as cultural theory was seeming to begin an inevitable decline—at least in the sense of its standing in academia. In an attempt to represent this historical detail, the sources selected to discuss cultural theory will deliberately predate the start of the transmission of *The West Wing*. The only significant exception will be Terry Eagleton's highly influential 2004 book, *After Theory*, published in the middle of the series' run.

Cultural theory may appear to have lost some of its significance within the contemporary era. Yet the core ideas that drove intellectual thought through the 1960s, the 1970s and beyond would still seem to retain a certain intellectual appeal, a certain kudos within the analytical interrogation of cultural texts.[9] According to Susan Sontag, all interpretation impoverishes and depletes the world; to Sontag, critical interpretation was merely the revenge of the intellectual upon the artist.[10] This could be seen as one point-of-view; however, an interpretation of a cultural production, especially when couched within a theoretical framework, does not necessarily have to be seen as an abstract construction. Instead, it could be seen as arguably enhancing the original, as this analysis of *The West Wing* will attempt to demonstrate. Hence the primary components of this book's argument will be an analysis of the series itself and a close reading of aspects of the 155 episodes, together with an analysis of the show from the perspective of cultural theory. In this way, the argument herein will aspire to offer an enhanced understanding of an already engaging, entertaining and thought-provoking text.[11]

In terms of its structure, the book will refrain from an overarching chronological commentary on the seven seasons of the show. Instead, the book will consider some of the main thematic elements identified within the discourse of the drama. As intimated above, the argument and analysis herein will consider such key thematic concerns as race, religion, sexuality and death; however, this will be in addition to a wide range of other issues. These will consist of the following: the issue of authorship, the depiction of disability, a discussion of narratological issues, the significance of pedagogy in the series, philosophical issues such as existentialism and phenomenology, film and television theory, historical authenticity, and intertextuality, together with a diverse range of other ideological issues. However, overarching all of this will be a discussion of *The West Wing* in terms of what it had to say about America, about American values and, most of all, about American politics.

Aaron Sorkin famously described *The West Wing* as "a valentine to public service,"[12] this remark perhaps summing up the overarching philosophy of the show. However, one might note that valentines are often unacknowledged, often unrequited and (perhaps most significantly) often unwanted. Thus, Sorkin's description could be seen as demonstrating both the flaws and the charms of the show. In other words, Sorkin might be accused of possessing a degree of naivety in having sent a valentine to public service in the first place. Yet such a sense of naivety might be seen as what has always been endearing about *The West Wing*. We celebrate its naivety; we rejoice in its innocence, its credulity and even its gullibility. For all its faults, *The West Wing* remains a consummate piece of television, one of *the* most significant of television dramas; and a cynical, skeptical, disparaging, and even world-weary audience still cares and still remains emotionally and intellectually involved.

1

Dramatis Personae
The Cast and Casting

It has been said that the correct casting of a film will simplify most of the subsequent directing decisions to be made during the making of the film. The same might be said of television drama, and, in the case of *The West Wing*, this would seem to have been validated. It would seem clear that, for all its faults, the show was astutely cast. If one looks at the main players, at the *dramatis personae*—Martin Sheen, Rob Lowe, John Spencer, Bradley Whitford, Richard Schiff and Allison Janney—it is now difficult to see any other actors taking the place of the actors who were actually cast.[1] One reason for this may have been the actors' provenance; with the exception of Martin Sheen and Rob Lowe, most of the ensemble cast were theater actors, perhaps because of Sorkin's early experiences as a playwright.[2] In this way the show avoided what might have been a more conventional and more stereotypical style of casting found in much of television drama. It may be true that some of the other, lesser players did not possess such a degree of acting kudos and individuality; nonetheless, *The West Wing* might still be appraised as being primarily character driven, the characters being all-important to the appeal of the narrative. In this sense one can plainly see Sorkin's ability to create believable and lasting protagonists—protagonists who successfully prevailed throughout the seven years in which the show was broadcast.

The opening episode of the series, "Pilot" (1/1), adeptly introduced the main protagonists, and, in so doing, also presented an initial impression of each of their character traits. For example, Sam Seaborn (Rob Lowe) first appeared in a fashionable Washington bar, and then in bed with a prostitute called Laurie. Laurie smoked cannabis after their erotic liaison, thus adding drugs as well as sex to the scene, which would later appear in direct contrast to Sam's clean-cut image. Leo McGarry (John Spencer) was first seen at home. There were a number of relevant details in his first scene—but one immediate issue was the fact that Leo had a maid who appeared to be black. The scene thus engaged with the sense of an ambivalence toward race the series would often display.³ CJ Cregg (Allison Janney) was first shown exercising in the gym, running on a treadmill and then—somewhat comically—falling off it; this detail would prove to be relevant as the series continued. Josh Lyman (Bradley Whitford) was first seen at work, seemingly having fallen asleep in his office overnight—a reference to the dedication President Josiah (Jed) Bartlet's staff consistently possessed toward their jobs. Toby Ziegler (Richard Schiff) was first shown on a plane, arguing with a stewardess over the use of his laptop computer—a scene that offered an indicator of Toby's morose demeanor. Mandy Hampton (Moira Kelly) was first shown in a high-powered car, recklessly driving and then (even more recklessly) "parking it," suggesting her bearing as a powerful and uncompromising woman. Finally, on his first entrance President Bartlet (Martin Sheen) was shown limping, walking with the aid of a cane, supposedly after falling off a bicycle; an alternate explanation would later become apparent.

Insomuch as *The West Wing* was so self-evidently character driven, and those characters appeared to be so true to life, it has therefore been suggested that some of the characters may have had a basis in reality. For example, CJ Cregg has been read as a cipher for Dee Dee Myers, President Bill Clinton's press secretary in the early years of his first term; similarly, Sam Seaborn would seem to have been based, to some extent at least, on George Stephanopoulos, the White House communications director during Clinton's first term; likewise, Mandy Hampton has been seen as being based on Mandy Grunwald, a media advisor for the Democratic party. However, such speculations would seem somewhat reductive. *The West Wing* was a fictional construct; it may have been influenced by real life, but not in such a simplistic way. Instead, it is likely that each character was drawn from a range of diverse and composite sources, both real and imagined. This can be seen in the character of President Bartlet himself; while *The West Wing* was undoubtedly influenced by the Clinton administration, Bartlet was *not* Bill Clinton. Instead he seems to have been an anomalous mixture of John Kennedy's Catholicism and charisma and Jimmy Carter's intelligence and idealism, although the actual model may have been the unelected (and perhaps unelectable) George McGovern, who lost to Richard Nixon in the 1972 presidential election.⁴ In this sense, the series could be described as a *roman à clef* (in literal translation, "a novel with a key")—a narrative in which actual and sometimes well-known people were presented via fictional names. However, this would only be seen within a limited framework and within certain restricted parameters.

There was one character who appeared to have an exact correlation with a historical figure. This was Governor Robert Richie, the Republican candidate who ran against Bartlet in the fictional 2002 election. It would seem that Richie was a somewhat clumsily rendered symbol for George W. Bush, a parody in response to Bush's victory over Al Gore in the real world's 2000 election.[5] Governor Ritchie was presented as "a plain speaking, apparently uncomplicated man," contrasted against "Bartlet's polymath intellectualism and complex moral integrity."[6] In this way, Richie was little more than a cipher to fulfill the stereotypical Republican role, a Bush-like candidate with the simplistic "ten-word answer" that Bartlet and his staff expected and then effortlessly demolished. However, it would seem that the satirical intent was overplayed, as David Barber put it:

> [It was] such a blatant dig at President Bush and his perceived stupidity that they might as well have cast Will Ferrell in the part.... As a character, Ritchie does not develop beyond being a cipher of Republicanism.... The problem with Ritchie as a character is that he is a cipher and his only function is to be denigrated by Bartlet and his staff.[7]

It has been suggested that Sorkin's so-called satire may have deliberately lacked subtlety[8]; in other words, the program makers may have wanted Bush to see the coded reference. However, all of this may have been to little avail, insomuch as "George W. Bush claimed never to have seen the show."[9]

Of the main characters, John Spencer as Leo and Richard Schiff as Toby were perhaps of the most complexity. Leo McGarry had a detailed and interesting back-story: he had independent wealth—a facet of the narrative that was never fully explained[10]; he was an alcoholic and had been addicted to prescription drugs for a number of years; and his wife was to subsequently leave him because, as Leo would freely admit, his job was more important to him than his marriage. In addition, Leo had a daughter who did not share his surname—again a facet of the narrative that was never fully explained.[11] Also, Leo was a perfectionist,[12] he was the best-dressed male player on the show, he could speak fluent Spanish, he had read the whole of Ernest Hemingway's output—twice—and he had flown combat missions during the Vietnam War. His character was interesting because of the ambivalences it raised; however, the most interesting facet of Leo's character was the fact that he unexpectedly died within the narrative of the series. John Spencer himself died unexpectedly of a heart attack on December 16, 2005. Spencer had already recorded several episodes that had not been broadcast. Hence it would appear that it was decided to use these episodes and then to fashion a fictitious death similar to the actual death of the actor. At the start of the episode "Running Mates" (7/10), Martin Sheen would ask what greater tribute they could make than to show Spencer's acting in the final scenes he shot for *The West Wing*. The alternate point-of-view would be to say this was the easiest and most economical way to proceed; it would otherwise have required costly rewriting and reshooting.[13] As if by way of compensating John Spencer's memory, in the episode "Requiem" (7/18), what appeared to be the entire cast of the series assembled for Leo's funeral.[14] This was a more fitting tribute, an effortless mélange of fact and fiction, and arguably one of the best scenes of the series.

Toby Ziegler was of interest as a character because he represented the conscience of the Bartlet administration,[15] a character who "functions as a constant reminder of Bartlet's failure to live up to the ideal."[16] Toby's stances on issues such as capital punishment and human rights, and his eventual decision to reveal the existence of a military shuttle, all showed evidence of this. In a more specific sense, an apt example of Toby's role as the administration's conscience occurred in the episode "In Excelsis Deo" (1/10). Herein Bartlet gently rebuked Toby's action in arranging a military funeral for a homeless veteran, a vagrant ex-soldier. Bartlet commented that they could not have every "homeless vet coming out of the woodwork," to which Toby responded: "I can only hope, sir."[17] A further example of Toby functioning as the moral conscience of the series occurred in the episode "The Crackpots and These Women" (1/5). In the middle of a basketball game between Bartlet and his staff, Toby, commenting on the president's need to win even a scratch game such as this, delivered the line: "This is a perfect metaphor. After you're gone, and the poets write, 'The Legend of Josiah Bartlet' let them write you as a tragic figure, sir. Let the poets write that he had the tools of greatness, but the voices of his better angels were shouted down by his obsessive need to win."[18] Such a challenging relationship continued throughout all seven seasons of the series. Bartlet's final act as president was to sign the letter giving Toby a pardon. However, a question remained: Had Toby pardoned Bartlet?[19]

Martin Sheen's portrayal of President Bartlet has routinely been seen in complimentary terms, for both the quality of Sheen's acting and the qualities of Bartlet himself as an ideal president (albeit a fictitious one) of the United States. Bartlet was routinely seen, for example, as the "liberal dreamboat" of our political fantasies,[20] or as "an immensely thoughtful, infinitely wise, deeply caring, thoroughly monogamous and unambiguously principled [president]."[21] Another commentator wrote: "Bartlet is neither an ineffectual idealist nor a tolerant realist, but navigates between the two poles throughout the series."[22] Bartlet was a three-term congressman, a two-term New Hampshire governor, an idealist, a moral man, a devout Catholic, a graduate of Notre Dame with former thoughts of becoming a priest, a Nobel laureate in economics, "a devoted father of three daughters, [and] faithful husband to his wife." He was "proficient in Latin, and a formidable student of history," and "a New England patrician with a direct link to a Founding Father."[23] This was the received wisdom; however, such an assessment arguably concealed the reality of Bartlet as a cynical political operator. Bartlet was a politician who had successfully run for office on several occasions; hence it was only logical that he should have other attributes that revealed him as not quite the "liberal dreamboat" of common appraisal. Bartlet does not appear to have had some of the character defects of recent presidents: for example, he was not a womanizer and he was not materially corrupt. Nonetheless, a more incisive reading of his character might be seen as revealing a number of significant shortcomings.

In an initial sense, there was the obvious issue that Bartlet had concealed the fact he had multiple sclerosis (MS) from both the American people and his closest colleagues. Bartlet had developed MS several years before becoming president. In the episode "The Fall's Gonna Kill You" (2/20), shortly after Bartlet's illness had finally been revealed, Josh Lyman was shown talking about the underhand methods of tobacco companies in withholding information about the damage their products caused. Josh commented: "They perpetrated a fraud against the American public." The intent was not explicitly stated, but it was clear that Bartlet had also perpetrated a fraud on the American public. In a later episode, "The Indians in the Lobby" (3/8), Bartlet was shown talking to Bruno Gianelli, his then campaign manager, about the politicization of his family. Bartlet told Bruno: "My family is off-limits." Bruno replied, with warranted bluntness: "Sir, your candor about a terrible illness was off-limits. Your regime of self-medication was off-limits. Due respect, you've used up your off-limits."[24] This was as harsh a censure of Bartlet by a character close to him as would be allowed in the series.[25] In addition, it was clear that Bartlet and his wife Abigail (Abbey) had had an agreement that, because of his illness, Bartlet would not run for a second term, although this backstory was never shown directly in the series. Abbey said, "You made a promise. We made a deal," to which Bartlet could only respond, "That was three years ago."[26] One might have been excused here in thinking that a deal is a deal, that it does not matter how much time has passed, and that Bartlet's word, even to his wife, could not be wholly trusted.

There were a number of other diverse issues; for example, there was the matter of Bartlet's illegal complicity in the assassination of Abdul Shareef, the defense minister of the fictitious gulf state of Qumar.[27] There was Bartlet's flouting of another, albeit lesser, law in the episode "Han" (5/4); in this episode Bartlet appeared to deliberately break U.S. law in not allowing Jai Yung Ahn, the North Korean pianist, to be given asylum. There was also Bartlet's ambivalent attitude toward the death penalty. In the episode "Take This Sabbath Day" (1/14), Bartlet made a political decision not to commute the death sentence of a federal prisoner convicted of the murder of two drug dealers. Bartlet was counseled by a Quaker, a rabbi and a priest, but still did not seem to have the courage to make the decision.[28] In addition, there was Bartlet's willingness to use his military power for personal revenge; in the second episode of the series, "Post Hoc, Ergo Propter Hoc" (1/2), Bartlet threatened to carpet bomb Syria, to "blow them off the face of the earth with the fury of God's own thunder." Bartlet was dissuaded from this action; however, the original intent was still apparent.[29] At times Bartlet's position as president appeared to make him almost megalomaniacal; in the episode "Night Five" (3/14), the psychiatrist Stanley Keyworth (who was acting as counselor to the president in an attempt to cure his insomnia) told Bartlet their two-hour session was over, that "they were done." Bartlet replied: "Stanley, I hate to put it this way, but I'm me, and you're you, and we're done when I say we're done." Keyworth replied: "No, I think you could use some assistance right now, sir. Use me, don't use me, but all I can offer you is this: I'll be the only person in the world, other than your family, who doesn't care that you're the president. Our time is up."[30]

In addition to this, Bartlet's personal manner was, at times, of questionable integrity, for example in Bartlet's relationship with his first vice president, John Hoynes. The relationship was a fraught one, perhaps because of the grudge Bartlet bore surrounding his original offer of the post to Hoynes. "You shouldn't have made me beg,"[31] Bartlet says in the episode "Enemies" (1/8). Later in the same episode, CJ mentions that she had heard Bartlet had "roughed up Hoynes in the cabinet meeting." CJ is correct; Bartlet deliberately embarrassed Hoynes, presumably because he could and because he wanted to. As part of such a seemingly vindictive trait, in a later episode, "War Crimes" (3/6), Bartlet would ask Hoynes: "Do you feel like having a beer?"—fully aware that Hoynes was a recovering alcoholic and could not drink. Elsewhere in the series, Bartlet's sarcasm often seemed to be present; for example, in Bartlet's derisive manner with the radio show host Dr. Jenna Jacobs in the episode "The Midterms" (2/3).[32] Bartlet was also routinely sarcastic with Toby. For example, in the episode "Here Today" (7/5), just prior to receiving Toby's letter of resignation, Bartlet commented: "What is that, the third one? Rip it up."[33] Finally, in perhaps one of his worst displays of arrogance, Bartlet seemed to deliberately humiliate his future son-in-law, Vic Faison, the fiancé of Ellie Bartlet, Bartlet's middle daughter. In what can only be described as a premeditated act of social cruelty, Bartlet deliberately put his "geeky, Buddy Holly–esque" son-in-law at a disadvantage; in a crude power play he led Faison into the Oval Office, just as the Joint Chiefs of Staff were leaving. The Joint Chiefs congratulated Faison on the wedding, but it was clear he was overwhelmed and humiliated by the experience.

There was perhaps only one scene, in the entire series, wherein Bartlet's character was fully revealed for what it was. This was a scene in the episode "The Short List" (1/9) between Bartlet and Joseph Crouch, the soon-to-be-retiring Supreme Court justice. The scene was as accurate a representation of Bartlet and his presidency as might be found; for this one instance the sentimental gloss was removed and Bartlet's actual character was revealed. The scene began with Bartlet, somewhat disingenuously, commenting that Crouch was too young to retire, to which Crouch replied that the president was "an excellent liar." The conversation then turned to the short list for the new Supreme Court justice, with Crouch disparagingly commenting that Bartlet would choose the safe option instead of appointing Mendoza, a Hispanic judge. Crouch then accused Bartlet of cowardice, in this and other decisions, stating how Bartlet had run "great guns in the campaign. It was an insurgency; boy, a sight to see, and then you drove to the middle of the road the moment after you took the oath … the middle of the road, nothing but a long line painted yellow." Bartlet seemed astonished someone would say this to him, and attempted to end the meeting, but Crouch insisted he have his say: "I wanted to retire five years ago. But I waited for a Democrat. I wanted a Democrat. And instead I got you! I've served on this bench for thirty-eight years. I took my seat the year you began college. I believe I've earned the right to say a word." Crouch then went on to urge Bartlet to consider Mendoza; Bartlet prevaricated and suggested he would do this when the next seat on the court was available. Crouch was derisive: "When the next seat opens up, you'll be writing your memoirs." In other words, Bartlet would then be out of office. Bartlet attempted to excuse his situation: "You know I imagine the view from your largely un-scrutinized place in history must be very different from mine. But I remind you sir, that I have the following things to negotiate: an opposition Congress, special interests with power beyond belief, and a bitchy media." Crouch dismissed this, saying: "So did Harry Truman." Bartlet agreed: "Well, I am not Harry Truman." This was a trap, with Crouch responding: "Mr. Bartlet, you needn't point out that fact"—and there the conversation ended. The scene was one of the few times in which Bartlet had no answer, wherein he appeared to lose the moral argument, and wherein all his faults and weaknesses were made clearly apparent. It could be argued that Bartlet never recovered from this attack, at least in the eyes of a perceptive viewer of the series. This scene has seldom been commented on in the critical literature on the series, but it is arguably a key scene—perhaps one of *the* key scenes of all seven seasons of the show.[34]

On the surface, Bartlet may have seemed to be a likeable character, and he was certainly popular with a large majority of the show's audience; however, on closer inspection he arguably had character flaws that were present, if not readily apparent. Once again this has seldom been noted in the critical response to the series, at least not in a concerted way. One reason for this may have been the fact that Bartlet was portrayed by Martin Sheen; it has become difficult to remove Bartlet from the actor who played him. Sheen appeared to accumulate so much prestige in the role as to preclude criticism. There were some elements of disapproval; for example, one critic described Sheen's performance as being "canned ham,"[35] arguing that he was portraying a president on an "upscale soap opera."[36] However, such criticisms were relatively rare; Andrew Stuttaford, writing in the *National Review*,[37] was one of the few real exceptions:

> If there is anyone more sanctimonious than *The West Wing*'s Jed Bartlet, it's the moralizing old ham who plays him. But prissy, preachy Martin Sheen wasn't always this way. There were times, back in the depths of the wicked, whacked-out 1970s, when today's straitlaced star was a boozer, a three-packs-of-cigarettes-a-day man, and who knows what else.[38]

Stuttaford went on:

> [Sheen] has been arrested, around 70 [times] at the latest count, often carefully choreographed for photogenic spectacle.... Sheen is a zealot: a man so convinced of his own rectitude that, for him, any compromise becomes a sin.... For a man supposedly dedicated to Christian values of reconciliation and love, Martin Sheen has a very sharp tongue indeed. George W. Bush, he says, is a "thug," "dull," "dangerous," "a bad comic working the crowd," a "moron," and a "white-knuckle drunk" in denial about his past difficulties with alcohol.[39]

However, disregarding such a "sharp tongued" critique of Sheen/Bartlet, together with the minor flaws of some of the other main players, in an overall sense it would seem fair to suggest that *The West Wing* was astutely cast. Furthermore, the characters played by the cast have proved to be both enduring and endearing. It was a character-led drama, this being one of the most significant strengths of the show, one of the reasons the show has endured so well—and why the show's audience continues to find the adventures of the protagonists within the narrative arc of the drama so endearing.

2

A Mosaic of Quotations
Intertextuality in The West Wing

The term intertextuality was first coined in 1966 by the Bulgarian-French philosopher Julia Kristeva. Kristeva argued that a literary or cultural text was not an isolated occurrence, but was made up of "a mosaic of quotations," and that any text should be seen as merely the "absorption and the transformation of another [text]."[1] In this sense, intertextuality was a significant aspect of poststructuralist thinking, rejecting the idea of a text as a "single, autonomous entity created by a single author."[2] In other words, the author was not seen as the "great originator, the creative genius, but rather a synthesizer: someone who draws together and orchestrates linguistic raw materials."[3] Therefore, in an overall sense, with the author decentered, a text would now be seen to consist of "multiple writings, and writings that are drawn from a range of discourses, already in circulation."[4] In terms of *The West Wing* and intertextuality, there was no doubting its narrative complexity—indeed, it is difficult to think of many other television dramas that possessed such an extensive inner world, such a believable alternate version of the real world. This is partially explained by the show's recurrent sense of intertextual echoing; the breadth and the depth of *The West Wing* allowed for a wealth of intertextual references, enabling a richness and a diversity to exist within the artistic discourses at play.

A number of previous dramas, films and television series can be seen as having a clear and obvious influence upon the show. The most direct influence derived from *The American President* (1995), a Rob Reiner film with a screenplay by Aaron Sorkin himself. The basic premise of the film and *The West Wing* was the same: both followed a liberal president and his staff within a somewhat idealized White House. It would seem that Sorkin was able to make use of material from the film; a number of plotlines would subsequently be used in the first season of *The West Wing*.[5] For example, some of the issues touched upon in the film and developed in the series related to gun control and to the issue of a proportional response to a military attack. In addition, the fictitious Global Defense Council was present in both dramas; the same plotline, of one of GDC's main lobbyists being "fired," was also present. The film's Sydney Ellen Wade (played to some effect by Annette Benning) seemed to be an early version of Amy Gardner in the series. Likewise, both texts had a Governor Stackhouse and a French President d'Astier; and both American presidents, Bartlet and Andrew Shepherd, had female press secretaries. Also, the opening scene of the film depicted a prototype for the many "walk and talk" scenes in *The West Wing*. There was the same use of the catchphrase "What's next?" Even the title of the coming television series was alluded to in the film, with Shepherd (Michael Douglas) commenting: "I'm more of a West Wing president."[6] Finally, a number of actors who would appear in *The West Wing* also appeared in *The American President*, including Martin Sheen,[7] Joshua Malina, Anna Deavere Smith, Nina Siemaszko, Ron Canada and Thom Barry.

In addition, there was the potential influence of an earlier film, *The Best Man* (1964). This was a political drama directed by Franklin J. Schaffner, based on the play by Gore Vidal, with a screenplay by Vidal himself.[8] This has rarely been seen as an influence on *The West Wing*; however, there would appear to be significant parallels, and it is possible it was a film with which Aaron Sorkin was familiar. The plot concerned a fictional 1964 Democratic convention in Los Angeles, where two candidates were attempting to obtain their party's presidential nomination: William Russell, played by Henry Fonda, and Joe Cantwell, played by Cliff Robertson. Fonda's character might be seen as an early model for President Bartlet: a liberal, intellectual president with a secret health issue. If *The West Wing* had been made some years earlier, then Fonda might have made a Bartlet of some significance. It being Gore Vidal, there were a number of acerbic aphorisms in the screenplay; for example: "There are no ends, only means"—"To want power is corruption already"—"All the characteristics of a dog except loyalty"—all somewhat different to the reach of a writer like Aaron Sorkin. Vidal died in 2012, and it is not known if he had an opinion of *The West Wing*, or if he ever watched it. However, given his interest in Washington politics, it is likely Vidal was at least aware of the series—replete with its "middle-brow orthodoxies."[9] Vidal's opinions of the series, however, must be left open to speculation—a cursory online search reveals no comments. Hence one can only imagine the Vidal-esque vitriol he may have unloaded upon the series.

Another political drama, which Sorkin was no doubt aware of, was *Washington Behind Closed Doors*. This was a six-part television series from 1977 based on John Ehrlichman's novel *The Company*. The series starred Jason Robards as President Richard Monkton, a transparent cipher for Richard Nixon, and Robert Vaughn as an H.R. Haldeman stand-in and Monkton's chief of

2. A Mosaic of Quotations 15

staff, demonstrating an arguably more realistic alternative to Leo McGarry's version of the role in *The West Wing*.[10] The eleven-part television series from a decade later, *Tanner '88*, directed by Robert Altman, was almost certainly an influence on Sorkin's ideas for *The West Wing*—he may have derived the idea that it was possible to portray idealism in American politics from this series. Another potential influence on *The West Wing* was the film *Thirteen Days*, directed by Roger Donaldson and released in 2000. The film came out while *The West Wing* was mid-way through its second season, but nonetheless the idealistic portrayal of President Kennedy as he maneuvered to avoid nuclear war during the Cuban Missile Crisis may have contributed to the idealistic portrayal of President Bartlet.[11] In the film, Bruce Greenwood was a strong contender for the best portrayal of President Kennedy—arguably better than Martin Sheen. The film had its faults; in a cynical light it might be viewed as a vanity project for its star, Kevin Costner, who played the role of Kenny O'Donnell. In the film, O'Donnell seemed to serve in a role close to that of chief of staff, while in reality Kennedy had no chief of staff, and O'Donnell was little more than a trusted appointments secretary. Other than this the film would seem to have been historically accurate, and, in an overall sense, *Thirteen Days* had exactly the same idealistic appeal as *The West Wing*.[12]

In a reversal of intertextual allusion, *The West Wing* would go on to prefigure a number of later television political dramas, primarily the following: *Commander in Chief* (2005–2006), *Scandal* (2012–2018), *House of Cards* (2013–2018) and *Designated Survivor* (2016–2019).[13] In the case of *Commander in Chief*, there were a number of deliberate parallels with *The West Wing*. For example, both series were based upon divergences from the real political history of America; both series made use of the 25th Amendment; in both series the president was a Nobel Prize winner; both series had a female press secretary; and finally, both series depicted a happily married president—although in the case of *Commander in Chief* the president was a woman, with a first husband rather than a first lady. In the case of *Scandal* there were obvious and intentional references to *The West Wing*. This could be seen primarily in the general *mise-en-scène*—the general look of the series. For example, the opening scene of the opening episode began in an up-market Washington, D.C. bar. This was a scene clearly and deliberately reminiscent of the opening scene of *The West Wing*. There was also the presence of Joshua Malina in both dramas, as Will Bailey in *The West Wing* and David Rosen in *Scandal*. Malina's presence could not help but act as a reference to *The West Wing*. In the case of *House of Cards*, its direct referent, especially in the first season, was the 1990 British television drama of the same name. However, there were also apparent influences from *The West Wing*—for example, the use of the Steadicam camera, together with a more stylized and minimalist representation of the White House. In addition, there seems to have been a deliberate burlesque of the "blasphemy scene" in *The West Wing* episode "Two Cathedrals" (2/22), with the parallel episode in *House of Cards* showing Frank Underwood actually spitting on the statue of the crucified Christ.[14] Such a degree of cynicism could be seen as a kind of antidote to the relentlessly agreeable qualities of President Bartlet—with President Frank Underwood fully living up to the vulgar initials of his name. Finally, there was *Designated Survivor*, a somewhat comic-book re-reading of *The West Wing*. The series took one insignificant plotline from the episode "He Shall from Time to Time" (1/12), wherein Josh and Donna attended to the line of succession, should the Capitol Building be "blown-up" during the President's State of the Union speech. "So who's it gonna be?" Donna asked. Josh then told Donna the designated survivor would be Roger Tribbey, the secretary of agriculture. In *Designated Survivor* the Capitol Building was blown up and the secretary of housing and urban development, Thomas Kirkwood, became president. This allowed Kirkwood, as played by Kiefer Sutherland, to create a president even more unctuous and liberal than President Bartlet.

In a wider sense, there were too many generalized intertextual allusions to note in any great depth, but a select number of instances might be considered. If one looks, for example, merely at the titles of certain *The West Wing* episodes, even here there was an eclectic sense of allusion to a diversity of sources. The episode "Mr. Willis of Ohio" (1/6) would seem to have been a deliberate recreation of Frank Capra's film *Mr. Smith Goes to Washington* (1939); and the title of the episode "Six Meetings Before Lunch" (1/18) would seem to have been a reductive allusion to a remark by the White Queen in *Alice through the Looking Glass*, who says: "Why, sometimes I've believed as many as six impossible things before breakfast." The title of the episode "The Fall's Gonna Kill You" (2/20) deliberately recalled the film *Butch Cassidy and the Sundance Kid* (1969); while the title of the episode "Stirred" (3/18) pointed directly to James Bond's martini—his cocktail of gin and vermouth being shaken not stirred—although Bartlet would question the quality of the drink. The title of the episode "No Exit" (5/20) was a reference to the 1944 play of the same name by Jean-Paul Sartre, an existentialist nightmare in which three people were locked together in a room for all eternity. Finally, the title of the episode "The Birnam Wood" (6/2) obviously referenced *Macbeth*. Shakespeare would appear again in numerous guises: *Julius Caesar* in "The Dogs of War" (5/2); *Hamlet* in "Shibboleth" (2/8); and *King Lear* throughout the show—as will be discussed at the close of this chapter.

Elsewhere, popular culture from a diverse range of sources was represented. For example, in the episode "17 People" (2/18) Toby's relentless bouncing of a ball against the office wall was obviously an homage to Steve McQueen in the film *The Great Escape* (1963); the closing scene of the episode "Hartsfield's Landing" (3/15) could not help but seem to portray a sur-

2. A Mosaic of Quotations 17

real outtake from Shirley Jackson's famous short story "The Lottery"; and the film *Groundhog Day* (1993) was clearly referenced in the episode "King Corn" (6/13). Of perhaps greater substance were the intertextual references at play in John Goodman's portrayal of President Glen Walken. One way of reading Bartlet's temporary successor would be to see Walken as a surreal re-reading of Walter Sobchak, the Dude's sidekick in the Coen Brothers' film *The Big Lebowski* (1998). This would appear to have been a deliberate reference. All the indicators were apparent within the two characters: the same bombastic presence, the same speech patterns, the same "staunch support" of veterans' rights—even down to the detail of Walken having a small, vaguely irritating dog in tow.[15] Finally, in the episode "The Dogs of War" (5/2), Leo's "cloak and dagger" meeting with Angela Blake in an underground car park somewhere in Washington, D.C. obviously pointed to *All the President's Men* (1976). There would seem to have been little reason for Leo to meet in such a location and at such a time—the intertextual allusion was all.

There were a number of other references to popular culture; for example, there were multiple references to a number of Bob Dylan songs, some direct,[16] some less direct. Some of the more nuanced references included Bartlet's comment in the opening episode, "Pilot" (1/1), "I forgot to open the garage door." Martin Sheen, an ardent admirer of Dylan's work, most likely saw the satirical reference to Dylan's song "Leopard-Skin Pill-Box Hat," which had the line: "You forgot to close the garage door." Similarly, in the episode "Isaac and Ishmael" (3/1), Abigail began her speech telling the story of the two eponymous characters with the phrase "God said to Abraham," perhaps knowingly quoting the opening line of Dylan's song "Highway 61 Revisited." Likewise, CJ's comment in the episode "Inauguration Part 2: Over There" (4/15), "The Chief Justice has lost his mind," seemed to echo a line from Dylan's song "Clothesline Saga." There were other references; for example, the scenes on the campaign bus in the episode "Welcome to Wherever You Are" (7/15) would appear to have been influenced by the 1992 film *Bob Roberts*, directed by Tim Robbins. This was a deliberately faux documentary that lampooned Bob Dylan in the 1960s, especially in regards to D.A. Pennebaker's film *Dont Look Back* (1967)—Robbins's film being a carefully nuanced attack on Dylan's artistic reputation as a supposed protest singer.

A further set of intertextual referents to which the series repeatedly returned were the films of Stanley Kubrick. Sometimes the reference was simply visual, as in the opening shot of the episode "Gaza" (5/21)—see Chapter 6 for a further discussion of this—or the party scenes in the episodes "Mr. Willis of Ohio" (1/6) and "Dead Irish Writers" (3/16), where the general *mise-en-scène* would seem to have been based upon the party scene at the start of *Eyes Wide Shut* (1999), Kubrick's last film.[17] Kubrick's film *Dr. Strangelove: Or How I*

Learned to Stop Worrying and Love the Bomb (1964) was either directly referenced or alluded to on a number of occasions, perhaps because it was the only Kubrick film set in (or underneath) the White House. For example, Bartlet in "Lord John Marbury" (1/11) remarks: "Well, bring on Dr. Strangelove and we're all set," and Admiral Fitzwallace in "20 Hours in America" (4/1/2) states: "I'm with Dr. Strangelove on keeping our military secrets secret." In addition, the scene between Bartlet and the Russian leader President Pyotr Chigorin in the episode "Evidence of Things Not Seen" (4/20) would seem to have deliberately mirrored a similar scene in *Dr. Strangelove* between President Merkin Muffley and Premier Dimitri Kissov. In a similar way, in the episode "Impact Winter" (6/9) there was an obvious allusion to *Dr. Strangelove* in the conversation about the need to breed in the bunker. "Somebody needs to repopulate," says one character, again directly mirroring a scene in Kubrick's film. The episode "17 People" (2/18) used the following captions to tell the story:

The Same Night
Two Nights After That
The Next Night
The Next Day
That Night

This seemed to reference a similar use of captions in another Kubrick film, *The Shining*.[18] In a more direct way, an exchange between Matt and Helen Santos in the episode "Here Today" (7/5) had obvious intertextual allusions to the same film. In the episode, Helen wanted to relax in the evening and watch a horror film, commenting: "All work and no play...," to which Santos interjected: "Are you calling me a dull boy?" There were numerous other references: *A Clockwork Orange* was mentioned by name in the episode "Freedonia" (6/15), while *Spartacus* was specifically referenced in the episode "Bad Moon Rising" (2/19), with CJ claiming in the film's famous line: "I am Spartacus."

However, the most interesting intertextual reference from popular culture was arguably the film *The Godfather* (1972); in fact, there were repeated allusions to all three of the *Godfather* films throughout all seven seasons of the show. There are too many instances to detail in a comprehensive manner, but the following examples might be commented upon. In the episode "He Shall, from Time to Time" (1/12), Leo protested, "This is not what I wanted," a line directly recalling Michael Corleone's famous line in *The Godfather Part 3* (1991). In the episode "20 Hours in L.A." (1/16), Josh's visit to Ted Marcus's mansion in Hollywood—together with Bartlet's subsequent demand that his "Deputy Chief-of-Staff" should not be "slapped" around—would seem to have been a direct and conscious reference to Tom Hagen's visit to Jack Woltz's Hollywood mansion in *The Godfather*. Later in Season 1, in the episode "Mandatory Minimums" (1/20), there was the first verbal reference to the film, when Josh told Sam: "Do you know what this is like? This is like *The Godfather*. When Pacino tells James Caan that he's gonna kill the cop. It's a lot like that scene, only not really."

In Season 2, in the episode "The Leadership Breakfast" (2/11), Leo claimed he was a "wartime *consigliere*." In *The Godfather Part 2* (1974), Tom Hagen had also aspired to be a "wartime *consigliere*," but having Irish ancestry he was not qualified to take that role; however, in *The West Wing*, Leo, also of Irish ancestry, did not seem to have had this difficulty. In Season 3 there were a cluster of references. For example, the congressional committee hearings in the episode "Bartlet for America" (3/10) seemed to be deliberately modeled on the committee hearings in *The Godfather Part 2*, with Leo taking the role of Michael Corleone.[19] "It ain't nothing but a family thing," Leo told his lawyer, Jordon Kendall, almost as if he were a member of *La Cosa Nostra*. In the following episode, "H. Con—172" (3/11), Leo would repeat the essence of the phrase, again to Jordon: "This is not your thing. It is my thing." In Italian the phrase *Cosa Nostra* literally means "our thing"—hence the implied reference to *The Godfather*.

In Season 5, in the episode "Constituency of One" (5/5), there were a number of somewhat gauche and almost artless references to *The Godfather*: Amy sent Josh a dead fish wrapped in newspaper; CJ somewhat ambiguously referred to the "Jewish-Connecticut Corleone" and Amy pondered if she was going "to come back from mass and find a horse's head on [her] desk." In Season 6, in the episode "Drought Conditions" (6/16), CJ would comment: "Nobody turns us down. We're like the Mob, but less violent." Finally, in Season 7, in the episode "Institutional Memory" (7/21), Santos attempted to persuade CJ to stay on in his administration, joking he would make her "an offer she couldn't refuse," a final reference to *The Godfather*—although in the event, CJ was able to turn down the offer and to escape unharmed.

In addition to such references from popular culture, perhaps the most significant intertextual allusion was to Shakespeare's play *King Lear*. This was arguably the most important instance of intertextuality in the series, and it would seem likely it was deliberately built into the fabric of the narrative from the beginning of the writing process. The main intertextual allusions to Shakespeare's play were self-evident: like Lear, Bartlet had three daughters, the youngest of whom seeming to be of most importance to him—in other words, for Cordelia read Zoey.[20] In a further parallel correspondence to *King Lear*, Bartlet was a head of state, a powerful, king-like man; yet nonetheless, like Lear, Bartlet underwent a crisis of confidence part way through the drama—with the two great men weathering both literal and metaphorical storms. Surprisingly, this somewhat obvious intertextual allusion has seldom been discussed within the literature on the show. There have been some intimations: for example, an unnamed journalist, writing in *The Economist*, commented that *The West Wing* was "essentially a fairy story about a benign ruler"[21]—and, in a sense, *King Lear* could also be seen as a fairy story about an inherently benign ruler. Michelle Mouton spoke of Zoey's "filial devotion,"[22] but she could just as easily have been talking of Cordelia's filial devotion to her father. Melissa Crawley spoke of Bartlet being "a shadow of a monarch long abandoned"[23]—and again the reference could just as easily have been made to *King Lear*. Later in her discussion, Crawley, talking of the episode "Ellie" (2/15), noted: "He will not permit someone to tell him that he loves one of his children 'less than the other.'"[24] The scene in question concerned Millicent Griffith, the surgeon general, a close family friend to the Bartlets, and also Ellie Bartlet's godmother. In the scene, Griffith told Bartlet that his daughter was afraid of him and perhaps questioned his affection. Bartlet responded: "I will not stand and allow someone to tell me that I love one of my children less than the others." This was the line Melissa Crawley was referring to, and it was as subtle an allusion to the way in which Shakespeare's play acted upon the show as would be found in the series. It was a clear reference to Lear's famous comment:

> Tell me, my daughters …
> Which of you shall we say doth love us most?[25]

In the famous storm scene in the middle of the play, Lear appeared to lose hold of his sanity. In *The West Wing*, Bartlet did not descend into actual madness. However, there was a storm scene—a scene with a similar sense of crisis within the drama. In the episode in question, "Two Cathedrals" (2/22), Bartlet may not have lost his reason, but his mental equilibrium was at least put into question, with Bartlet lambasting and cursing God in Latin while an unseasonal tropical storm lambasted the church he was standing in.[26] Bartlet's anger was certainly Lear-like. Like Lear, Bartlet would eventually go out to confront and, in a sense, be baptized by the storm—a kind of storm that had not occurred in the last hundred years and that could bring forth a spectral representation of Mrs. Landingham. Here in these scenes, such a sense of intertextuality within disparate cultural texts could be said to have enhanced the narrative being told. There were other indicators: for example, the episode "Abu el Banat" (5/9)[27] was concerned with the political ambitions of Elizabeth, Bartlet's oldest daughter, or at least her political ambitions via her husband.[28] As such, it was perhaps relevant to note that the title of the episode was a Bedouin phrase meaning "father of daughters"—again an obvious and arguably conscious reference toward Shakespeare's play. Finally, in the closing episode of the series, "Tomorrow" (7/22), in the closing scene of the entire drama, Bartlet was shown in the presidential helicopter, returning to New Hampshire after eight years in office. As Bartlet was returning home, the "ex-king" was told by Abbey that his three daughters were awaiting him: "The girls are gonna be waiting for us when we get to the farm this evening. It's supposed to be a surprise. Act like it." Bartlet appeared to be displeased: "Tonight? I was looking forward to some peace and quiet." Abbey replied, in what would seem to be another conscious reference to Shakespeare's play: "They just wanted to show you their love and support in your hour of need." *King Lear* was—in essence—a play about the conflict between parents and children; and here, in this final scene in the show, there was a final reference to such a conflict—however moderate it may have been—between Bartlet and his daughters.

Of course, all cultural texts exhibit intertextual properties, but in the case of *The West Wing* there was an unusually complex and subtle interplay of referencing taking place: intertextual references from both high and popular culture; intertextual references that wove multifarious threads throughout the show's entire narrative; and intertextual references that continually succeeded in enhancing the overarching qualities of *The West Wing* as a cultural text. In itself, intertextuality can be either conscious and citational, or wholly unconscious, or even—at times—deliberately plagiaristic. In the case of *The West Wing* there was little sense of plagiarism; intertextual references within the show were most commonly consciously placed—sometimes in a particularly skillful way. At times the intertextual references seemed unconsciously positioned; however, although the show made use of a wide and diverse arena of sources, it did so in a decidedly valid way, and thus, whatever other criticisms might be made, it remains a television drama of genuine originality.

3

Historical Fictions
A Parallel Universe

One of the fascinating aspects in watching and studying *The West Wing* concerns the complex interplay between the real and the imaginary histories at play within the discursive practices of the series. In other words, it would seem evident that *The West Wing* was deliberately situated within the real world, but also outside of it; that is, it appeared to inhabit a familiar but different universe to our own. In this sense, *The West Wing* could be said to represent a parallel reality, using elements of historical reality while also presupposing other divergent realities. Such a technique allowed the series to create plots that envisaged believable yet fictionally based storylines; for example, most of the nation states in *The West Wing* were real, but when necessary fictitious states could also be used. In a similar way, some of the figures on the world stage seemed to be based on actual people, while the majority were analogous but fictitious facsimiles. What was impressive was the careful way in which reality and alternative realities were constructed in a creative and credible fashion. There were some inconsistencies, but in general *The West Wing* offered a convincing fictional reality, as will be discussed in this chapter.

A careful reading of the series would seem to suggest a disjuncture had occurred between our reality and *The West Wing*'s at some point around Richard Nixon's resignation from office on August 9, 1974. As will be seen, there were numerous references to historical presidents up to Nixon, but only fictional presidents were referred to after this date. In addition, there was a disparity in the dates of presidential elections. Since the time of George Washington, such elections have occurred in a consistent four-year cycle; however, President Bartlet was elected for the first time in 1998. This occurred either two years earlier or two years later than a real presidential election, whichever way one chooses to look at it. In other words, the show featured a deliberately skewed election cycle compared to the one found in the real

3. Historical Fictions 23

world. It would seem clear that the writers of the series intentionally put this anomaly in place. While it is not possible to know for certain why this was done, it is possible to speculate how this anomaly may have occurred.[1]

As far as can be ascertained, few published sources have ventured to offer an explanation for such an anomaly. However, in October 2005 the website alternatehistory.com offered as convincing an account as might be imagined. One contributor to the site, referred to only as "Roedecker," presented a persuasive explanation. The theory hinged on the idea that the 25th Amendment to the U.S. constitution did not occur at the same time in *The West Wing*'s alternative universe. In our version of reality, the 25th Amendment to the constitution of the United States was ratified on February 10, 1967; the amendment clarified presidential succession and the procedure for nominating a vice president, should this be necessary. In essence it made it compulsory to appoint a vice president if the incumbent had died, resigned or was otherwise not able to continue to fulfill his (or her) position. For example, between the assassination of President John F. Kennedy on November 22, 1963, and the inauguration of Hubert Humphrey as vice president on January 20, 1965, there was no vice president. Had Lyndon Johnson died, or been unable to continue as President, the next in line would have been John McCormack, then the Speaker of the House of Representatives. Hence, if the 25th Amendment had not been ratified in 1967, after the resignation of Vice President Spiro Agnew on October 10, 1973, it would not have been mandatory for Richard Nixon to have appointed a new vice president; therefore, the then Speaker of the House, Carl Albert, would have assumed the presidency on Nixon's resignation.[2]

This would have meant that a member of an opposing party (Albert was a Democrat) would have assumed the presidency after the president had vacated the office. In this fictitious and speculative scenario, it is conceivable that Albert, aware that the country had voted overwhelmingly for one party, but had a president of the opposing party, might have put measures in place to call an early election[3]; hence resulting in skewed dates of presidential elections, as found in *The West Wing*. It might be noted that the 25th Amendment was specifically discussed in *The West Wing* in the episode "Twenty-Five" (4/23), which might appear to somewhat negate this theory. However, as no specific dates were mentioned it is possible to presume—in the fictitious universe inhabited by *The West Wing*—that the amendment was passed at a later date; in other words, at some point after Nixon's resignation. This would have enabled the scenario set out in this explanation to have occurred.

Who would have won an election of the kind described above is uncertain. However, what is known is that, in *The West Wing*'s universe, the next president would have been a Republican. In the episode "Lies, Damn Lies and Statistics" (1/21), CJ commented, albeit only in passing, that there had been four Republican presidents in the last 30 years.[4] CJ was talking in the year 2000; hence, 30 years before would have been 1970. The four Republican presidents would therefore have included President Nixon. It would also have included the fictitious Republican President Owen Lassiter (the president before Bartlet) who served for two terms from 1991 to 1999—this being clearly referenced in the series. It is also known (again from direct information offered in the series) that a one-term Democrat, President D. Wire Newman, was in office from 1987 to 1991. This leaves a twelve-year gap from 1975 to 1987, wherein two presidents (therefore, both Republican) served in office. Roedecker speculated this would have been President Gerald Ford (1975–1979) and President Ronald Reagan (1979–1987); however, this was mere speculation and not of great significance, as neither Ford nor Reagan were ever specifically referenced in the show. What was of relevance was that two Republican presidents served in office during this time, hence completing the line of succession, and hence putting in place a tenable explanation for the change in the election cycle in *The West Wing*.

If the timeline of the series diverged from the historical record at the end of the Nixon presidency, as such a persuasive account would suggest, then it might be fair to propose—given chaos theory—that many subsequent events that occurred in our world did not occur in the alternative world of *The West Wing*. One obvious example being the events of September 11, 2001; as will be seen in Chapter 8, there was a response to this event—but one couched in a deliberately ambivalent way. In the episode "Isaac and Ishmael" (3/1), written and broadcast only three weeks after 9/11, it was clearly apparent that a devastating event had just occurred in *The West Wing*'s world, but this was an event that was never fully explained. Insomuch, one of the least obvious, but perhaps one of the most intriguing aspects of the series, was the sense that storylines were taking place within an alternative reality, wherein national and world events were similar but not quite the same as in the actual world. In the case of the events of a quasi–9/11, there was a genuine sense of a beguiling back-story, of events occurring behind the scenes, events that were narratively enticing but unavailable to the viewer. However, in contrast to this, there were instances when the authenticity of an alternative historical discourse was not as convincing; for example, in the episode "20 Hours in L.A." (1/16), real-life personalities such as Jay Leno and David Hasselhoff played themselves, a narrative detail that complicated and, to some extent, lessened the relationship between the real world and the alternative world of *The West Wing*. That is, if history had diverged in 1974, would such celebrities as Leno and Hasselhoff have become celebrities? If Jay Leno was a famous chat-show host and David Hasselhoff a famous actor, then would it not be expected that Bill Clinton—rather than Josiah Bartlet—would be president?[5]

A further way in which the series appeared to have less veracity in its construction of an alternative history lay in its use of fictitious countries. There were two specific examples: the Republic of Equatorial Kundu, first featured in the episode "In This White House" (2/4), and the fictitious Middle Eastern state of Qumar, which was introduced during the third season of the show. Both fictitious states would seem to have had obvious counterparts in the real world: Kundu would seem to have represented Rwanda, while Qumar would appear to have been an amalgam of several Middle Eastern states (Qatar in terms of the derivation of its name, together with elements of Saudi Arabia and Iran in terms of its political position and its fundamentalist ideology).[6] The obvious question then arose: Why would the writers of the series have done this? It certainly did not have any rational coherence in terms of the carefully constructed alternate timeline; even if history had diverged sometime in the 1970s this would not account for the two new states appearing. It might have been thought, in terms of the scope of such polemical storylines—genocide and state terrorism—that it was necessary to reach beyond actual countries. However, for Aaron Sorkin and others to have created two fictional states—which were to play significant roles in a number of episodes—arguably offered the discourse more of a comic-strip feel than that of a serious television drama.

In the case of Kundu, a fictitious country was necessary insomuch as the storyline appeared to be a retelling of the Rwandan genocide of 1994: between April and July of 1994, an estimated 800,000 people were killed in Rwanda, the Hutu section of society killing significant numbers of the Tutsi section of society. The United States, under President Bill Clinton's administration, is said to have known genocide was taking place, but did little to prevent the mass killings. In the retelling, however, Bartlet did take assertive measures— eventually acting to prevent further human slaughter on a mass scale.[7] In the case of Qumar, the reason for the use of a fictitious country was not that *The West Wing* was retelling past events; the reason perhaps lay in the desire to have a greater artistic freedom, specifically the freedom to generate more melodramatic storylines, as Philip Cass put it:

> Why create a fictional country? I suggest that if a country is fictional, its leaders can be safely assassinated and its people bombed or invaded as required. In a cycle of stories that begins at the end of Season 3 and reaches into Season 5, Bartlett and his advisers decide to assassinate the Qumari Defense Minister, Abdul Shareef, who, it is revealed, is secretly backing terrorist organizations plotting against the United States.[8]

This was seen to good effect in the episode "The Dogs of War" (5/2), in a scene wherein Leo, Secretary of State Lewis Berryhill, and the Qumari ambassador, Umar Usef, met in the White House. It was clear, in this scene at least, that Qumar was being used as an obvious cipher for Saudi Arabia. This could be seen, for example, in the tone and in the content of the language Leo used: "Your government actively supports the Bahji. In addition to stoning adulterers and banning anything written after and including the Guttenberg Bible, they preach the overthrow of our government and violence against our citizens."[9] To have explicitly referred to Saudi Arabia (within a fictional discourse) would have perhaps reached for too extreme a polemical posture, hence the argument for creating a fictitious nation state could be understood.

In this way, the series might have been seen to have lost a degree of creative integrity; insomuch as it was difficult, as already intimated, to construct a scenario in which the two fictitious nations states in question could have existed in any believable way. In addition, and to return to the placing of contemporary celebrities into the narrative discourse of the series, it might be noted that elsewhere in the show, in contrast to this apparent aberration, when real figures (for the most part political figures) appeared, there was generally a reasoned argument to support their inclusion. For example, Yasser Arafat was specifically mentioned by Bartlet in the episode "On the Day Before" (3/5)[10]; in a similar way, Fidel Castro was a real figure in the universe of *The West Wing*, as was Queen Elizabeth II, as was Muammar al-Gaddafi and so on.[11] The corollary here rests on the premise that such figures were already apparent and existent in the real world, before the so-called divergence into the fictitious universe of *The West Wing*.

Hence, for example, all the recent presidents of the United States, up to and including Richard Nixon, were alluded to.[12] There was a direct reference to President Nixon in the episode "Six Meetings Before Lunch" (1/18), wherein Mandy, attempting to find a way of replacing a dead panda bear, commented: "Hsing-Hsing. That was his name.... Hsing-Hsing was given to us as a gift by the Chinese government when Nixon..."[13] In addition, there was a further specific reference in the episode "17 People" (2/18). Toby, during a discussion of the potential replacement of John Hoynes as vice president, stated that Hoynes could be "dropped from the ticket in 2002." Toby then went on to speculate: "Because I thought maybe it was an Eisenhower-Nixon..."[14] Other than these two instances, Nixon was only alluded to via a number of satiric references to the Watergate scandal; for example, in the episode "Bad Moon Rising" (2/19), the meeting between the president, the chief of staff and the president's counsel (Bartlet, Leo and Oliver Babish) appeared to deliberately resemble a meeting between Nixon, H.R. Haldeman and John Dean. The joke was compounded by Babish's comedic destruction of a recording device with a gavel just before the meeting began. In addition, there was Josh and Will Bailey's short exchange in the episode "7A WF 83429" (5/1), welcoming the new (and temporary) administration of President Walken. Josh asked: "Do we have any hidden cameras and tape recorders in there?" Will replied: "Not since the mid–1970s."[15]

Perhaps the most interesting and the most significant aspect of *The West*

Wing's alternate universe was the way in which the spirit of President Kennedy was repeatedly evoked. Kennedy was a constant presence throughout the series, from the opening episodes to the final episode itself. For example, the third episode of the opening season, "A Proportional Response" (1/3), originally had a direct reference to Kennedy by name[16]; in the episode "The State Dinner" (1/7) the John F. Kennedy aircraft carrier was specifically referenced; the Kennedy Center was referenced in numerous episodes[17]; Kennedy's famous desk was mentioned in the episode "18th and Potomac" (2/21); Kennedy was explicitly mentioned by name in the episode "Bartlet for America" (3/10)[18]; and two episodes later, in "100,000 Airplanes" (3/12), Bartlet notably referenced Kennedy's famous proclamation of landing a man on the moon: "A President stood up. He said we will land a man on the moon before the end of the decade ... we didn't know anything ... but a President said we're going to do it, and we did it." Kennedy was mentioned again in the episode "The Black Vera Wang" (3/20), wherein Donna noted: "Twenty years ago, seventy-five percent of the people who graduated from the Kennedy School of Government took jobs in public service." In the episode "Access" (5/18), Kennedy (along with his press secretary, Pierre Salinger) was actually shown on archival footage. In the episode "A Change Is Gonna Come" (6/7), Bartlet once again mentioned Kennedy: "John F. Kennedy once said, 'A nation reveals itself not only by the men it produces, but also by the men it honors.'" Kennedy was also mentioned numerous times in the episode "Ninety Miles Away" (6/19); and finally, was mentioned in the last episode of the series, "Tomorrow" (7/22), in a conversation between Bartlet and Santos, wherein they discussed inauguration speeches. Santos commented: "There's no 'ask not what your country can do for you,' JFK really screwed us with that one, didn't he?"[19]

In the context of such multiple and recurring references, it would seem clear that Kennedy's legacy was a significant influence on the series. The explanation of why this was so important might be summed up in a single word: "Camelot." As Melissa Crawley put it: "The narrative of the series is mythic, a modern-day version of Camelot, wherein loyal servants are guided by a righteous king."[20] In the course of the series, Camelot was sometimes directly referenced; for example, in the episode "Running Mates" (7/10), Josh depicted Matt Santos and his wife, Helen, as a young and attractive couple, commenting that it was "Camelot for the 21st century." However, the key reference was to be found earlier in the series, in the twin episodes "20 Hours in America" (4/1/2). Here Bartlet was shown delivering a campaign speech, which ended as follows: "This is a time for American heroes. We will do what is hard. We will achieve what is great. This is a time for American heroes and we reach for the stars.... God bless you and God bless the United States of America." The speech, albeit verging on the maudlin, had clear overtones of Kennedy-esque rhetoric, with the expression "this is the time for American heroes" becoming something of a campaign catchphrase. Mallory O'Brien, the seemingly forever unrequited love interest of Sam, somewhat surprisingly appeared to find the phrase—and the speech—both inspiring and even erotic, telling Sam: "'This is a time for American heroes and we reach for the stars.' I'm weak." Sam replied: "Yes. I think I stole that from Camelot." Sam states that he stole the line from Camelot, but he most likely did not mean the musical, but rather the Kennedy administration.[21] In such a way the line might be considered significant, at least in terms of the political influences upon the show. In a sense it might be said that the entire series was stolen from Camelot, insomuch as Bartlet's White House might be seen as a recasting of the better parts of the Kennedy administration.

The epithet "Camelot," which became such a ubiquitous sobriquet for President Kennedy's period in office, was first suggested by Jacqueline Kennedy, in an interview in *Life* magazine, just a few days after the assassination.[22] In the interview, conducted by the journalist Theodore White, Jacqueline Kennedy explained how she and the president had enjoyed listening to the cast recording of the Alan Jay Lerner and Frederick Lowe musical *Camelot*—in particular the title song, in which Richard Burton as King Arthur had sung of one brief, shining moment that had been known as Camelot. In what may have been a calculated move at mythmaking, the president's widow succeeded in offering a one-word description of the Kennedy administration, one that has endured ever since. The musical, which had opened in 1960, shortly before Kennedy's inauguration, told the story of King Arthur and his roundtable. It was perhaps not one of Lerner and Lowe's most inspired works; however, the comparison between the high ideals of King Arthur and President Kennedy, both slain "kings," proved to be a lasting epitaph, a one-word description that has come to represent—and arguably distort—an entire era.

The intertextual allusions to Kennedy also operated within the scope of a more gruesome arena: President Kennedy achieved such a romanticized status—a shining knight of Camelot—partly because of his untimely and grotesquely violent death. Albeit in a subtle way, the narrative discourse of *The West Wing* appeared to be fully cognizant of this. In the episode "Mandatory Minimums" (1/20), during a speech about candidates for the Federal Election Commission, Bartlet told the following story: "My father was very fond of the analogy of the Irish lads whose journey was blocked by a brick wall, seemingly too high to scale. Throwing their caps over the wall, the lads had no choice but to follow. How many times in the great history of our country have we come to a wall seemingly too high to scale, only to throw our caps to the other side?" In a speech extolling the benefits of the space program, in San Antonio, Texas, on November 21, 1963, President Kennedy told the same story:

3. Historical Fictions 29

Frank O'Connor, the Irish writer, tells in one of his books how, as a boy, he and his friends would make their way across the countryside, and when they came to an orchard wall that seemed too high, and too doubtful to try, and too difficult to permit their voyage to continue, they took off their hats and tossed them over the wall, and then they had no choice but to follow them.[23]

In real life, Kennedy's speech was given on the day before his assassination; in the fictional world of *The West Wing* there would be an assassination attempt on the president in just two episodes' time. In addition, it might be noted that Bartlet did not often refer to his literal father in such a fashion; therefore, it could be argued that Bartlet was not referring to his actual father, but was referring to his presidential father, at least within the fictitious discourse of the show.[24]

In a wider sense, the Kennedy assassination resonated within the general discourse of the series, as it arguably resonates within the general discourse of American culture itself.[25] The fictional assassination attempt on Bartlet has been criticized for lacking the dramatic weight it might otherwise have had. However, the storyline in itself was not unbelievable, if one considers that four out of the 45 presidents of the United States have been assassinated, all via gunshot wounds—a less than inviting 8.9 percent chance of being violently killed in office. In addition to this, the assassination attempt resonated within the series because the assassination of President Kennedy remains such a beguiling subject area. While it will most probably never be satisfactorily resolved, the assassination of President Kennedy remains one of the few conspiracy theories that may possibly have some credibility.[26] For example, although overtly manipulative, Oliver Stone's film *JFK* (1991) put forward what might be seen as a counter-myth, an alternative to the Warren Commission's "official myth." Other sources, for example James Ellroy's novel *American Tabloid*, covered similar ground to Stone's film, offering an alternative version of events to the official account. As such, both Stone's film and Ellroy's novel represented a way of looking at the complexity of the violence within America's darker political spaces; no doubt cognizant of such sources, *The West Wing*'s use of an attempted presidential assassination resonated within the underlying psyche of American culture.

* * *

In terms of the chronological structure of the series itself—in other words, the way in which Bartlet's fictional presidency followed its own historical timeline—this was only of limited concern. This was the case as *The West Wing* generally followed an uncompromisingly chronological configuration to detail the eight years of Bartlet's two terms in office. However, there were some elements of interest: for example, there was a consistent use of analeptic scenes, together with one significant example of prolepsis. In addition, the rare but deliberate use of narrative ellipsis was of interest[27]; here one might note the intentional narrative exclusion at the start of the series—the opening episode would seem to have been set sometime in August 1999, around eight months into Bartlet's first term. In addition, throughout the series there were instances of exact dates being specified, such dates seeming to deliberately match the dates on which the episodes in question were first broadcast.[28] For example, in the episode "In Excelsis Deo" (1/10), during a discussion of the upcoming millennium, the date was given: Thursday, December 23 (the episode being broadcast just eight days before this); likewise, in the episode "Enemies Foreign and Domestic" (3/19), the date on one of CJ's emails was April 30, 2002, only one day behind the date of the episode's original broadcast.[29] As such, the deliberate placing of the series within a precise and detailed timeframe, along with the generally consistent sense of allowing time to pass at the same time as real time, added to the sense that *The West Wing* inhabited a real world parallel to our own.[30]

In an overall sense, the parallel historical timeline of *The West Wing* could be seen as offering the opportunity to explore a mythic discourse. Ruth Wodak, citing Roland Barthes in *Mythologies*, argued that *The West Wing* had attempted to do just this: "I assume that the worlds created in such fictional dramas serve as a second reality or a *myth*."[31] Wodak suggested that such myths, such second realities, provide a space wherein "complex problems" can find solutions, via "seemingly wise politicians" for the audience's "positive values."[32] Thus, it would appear that, in essence, the mythic discourse the series offered was a world as it should have been: what the White House might have been like had John F. Kennedy lived 30 years later and lacked the character flaws he possessed and, of course, had he avoided assassination. Hence, the success of the series can be explained very simply: it was a wish fulfillment for an ideal White House and an ideal presidency. Such an overarching historical structure may not have been wholly part of a conscious design by Sorkin and the show's other writers; however, this is arguably one way in which we, the viewers of the series, might reasonably interpret the show. As will be seen in the next chapter, reader response theory allows the reader the opportunity to fill in the blanks of any cultural text. In other words, it allows us to construct a believable version of events in our own minds, both in terms of a way of understanding the text and (specifically in the case of *The West Wing*) as the opportunity to construct a believable version of events, and to explain the alternate universe that the cultural text in question appeared to inhabit. The expanse and duration of *The West Wing* allowed the viewer not only to infer intertextual resonances, and to put to use all the diverse hermeneutic devices available, but also to place the fictional world into an authentic relationship with the real one—this perhaps going some way to explain the underlying appeal of the show.

4

Death of the Author
Aaron Sorkin as Auteur?

Who is the author of *The West Wing*? There would seem to be a simple answer: Aaron Sorkin; at least this would seem to have always been the general consensus of opinion. In other words, Sorkin has consistently been seen as *the* one significant creative force behind the series. In terms of the critical response to *The West Wing*, it is difficult to find many dissenting voices to this premise: few journalistic sources have contradicted this claim, and likewise, the academic response has generally lent to this way of thinking. For example, Melissa Crawley commented: "The series has always been a product of Mr. Sorkin's personal vision."[1] Cassandra Belek agreed:

> Sorkin is not only the "author" of *The West Wing*, but he had the largest role in its early production and in establishing the pace, tone, and messages of the series.[2]

David Barber noted, however:

> From season five until the end of the series, producer John Wells took over from Sorkin as the show runner, the person who made the decisions about the form and trajectory of the plotlines and the overall style of the series.[3]

In addition, of the monographs written on the series, a number have deliberately signaled Sorkin's significance in their titles; for example, Thomas Fahy's *Considering Aaron Sorkin: Essays on the Politics, Poetics and Sleight of Hand in the Films and Television Series* and Melissa Crawley's *Mr. Sorkin Goes to Washington: Shaping the President on Television's* The West Wing. Other authors have likewise promoted the view of Sorkin's significance to the creative process; for example, Paul Challen, in his book *Inside the West Wing: An Unauthorized Look at Television's Smartest Show*, noted how Sorkin's name resonated in a way those of other television script writers did not: "It's a good bet that the majority of even serious TV viewers barely know the names of the writers of their favorite shows, let alone details of their personal lives."[4]

Also, there would seem to have been a move to overestimate Sorkin's actual authorial contribution to the series; for example, Melissa Crawley claimed that "in four seasons he [Sorkin] wrote or co-wrote 86 out of 88 episodes."[5] This was not strictly accurate and somewhat misleading, albeit most likely unknowingly. In a similar way, Peter C. Rollins and John E. O'Connor's *The West Wing: The American Presidency as Television Drama* put forward the claim that Sorkin was the author of 72 of the then extant 73 episodes,[6] while Jason P. Vest went so far as to inexplicably state: "I award Sorkin a single writing credit even for scripts that he did not solely write."[7] Trevor and Shawn J. Parry-Giles, in their book *The Prime-Time Presidency: The West Wing and U.S. Nationalism*, stated that *The West Wing* was written "almost exclusively for four seasons by Aaron Sorkin."[8] To differing degrees of inaccuracy, all these sources overestimated Sorkin's authorial contribution.

As the series no longer has an official website, the most reliable source to account for the actual writing credits would seem to be the booklet included in the DVD box set *The West Wing: Complete Seasons 1–7*.[9] The writing credits here are consistent with the credits in the opening and closing titles of each episode. From the information given, the writing credits were as follows: of the 89 episodes in Seasons 1–4, Sorkin was credited with 31 sole writing credits and 54 co-writing credits.[10] Hence Sorkin was the sole writer on only a little more than a third of the 89 episodes in Seasons 1–4; and thus, while Sorkin has generally been seen as the significant creative force behind the series, there are at least some valid questions to ask as to just how significant this contribution was.[11]

In addition, the issue of authorship is clouded still further when the role of staff writers is taken into account. Melissa Crawley commented:

> For Sorkin, the job of staff writers is to organize research and contribute ideas and issue-based arguments. He comments: "The most difficult part [is] that I'm going to cramp their style creatively—almost completely, that I'm going to be writing the scripts and that they're going to be doing something else."[12]

Because of this, there was further uncertainty over Sorkin's contribution as *the* writer of the show; according to Eli Attie, the writing staff would pitch story ideas to Sorkin—those that were chosen would be written up and Sorkin would then incorporate this material into the finished script for each episode. Attie: "He [Sorkin] very much wrote and shaped the vast majority of scripts, but from a lot of smart, heavily researched material from a very hardworking staff."[13] In addition, consultants such as Dee Dee Myers contributed political jargon and "twists and thematic concepts"[14]—while in the fourth season other writers, such as Attie and Kevin Falls, would write some of the scripts, which Sorkin "would polish and/or rewrite."[15] As Peter de Jonge put it:

4. Death of the Author 33

> To maintain his elusive parallel universe, one that feels contemporary but is also impossible to pin down in time, Sorkin employs a half-dozen former high-ranking politicos and keeps a close watch "on the dials and gauges." To come up with the four or five story lines the show burns through each episode, the staff reheats old issues from the archives or imagines something plausible enough to have actually happened.[16]

All of this would suggest a much more collaborative writing process than the raw credits would indicate, hence once again serving to question the level of Sorkin's reputation as author of the series.

In terms of the contribution of staff writers, this issue was brought into further focus via the controversy surrounding the writing credits for the episode "In Excelsis Deo" (1/10). The episode was based upon the experiences of Rick Cleveland, one of the several staff writers then working on the series. Cleveland's father had been a Korean War veteran, who spent his final years as a vagrant living on the street; Cleveland had used this as the overarching plotline of the episode. In September 2000, the episode won an Emmy for best script; however, there was a controversial incident, reported in the *New York Times*, that Sorkin had "ushered" Cleveland off-stage before he could deliver an acceptance speech.[17] An online discussion then ensued between Sorkin and Cleveland, with Sorkin, somewhat condescendingly it must be said, explaining that he gave his writers a "story by" credit on a "rotating basis" by way of a "gratuity."[18] What this incident may have revealed, more than anything else, was the degree of power Sorkin held over his writing staff. Peter de Jonge has written of Sorkin's "intense reluctance" to share writing credits with other writers on the show[19]; and Pamela Ezell wrote of "Sorkin's tendency to dismiss the contributions of all other staff writers as 'research,' and to insist that he [was] responsible for the quality of each episode."[20] Thomas Fahy commented how there was a sense in which it was accepted that the writing on the show originated wholly with Sorkin:

> We don't think about the team of writers ... or the staff generating story ideas for *The West Wing*, we think only of Sorkin. Whether intentionally or not, Sorkin has made himself and his image an integral part of his work.[21]

Once again, what all of this revealed was that the issue of authorship on *The West Wing* was not as "clear-cut" as might be commonly supposed.

* * *

In 2003, Sorkin published two books of scripts from the first four seasons of the show; these consisted of the following fourteen episodes:

Pilot (1/1)
A Proportional Response (1/3)
In the Shadow of Two Gunmen Part 1 (2/1)

In the Shadow of Two Gunmen Part 2 (2/2)
17 People (2/18)
Two Cathedrals (2/22)
Isaac and Ishmael (3/1)
Bartlet for America (3/10)
Posse Comitatus (3/22)
20 Hours in America Parts 1 and 2 (4/1/2)
Holy Night (4/11)
Commencement (4/22)
Twenty-Five (4/23)

The act of publishing the fourteen scripts served to confirm Sorkin's position as the authorial voice of the series; this being for the simple reason that Sorkin's signature was therefore established still more clearly upon his work. Therefore, it might be noted that all fourteen scripts chosen for the two volumes were from episodes credited to Sorkin alone; note that there were only seventeen other scripts with such sole Sorkin accreditation, hence the choice of scripts could be seen as being a careful and calculated design to promote Sorkin's authorship.[22] In contrast, it should be noted that the published scripts were almost identical (as far as can be ascertained) to the dialogue as broadcast in each of the episodes. Hence the question could be raised as to whether Sorkin's original scripts had been revised and altered during the shooting process; that is, changed and amended outside of Sorkin's express authorial control. In other words, it is possible that the scripts, as extant in published form, were mere transcriptions of the broadcast episodes, and did not necessarily share an uncompromising relationship with Sorkin's original scripts.[23] It might be noted that the second volume of shooting scripts, with examples from Seasons 3–4, gave detailed information on the script revision process: dates and differing page numbers, different colored pages and so on, but this still did not answer the question surrounding the actual derivation of the published scripts. The point at play here is the idea that if changes had been made during the shooting stage, as routinely occurs during the making of the majority of feature films and television dramas, then such changes may therefore have been outside of Sorkin's textual authority, thus serving to lessen his significance as creator of the series.[24]

* * *

Aaron Sorkin (together with the show's producer, Thomas Schlamme) unexpectedly left the series at the end of Season Four. The reasons for this sudden and unexpected departure have never been fully explained, but it is clear both had planned to stay longer, according to Sorkin himself:

4. Death of the Author 35

> Tommy and I had wanted to take the show to its 100th episode [this would have equated to the 12th episode of Season 5] before handing it over to John, Chris, Alex and Kevin and riding into the sunset. But for various reasons of no interest it was not to be.[25]

Of course, many people may well have had an interest in the reasons for two of the most significant figures behind the series suddenly leaving.[26] However, a more viable area for debate might arguably focus on the way in which Sorkin's untimely departure related to issues of authorship; in other words, a comparison between the so-called "Sorkin seasons" (Seasons 1–4) and the subsequent seasons (Seasons 5–7) without him. Few critics have commented directly on this subject area, but David Barber, for one, noted:

> In its fifth season *The West Wing* staff deal with crises and situations in, amongst other places, North Korea ("Han"), Saudi Arabia ("The Stormy Present") and Israel and Palestine ("The Warfare of Genghis Khan," "Gaza" and "Memorial Day"). This contrasts with the fictional construction of Qumar in the third and fourth seasons bringing the series into closer proximity with the real world and with current affairs.[27]

This was a valid point; in addition, there was an argument to be made that there was, in fact, relatively little discernible difference between the first four seasons with Sorkin and the final three seasons without him, either in terms of the quality of the storylines or in terms of the quality of the dialogue.

It could be argued that the post–Sorkin storylines were of an equivalent quality; however, to claim that the quality of the dialogue did not change in the post–Sorkin seasons might not be so plausible. There have been suggestions that Sorkin's dialogue was almost Shakespearian, at least in terms of its rhythm and its meter; Richard Schiff stated: "Aaron is very open to ideas, to rewording his words. But you have to understand that he writes poetry and he writes music. If you come up with an alternative, it better be in meter."[28] This was not to suggest that prime-time television drama was being delivered in iambic pentameter, but nonetheless there was unquestionably an individual quality to the cadences Sorkin used. Michael A. Wolff put this well, commenting on the way Sorkin's characters constantly bantered:

> The art of banter, which is both a workplace and television writer's art, the true insider's patois (there's a special rhythm to the banter in the show, a staccato syllabification), [this] may be at the heart of *The West Wing*'s success.[29]

However, a comparison of the actual dialogue in the Sorkin and post–Sorkin seasons in fact suggests relatively few discernible differences. For example, would even the most discerning of viewers have noticed a change in the quality of the dialogue in "Enemies" (1/8), "Swiss Diplomacy" (4/9) and "The Long Goodbye" (4/13), episodes in which Sorkin had no hand in the writing? There have been some claims made that Sorkin's writing represented "the best available on prime-time television"[30]—however, Sorkin was capable of falling far below such a standard of writing. To take one example, in the episode "Red Haven's on Fire" (4/17), the scene in the White House with the families of the hostages in Kundu was arguably one of the most ineptly written of all seven seasons. Hence the accepted wisdom that it was Sorkin's rhythmic, metrical and complex dialogue that lay behind the success of the series may not have been wholly correct.

Insomuch as Aaron Sorkin has frequently been envisaged as the authorial voice behind *The West Wing*, a brief discussion regarding the concept of *auteur* theory would appear to be relevant. It might first be noted that Sorkin only wrote scripts for the show, he did not act as director.[31] In other words, he had no input into the visual aspects of the drama: the use of the camera, the lighting and the general *mise-en-scène*. Likewise, Sorkin had little input on the use of music, the set design, the editing and all the other myriad creative facets of making a television drama; Sorkin's contribution consisted only of the written word.[32] As such, it would seem erroneous to perceive Aaron Sorkin as an *auteur* figure; as intimated, Sorkin merely had partial or whole writing credits for most of the first four seasons of the series. If there was a personal signature to be fixed to *The West Wing* the following names might be mentioned: Thomas Schlamme,[33] Alex Graves[34] and Christopher Misiano[35]; between them they directed 82 episodes of the show, over half of the total 155 episodes. As directors they arguably had a more significant role than Sorkin's total of only 30 sole-authored and 54 co-authored teleplays; hence once again serving to diminish Sorkin's generally accepted reputation as the "author" behind *The West Wing*.

* * *

To explore this topic from a theoretical perspective: a significant challenge to the authorial voice came about in 1968 via the publication of Roland Barthes's influential essay "The Death of the Author."[36] In this short essay, an essay that has been seen as marking the beginnings of poststructuralist thought, Barthes questioned the very concept of authorship. Barthes argued that it was language that speaks, not the author, and that "a text's unity lies not in its origin but in its destination."[37] There are always a multiplicity of readings to a text, meanings of which the author is mostly unaware, and it is only when the text is read that such meanings begin to become apparent; in other words, the reader can construct any meaning he or she wishes to construct. The weight of Barthes's argument might thus be seen as dismantling much of the basis of *auteur* theory, albeit in a wider arena than that of cinema or television. This might be argued insomuch as "Death of the Author" was more sophisticated than a mere simplistic dismissal of biographical intent. At its most radical it called into question the way we view not only authors but also so-called "individuals." It spoke of a fundamental questioning of the notion of personality, a fundamental questioning of the self. In what sense can an author, or indeed anyone, be said to be an autonomous, coherent individual? Barthes suggested that the reader, the "I" who approaches a text, was not merely an individual "I," but a plurality of "I's"; in other words, a compound of other multiple readers, of other multiple texts and other multiple codes. Barthes suggested this plurality was almost infinite, and that the reader approaches any text with knowledge of all the other diverse texts they may have previously experienced.[38]

On a less esoteric level, Barthes's theoretical premise could be seen as pointing to a consideration of the moment when an author prepares to create a cultural text. One might note that he or she has only a token understanding of what they are about to write about. Barthes argued that authors were only "minimally aware" of all the myriad complexities of conscious and unconscious thoughts at work in their minds as they submitted words to paper. Hence within any text, there was no sacred meaning, rather it would be the "Barthesian" reader who would create a myriad of potential meanings. While not, strictly speaking, containing infinite possible interpretations, a text would possess as many interpretations as there were readers to read it. In addition, each time we read a novel or view a film, so Barthes argued, we are changed in a small way; our way of thinking being either challenged or reinforced. Hence Barthes would argue that meaning was, in fact, recreated anew via each specific encounter between a reader and a text. Thus intertextuality would seem to be all embracing, as Barthes says of the author: "His only power is to mix writings, to counter the ones with the others."[39] The text thus has no "authority"; there is nothing to constrain a reader constructing any meaning he or she wishes. The author is simply one voice among many, and there is no reason why his or her voice is any more relevant than anyone else's. In this way the author is no longer considered as the sole arbiter of meaning—the author is no longer thought of as the creator—but rather a synthesizer, someone who draws together and orchestrates raw linguistic materials into a "mosaic of quotations"—or, as Barthes preferred, a "tissue of quotations." In other words, all texts are drawn from the vast repository of other texts from a diverse range of cultural repositories. In essence, Barthes's argument seemed to suggest meaning was endlessly deferred; that a text was merely a combination of signs whose ultimate meaning was forever unattainable. The potential meanings of a cultural text were dependent on the linguistic permutations of the reader of that cultural text; as Barthes concluded: "The birth of the reader must be at the cost of the death of the author."[40]

In addition to the poststructuralist arguments of Roland Barthes, there were also a range of theoretical models assembled under the term "reader-response theories." These consisted of a number of approaches looking still further toward the significance of the reader's role in cultural productions, often privileging the reader over the writer. To the general observer this may have seemed like an affront to common sense; however, such theories have been generally accepted as having significant arguments to make. One of the main preoccupations of cultural theory has been to have less concern with the author and to privilege what the text was actually saying; to take an example: Wolfgang Iser's argument points to the problematical issue that no reading can ever exhaust the full potential of a text, that the best a reader can do is to fill the gaps inherent in the text.[41] Similarly, another theory suggests that all cultural texts are polysemantic, and therefore all a reader can do is to provide a reductive interpretation of their own individual making, within their own "horizon of expectation."[42] In terms of *The West Wing*, reader-response theory has seldom been heard within a critical discussion. There were some exceptions; for example, Trevor and Shawn J. Parry-Giles stated: "Regardless of their predisposition toward *TWW*, viewers produce meanings that are negotiated and reflect their engagement with the text as thinking active agents."[43] In a similar way, Philip Cass commented: "The fictional events [of *The West Wing*] may be perceived by another audience to have quite definite parallels with real events in their lives" when such "stories will have acquired entirely different levels of significance."[44] However, perhaps of more interest was Rebecca Williams's argument that the fans of television shows could, to some extent at least, have a potential influence on the narrative of the text.[45] Williams argued that *The West Wing* was a clear example of this and, via the use of Donald Winnicott's theories of object transference and limerence,[46] she offered a convincing argument to explain fan identification with the fictional characters in *The West Wing*.[47] If one takes this latter idea into account, then the prominence of the authorial voice within the text of *The West Wing* arguably becomes still further compromised, at least if one accepts this line of reasoning.

To approach an overall observation as to the issue of authorship in *The West Wing*: it must first be admitted that Aaron Sorkin would seem to have secured the place, at least in terms of the general viewing audience, of being "the author" of the show. However, on consideration this would appear to be a problematical point-of-view. Sorkin had the initial idea to write a television drama about the president and his staff within a fictional White House[48]; it is also clear that Sorkin sketched the original characters; in addition, it would seem that Sorkin provided at least some of the main plotlines; and finally, there was the dialogue—Sorkin's indisputable ability to create convincing and memorable lines for his characters. However, there was another side to the argument: as this chapter has attempted to contend, the romanticized view of the author as an individual genius, a fountain of creativity, producing a literary masterpiece of highly original material, was an overly simplistic notion. Nonetheless, as if to confound this, in "Tomorrow" (7/22), the final episode of the series, Aaron Sorkin was shown sitting in the audience at the new president's inauguration. It was as if the author had returned to the stage to help in drawing our revels to an end. This may likely have been the deliberate intention, but the notion of perceiving of Sorkin as the creator behind the series may, in a final conclusion, have been erroneous, and may have ultimately had more of a commercial motive than anything else. At best Sorkin, as with any other author, acted as a mere arranger of materials—to envisage anything else would be to engender a naive and almost gullible approach to the notion of authorship.

5

On a Wing and a Prayer

Bartlet Deconstructs the Old Testament

One of the most memorable scenes in the second season of *The West Wing* occurred in the episode "The Midterms" (2/3). The scene concerned an encounter between Bartlet and a character called Dr. Jenna Jacobs at a reception in the White House for radio talk-show hosts. The character of Dr. Jacobs has been seen as being a cipher for Laura Schlessinger; at the time of the broadcast, Schlessinger was a talk-radio host who had an ultra-conservative stance. For example, she was accused of being excessively homophobic—referring to homosexuality as "deviant" and a "biological error." It is well known that Sorkin based the scene on the anonymous "Letter to Dr. Laura," which at the time of the episode was a well-known open email to Schlessinger. As such, Sorkin was deliberately plagiarizing this source to foster what was undoubtedly a powerful scene; however, it might be noted that the email itself (written by an unidentified website author) can be traced to numerous published sources, dating back to at least the 1990s, that repeated the same familiar scriptural references.[1]

The scene began with Bartlet addressing his guests; thanking them for coming, joking in a good-natured way; but then he seemed to become sidetracked, looking at Jacobs: "I'm sorry, you're Dr. Jenna Jacobs?" Jacobs responded: "Yes, sir." With a degree of cynicism, Bartlet commented: "It's good to have you here"—going on to scrutinize Dr. Jacobs's qualifications, asking if she was a medical doctor. Jacobs responded that she had a PhD. Bartlet speculated it might be in psychology or theology or social work; but it turned out that Jacobs had a PhD in English literature. Bartlet went on: "I'm asking, because on your show, people call in for advice and you go by the name of Dr. Jacobs.... And I didn't know if maybe your listeners were confused by that, and assumed you had advanced training in psychology, theology, or health-

5. On a Wing and a Prayer

care." Jacobs denied this: "I don't believe they are confused, no sir." Bartlet continued: "Good. I like your show. I like how you call homosexuality an abomination." Jacobs countered by saying: "I don't say homosexuality is an abomination, Mr. President, the Bible does." Bartlet: "Yes, it does. Leviticus." Jacobs: "18:22." After this agreement that they both knew "chapter and verse," Bartlet then launched into the famous list of Biblical injunctions, following which would entail: being allowed to sell his youngest daughter into slavery, as sanctioned in Exodus 21:7; sentencing Leo to death for "working on the Sabbath," as forbidden in Exodus 35:2; and requiring that the Washington Redskins wear gloves to avoid touching the skin of a dead pig, as prohibited in Leviticus 11:7. Bartlet went on: "Does the whole town really have to be together to stone my brother, John, for planting different crops side by side? Can I burn my mother in a small family gathering for wearing garments made from two different threads? Think about those questions, would you? One last thing, while you may be mistaking this for your monthly meeting of the Ignorant Tight Ass Club, in this building, when the President stands, nobody sits."

A number of observations can be made from the scene: first, Bartlet appears to "know his bible" (the attentive viewer would have already recalled he had read it from "cover to cover")[2]—however, the way in which Bartlet made use of this learned knowledge was, to say the least, open to question. Second, Bartlet scarcely seemed to play the polite and gracious host within the scene, being first sarcastic and then deliberately abusive to his guest.[3] In contrast to this, it might be noted that Jacobs remained polite and courteous throughout the scene, attempting—when she was able—to answer the president's questions as honestly as she could.[4] While the scene has generally been seen as demonstrating Bartlet's intellect and his debating skills, a more considered appraisal might have seen the president as a bully, using his position to belittle a person who was, in essence, a guest in his own home.[5]

At the time of the broadcast the scene provoked a wide range of comments on a number of websites, in addition to further responses made later in the published literature. However, the most interesting and challenging reaction to the scene, was arguably made in an article entitled "President Bartlet's Fallacious Diatribe," written by Hank Hanegraaff and originally published in the *Christian Research Journal* in 2001. Hanegraaff was a radio talk-show host himself, in addition to being an outspoken advocate of evangelical Christianity. Hanegraaff's essay began in a measured and balanced manner; he described the way in which Jacobs was submitted to a "tirade" of criticism, noting the barely concealed disdain Bartlet seemed to have for her academic qualifications. Although Bartlet did not explicitly say so, he suggested her PhD in English literature was irrelevant, with the implication she was therefore unqualified to offer advice to her listeners.[6] According to

Hanegraaff, the scene demonstrated how hypocritical Bartlet's seemingly liberal comments were; Sorkin no doubt intended Bartlet to have the higher moral stance, but even a cursory reading would seem to suggest this was not the case.

The scene approached its dramatic core at the point when Bartlet commented: "I like how you call homosexuality an abomination." As intimated above, both Bartlet and Jacobs were fully cognizant of the scriptural reference, Bartlet providing the book, "Leviticus," Jacobs providing chapter and verse, "18.22."[7] The biblical reference itself was not quoted in the episode, but the citation, from the *King James Bible*, was as follows: "Thou shalt not lie with mankind, as with womankind: it is abomination" (*KJB* Leviticus 18.22). As such, Jacobs would seem to have been correct; the Bible *did* say homosexuality is an abomination. In terms of specific nomenclature, Leviticus, as a third to fifth century BCE text, obviously did not use the term "homosexuality"—such a term only having been coined as late as the 1860s. However, to lie with mankind as with womankind represented as close to a proxy translation as might be wished for.[8] It might be noted that Bartlet did not bother to argue within a wider context; in other words, to argue that the proscription against same-sex relationships in an ancient Judaic text might have had more to do with a reaction to the influence of Greek culture, rather than with the law of God. Instead, Bartlet attempted to undermine the idea that homosexuality was an abomination by proceeding upon a detailed exegesis of other Old Testament proscriptions, launching into what Hanegraaff described as a "diatribe" on Mosaic law—a diatribe against some of the more questionable teachings of the Old Testament.

Bartlet's "diatribe" began by referring to Exodus 21:13, suggesting he might have been interested in selling his youngest daughter into slavery, and hence suggesting the Bible sanctioned such a practice. However, the actual verse read as follows: "And if a man sells his daughter to be a maidservant, she shall not go as the menservants do" (*KJB* Exodus 21.13). The verse was somewhat equivocal. Hanegraaff made the point that "the Bible does not commend slavery; rather, it recognizes the reality of slavery" and that "slavery within an Old Testament context was sanctioned due to economic realities rather than racial or sexual prejudices."[9] This would seem to have been a valid point; in other words, that a scriptural text must be read within the context of its own time and within the scope of its own discursive practices. There was also the point that Bartlet, as an American president of a nation state that had only abolished slavery 135 years before, was hardly the most appropriate person to lecture anyone about the depravities of slavery.

Bartlet then turned to Exodus 35.2, the moral obligation to keep the Sabbath day—and to observe this ruling even to the extent of condemning those who violated it to death. The verse from Exodus read as follows:

5. On a Wing and a Prayer 43

> Six days shall work be done, but on the seventh day there shall be to you an holy day, a Sabbath of rest to the Lord: whosoever doeth work therein shall be put to death [*KJB* Exodus 35.2].

The reading from Exodus would seem to have been unequivocal and beyond argument—the instruction appeared to be clear—with Bartlet being correct on all counts.

Bartlet then went on to refer to Leviticus 11.7, which he describes as stating that the act of touching the skin of a dead pig was unclean, and suggesting that if this were true, NFL football players, such as the Washington Redskins, or college players at Notre Dame, should wear gloves when playing on the Sabbath. The verse in question was somewhat equivocal, but read as follows: "And the swine, though he divided in the hoof, and be cloven-footed, yet he cheweth not the cud: he is unclean to you" (*KJB* Leviticus 11.7). Hanegraaff put forward the somewhat pedantic, but nonetheless accurate argument: "Footballs used in college and the professional ranks are not even made of pigskin. Rather, they are made of cowhide."[10] However, there was the idea here that Christian believers would not be bound to follow such restrictions; there being no proscription against eating pork, for example, for followers of Christianity, as there was for most followers of Judaism.

The scene continued, with Bartlet moving on to allude to further supposed scriptural proscriptions, asking whether he should stone his brother for "planting different crops side by side" or burn his mother "in a small family gathering for wearing garments made from two different threads." In these instances Bartlet did not offer specific biblical references; here there was no chapter and verse. Hence it was problematical to ascertain both the source and the veracity of such particular examples of biblical exegesis. According to Hanegraaff:

> Nowhere in Scripture is there any suggestion that we should kill family members for failing to heed Levitical laws regarding seeding and sewing.... Scripture simply uses the object lessons of seeding crops and sewing clothes to illustrate the spiritual and social distinctions between the kingdom of darkness and the kingdom of light.[11]

Hanegraaff summarized his argument by noting: "There is a quantum difference between enduring moral principles such as those regarding homosexuality and temporary ceremonial practices relegated to a particular historical context."[12] Herein was the core of Hanegraaff's argument, insomuch as his line of reasoning had a degree of credibility: an incisive argument that undercut Bartlet's somewhat disingenuous interpretations of Old Testament teachings. Many fundamentalist Christians do follow biblical texts in a consistently literal way, not caring to account for the subtle finesse Hanegraaff allowed; nonetheless, this may have been the constituency Bartlet was pointing toward, a fundamentalist quarter rather than a more literate and sophisticated audience—the audience *The West Wing* purported to attract.

As his own doctorate was in economics, Bartlet might have been better off quoting the Old Testament's views on usury—on the practice of lending money at unreasonably high rates of interest:

> If thou lend money to any of my people that is poor by thee, thou shalt not be to him as a usurer, neither shalt thy lay upon him usury (*KJB* Exodus 22.25).

As usury might arguably be seen as one of the central tenets of capitalism, and capitalism hence in direct contravention of biblical teaching, it would have been of interest to see how Bartlet approached this topic. For example, one might speculate how many fundamentalist Christians in the United States (one of *the* most capitalist of nation states) generated wealth via interest-bearing banking and investment accounts—hence arguably in direct contravention of biblical teaching.

In a similar context, it was of interest that the scene between Bartlet and Dr. Jacobs did not directly allude to abortion, perhaps one of the key polemical issues in terms of the debate between politicians and evangelical Christians in America. It was perhaps significant that the issue of abortion was seldom discussed in the series as a whole; in fact, out of the 155 episodes, only three dealt with the issue of abortion in any depth.[13] The three episodes in question were: the opening episode, "Pilot" (1/1), the episode "In God We Trust" (6/20), and an episode from the final season, "The Al Smith Dinner" (7/6). In the former Bartlet was depicted as having a conveniently subtle attitude to abortion—this was seen in Leo's comment to Al Caldwell (a moderate leader of a right-wing Christian organization) that Bartlet had "spent eight months [presumably the presidential campaign] traveling around the country discouraging young women from having abortions."[14] Caldwell then intimated that Bartlet had not specifically come out against abortion—to which Leo responded: "He [Bartlet] doesn't believe it's the government's place to legislate this issue."[15] Bartlet therefore appeared to have it both ways, to be both pro-choice and anti-abortion. Leo also had a contribution to make in "The Al Smith Dinner." Leo offered this comment: "The Bible is silent on the issue; not one word that says it's the destruction of a human life."[16] Leo's comment seemed to echo the general discourse of the conversation between Bartlet and Dr. Jacobs regarding biblical proscriptions—as such this line might have brought an appropriate edge to the discussion, had it possessed a biblical provenance.

Hanegraaff's article was carefully researched and succeeded in making a number of incisive points about the Bartlet/Jacobs scene. Hanegraaff was also incisive in observing that Sorkin's script, within this scene, was not wholly original:

It seems his tirade was lifted in large part from a widely circulated e-mail that appears on a multitude of gay/lesbian Web sites [sic], in which many of the same questions are posed to Dr. Laura.[17]

In an overarching sense, Hanegraaff's article succeeded in making a robust and penetrating critique of Bartlet's behavior; however, toward the end of his article the impartiality of the discourse put forward seemed to lessen; Hanegraaff began this section of his article by stating:

> From the perspective of Scripture, Christ made it crystal clear that the ceremonial aspects of the law would be fulfilled through His life, death, and resurrection. He made it equally clear that the scriptural injunctions against sexual perversions— including homosexuality—were universal and enduring.[18]

From outside the perspective of scriptural teachings such a claim would seem to be problematic. As has been seen, there were proscriptive laws against same-sex relationships in the Old Testament; however, a reading of Christ's teachings in the New Testament would suggest no specific proscriptive references or even allusions to homosexuality. It was of interest that Hanegraaff offered no specific citations (no chapter and verse) to back up this claim, for the simple reason that none exist. In fact, a reading of Christ's teaching within the New Testament revealed something close to the contrary. During the three years of his ministry, Christ—who lived primarily in the company of men, who had no reported relationships with women, who had an apostle whom he is said to have loved—made no comment on this subject area. Christ did allude to the primacy of marriage (see, for example, Matthew 19.4–6), but he made no explicit comments against same-sex relationships.

However, Hanegraaff's argument went still further, his line of reasoning becoming more and more severe, and it is thus worth quoting the following section in full:

> Sexual liberation has brought homosexuals out of the closet into a shadow of physical affliction where a score of diseases lurk. And as if this were not gloomy enough, the more deadly spectre of HIV infection deepens the shadow, not only for the ever-growing number who die but also for those who are left behind to grieve and to wonder who will die next. We would do well to recognize that the God of the Bible does not condemn homosexuality in an arbitrary and capricious fashion. Rather, He carefully defines the borders of human sexuality so that our joy may be complete. It does not require an advanced degree in physiology to appreciate the fact that the human body is not designed for homosexual relationships. Spurious slogans and sound-bites do not change the scientific reality that homosexual relationships are devastating not only from a psychological but also from a physiological perspective: Irritation of the sensitive rectal mucus layer causes a host of reactions, including diarrhoea, cramps, haemorrhoids, prostate damage, and ulcers or fissures which in turn invite infection. The thin cell layer of the rectum is easily perforated, and its insensitivity to pain can lead to serious complications before a person is aware of any harm.[19]

Such a point-of-view would seem to have been uninformed as to basic human behavior; for example, a same sex male couple will not necessary indulge in anal intercourse. In fact, anal sex may more accurately be seen as an act practiced by both "gay" and "straight" couples, with a probably greater incidence among heterosexual pairings.[20] Yet, what was of interest was the underlying sense of abjection in Hanegraaff's argument, the way in which he had difficulty in disguising a sense of repugnance, one that reached a kind of zenith of abhorrence in the way he finished this part of the article:

> This is just the tip of an insidious iceberg. Common nonviral infections transmitted through homosexual activity are "amebiasis, giardiasis, gonorrhea, shigellosis, chlamydia, syphilis and ectoparasites." Viral infections include "condylomata, herpes, hepatitis B and hepatitis A." Like bacterial infections, these diseases are easily transmitted by oral-genital contact, genital-anal contact and oral-anal contact. Suffice it to say that while there are attendant moral and medical problems with sexual promiscuity in general, it would be homophobic in the extreme to obscure the scientific realities concerning homosexuality. It is a hate crime of unparalleled proportions to attempt to keep a whole segment of the population in the dark concerning such issues.[21]

In the end, such a one-sided analysis of homosexuality eloquently made the very point Bartlet had been attempting to make in the scene under discussion: that a literal interpretation of biblical scripture could not be sustained within any kind of arena approaching a rational debate. Hanegraaff's rationale, in the latter part of his essay, arguably represented another kind of abomination; in other words, it was an ignorant, unfounded and irrational view of human sexuality, one that undermined his earlier cogent argument and hence could not help but reduce the overarching intent of his otherwise convincing essay.

* * *

Of perhaps greater interest (greater interest, that is, than Hanegraaff's irrational fears of sexually transmitted diseases) were some of the other facets to the scene in question besides Bartlet's deconstruction of Old Testament teachings and the *reductio ad absurdum* of simplistic Biblical exegesis. In critical appraisals of the scene such issues have routinely been the focus of attention, but other issues were also of interest: for example, Jenna Jacobs's appearance, her green outfit and her general demeanor; likewise, Bartlet's appearance and demeanor, especially the baton-like, rolled-up paper he held throughout the scene. Dr. Jenna Jacobs was deftly drawn as both an intellectual and a "glamorous" woman. As previously intimated she seems to have been based on Dr. Laura Schlessinger, but this was beside the point; Jacobs herself was an intelligent and impressive woman—her apparel and her brief exchange with Bartlet fully demonstrating this. Jacobs was clearly envious of Bartlet's gender and power, as the color of her outfit perhaps indicated, but it was the subtle and complex way she was portrayed (by British-born actress Claire Yarlett) that remains in the memory.[22]

In this sense, and from a feminist point-of-view, the scene offered an example of how Bartlet was required to demonstrate his mastery over a potentially dominant female figure. Bartlet appeared to effortlessly demolish Jacobs's reputation and character, Bartlet's superiority suggesting Jacobs was little qualified to talk on morality or ethics—and that he (with a word-perfect knowledge of the Old Testament) was her superior. As such, and within the blatantly phallocentric discourse of Sorkin's script, this was always going to be the only possible outcome; with Bartlet being Bartlet, he could not afford to allow an intellectual woman who shared a different world view to escape censure. Bartlet nonetheless appeared to need constant support to effect this seemingly effortless act; not only was he the president of the United States, inhabiting his own environment, with all the prestige this implied, Bartlet required a still further expression of dominance. Throughout the scene Bartlet held a rolled-up—and hence rigid—file of paper, with which he gesticulated throughout the course of his conversation with Jacobs. This may not have been immediately noticeable on a casual viewing, but its sense of dominance demonstrated obvious phallic pretensions. One was reminded here of Tom Cruise's character in Rob Reiner's film *A Few Good Men* (1992), scripted by Sorkin from his stage-play of the same name. Unusually for a Tom Cruise film there was no clear love interest in the narrative; hence, as if to preserve his masculine prowess, Cruise's character was constantly positioned holding a (phallic) baseball bat—both within and without the sporting scenes of the film.[23]

In an overarching way, the "abomination" scene in the episode has commonly been perceived as one in which Bartlet effortlessly put the Christian right in their place; demonstrating this via his command of the Bible and his multiple (albeit questionable) examples of scriptural provenance to prove his point. However, the contrary position would be to see the scene as Bartlet acting, once again, as the bully, lecturing and harassing another party who was not permitted to respond in any kind of equitable way. In an overall sense it would seem that Bartlet's approach was calculated and cynical; as Hanegraaff's article makes clear, all Bartlet succeeded in doing was to expose how a simple-minded interpretation of Biblical quotation can be made to look foolish. Yet, there was no attempt to make a measured analysis of biblical scripture; in other words, to actually endeavor to encompass the issue in anything approaching a meaningful way. In addition, and by way of a final note, there was also the issue of labeling, of depicting the other as "the other," with "the other" routinely being inferior to Bartlet and his staff. As Harold K. Bush put it: "It is worth noting how the series often reinforces certain kind of stereotypes, especially of Evangelical Christians, Republicans, and to some extent of Arabs and Muslims."[24] As such, the episode, or at least the specific scene within the episode, demonstrated an inherent bias that was continually present within *The West Wing*. It was a bias with which much of the viewing audience might have agreed, but it was a bias nonetheless: the unchallenged notion that Bartlet and his staff knew better than their opponents; especially those with radically different perspectives, either from a religious, cultural or racial basis.

6

Cinematic Television
The Mise-en-Scène *of* The West Wing

One of the strengths of *The West Wing* was undoubtedly the way in which it was photographed. It was a television series, but it appeared to possess the production values similar to those of a feature film.[1] One of the most significant figures here, in this context, was Thomas Del Ruth; Del Ruth was director of photography for the majority of the episodes during the first six seasons of the show. Del Ruth's "cinematic style"[2] could readily be seen in the use of soft-focus and diffused lighting, as well as in the inventive use of tracking shots, the so-called "walk and talk" shots that were so ubiquitous throughout the series. The other significant issue that provided the "look" of the show was undoubtedly the quality of the set design; primarily the sets built to represent the interior of the White House, a wholly convincing representation of the West Wing that gave the series its title.[3] In this way the series presented a consummate and sophisticated televisual experience: a set that seemed wholly realistic and true to life and was photographed with authenticity and sophistication. All of these facets built to create a *mise-en-scène* that provided one of *the* key signatures of the show.

In terms of the camera itself, the series made significant use of the Steadicam; this was seen from the very beginning of the drama, in the Steadicam shot of Leo McGarry entering the White House in the episode "Pilot" (1/1). During the course of what appeared to be one long, continuous shot, some 3.26 minutes in length, Leo had twelve different conversations, encountered what has been estimated as over a hundred extras, and passed through numerous different rooms and work spaces—all of this on his way through the White House toward his office.[4] Of still further interest was the famous Steadicam scene near the beginning of the episode "Five Votes Down" (1/4): lasting 2.51 minutes, this was successfully rendered in a single, uninterrupted shot.⁵ Janet McCabe claimed the scene to be "one of the longest and most complicated Steadicam shoots" to be shot in the series.⁶ The scene was shot at the Ambassador Hotel in Los Angeles, the same location as the assassination of Robert Kennedy in 1968. This was a somewhat gruesome detail, given the fact that the scene began with Bartlet delivering a speech on gun control—and that Bartlet appeared to walk through the same hotel kitchen in which Kennedy had been shot and killed. It was almost as if the series had shown Bartlet's motorcade imprudently driving through Dealey Plaza; however, in its defense, it is likely that relatively few viewers at the time of the original broadcast of the episode would have been aware of the somewhat gruesome provenance of its setting. Nonetheless, whatever its derivation, the scene demonstrated the quality and the precision with which the show was photographed.

In a wider context, it might be argued that the Steadicam camera was used in *The West Wing* to as great an effect as any film or television series since Stanley Kubrick's *The Shining* (1980)—the film that had first forged such a new way of filming.⁷ Elsewhere in the series, the use of the camera appeared, at times at least, to have had an almost "Kubrickian" precision and quality. One of the most apposite examples was the celebrated crane shot at the beginning of the episode "Gaza" (5/21); the episode began with a close-up shot of a young Palestinian boy—ostensibly in Gaza—kicking a football from a vertiginous cliff, in synchronized time to the entrance of a helicopter flying overhead. The key feature of the scene, and what made it so remarkable and even "Kubrickian," was the way in which the arc of the football and the arc of the incoming helicopter appeared to match each other within a symmetrical frame. The series began just outside of Stanley Kubrick's lifespan—but had he lived to see it there is a probability that Kubrick may have appreciated at least some of the visual aspects of the series.⁸

In terms of *The West Wing*'s visual grammar, one of the key elements resided in the way in which the show was lit. In other words, there was a distinctive and inventive style to the use of lighting throughout the course of the show's run, what Michael Dumlao described as "some of the most evocative uses of lighting ... ever experienced in television."⁹ The lighting, at times diffused, at times impressionistic, at times almost *film noir*-esque, had an evocative quality throughout the series—especially the use of light and shade, what Janet McCabe described as: "the chiaroscuro shafts of contrasting light and shadow."¹⁰ There were exceptions to this signature style; for example, in the episode "Enemies" (1/8) there was an innovatively lit scene in Josh's office: as Josh was talking to Mandy, there was a back-lit sunset, which offered the scene a wholly different character to the show's usual approach. There were also episodes in which the typical use of the camera and the lighting were deliberately subverted; this could be seen, for example, in the convention scenes during the episode "2162 Votes" (6/22). As Thomas Del Ruth commented, this particular episode featured "kinetic handheld camera movement and harsh spotlight, [which] contrast[ed] with the traditional *West Wing* look."[11] However, in terms of the overall lighting of the show, it mostly retained a distinctive signature: a rich, dark, soft demeanor; a factor that may well have contributed to the enduring character of the series.

In addition to the use of lighting in the series, there was also the issue of the actual quality of the image, as perceived by the viewer, either via live television of the time, or via the subsequent release on videotape, DVD and then online streaming. While the series consistently possessed the look of a feature film (cinematic television in other words), in contrast to this—literally in contrast—there was a lack of definition to the picture quality, a sense of soft focus to the images as presented on screen. It would seem that this was intentional; such a style of diffused representation would seem to have been a deliberate design to inform the quality, the disposition and the character of the show. In this sense it is perhaps of interest that, as of the time of writing, the series has not been released in Blu-ray format. The most likely reason is that there would have been little significant improvement in the quality of definition, simply because of the inordinate soft focus of the original film stock, and hence this would not allow for an enhancement in the clarity of the image. In this way, and in the age of high definition television, *The West Wing* retains a distinctive character. It was a television series, but one of its lasting qualities indicates an identity beyond such constraints.[12]

In a wider context, outside of issues of picture definition and the concept of Thomas Del Ruth's "dark" lighting, there are other points to make around the quality of the cinematography. According to Del Ruth himself, "the drama's visual style [was] romantic." This was perhaps as accurate an appraisal as any; a romantic style was apparent in the soft focus, the subdued lighting, the sumptuous White House sets and the ubiquitously fluid camera movement. All of these qualities enabled *The West Wing* to rise above the usual mode of television drama. However, while the style may have been described as romantic, the use of the camera frequently verged toward the conservative, insomuch as there were relatively few complicated practices put into play. For example, there were few uses of composite dissolves,[13] there was little use of deep focus, there was little use of freeze frame,[14] there was no use of split screen technique and so on. Instead the series generally followed a relatively conventional mode of expression in the way it presented its *mise-en-scène*. Nonetheless, as with the aforementioned opening shot of the episode "Gaza," this was not to say that the show possessed no instances of innovative camera work. For example, the episode "Take This Sabbath Day" (1/14) presented a range of cinematic scenes: an atmospheric rendering of the Supreme Court, the scenes of Air Force One (albeit partially created via CGI), the scenes within the synagogue, even the scenes of the White House in the snow—all were rendered in an impressive way. Similarly, the episode "The Midterms" (2/3) began with an impressive and technically proficient scene, a two minute continuous shot of CJ walking through the West Wing; likewise, the episode "Shutdown" (5/8) included one of the series' most imposing location shots—a cinematic walk to Congress by Bartlet and his staff; in "Abu el Banat" (5/9) there was an innovative crane shot of the Christmas tree on the White House grounds; there was a surprising white screen opening to the episode "Opposition Research" (6/11); there was the use of hand-held cameras at the beginning of the episode "2162 Votes" (6/22); finally, there was the use of montage in the episode "The Mommy Problem" (7/2), and then, to much greater effect, in a cinematic montage of Washington, D.C., at the start of the episode "Tomorrow" (7/22), followed by a montage of scenes featuring the show's main characters, all adding to signify a sense of closure to the narrative.

In addition to the general sense of conventionality in the use of the camera, a further range of traditional techniques could be found within the series. For example, there was the use of establishing shots; in other words: a tendency to use establishing shots to open each of the four main acts in each episode.[15] Also of interest was the issue of ASL (average shot length). The issue of ASL has been much discussed within film and television studies in recent times, and it has been noted that shot lengths are becoming shorter and shorter. In this way, it might be noted that although *The West Wing* included a number of deliberately long-held scenes; it also included, as Jason P. Vest put it, "numerous short scenes that Sorkin [placed on top of] each other [to] produce an impressionistic experience."[16] As far as can be ascertained, research has not been undertaken to define the average shot length of the series; however, from a cursory consideration, a reasonable conjecture would be to presume that the series had something approaching an average ASL, at least in terms of other current television dramas.

The West Wing was also conventional in its use of voice-overs, especially in the way the voice was gendered; the voice-over in film (and television) has always been predominantly male, the female voice commonly being restricted to the corporeal body rather than abstract verbal communication. In *The West Wing* this was generally the case. Voice-overs were mostly restricted to the famous phrase "Previously on *The West Wing*" at the beginning of each of the show's episodes,[17] and of these instances only a small minority had a female voice-over, usually either Allison Janney as CJ or Janel Moloney as Donna.[18] As will be seen in Chapter 18, in a discussion of feminist issues within the series, the significance of the female voice would appear to have been continually reduced and displaced throughout the narrative of the series.

Television might be said to represent one of the most eloquent examples of Theodore Sturgeon's famous dictum: "Ninety percent of everything is crap."[19] In such a way, television has been described as representing the lowest of low cultural common denominators. Hence one of the most significant qualities of *The West Wing* was the way in which it was able to demonstrate such a degree of artistic and imaginative excellence. In a theoretical context, within a postmodern reading, television has always consisted of surface rather than depth, literally so: it consists of little more than the rapid movement of a myriad of pixilated images on a flickering screen, albeit a series of pixels arranged in an exquisitely complex order—the ultimate pointillist painting. In addition, television—like popular music—has never had a modernism to be "post to," but with its ever-changing flow of almost ubiquitously banal imagery, television remains a decidedly postmodern part of our culture.[20] In David Lyon's argument, television can be seen as both a "driver" and a part of consumer culture,[21] insomuch as television and consumer culture belong together and have grown symbiotically since World War II. This notion links with Jean Baudrillard's idea that the postmodern splits away from the modern when the product of demand—of consumers—becomes central,[22] with television acting as "the production of needs and wants, the mobilization of desire and fantasy," acting in this role as a "politics of distraction."[23] Hence television must be seen as residing at the center of the hegemony of consumerist popular culture, if only for the reason that the vast majority of television—especially American television—"lives and dies" via its success in the commercial market. By way of an antidote to all of this, *The West Wing* arguably offered an example of how such cynical capitalist and consumerist forces could be overcome; the show managed to prevail within the tarnished environment of network television drama, not to mention the ever-present demands of a consumer-driven discourse, to engender a cultural production of authentic and lasting prestige.

As intimated at the start of this chapter, *The West Wing* could therefore be described as a major network television drama that possessed more the diverse traits of a high-quality feature film than a standard television series. If this was the case it was a very long feature film, some 155 hours in length,[24] but throughout its seven-year run the show consistently demonstrated a richly cinematic view of the world. It could be argued that one of the reasons why *The West Wing* was such a convincing dramatic narrative was because of the cinematic way in which it was photographed; albeit in conjunction with a diverse range of other facets to the drama, such as the scripts, the acting, the sets and so on. The many millions of viewers of the series—both of the original broadcasts and of later recorded forms—arguably believed (in the characters and in the drama) because of the sense of authenticity provided by the photography—by the *mise-en-scène*. In a final consideration, this ultimately afforded *The West Wing* one of its most enduring artistic and creative properties.

7

The Signifier and the Signified
Structuralist Readings

Structuralism was an intellectual movement that began in France in the 1950s, primarily located within the work of the anthropologist Claude Lévi-Strauss and the literary critic Roland Barthes. In essence it was the belief that things could not be understood in isolation, that they have to be seen in the context of the larger structures of which they were a part. In other words, structuralism argued that individual units of any system had meaning only by virtue of their relationship to one another. In a wider sense, structuralism might therefore be said to have been an attempt to apply logic to the human subject and to the creations of the human subject. According to Terry Eagleton, structuralism scandalized the literary establishment because of this claim, because of its neglect of the individual, because of its clinical approach to the "mysteries" of literature and because of its seeming incompatibility with common sense.[1] However, the counter argument would be to observe how traditional criticism had previously attempted to do little more than look into a window on the author's psyche, while structuralism, in Eagleton's argument, appeared to look into a window on the universal mind. Hence "meaning," in its conventional sense, does not exist; as Eagleton put it: "However far back we push, however much we hunt for the origin of meaning, we will always find a structure already in place."[2]

Eagleton's assertion might be open to argument, but what is clear is the fact that signs depend upon their location for their meaning; for example, a skull and crossbones on a bottle might indicate poison, while a skull and crossbones on a flag might indicate a pirate ship. In other words, meaning is not the result of a specific correspondence between signifier and signified, but rather the difference and the relationship between signifier and signified. For example, at a traffic light there is nothing inherently "go" about green or

7. The Signifier and the Signified

"stop" about red; what is significant is the relationship between the two and our understanding of that relationship. In a broader sense, structuralist readings allowed for a more extensive form of hermeneutic readings to be made about narrative discourses; for example, Claude Lévi-Strauss argued that mythological stories from *all* human societies had a set of recurrent themes (incest, fratricide, patricide, cannibalism), that myth was a kind of "collective dream," capable of being encoded and then decoded, and that myths therefore reveal the essential similarity of human nature across the world.[3] A structuralist reading thus enables one to perceive such significant patterns, and to draw conclusions from "such patterns about the culture that is being investigated."[4] Therefore, and in a still broader sense, Roland Barthes's argument that all fictional dramas serve as an alternate reality, with something close to mythic qualities,[5] has always been one of the key aspects of structuralism, and one that will be explored within this chapter.

In terms of *The West Wing*, a structuralist reading offers a wide range of rewarding interpretative opportunities. Some obvious ways to begin would be: to consider the binary oppositions (so beloved of structuralists) within the show; to consider the use of proper names throughout the series; to take a further look at the intertextual resonances in the show; to analyze generic conventions; and to deliberate on the underlying narrative structures in play, together with reflecting on the linguistic comparisons, semiotic patterning and the underlying patterns and motifs present within the narrative.[6] This chapter will also offer a discussion of the use of language itself, specifically, an analysis of the use of Latin in the episode "Two Cathedrals" (2/22); and then finally—after a brief foray into the phenomenological implications within the series—a concise structuralist reading will be made via an exploration of the way the series dealt with a particular article of masculine attire, what might be termed the phallic semiotics of the necktie.

The beginning and ending of *The West Wing*, taking into account its entire seven-year run, had a number of relevant pointers.[7] For example, the first words of the series consisted of an innocuous voice-over by a waiter in the Four Seasons Hotel in Georgetown: "Two Absolut Martinis up, and another Dewars rocks."[8] This opening scene concerned an encounter between Sam Seaborn and a newspaper reporter, meeting off-the-record to discuss Josh Lyman's future at the White House after he had insulted a conservative Christian spokesperson live on television. However, from a structuralist perspective what was of interest was the way the opening episode ended, with another reference to alcohol. Bartlet asked Mrs. Landingham: "What's next?" Mrs. Landingham listed the evening's schedule: "Governor Thomas and the Majority Leader have asked to be conferenced in, and the group from NASA is assembling for their photo-op. At seven o'clock you have, uh, cocktails."[9] Although Leo, Bartlet's chief of staff, and John Hoynes, the vice president, would both be shown to be recovering alcoholics, alcohol would not play a particularly significant role in the series. However, within these references to alcohol (at two such significant points in the opening episode) there was a subtle reading to be made: the idea that alcohol (and alcoholism) *does* play a significant role within the discourse of American life, especially within American political life.[10] Hence a closer attention to such subtle structural issues arguably pointed out a subtextual theme that might otherwise have remained unobserved.

Also within the opening episode of the show, one sphere of action related how Bartlet had fallen off a bicycle and sprained his ankle. The reason for Bartlet "riding his bicycle into a tree" was supposedly the result of a paroxysm of temper, caused by the president's twelve-year-old granddaughter, Annie, receiving, a "Raggedy Ann Doll with a knife in its throat," the doll (and the knife) having been sent by a conservative Christian group. However, this occurred off-screen, and in retrospect the actual reason for the accident may have been due to other causes; in other words, to the effects of multiple sclerosis, albeit unknown to the audience, unknown to the characters in the narrative, and perhaps even unknown to the writers of the series.[11] Hence within a structuralist reading, the sense of a fall at the very beginning of the narrative could be seen as gathering a further resonance. In a symbolic mode, Bartlet's entrance into the narrative, using a cane, could also be seen as resembling that of the wounded king from folklore. This was an idea that would find greater relevance as the course of the story enfolded, with the fall representing a fall from grace, almost as if in a biblical sense, albeit once again embedded within a deeply symbolic mode.

* * *

In terms of binary oppositions, a structuralist analysis of *The West Wing* offered a diverse range of other readings. It is unlikely that the writers and the audience of the show would have been wholly interested in such oppositions; however, a structuralist reading at least offers the opportunity to uncover a range of issues that were not wholly apparent. It would seem that binary oppositions, in and of themselves, are self-evidently existent; the concept of a word would not exist unless it had a binary opposition; for example we cannot have the idea of "good" without its opposite, "evil," or "male" without "female," or "light" without "darkness" and so on.[12] This property could be seen throughout *The West Wing*—with such oppositions often revealing the superiority of one over the other; for example, male and female, white and black, heterosexual and homosexual, Catholic and non–Catholic, aggressor and non-aggressor and so on. The list of such oppositions is a long one and they are too numerous to consider in detail here; however, some will be discussed in the succeeding chapters: male and female within a discussion of feminism in Chapter 18, white and black within a discussion of race in Chapter 12, heterosexual and homosexual within a discussion of gender in Chapter 13, Catholic and non–Catholic within a discussion of religion in Chapter 11, and aggressor and non-aggressor within a discussion of international law in Chapter 18.

At a more specific level, a number of other oppositions might be cited: for example, the binary single and married. A minimal analytical survey reveals how a significant majority of the characters in the series were unmarried and unattached—the relevance of this having subtle implications, as will later be discussed.[13] In a similar sense, there was the continual opposition of Democrats and Republicans, Democrats being consistently "good," Republicans being consistently "bad." The show was often charged with a degree of political bias because of this relatively simplistic partiality; however, it should be noted that there was a degree of subtlety in such sympathetic Republicans as Arnold Vinick and Ainsley Haynes. Finally, Lévi-Strauss believed the most important binary opposition to be nature and culture: "nature" being the way things are—"culture" being the way we make them out to be; in *The West Wing* this would be played out consistently across the show's run, as the observant viewer may well have perceived.

* * *

Roland Barthes famously declared that the proper name was "the prince of signifiers" and that its "connotations" were "rich, social and symbolic."[14] Within a structuralist discourse words themselves are rich, social and symbolic; however, to Barthes the proper name was of still more specific importance. This can readily be seen within *The West Wing*, if one looks at some of the main characters. Beginning with the president himself, the name Josiah Edward Bartlet was said to have derived from Josiah Bartlett, a supposed ancestor of the fictitious Bartlet—the original Bartlett having been the fourth governor of New Hampshire from 1790 to 1794 and a signatory to the Declaration of Independence. Otherwise, the name Josiah, together with the name of the first lady, Abigail, were names that would not have been out of place within a Puritan discourse, as if they might have been present at the Salem witch trials.[15] A number of the names of other characters had connotations of ethnicity: for example, "Leo McGarry" obviously suggested Scottish or perhaps Irish ancestry; two of the president's other aides, Toby Ziegler and Josh Lyman, had names that may have pointed the viewer to a Jewish ethnic identity. In the case of Toby, his surname could not help but have another resonance; the name echoing that of Ron Ziegler, President Nixon's press secretary.[16] In the case of Josh Lyman, the first name, Josh, could obviously be seen as indicating one who teased, who was not always serious; while the surname, Lyman, could be seen as suggesting a less than veracious demeanor, both attributes to some extent resembling Josh's actual character. This would not be to imply that this was either a conscious or unconscious decision, simply that the actor, the scriptwriter, and the audience itself—via an act of osmosis—came to see these qualities via the naming of the character. In a related sense, Sam's name, Sam Seaborn, seemed to suggest a sense of wholesomeness and even whiteness. Similarly, the name Mrs. Landingham—Dolores Landingham—seemed to represent security, a way of grounding Bartlet from his youth to his presidency.

In terms of the use of female names, an initial point of interest was the use of gender-ambivalent names for a significant number of female roles, as in the following:

- CJ Cregg
- Joey Lucas
- Mallory O'Brien
- Andy Wyatt
- Ainsley Hayes
- Jordon Kendall

- Hogan Cregg
- Ricky Rafferty
- Lou Thornton
- Laurie (no given surname)
- Ginger (no given surname)

Whether such gender-ambivalent names had a particular relevance remains open to speculation, but it is perhaps relevant to note that there was no corresponding ambivalence in the naming of male characters.[17] Elsewhere, female characters were often somewhat demeaned by their names; for example, both of Toby's assistants, Ginger and Bonnie (neither had designated surnames), had names that vaguely resembled the names of pets, rather than people. To this one might add the names of female characters such as Mandy and Donna and Ronna—all shortened "pet-names" with vaguely demeaning connotations. Also, it might be noted that the full names of such characters—Madeline Hampton and Donatella Moss and whatever Ronna Beckman's first name may have been shortened from—were rarely if ever used.[18]

One of the most interesting names in the series was that of Mallory O'Brien. Aside from having a gender-ambivalent first name, Mallory's surname was also of interest. Given that Mallory was Leo McGarry's daughter and that she was unmarried, Mallory's surname might have been expected to be McGarry, but instead it was O'Brien, her mother's family name. This was never fully explained within the series; on a simplistic level Mallory's surname could not have been McGarry, as the trick of Sam not realizing she was Leo's daughter (as played out during her first appearance in the opening episode) would not have worked. Aside from the beguiling nature of her name, Mallory was one of the most intriguing of the show's minor characters; played by Allison Smith, Mallory appeared in a total of only eleven episodes of *The West Wing*, but this spanned all seven seasons, with Mallory's char-

7. The Signifier and the Signified

acter appearing in both the first episode, "Pilot," (1/1) and the final episode, "Tomorrow" (7/22). From the beginning to the ending of the series, she could therefore be seen, via her Arthurian name,[19] as a consistent reminder of the Camelot presence within the show; a subtle allusion to JFK's influence on the parallel court of President Bartlet's idealized "roundtable." This was an apt example of Barthes's argument; Mallory's name *was* rich, social and symbolic. This may or may not have been the conscious intention of Aaron Sorkin (or whosoever chose the name Mallory), but nonetheless the name resonated throughout the series; from the first to the last episode it provided a consistent allusion to the captivating quality of JFK's presidency.

Elsewhere, the use of names was of interest for a number of other reasons; for example, in terms of the issue of race. This was evident in the naming of the president's personal aide, Charlie Young. Here was a black man with a commonplace first name and a surname betraying his youthfulness—together with an overarching sense of the ordinary—and hence there seemed to be a degree of condescension, albeit in an unintended way. The two other main black characters, Admiral Percy Fitzwallace and Dr. Nancy McNally, both had significant names, insomuch as both appeared to have clearly recognizable slave names. Both names seemed to have a Scottish/Irish derivation, which was obviously less than likely to reflect an authentic ethnic lineage.[20] Otherwise character names worthy of attention included: the somewhat archly name psychiatrist Stanley Keyworth; the White House curator Bernard Thatch; the White House counsel Oliver Babish; Ann Stark, a former friend of Toby's; Tabitha Fortis, the new Poet Laureate; and Roy Ashland, the chief justice of the Supreme Court. In addition, some of the other names took on an almost Dickensian sense of exaggeration, such as: Bertram Cravenly in "Inauguration Part 1" (4/14); Mark Farragut in "The Indians in the Lobby" (3/8); Wendell Triplehorn in "Swiss Diplomacy" (4/9) and so on. Finally, the names of the twins of Toby and Andy—Molly and Huck—may initially have seemed to have been names with an interesting literary derivation, from Molly Bloom and Huckleberry Finn. However, Molly was named for Zoey's murdered secret service bodyguard, and Huck—although his name was short for Huckleberry—was named for Andy's grandfather.

* * *

In terms of the use of language itself, one of the most salient issues within *The West Wing* was the relative lack of profanity, the relative lack of expletives. As will be discussed in Chapter 15 within a comparison of the show to *The Wire*, because of network television restrictions *The West Wing* was not able to use authentic "street language."[21] However, an analysis of those expletives that were used, however mild, would appear to be of interest. For example, there was a relatively common use of scatological imagery, especially the use of the word "pissed," not to mention "piss," and even "pissy."[22] To take just one episode, "Bad Moon Rising" (2/19): here Donna commented that someone was "pretty pissed," CJ noted that Toby was "pissed," Jamie Hotchkiss, a journalist, told CJ he was "pissed," and finally, Leo told Oliver Babish he was "acting a little pissy," to which Babish replied: "Yeah, well, I'm pissed." This particular word, within an American context, did not possess the same taboo quotient as it did in British usage. In the United States, the word would routinely mean irritated or frustrated—seemingly lacking the context of inebriation, as found in the United Kingdom, which ultimately derived from the literal meaning: an onomatopoeic word for urination.

In a similar, if more extreme example, there was the use of the word "wanker." To a British audience, familiar with the linguistic demureness of the series, this may have come as something of a surprise. The usage occurred in the episode "The Birnam Wood" (6/2), wherein Josh was complaining to CJ about Donna's "IRA boyfriend." CJ questioned: "The dashing photojournalist?" Josh responded: "Yeah, I think the professional term is wanker." Josh was describing a hospital visit to Donna, in Germany; the dashing photojournalist was Colin Ayres, a Northern Ireland photographer (played by Jason Isaacs) with whom Donna had had a brief romance. In American English the word in question was generally used to describe a useless person; while in British English the word had the same meaning, but also acted as a ubiquitous synonym for masturbation, a "wanker" literally being someone who wanks, someone who masturbates. However, the word in an American setting lost some of its taboo quality, hence its use in the otherwise restricted linguistic discourse of *The West Wing*.

There were a number of other instances: in the episode "Manchester Part 2" (3/3), Toby stopped just short of uttering a very taboo expletive: "I'm from the United States of suck my...," while in the episode "The Women of Qumar" (3/9), CJ told Toby: "You know, if I was living in Qumar I wouldn't be able to say 'Shove it up your ass, Toby.' But since I'm not, shove it up your ass, Toby." CJ also had two instances of expletive language in the episode "Internal Displacement" (7/11), first castratory and then onanistic: "Let's chop the financial balls off these genocidal bastards" and "I feel like I'm handing out towels at the Playboy mansion." Finally, Charlie had several usages of euphemistic language; while the series lacked any usage of the common Oedipal expletive, it was at least alluded to in the episode "The Red Mass" (4/4). Charlie: "At several points he suggest[ed] that I might have an improper relationship with my mother." A remark of higher satiric value occurred in the episode "Privateers" (4/18). Referring to Jean-Paul (the French student who had succeeded Charlie in Zoey's affections), Charlie made the following comment: "Zoey's being indicted into the DAR and there's a reception. And Jean-Paul thinks it's unnatural, and he's the son of a count." This was arguably one of the funniest lines

7. The Signifier and the Signified

in the entire series, "a son of a count," whether intended or not, was satirically amusing. It was perhaps germane that a black character, Charlie, came closest to using such so-called street language or four-letter-word nomenclature (the barely disguised references to "motherfucker," and "cunt").

However, as to the most extreme use of linguistic profanity in the series, this came from an unexpected source, Mrs. Landingham, in the episode "Two Cathedrals" (2/22): "Mr. President, your father was a prick." As intimated, the unadorned, undisguised and explicit use of the word "prick" perhaps remains the most jarring use of language in the series.[23] From a psychoanalytic perspective this was significant, as Bartlet's father was, in a literal sense, a prick, or at least he possessed the signified object, what Jacques Lacan referred to as the "ultimate signifier," with which to generate his offspring. The implication of this issue will be discussed in greater depth in Chapter 22, within a discussion of psychoanalytical theory; however, Mrs. Landingham's comment and her succinct deliberations upon Bartlet's father and his qualities as a human being were well made, and to some extent offered an explanation of some of Bartlet's actions in the series.

By way of a final consideration of the use of explicit language, one might point to a usage of language other than English. The usage in question came in the same episode, "Two Cathedrals" (2/22), in the celebrated scene wherein Bartlet had the National Cathedral in Washington, D.C. sealed, and then berated God for allowing the meaningless death of Mrs. Landingham. The final section of Bartlet's tirade was delivered in Latin, therefore allowing for a more candid and overt discourse. However, because of Martin Sheen's less than perfect command of Latin pronunciation, it is not easy to know what he was saying. A transcription/translation of the speech was published in both *The West Wing Script Book*[24] and in *The Official Companion to The West Wing*.[25] It reads as follows:

> Haec credam a deo pio? A deo iusto, a deo scito? Cruciatus in crucem. Tuus in terra servus, nuntius fui. Officium perfeci. Cruciatus in crucem. Eas in crucem!
> Am I really to believe that these are the acts of a loving God? A just God? A wise God? To hell with your punishments. I was your servant here on Earth. And I spread your word and did your work. To hell with your punishments. To hell with you!

However, while this represented the official version, it was only an approximate transcription of what Bartlet was saying—or attempting to say. A close reading of the scene would aspire to offer a more literal translation of Bartlet's invective "tirade" to God:

> *Gratias tibi ago, domine*
> I give thanks to you, Lord.

Note Bartlet's ubiquitous sense of sarcasm in this opening comment—note also that this opening comment was deleted from both of the official sources.

> *Haec credam a deo pio, a deo justo, a deo scito?*
> Am I to believe these things from a loving god, a just god, a wise god?

This agreed with the official sources.

> *Cruciatus in crucem*
> To hell with your punishments.

This could be translated as such, but to put this literally it was saying, "Put punishments onto a cross."

> *Tuus in terra servus, nuntius fui; officium perfeci*
> I was your servant, your messenger on the earth; I did my duty.

Again, this was similar to the official sources.

> *Cruciatus in crucem eas in crucem*
> To hell with your punishments and to hell with you.[26]

As above, this could be translated as such, but in a literal sense it was saying something much more polemical, something that appeared to literally say: "You were punished on a cross, get back on the cross," which was arguably more offensive to God, to Christ, to believers in Christianity and even to atheists. God, of course, offered no reply to these presidential goadings—in either English or Latin—but nonetheless the scene remains one of the most iconic from the entire run of the series.

In an intertextual arena, Sorkin's use of untranslated Latin may have been influenced by a similar usage in Benjamin Britten's opera *The Turn of the Screw* (1954). Within the libretto there was a scene found nowhere in Henry James's novel, but one that expanded on the implied moral corruptness of the source narrative—the oblique suggestion of child abuse. As in *The West Wing*, the scene in the opera also contained lines of untranslated Latin; the Latin verse in the opera went as follows:

> Oh, clunis, caulis, follis, vectis, cucumis, fustis.

This being translated as:

> Oh, anus, cabbage stalk (penis), bellows (scrotum), crowbar, cucumber, knobble sticks (phallic symbols).

This was followed, in English, by the phrase:

> Bless ye Lord.

Thus it became, in the words of one critic, "a gay Christian male's earnest claim for a kind of sanctity of the gay male body, unrecognized by Britten's church."[27] Whether Sorkin (and other writers on the show) were aware of Britten's opera and the use of Latin to disguise blasphemies and obscenities is open to question; however, the similarities were present if one wished to see them.

* * *

7. The Signifier and the Signified

By way of a final exploration of the structuralist elements within *The West Wing*, one specific example will be considered; in this case, the signifier being an item of male apparel, the necktie.[28] As is well known, the necktie has often been seen as having strong phallic indicators. Freud himself noted this in an essay on fetishism in 1927; as Joanne Finkelstein noted:

> Freud confidently described the necktie ... as a strong symbol of the phallus ... the conventional long tie runs from the prominent male larynx, along the torso and terminates as a signal to the male sex organ.[29]

In other words, if one looks at this particular signifier within a semiotic arena, the necktie becomes an extended, thin object hanging down from a male body, with an arrow pointing directly toward the phallus—hence representing what might be seen as an obvious indicator of phallocentric dominance. It should be noted that the necktie has always been an item of clothing with little practical usage—being of mere decoration; also, it should be noted that boys begin to wear ties around the age of puberty, that girls and women seldom wear ties, and that if they do there is often a sense of transgression. This sense of transgression possibly arises because of the sense in which the tie—as worn by girls and women—points to something that is not there—there being no phallus to signify; hence a jarring sense of something close to a sense of fetishism.[30]

In *The West Wing*, the necktie was—unsurprisingly—predominantly worn by men, with such men routinely being powerful, white, and predominantly of an educated class, hence identified with authority and sobriety, with the "establishment," and with a certain kind of professional esteem. This resonated with the sense in which, for most of the 20th and into the 21st century, the tie has been associated with the professional male in Western society. Hence a minimal semiotic reading, within a larger structuralist discourse, would be to conclude that such a particular form of male apparel (and, as Shakespeare put it, the apparel oft proclaims the man) has an authentic significance. Therefore, to follow the discursive practices of the necktie, throughout the course of the show, may provide some rewarding conclusions, at least within a structuralist reading.

The necktie was present throughout the series, and it would be unwieldy and burdensome to detail each example, but the main instances could be set out as follows. In the opening episode, "Pilot" (1/1), Josh and Donna had the following exchange. Donna: "You shouldn't have worn that tie on television. It bleeds." Josh: "I don't think it was the tie that got me in trouble." The same concern (or even fear) would be repeated in the episode "The Hubbert Peak" (6/5), wherein Annabeth would inform Toby: "That tie's gonna bleed." Likewise, in the episode "Game On" (4/6), Bartlet was shown preparing for the debate with Governor Richie, his Republican opponent in the 2002 presidential election; and in this episode the choice of his necktie almost took center-stage. First, there was a near obsessive zeal to locate the tie Bartlet had worn in the debate during his first campaign. The tie had been borrowed from Josh, with Charlie having the job of searching for this lucky tie. The search may or may not have been successful; however, for willful reasons of her own—just as Bartlet was about to take to the stage for the debate—Abbey took a pair of scissors and deliberately cut Bartlet's tie in half. Why Abbey should have decided to do this was never explained, no motive was given; but her action caused some consternation. With only seconds to go before the debate was to begin, Bartlet was forced to use a last-minute replacement tie, again borrowed from Josh. From a semiotic point-of-view there were a number of obvious symbolic resonances at play, especially as Bartlet had earlier commented that there was "a lot of juice in that tie." In a sense the "king" had been symbolically castrated by the "queen"—his precious bodily fluids (the juice in the tie) had been deliberately spilt, albeit only in symbolic form and for symbolic reasons. In other words, Abbey had deliberately cut the tie to give Bartlet more strength, to demonstrate that lucky neckties (replete with their symbolic connotations) were not relevant to his performance in the debate.

The significance of the necktie as a symbol of power was further explored in the episodes "7A WF 83429" (5/1) and "The Dogs of War" (5/2), the episodes wherein Bartlet was forced to "recuse" himself as president. What was of interest was that in the scenes wherein Bartlet was temporarily deprived of power, he was shown without a tie. Bartlet was depicted in a number of scenes in the private residence of the White House, literally out of office, often in the kitchen (a clichéd feminized space), without a tie, without his attribute of masculine apparel, and hence without the symbolic trope of phallic authority. In contrast, Bartlet's temporary successor, President Walken, was consistently shown wearing a tie; this being accentuated in the way CJ straightened Walken's necktie, just prior to his giving an important press conference. Of course when Bartlet was eventually able to resume power he was shown wearing a necktie; having regained his power and dominance he was able to demonstrate his phallic authority in symbolic form.[31]

In the episode "And It's Surely to Their Credit" (2/5), Bartlet and Abbey had a rare opportunity for an erotic encounter. In the scene in question Abbey was hoping for some romance: "A couple of cocktails, Mel Torme." Bartlet was more interested in expediency, in having sexual intimacy while the time allowed: "Abbey, you have two minutes, or I swear to God I'm gonna get Mrs. Landingham drunk." Abbey responded: "Okay, I'm going to the bathroom. Where I am gonna change into a special little garment I think you might enjoy! Loosen your tie. Loosen whatever you'd like." The fact that the scene ended with the instruction for Bartlet to loosen his tie was of relevance; a subtle detail that perhaps required no further explanation. At times the concern with neckties had a more homosocial context, as in the following exchange between Toby and Josh in the episode "The U.S. Poet Laureate" (3/17). Toby asked if his tie was all right; Josh appeared confused. Toby: "This necktie, does it go with the jacket?" Josh: "God, I don't know Toby.... The tie is fine, why?" Toby then confessed: "I'm meeting someone."[32] The significant point here was the fact that Toby was romantically attracted to the poet Tabatha Fortis (played by Laura Dern), hence the correct necktie, replete with the phallic signal it entailed, was of relevance.

Finally, in the last episode of the series, "Tomorrow" (7/22), the necktie was significant in the case of two different scenes. First, in a scene between President-Elect Matt Santos and his wife, Helen, Helen was helping to tie Santos's necktie while they discussed a means of ensuring their privacy during the coming presidency. Helen: "We're gonna have to figure out some kind of signal when we want privacy." Santos: "Like a necktie on the doorknob?" While it was not explicitly stated, it was clear that both were talking about sex, and how to preserve some private space for intimacy during their stay in the White House. Hence the idea of using a necktie on a doorknob to signal "do not disturb" was laden with symbolism. The second usage was more inclined toward dominance and power than toward blatant sexual imagery. It occurred in one of the last scenes of the series, wherein Bartlet explained to Charlie how he had chosen a farewell gift to mark the end of his presidency: "I considered getting you a tie with the scales of justice on it. Figured you'd use this more." Bartlet's actual gift to Charlie was his old copy of the Constitution; insomuch as Charlie had made the decision to study law at Georgetown University. However, a necktie with the scales of justice would arguably have provided, in symbolic form, a way of substituting one emblem of power for another.

* * *

A further range of structuralist readings could be made of the series; for example, there were a number of subtextual tropes within the show's run that may not have been wholly apparent outside of a semiotic reading. One apt example was CJ Cregg's goldfish; the fish (and its bowl) appeared in the ninth episode of the first season and remained a subtle presence for much of the show's remaining run. A semiotic analysis might well have questioned what this ubiquitous trope represented. The goldfish had begun as a gift by Danny Concannon to CJ, a comedy of errors over her liking for a kind of crackers called "Goldfish."[33] However, what the goldfish in its bowl might actually have represented remained open to interpretation. If one was to take a less than charitable reading, a somewhat disparaging point-of-view, then Gail, as the goldfish was called, could perhaps have been viewed as representative of the mindlessness of the average voter, continually observing events unfolding in the White House, but with no ability to understand what was actually going on, having only the apocryphal three-second memory of a goldfish.[34] There were many other instances, too numerous to include[35]; however, one might conclude with an appreciation that all narrative is, to some extent, circular. As Sam Seaborn re-entered the White House, in the closing moments of the drama, to begin work for a different administration, he commented: "Home, sweet home." Hence the story appeared to come back upon itself, the end becoming the beginning.

8

"This pitiful exercise"
Temporal Rupture in the "Isaac and Ishmael" Episode

The third season of *The West Wing* had been scheduled to begin screening during the last week of September 2001. The first five episodes of the season had been filmed, and Aaron Sorkin was in the process of writing the sixth episode—what was to have been a Halloween show, with children "trick or treating" in the White House.[1] However, on September 11 the world changed, and the producers of the show were placed in something of a predicament. It would appear that Sorkin's first response had been to delay the date of the season's opening[2]; but it would seem that the commercial pressures of network television prevailed and another solution was required.[3] Sorkin was therefore forced to conceive of another response; insomuch as it was clear that images of 9/11 would not fit well with images of "Josh and Donna flirting and Sam and Toby wisecracking and Leo and CJ stampeding down a corridor."[4] Hence Sorkin wrote an episode outside of the timeframe of the series, a textual device that would enable him to construct a drama that would represent what was "in the air" at the time, as Sorkin put it:

> The only thing I could think of to do was to write an episode that somehow recreated the conversations that we were all having at our kitchen tables, at our offices, at our schools. And it had to be done very quickly, so this is what I decided to do—to talk about the history of terrorism.[5]

Sorkin would go on to elaborate on this decision:

> The attacks had profoundly affected everyone in the country except these characters, who suddenly were living in a world that no longer existed.... It would be the show's version of bowing its head. It would never reference the World Trade Centre or the Pentagon or Pennsylvania or airplanes, but we'll know something happened recently and everyone's been on edge.[6]

John Wells, the executive producer of the episode, recognized in "Isaac and Ishmael" both the need to respond and the need to acknowledge the exceptional nature and "temporal rupture" that 9/11 had wrought:

> Obviously, everybody in entertainment and series TV have been trying to figure out what's the appropriate response, such as what needs to be said on "West Wing"....
> We didn't feel comfortable going back to our fictional White House without taking a moment. Hopefully, we can say something that's useful.... Hopefully, it will make people talk and think.[7]

In other words, *The West Wing* had to find a way of dealing with the effects of 9/11 if it was to remain credible.[8] With this in mind, Sorkin quickly drafted the new episode. According to the script revision history given in the published shooting script, there were eight revised drafts of the script, beginning on September 21 and ending on September 28.[9] In the next few days the episode was filmed and edited, and then subsequently broadcast on October 3, 2001, just three weeks after the events of 9/11.

In terms of viewing figures, the episode was a significant success, with a reported 25 million people watching as it was first broadcast in America.[10] The high viewing figures mirrored the level of critical attention, both in the popular media of the time and then in the subsequent academic response. In terms of the academic response, it would appear that more attention was paid to the "Isaac and Ishmael" episode than any other episode. In fact, it is not too much of an exaggeration to say that this episode has gathered almost as much critical attention as all the other 154 episodes put together.[11] However, in retrospect, such intensive critical attention was perhaps inopportune, as it would seem that the episode has not aged well, at least not outside of its immediate context of 9/11. From a more considered perspective, the difficulties of producing the episode in such conditions, and within such a short time-frame, have become apparent. Perhaps the only redeeming feature of such a degree of critical attention was the effect of strengthening and illuminating an appreciation of the series as a whole, at least within a scholarly context; in fact, an awareness of the depth of research into the episode was one of the reasons that prompted this present book.

The initial response to the episode included the following journalistic comments: Tom Shales of *The Washington Post* described the episode as a "lecture" that came across as "pretentious and pietistic hubris"; the *New York Post*'s headline declared: "'West Wing' Wimps Out on Terror"; *Time* magazine called it "God-awful in its condescending pedantry"[12]; while, in a similar vein, *USA Today* called the episode "a crashing and condescending bore."[13] Cory Barker, in an online article at tvsurveillance.com, noted: "The discord between the deaths of many real people and the overwrought speeches given by fictional [characters] ... is awkward and somewhat uncomfortable,"[14] while Keith Topping, author of *Inside Bartlet's White House*, commented on how "'Isaac and Ishmael' forgoes *The West Wing*'s usually incisive critique to deliver a tidal wave of soapboxy rhetoric." In an academic response, Rachel Gans-Boriskin and Russ Tisinger commented that the episode was "troublesome in its simplicity and jingoism."[15] Philip Cass noted: "somehow the programme was gutless, a well-intentioned but empty polemic made by well-meaning people appalled by, but too nice, to know how to react to such a horrific event."[16]

There were some positive responses; for example, Melissa Crawley argued the episode "secured its place in the complex interaction between the reality and the performance of politics."[17] Robert Jones and George Dionisopoulos noted that the episode had been met "with a decidedly captious critical reaction," adding that "traditionally, cultures turn to their storytellers in moments of crisis because their narratives can offer a type of explanation and solace that may not be available with rationality."[18] For Trevor and Shawn J. Parry-Giles the episode was unique for its "direct response to the 9/11 terrorist attacks,"[19] and they argued that "what results is … a more nuanced and detailed discussion of the origins of terrorism."[20] David Barber noted how the episode was structured "with questions rather than answers, attempting to explore the 'emotional terrain' of America after 9/11 rather than to suggest a viable reaction to the attacks."[21]

* * *

The episode opened in an atypical fashion, wholly different to the usual format; instead of the rousing opening musical theme there was only a brief musical interlude, five plangent piano notes, after which the main actors of the show appeared, in turn, in front of a black background—the actors performing out of character, appearing as themselves, and directly addressing the audience:

> MARTIN: Good evening, I'm Martin Sheen, and I'm with the cast of *The West Wing*. For those of you who tuned in tonight to see our season premiere, you won't. That'll be next week.
> ROB: We're eager to get back to our continuing storylines, but tonight we wanted to stop for a moment and do something different.
> ALLISON: You'll notice a few things different about the show tonight. For instance, in place of our usual main title sequence, we'll be putting phone numbers up on the screen where you can pledge donations to groups that are able to help with victim assistance.
> JOHN: By now, nobody needs to be convinced that when they named New York's Finest and New York's Bravest, they knew what they were talking about. That's why we're pleased to tell you that the profits of tonight's episode will be donated to New York Fire-fighters, 9/11 Disaster Relief Fund, and the New York Police and Fire, Widows and Children's Benefit Fund.
> DULÉ: A helping hand from our family to theirs.
> BRADLEY: Now don't panic, we're in show business and we'll get back to tending

our egos in short order, but tonight we offer a play. It's called "Isaac and Ishmael." We suggest you don't spend a lot of time trying to figure out where this episode comes in the timeline of the series. It doesn't. It's a storytelling aberration, if you'll allow.
RICHARD: Next week, we'll start our third season. That's when you'll see stories about a re-election campaign, an MS disclosure, an embassy in Haiti …
STOCKARD: Repealing the estate tax …
ROB: A fight against Big Tobacco …
DULÉ: A fight to get our friends back …
JOHN: Funding the NEA …
ALLISON: A veto override …
STOCKARD: A marriage in trouble …
JANEL: And I get a boyfriend.
MARTIN: That's all for us. Thank you for listening, and may God bless the United States of America.[22]

There was a sense here, in the direct address to the audience, of breaking the pretense of the so-called "fourth wall," of deliberately disrupting a carefully constructed narrative artifice. As such, Bradley Whitford's comment on the episode being a "storytelling aberration," advising the viewing audience not to spend a "lot of time trying to figure it out" was of interest. Such advice could be offered; however, there would seem to be an inherent problem in couching the "play" both inside and outside of the drama's narrative, a "play" that was "completely detached and unrelated to the first two seasons of *The West Wing*"[23]—but also self-evidently part of that same invented world. In other words, an "aberration" in the narrative could not help but affect the believability of the narrative as a whole; and, as such, could not help but blur the distinction between what was real and what was not. As Ruth Wodak put it: "Here we encounter an interface between fiction and reality in a much more explicit way than in any other episode."[24] The "play" raised concepts of postmodern theory surrounding the self-awareness of the text as a text, but, as will be seen (in Chapter 16), *The West Wing* was not a postmodern text—at least not in a self-reflexive way—hence the potential damage to the audience's appreciation of the narrative as a whole.[25]

As discussed in Chapter 3, one of the main attractions of *The West Wing* was that it appeared to exist within the margins of a convincing alternate universe; that is, it took place in what appeared to be our present, but in fact played out its drama in a parallel reality, an alternate and somewhat idealized depiction of our own world. Hence, to have placed a further alternative reality onto a narrative that already existed within an alternative reality seemed to stretch credibility. This might be compared to the practice within Superman comics in the 1960s that regularly had imaginary stories (stories outside of the regular continuity) placed within what was already an imaginary world.[26] In the context of the comic book genre this almost risible device was

8. "This pitiful exercise"

easy to accept, but in the case of a drama like *The West Wing* this was more problematical. It was clear in the episode that some kind of major incident had occurred equivalent to a 9/11 event. There were clues: at one point in the episode Josh mentioned, "We have crashed five times in three weeks," "crashed" referring to an emergency shutdown of the White House. If the date was the same as the broadcast date, then three weeks would have traced back to September 11 itself. It would seem something had happened within the alternative world of *The West Wing* at this time—if not the attacks on the Twin Towers, the Pentagon and the United 93 flight, then something similar. However, this was an imaginary event within a fictitious drama; it would not be referred to anywhere else in the series; and hence it was an aspect of the narrative with little or no dramatic relevance to the viewer.

If 9/11 did not occur in *The West Wing's* universe there were, nonetheless, consistent allusions to the event throughout the series. For the most part, these came after the "Isaac and Ishmael" episode. However, there was one prior incident: Osama bin Laden was mentioned by name in the episode "In the Shadow of Two Gunmen Part 1" (2/1), a full year before 9/11. Nancy McNally, Bartlet's National Security Advisor, commented: "It's worth mentioning that at this moment we do not know the whereabouts of about a half dozen cell leaders, including bin Laden." In addition, in the episode "100,000 Airplanes" (3/12), Bartlet's State of the Union speech included the following lines: "We are faced with a new challenge ... we meet and master new forms of aggression ... in the face of oppression and global terror ... we say here tonight with one voice. There is no corner of this earth so remote, no cave so dark, that you will not be found and brought to light and ended." The speech was heard only in the background on television, yet it was obviously cognizant of the "War on Terror," and Bartlet could easily have been talking about bin Laden. Finally, in the episode A Good Day (6/17), nearing the end of his presidency—and talking about the increasing deficit—Bartlet commented: "First term, we made so much progress we were talking balanced budget [then] the economy slowed [and] costs spiraled. Security at home, terrorism.... I couldn't control it." Here it would seem clear that such comments were an allusion to events analogous to 9/11. In this sense, while the episode "Isaac and Ishmael" has been described as "a play," a one-off drama, it could also be read as a play of a different kind; as if it was "playing" the audience—deliberately acting in a ludic, provocative and arguably misleading way.

* * *

In a wider context, the episode seemed unashamedly patriotic. As with the series as a whole, but here in a much more exaggerated form, the argument was simple: America was a nation "blessed by God with the protection of two vast oceans"; it was nothing less than "the greatest country in the world."²⁷ This was one way of looking at the issue, and a concept many Americans might have agreed with; however, an alternative point-of-view was not on offer. An example of such a dogmatic way of looking at the world occurred during an exchange between Sam Seaborn and one of the students in the mess hall. The student posed the question: "What do you call a society that has to just live every day with the idea that the pizza place you are eating in could blow up without any warning?" Sam replied: "Israel"—a response so simplistic in its flippancy as to be almost risible.²⁸ What was significant here was that the same jejune level of political discourse was sustained throughout the episode. As Thomas J. Gillan noted, the episode created

> a dichotomy for viewers: the good American Way and its customs against the evil ways of religious fanaticism, the potential of an America with a redemptive view of history, always leading towards progress, against the backwardness of barbarism.²⁹

A similar degree of latent bias could be seen in a question from another student, who asked: "So, what's the deal with everybody trying to kill us?" It was a question that was at least put forward, but it was a question to which no real answer was provided.³⁰ As Philip Cass put it:

> Ultimately, the only answer that Josh, Sam and the others can offer the students is pluralism, the pious notion that people will stop being fanatics if they are confronted with a variety of religious, political, ethical and moral options.³¹

Josh stated that the reason "they"—certain groups of people from elsewhere in the world—hated America was because of America's "freedom." However, as Rachel Gans-Boriskin and Russ Tisinger pointed out: "Absent from this refrain was mention of any of the economic or political reasons that might have provoked certain groups to have grievances with the United States."³² There was barely any sense of the episode "turning its gaze" inward on the place of the "United States in the world."³³ As Jack Holland put it, there was a sense in which the episode suggested that Americans were attacked "because of who they are, not what they [had] done."³⁴ In essence, the question of why America was subject to the terrorist attack on 9/11 was completely sidestepped; it was lost in the overarching and simplistic proclamation that the United States of America was "the greatest country in the world,"³⁵ a claim that the contributors to the episode may actually have believed, but which nonetheless remains questionable.³⁶

When one considers the episode's consideration of terrorism itself, the discursive practices appeared to become still more biased. For example, one of the students asked Sam if he knew a lot about terrorism. "I dabble," said Sam. The student asked what struck Sam the most, to which Sam replied: "Its 100% failure rate." History, however, would seem to argue against Sam's claim. To quote Mao Zedong, albeit by way of Alabama 3, "Change must come through the barrel of a gun."³⁷ Mao was talking about the means the Com-

8. "This pitiful exercise"

munist Party of China must adopt to take control of the government, but the same idea holds for terrorism. It is an unpalatable fact, but violence, whether by nation states or by so-called terrorists, can and does succeed.[38] Another student asked Sam: "What about the IRA?" Sam replied, "The Brits are still there. The Protestants are still there." Sam's remark was so inaccurate as to be incoherent.[39] It overlooked the fact that the Catholic community in Northern Ireland was (and is) now represented in a power sharing government, and that Sinn Fein, once the so-called political wing of the IRA, now played a significant role in government. It is unlikely this would have happened without the terrorist campaign of the IRA throughout the so-called Troubles.[40]

However, the facetious pronouncements on terrorism were not restricted to Sam's limited knowledge of Irish history. For example, Toby pronounced that the first terrorist was one al Hassan ibn al Sabah, an eleventh-century Shiite cultist, who may have provided the world with the etymology of the word "assassin." As Keith Topping noted, citing just one exception, this was "to overlook the Zealots, a thousand years earlier, the Jewish sect who waged a terrorist war against the Romans."[41] Finally, there was Josh's famous (or perhaps infamous) comment: "Answer the following question: Islamic extremist is to Islamic as 'blank' is to Christianity. [Josh then wrote 'KKK' on the flipchart.] That's what we're talking about. It's the Klan, gone medieval and global." Disregarding Josh's flawed syntax, the analogy to the Ku Klux Klan was inaccurate, as Philip Cass put it: the use of the term "medieval" was not appropriate, because "organizations like Al-Qaeda are very much part of modernity."[42]

The antidote to all of this would have been if Noam Chomsky could somehow have been conjured up from behind Josh's absurd flipchart, to appear and to offer a more coherent and balanced point-of-view.[43] Chomsky, as one of the leading voices of "left-wing intellectual dissidence in the United States,"[44] may have had something different to say. In his book *9/11: Was There an Alternative?* published in November 2001, in the immediate aftermath of the attacks, Chomsky presented himself as one of the few voices to offer an alternative narrative to the prevailing mood:

> INTERVIEWER: Is the nation's so-called war on terrorism winnable?
> CHOMSKY: If we want to consider this question seriously we should recognize that in much of the world the US is regarded as a leading terrorist state, and with good reason. We might bear in mind, for example, that in 1986 the US was condemned by the World Court for "unlawful use of force" (international terrorism) and then vetoed a Security Council resolution calling on all states (meaning the US) to adhere to international law. Only one of countless examples.[45]

Chomsky's voice was, of course, not heard in the episode; in fact, as far as can be ascertained, Chomsky's voice was not heard at all in the entire run of *The West Wing*. This was perhaps surprising for a so-called liberal show—insomuch as Chomsky, as intimated above, has generally been regarded as one of America's foremost liberal thinkers.

In this way, far from supporting a liberal point-of-view, the episode could be read as supportive of the subsequent actions President George W. Bush was to take. In his article "When You Think of the Taliban, Think of the Nazis: Teaching Americans 9/11 in NBC's *The West Wing*," Jack Holland argued that the episode "contributed to a narrowing of political dialogue after 9/11,"[46] and that "*The West Wing* helped to reinforce and sustain the efforts of the Bush Administration, further narrowing the space for debate and chances of alternative framings in the post–9/11 moment."[47] Holland argued that by portraying an enemy that was "motivated by pure hatred, rather than any political grievance (justified or otherwise), [*The West Wing*] ensured that questions of American blame were kept 'off the table' and beyond the limits of acceptable reflection after 9/11."[48] The implication was that the episode, albeit in a minor way, contributed to the general mood of public opinion; as Holland put it:

> By helping to establish what would become a largely agreed-upon background of discursive meanings, *The West Wing* through the "Isaac and Ishmael" episode contributed to the possibility of the "War on Terror" and actively shut down the scope for debate in American politics and society after 9/11.[49]

Other critics concurred; for example, Rachel Gans-Boriskin and Russ Tisinger commented that *The West Wing* may have "contributed to public support for military action in Iraq"[50] and that "in the months after the terrorist attacks" *The West Wing* "pursued a foreign policy more hawkish than even that of the Bush administration."[51]

Jack Holland's article also raised the question of whether the suicide bombers on the planes were as cowardly as they were portrayed, and how such an issue was "a politically charged topic in the shadow of the fall of the Twin Towers."[52] Holland was referring to George W. Bush's remark that 9/11 was a "cowardly act." In a similar way, in the "Isaac and Ishmael" episode, Bartlet stated: "We don't need martyrs right now. We need heroes. A hero would die for his country, but he'd much rather live for it." However, sometimes "a hero" may have no choice but to act as a martyr or as a suicide bomber. In a specific context, it could be argued that the American passengers on United 93 were suicide bombers, of a sort at least, although they, of course, have seldom been seen as such. The United 93 passengers, aware that their plane had been hijacked, aware that other planes had struck strategic targets, and aware that their plane was probably heading for a high value target, decided to overpower the hijackers before the plane could reach its target. The passengers eventually succeeded in overwhelming the terrorists

8. "This pitiful exercise"

and the plane crashed, killing everyone on board. In a strict sense this was suicide, for the passengers would have lived a short period longer if they had not taken this action. The passengers were seen as American heroes; but what if the "terrorists" thought they had no choice, as the Americans on the United 93 flight thought they had no choice? In other words, the nineteen terrorists who hijacked the four planes on September 11, 2001, may have argued they had no other choice in their fight against America. However, this had little if any significance within the narrative of brave American heroes and cowardly suicide bombers, either in the fictional world of *The West Wing*, or in the real world as we know it.[53]

* * *

The episode is mostly remembered for the scenes of Josh, together with other White House staff, conducting the impromptu seminar with the group of high-school children; however, arguably of more significance was the other plotline: Leo's interrogation of a suspected terrorist working in the White House. Leo McGarry was perhaps the least liberal of Bartlet's staff (he had seen combat as a pilot in the Vietnam war, he held a consistent "hawkish" stance in terms of military operations and he would later prove to be anti–Palestinian during the Middle East peace summit in Season 6); nonetheless, the prejudiced and near-racist attitude Leo adopted in the episode was most likely something of a surprise to many viewers.[54] The Leo of "Isaac and Ishmael" appeared excessively apprehensive and almost paranoid, interrogating Raqim Ali (Ajay Naidu) in a ruthless and almost xenophobic manner.[55] This issue was discussed by Jasbir Puar and Amit Rai in their essay "Monster, Terrorist, Fag: The War on Terrorism and the Production of Docile Patriots." In the article, Puar and Rai argued that the American media had turned "American viewers into docile patriots by presenting the 'enemy' as a dangerous 'other,' by reinforcing racial and ethnic stereotypes, and by connecting the 'terrorist' to conventional imagery of the monster and sexual deviancy."[56] This argument offered some sense of an explanation, but even so, the change in Leo's character remained a jarring aspect to the narrative.

Leo's prejudices did not go unchallenged, with Raqim accusing his near-racist interrogator of having "the memory of a gypsy moth." It would appear that Raqim had been present during the assassination attempt at Rosslyn,[57] making the point that white Americans had been responsible and their primary target had been an African American; this being an obvious critique of racial profiling. After a protracted interrogation, it subsequently became apparent that Raqim was innocent, and that he merely shared his name with the pseudonym of a suspected terrorist.[58] After this discovery, Leo was unable to provide an adequate explanation for his previous behavior. All he could do was mutter incoherently: "You know, we're obviously all under ... uh ...

greater than the usual amount of … you know…" Leo did go so far as to tell Raqim he apologized for making certain bigoted slurs; however, Leo did not make a full apology for his actions. In fact, his last line (the last line of the episode) was couched within a deliberately ambiguous discourse: "Hey kid, way to be back at your desk." If one discounts the flawed syntax of the expression, together with the condescending use of the word "kid," the line could be seen as pointing to the "diligence and work ethic" of Americans,[59] but Raqim did not respond to the remark, merely staring at Leo in a dignified way until the fade-out. At an earlier point in the episode, Raqim had referred to the racist actions taken against him as being a "pitiful exercise"—a phrase a cynic might have said summed up some of the more extreme issues and arguments put forward in the episode itself.

* * *

In an overarching sense, it would seem fair to reaffirm that the episode has not endured well. As intimated, there were extenuating circumstances: the makers of the show had no other choice but to make a response to 9/11; and they had relatively little time to accomplish the task. As such, the episode, "a contested interpretation of the story of Abraham,"[60] was flawed from the outset, from the facile title on down—a title that appeared to indicate "a framing of September 11 through a religious lens rather than a political one."[61] In retrospect, this was perhaps one of the episode's most significant failings, insomuch as it was not able to engage authentically with the actual political context of 9/11. Abbey's "bedtime story"—for the high-school children in the episode and perhaps for the wider American public in general—was an unsophisticated, overly patriotic and blinkered exercise; insipid in its self-serving platitudes, it managed to be both patronizing and naive at the same time.[62] If one were to take a rigorously unbiased approach, it was also a narcissistic exercise, both self-absorbed and self-important. At the start of the episode, Bradley Whitford joked about the need for the cast to get back to tending their egos; this was meant to be ironic, but there was a literal aspect to the comment as well. There was a sense that the episode, whatever it may have been aspiring to, was also something of a vanity project, so glib and so unconvincing was the general discourse.[63]

In its defense, there were some elements of worth; for example, near the end of the episode one of the students asked Josh if he favored the death penalty. Josh said he did not. The student asked what he would do instead, to which Josh responded: "I'd put them in a small cell, and make them watch home movies of the birthdays and baptisms and weddings of every single person they killed, over and over, every day, for the rest of their lives." However, for the most part the episode was unable to engage within the context of a sophisticated discourse. As Jaap Kooijman argued, while the episode attempted "to present a nuanced perspective on terrorism, Muslim fundamentalism, and the practice of racial profiling," it succeeded in merely presenting "freedom and democracy as exceptionally American values" with little room to reflect critically "upon the nation-state USA and its role in international politics."[64] In this sense, the episode could be seen as representative of *The West Wing* as a whole—all its strengths and all its weaknesses were present within this episode—albeit in a highly exaggerated form. To describe the episode as being a "pitiful exercise" might be overly critical, but now, with the benefit of hindsight, and with its many faults on show, one might conclude it would have been better if the episode had not been made.

9

Bourgeois Wing
Marxist Readings

As far as can be ascertained, the name of Karl Marx was not mentioned in any of the 155 episodes of *The West Wing*.[1] This was perhaps surprising, given that Bartlet was head of state of one of the world's great capitalist societies, and that—in addition to this—he was also a Nobel Prize winner in economics. As such, Marx was, as the saying goes, conspicuous via his absence—and this was surprising if one considers the influence Marx's work has had on intellectual debate in the West, his influence on economic and political thought. However, notwithstanding this absence from the text, it is still possible to generate a Marxist reading of the series, albeit against the grain of the textual structure of the series. Of course, in adopting a Marxist ideology within the context of an American text, or even merely within an American environment, one must be aware of an inherent bias against such an ideological doctrine. This obviously reached its most extreme response after World War II, in the so-called McCarthy era of the 1950s, wherein a significant number of Americans seemed to hold so one-sided and prejudiced a view as to seem almost ignorant of Marx's actual philosophy. In this way, the paucity of materials within the series is, in and of itself, significant; and, as such, a Marxist reading of *The West Wing* would appear to be worthy of discussion.

Marxism, according to its well-known definition, had the objective of bringing about a classless society, based upon the common ownership of the means of production, distribution and exchange. This objective now seems almost absurd in its idealism; so much so that Michel Foucault went so far as to argue Marxism only made sense within the arena of its origins in the 19th century. In other words, as Foucault intimated, Marxism exists in 19th century thought as a fish exists in water; it ceases to breathe anywhere else. In the real world of economic competition, it now seems apparent that Marxism will never be able to compete against even the most ordinary of capitalist states. Nonetheless, the idealistic aspiration behind Marxist theory still abides—and the world would be a much more equitable place if we were somehow able to follow its edicts. To put the argument into a somewhat simplistic forum: a right wing point-of-view would be classed as imperialists or capitalists, people who attempt to convert as much of their world to their own material and financial advantage as possible[2]; the left wing point-of-view would be classed as communists or socialists, people who believe in cooperation for the greater good of all members of society.[3] Neither system works, the least unfair and the least inefficient being a kind of benign social democracy. However, as Winston Churchill once said: democracy is the worst form of government except for all the others—hence we make do with the best of the worst. The Churchill quotation was, in fact, used in the series[4]; and, to be fair to *The West Wing*, there was an underlying awareness of the relevance of the line when considering the impracticalities of a Marxist form of government.

In terms of social class, always a significant element of any cultural text, in *The West Wing* this played out in an understated way. According to Marx, there were three main categories within the makeup of the social order: first, the aristocracy—the land-owning members of society[5]; second, the *bourgeoisie*—the owners of the means of production; and finally, the proletariat—the workers—those members of society that actually provided the wealth of society. Marx argued that the *bourgeoisie* had infiltrated all levels of society—to the extent that theirs were the only values that were accepted. In a similar sense, this occurred in the way such values infiltrated cultural and artistic structures within society. Hence a Marxist ideology would see writers and artists as part of the same social context, upholding a capitalist society, even though the individual writers and artists would not necessarily be aware of this. To consider, for example, the literary novel in the late 19th and into the 20th century: such works as Émile Zola's *Germinal*, D.H. Lawrence's *Sons and Lovers*, and John Steinbeck's *The Grapes of Wrath* offered a different point-of-view in challenging capitalism, but these were rare exceptions—and such challenges are even rarer in television, especially American television. As such, it is clear that *The West Wing* itself did not challenge the hegemony of capitalism, either consciously or unconsciously. A comparison will be made, within this book, between *The West Wing* and *The Wire*, and such a comparison might be useful, insomuch as *The Wire*, in contrast to the vast majority of other American television drama, at least raised questions pertaining to the injustices of capitalism and its deleterious effects on society—raising questions surrounding the relationship between lawful society and so-called criminality. This was a strategy with which *The West Wing*, to put it mildly, did not collude.[6]

In this sense, the Marxist view of the individual, within a capitalist society, was that of a mere commodity, a mere economic unit. The capitalist employers were not interested in their employees as people, but merely as a means of producing wealth. Louis Althusser, the literary critic said to have been more Marxist than Marx, argued that people within a capitalist system only think they are free, only think that they are unique individuals able to control and determine their destinies; this being to enable the system to operate efficiently, as it was more convenient to allow such workers to believe this was the case. In a similar sense, Antonio Gramsci, another significant Marxist theorist, argued that the ruling classes have been able to retain control not through direct coercion, but via indirect means; under such control people were willing to work within their own subordination, willing conspirators within their own exploitation. As intimated above, one of the main ways this was achieved was via artistic productions, via the media, and via the total sum of what we define as culture, all of which subtly reinforces and justifies "the way things are" and hence naturalizes and legitimizes the status quo. We may believe we are free agents, but in reality we are controlled via a range of structures—some subtle, some unsubtle—and, as such, the large majority willingly maintains a system that concentrates wealth and power in the hands of a small minority.

In *The West Wing* this was seen to significant effect. Within the series there was an unspoken acceptance of the capitalist society of the United States; this was consistently unquestioned and unchallenged throughout the drama. While the United States is a free republic, lacking a monarchy and an established class system,[7] it is nonetheless a society fueled by capital, comprising those who have it and those who do not. This was a form of society that was never fundamentally challenged either by Sorkin or by the numerous other writers who wrote for the show. Thus, and to restate the point: cultural productions—such as mainstream television drama—would not be expected to challenge such a status quo. The issue of the relationship of the media to the capitalist society it inhabits would once again seem to be of relevance; writers and artists, as part of their social context, would be expected—far from challenging the iniquitous excesses of the capitalist society they inhabited—to uphold the values of that capitalist society.[8]

In terms of the issue of social class within *The West Wing*, this was of some interest. As might have been expected, the great majority of the main characters in the drama came from what might be termed the *bourgeois* element of society; in other words, predominantly highly educated and privileged members of American society.[9] For example, the president was a landowner, he professed a lineage back to the founding fathers, and he had great personal wealth.[10] In terms of other characters, there were similar social and monetary qualities on show. For example, Leo McGarry appears to have had a significant amount of personal wealth; this was never explicitly explained, but was apparent throughout the series. For example, in the episode "The Indians in the Lobby" (3/7), Bartlet, talking about an initiative to provide low-cost cell phones to neighborhood watch groups, commented: "There's nothing wrong with the policy, it's just too small. I could fund this initiative out of my pocket." Toby pointed out it cost ten million dollars, to which Bartlet responded: "Leo could fund it out of his pocket." In a similar way, albeit not to the same extent, the majority of the other main characters—Josh, Toby, CJ, and Will—all appeared to be relatively financially secure, and all were certainly highly educated.[11] In fact, the only main character who did not fall into this category, the only character to come from a poorer background and from a background of poor education, was Charlie, and Charlie was, of course, black.

As such, a Marxist reading might question how all of these characters had gained their wealth in the first place. As Terry Eagleton once noted, if one traces back the ownership of property far enough, it was taken by force and violence. In a more acute way, the French novelist Honoré de Balzac stated: "Behind every great fortune lies a great crime." In this light one might ask how Bartlet and his family gained their material wealth, or what "great crime" lay behind their "great fortune." To Eagleton the answer would have been relatively straightforward. In a discussion of England and the subsequent emergence of the British Empire, Eagleton noted:

> England achieves its point of economic "take-off," arguably on the back of the enormous profits it reaped from the eighteenth century slave trade and its imperial control of the seas, to become the world's first industrial capitalist nation.[12]

It is clear that the same history would be relevant, perhaps even more so, for America. Bartlet's ancestors may well have been slave owners—his wealth may have derived from a form of capitalism that would now seem almost shameful within a civilized society. Hence, and while this is only speculation, this may have been the "great crime" (in Balzac's phrasing).[13] As intimated above, *The West Wing* had little sense of questioning the excesses of the American capitalist system. There was no sense, for example, of accepting a "sufficiency of goods."[14] In *The West Wing* there was little sense of protesting the iniquities of capitalism, the majority (if not all) of the main protagonists in the drama simply accepted the status quo—accepted the extremes of exploitation.

This would seem to be approaching the essence of the argument; in other words, when taken to an extreme, excessive capitalism and criminal actions threaten to blur into one, with crime becoming merely an exaggerated form of capitalism, at least from a Marxist point-of-view. Such a proposition was seen to greater effect in *The Wire*, where there was little moral difference between the criminal and the non-criminal, between the drug dealers and the police—not to mention the corrupt businessmen, the corrupt politicians, the corrupt judges and so on. However, this was not the case in *The West Wing*. Here a more aspirational perspective still prevailed; here there was still a sense that the main structures of American life remained uncorrupted. Such an idealistic point-of-view was often upheld by the critical response to the show, especially within an American academic forum. For example, Christina Lane was able to comment: "Bartlet makes his final decision to run again on behalf of the underrepresented working classes."[15] This was a questionable evaluation, and would appear to have been an argument from a critic embedded within the same ideological system—and, as such, it pointed to the way in which artist and critic were merely part of the same hypocrisy. An opposing argument could easily have been made that Bartlet decided to run again for reasons far removed from any sense of wishing to improve the position of "the underrepresented working classes."

* * *

One of the key issues Marx made use of, in his theory of alienation, was that of work—the drudgery of work. To a certain degree, this could be witnessed in *The West Wing*'s attitude to work. While Marx argued that work tended to alienate the individual, estranging the human subject from their creative and heuristic selves, in *The West Wing* this was somewhat different. Within any capitalist system there is always a necessity to work, to produce, and hence the vast majority of the population can only express themselves via their labor, this being the only way they have in which to define themselves within a capitalist system. As intimated above, capitalism has prevailed by persuading the majority—whom it economically exploits—to define its interests as narrowly as possible. In the past, this was accomplished via the levels of pay received, levels that were often close to a life of deprivation. In more recent times this has been achieved via a range of subtle strategies; by way of the creation of discourses of counterfeit desires that the individual believes will make them happy. In other words, we buy into the system: we go to school, we go to university, we achieve the required qualifications, we obtain the jobs we believe we want, and some even obtain jobs that seem to offer some kind of fulfillment—although the majority enters a life of drudgery. We do all this to acquire money, because we believe money will make us happy. In short, we are seduced by money and all it can offer, we neglect Eagleton's idea of a "sufficiency of goods," and we work—because work enables us to obtain money, and hence at least the hope of happiness.

In such a context it might be noted that the opening sequence of each episode of *The West Wing* consistently showed the main characters at work. As Melissa Crawley observed, this sequence portrayed "the characters in action in the workplace," with the still photographs showing "them in earnest or contemplative moments in their offices, on the telephone, in meetings or in other work moments."[16] A Marxist interpretation might conclude that this was a somewhat less than subtle message, a subversive pointer to the show's audience that "work was good." In other words, the opening sequence repeatedly insisted that here were good people doing good work—and furthermore, this was to be admired and respected. Susan J. Douglas, in an entertaining and perceptive online posting in 2002, "The West Wing's Workaholics," argued *The West Wing* "celebrates, fetishizes, if you will, workaholism."[17] Douglas went on to note how overwork was "made to seem exciting and glamorous" and compared this to the reality of the actual workplace:

> Unlike the multi-tasking we grunts are stuck with—chained to our desks, often alone, reading e-mail while listening to voicemail and on hold with automated phone information centers—this *West Wing* work happens in motion, on the fly: It's almost breathless. The pace and editing alone confirm that working constantly is enviable and thrilling.... I think we all want to pretend for an hour a week that overwork is glamorous and exhilarating; it makes many of us feel better about our own overtime. Let's just not lose sight of what else is getting legitimated as well.[18]

What was "getting legitimated," at least within the context of a Marxist reading, was the exploitation of workers, an issue so blithely evaded in *The West Wing*. Douglas's post concluded by commenting that although the show "celebrates liberal politics and even, at times, social justice" there was another point-of-view: "It also canonizes the expectation that staying late at work is more important than going to your kid's science fair—or even seeing an old friend."[19] Douglas's post, although light-hearted, eloquently made the point that the show was insidiously reinforcing the message that we must all work harder. As such, Douglas's post (without mentioning Marx) offered an incisive Marxist analysis of how we are all programmed to act within the capitalist system. As will be discussed in Chapter 13, few if any of the main characters in the series appeared to have viable private lives, or to have settled marriages with partners and children. Instead they were all—without exception—in love with their jobs, working diligently for their president. A Marxist analysis of such a situation might reasonably question exactly why they would be so willing to do this.

* * *

In a different context, and outside of Marx's discussion of economic philosophy and class struggle, Marxist theory was also relevant to *The West Wing* in terms of a religious discourse. In his manuscript *Critique of Hegel's Philosophy of Right*, Marx delivered, as if almost in passing, this assault on organized religion:

> Religious suffering is, at one and the same time, the expression of real suffering and protest against real suffering. Religion is the sigh of the oppressed creature, the

heart of a heartless world, and the soul of soulless conditions. It is the opium of the masses.

Religion, by this definition, would be defined as little more than a drug addict injecting a needle into their vein, a narcotic to enable one to forget the realities of life, and hence find solace in the sedative effects of a soporific solution. Marx was also of interest in his overarching account of the corrosive effects of religion on the human subject: the idea that human beings should be in communion with one another not with a religious figure—with a supposed deity.[20] In this way Marx saw society and culture as largely organized to uphold a capitalist point-of-view, with religion offering a form of false consciousness to distract the masses away from the real material issues of history. As intimated above, in the case of *The West Wing*, this scenario was played out with some degree of repetition; the issue of faith would be of significance throughout the drama.[21]

* * *

In summary, Marxism, one of the most significant of the grand narratives, played a relevant role within the ideological discourse of *The West Wing*. Although not referenced in a direct way, Marxist concepts were, nonetheless, of relevance throughout the drama. The philosophy of Karl Marx (together with that of his co-author Friedrich Engels) could thus be seen as providing one means of understanding the underlying assumptions prevalent throughout the narrative of the series. While *The West Wing* has frequently been criticized for its liberal and left-wing bias, a Marxist reading would argue this was not the case and that, in reality, the ideological discourses at play within *The West Wing* were far from liberal. In fact, the political dialogue put forward in the series upheld what might be termed more of a right-wing agenda, at least in the context of upholding capitalist ideals. At times this was specifically confirmed; for example, the episode "Somebody's Going to Emergency, Somebody's Going to Jail" (2/16) subtly supported the House Un-American Activities Committee investigations of the 1950s. The storyline concerned Sam's attempt to clear the name of a character called Daniel Gault, who had been accused of espionage in the 1950s. Sam was initially convinced that Gault had been the victim of a McCarthyist witch-hunt; however, it eventually transpired that Gault *was* a spy—a spy who had deliberately disclosed information to the Soviet Union.[22] Hence far from espousing a liberal point-of-view, in the case of this particular episode there was a clear suggestion that communist infiltrations *had* occurred. This was perhaps relevant insomuch as Hollywood, itself, has often acted as a refuge for a liberal perspective within American life—Hollywood being one of the first targets of Joseph McCarthy's accusations of communist sympathies. Such a narrative detail, within the episode in question, was just one example to contradict the underlying liberal viewpoint the series was said to uphold. *The West Wing* was sometimes lampooned in the media as being more akin to *The Left Wing*, but a Marxist reading of the show would suggest this was an inaccurate appraisal, and that this was far from the case.

10

"The greatest country in the world"
Misconstrued Politics

In the opening episode of the first season of *The Newsroom* (2012), in what was perhaps one of Aaron Sorkin's most inspired soliloquies, the show's main protagonist, Will McAvoy (Jeff Daniels), deconstructed the notion of America being the greatest country in the world. McAvoy started by saying there was "absolutely no evidence to support the statement that we're the greatest country in the world," then going on to state that America was 7th in literacy, 27th in math, 22nd in science, 49th in life expectancy and 178th in infant mortality.[1] According to McAvoy's statistical appraisal America led the world in only three categories: "The number of incarcerated citizens per capita, the number of adults who believe angels are real, and defense spending, where we spend more than the next twenty-six countries combined." McAvoy went on to say America used to be the greatest country in the world: when it stood up for what was right; "when it fought for moral reasons; when it waged wars on poverty, not poor people." He continued: "We reached for the stars ... we aspired to intelligence, we didn't belittle it ... we were able to be all these things, and to do all these things, because we were informed, by great men, men who were revered. First step in solving any problem is recognizing there is one. America is not the greatest country in the world anymore." Writing a number of years after *The West Wing*, Sorkin may have drafted this "epic" speech as part of a response to the "horrors" of the George W. Bush administration, and with a subsequently more cynical perspective on the moral standing of America. However, the same writer, within the overarching ideological discourse of *The West Wing*, would seem to have held more to the view that America *was* the best country in the world; this being the overarching sense of America's standing in *The West Wing*.

In such a context, it might be fair to argue that a significant percentage

10. "The greatest country in the world" 87

of Americans would agree with the proposition that America was the greatest country in the world: as Phillip Cass put it, the United States has consistently seen itself "as a country ... that is exceptional.... *The West Wing* is convinced of American exceptionalism, of its goodness and of its ability to solve all the nation's ills through an idealized process of rational debate, negotiation and good works."[2] This proposition would seem to be a convincing one, insomuch as it appeared to be a trope that prevailed throughout most of *The West Wing*'s narrative. For example, this was seen, in its more exaggerated and idealistic form, via Rob Lowe's portrayal of Sam Seaborn. As Melissa Crawley put it: "Through the character of Sam, Sorkin makes government a symbol for something larger: 'This country is an idea and one that's lit the world for two centuries.'"[3] However, in contrast to this, while a considerable number of people within America might agree with such a proposition, it might also be fair to argue that a considerable percentage of people outside of America would disagree with it.

An apt example of such a dichotomy of views occurred in the episode "Internal Displacement" (7/11). As usual, there were a number of storylines at play within the episode, both within a personal and a political context. In a personal context one storyline concerned Danny building up the courage to propose to CJ; in another the president's son-in-law, Doug Westin, who was running for the House of Representatives, was revealed as having had an affair with his family's nanny. In a political context the episode concerned the attempts of the White House (under the aegis of CJ) to prevent a Chinese veto on a UN resolution on the genocide taking place in Darfur, in West Sudan. However, politics being politics, there was no possibility of the United States taking any action to prevent the genocide. CJ was visited, later in the episode, by Steven Laussen from the organization Refugees' Rights Allowances. After some opening pleasantries, Laussen asked: "You're aware of the situation in the Sudan?" CJ agreed they were; Laussen asked: "Has there been any official response from this administration?" CJ responded: "We condemned it." Laussen asked: "What do you want to hear? You want to hear the numbers first, or the horror stories?" CJ: "Neither." Laussen gave her the details anyway: "Three million displaced, 400,000 dead, children forced to watch their mothers raped and their fathers killed ... on this planet, on your watch." CJ responded with a simple: "Yeah." Laussen stated the need for strong preemptive action by the Bartlet Administration, but it was clear that CJ, as chief of staff, was not going to involve Bartlet. The scene ended with Laussen saying: "I want my five minutes with the President"—and CJ telling him: "This was your five minutes with the President. I'm sorry, Steve. I have a meeting."[4] The scene, which was arguably as well written as any of the exchanges during Aaron Sorkin's time, succinctly demonstrated the cynicism of politics in *The West Wing*. What was clear was Bartlet's administration had no intention of undertaking any kind of military operation that would reduce the genocide in Darfur. As such, it was clearly apparent that CJ did not wish to be swayed emotionally, she did not want the numbers, and she did not wish to hear the horror stories.[5] It would seem that the meeting was a mere courtesy, and the fact that the fictitious president in *The West Wing*—along with President George W. Bush in the real world—chose not to take any action could not help but further weaken the claim that America was the greatest country in the world.

This was compounded in a later scene in the same episode, wherein CJ, once again holding center stage, was discussing the situation in Sudan with the Chinese ambassador, who told her: "You have always taught us that liberty is the same thing as capitalism, as if life, liberty and the pursuit of happiness cannot be crushed by greed. Your American dream is financial, not ethical." As will be seen in Chapter 12, the American Declaration of Independence has always been a problematical aspiration for America to live up to. There is a sense in which America can never fully embrace its own history: the genocide of Native Americans, the enslavement of tens of millions of African Americans, and then, coming into more recent times, the Kennedy assassination, the defeat in Vietnam, the Watergate scandal, the Iran-Contra affair, the First Iraq War, the attempted impeachment of Clinton, the controversy over the 2000 election, the Second Iraq War—and so on.[6] In any case, it would appear that CJ's pragmatic political scheming, within the narrative discourse of the episode, eventually found a degree of success. However, as was often the situation in *The West Wing*, this aspect of the narrative was not followed-up; as if by sleight-of-hand the drama then moved on, with this strand of the narrative failing to be revisited.[7] In terms of plot development, the only enduring narrative detail that would have relevance in the episode was whether or not the president's son-in-law was "banging the nanny."

* * *

It could be argued that some of the contradictions inherent within America lay, to some extent at least, in its size and power, both in an economic and in a military sense. As Philip Cass put it: "The world of *The West Wing* and its fictional President Josiah Bartlett [sic] works safely within the established—and real—paradigm of American imperial power."[8] Cass went on to argue:

> Bartlett's [sic] occasional references to the *Pax Romana* make it clear that he sees the United States as fulfilling a hegemonic role. For a supposedly liberal president—and for an overtly liberal series—this presents a paradox, but these internal contradictions are never questioned. Never once do Bartlett [sic] or any of the other fictional characters seriously challenge the "real" system.... *The West Wing* is clearly a cultural product designed to reinforce and bolster the myth of the supremacy and superiority of the American political establishment.[9]

10. "The greatest country in the world" 89

In the episode "The Lame Duck Congress" (2/6), Bartlet would make the comment: "We forget it's not a democracy, it's a republic. The people don't make the decisions, they choose the people who make the decisions." In this Bartlet was obviously correct, but the question that arises is whether America was a democratic republic or an imperial republic. Thomas Paine, who is said to have been the first person to have used the term: "The United States of America," espoused the idea that the only morally acceptable constitution was that of a democratic republic—of which America was a prime example.[10] There have been numerous responses from an intellectual arena to contradict this appraisal; for example, Susan Sontag perceived of America's energy as being built on the energy of violence, and described how such energy was often "sublimated into crude materialism and acquisitiveness."[11] Frantz Fanon, an early theorist of postcolonialism, had a still more pessimistic appraisal: "Two centuries ago, a former European colony decided to catch up with Europe. It succeeded so well that the United States of America became a monster, in which the taints, the sickness and the inhumanity of Europe have grown to appalling dimensions."[12]

It could be argued that *The West Wing*, disavowing such pessimistic accounts of the American republic, at least attempted to offer an even-handed argument in response to the sentiment referenced in the title of this chapter. One strategy it undertook to enable this was the means by which the series presented a seemingly realistic picture of political strategies, and the ways in which such strategies were put into action. As intimated above, there was a sense, throughout the series, of political expediency, a cynical but nonetheless accurate portrayal of how a government attempted to pursue its policies. An early example occurred in the episode "The Short List" (1/9), the episode concerning the opportunity to appoint a new Supreme Court judge. The initial nominee, Peyton Cabot Harrison III, was referred to as a "quick nomination," "good for us," "a home run," and a nomination that would give the administration "a seven to ten percent bump" in the polls. This was good news for Bartlet and his staff—but not necessarily for the country. This was the core of the episode—at least in terms of political expediency—and it was a facet of Bartlet's administration throughout the series. However, this would have been to disregard the idealism for which Bartlet's staff were so celebrated; the liberal zeal of Sam, Josh, Toby, CJ and so on. Yet, in contrast to this supposed idealism and liberal zeal, Bartlet's staff often tended to look more toward the solution that would solidify their president's office.

An apt example of such a practice could be seen in the relationship between Bartlet and his first vice president, John Hoynes. This was of interest, insomuch as it offered a relevant perspective on the diverse ways in which political realities were played out in the series. Hoynes was generally depicted as something of a cardboard villain; he appeared to be an outsider to the inner workings of the Bartlet presidency, a cynical politician holding a grudge at having lost the 1998 presidential nomination, and was only interested in his own future political opportunities. In addition, Hoynes was portrayed as a reckless womanizer, something of a sub–John F. Kennedy in terms of appearance and sexual predilections. On two different occasions Hoynes's philandering was to have serious implications: the first resulting in his resigning as vice president, the second damaging his campaign to become the Democratic nominee for the presidential election to succeed Bartlet, in 2006. A different interpretation might have been to see Hoynes as demonstrating a consistent degree of loyalty toward the president, with the president, or at least his staff, demonstrating a consistent sense of disloyalty to Hoynes.[13] In such a context, one might note Hoynes's initial reaction on being offered the opportunity to run on Bartlet's ticket as vice president. Hoynes did not immediately accept Bartlet's offer, which was to become the main cause of friction between the two men. However, it should be noted that Hoynes had just been informed that Bartlet had multiple sclerosis, and had been concealing the fact—in other words, he was being asked to be vice president by a man who had procured "a massive fraud" on the American electorate. Hence Hoynes could be seen as responding in an understandable way: he had lost the nomination to a dishonest candidate; a candidate who would—in all likelihood—not have gained the nomination if his illness had become known. In taking this into consideration it could be argued that it was Hoynes that acted in the honorable way; in other words, that Hoynes kept Bartlet's confidence and agreed to serve as vice president—albeit with the indignity of the knowledge of Bartlet's disingenuous actions.

In this way, there was an implication that Hoynes may have been a better president than Bartlet; as noted, Hoynes had the looks and stature of a Kennedy-esque figure; hence, in a different world, he might have offered *The West Wing* a different kind of president. The exit of Hoynes from the series seemed rushed and lacking in imagination; as intimated above, there was a somewhat clichéd and predictable reason for his resignation: a sex scandal. There was a sense here that Sorkin, and the writing team, may already have devised the season's closing plotline: Zoey's kidnapping and Bartlet's subsequent recusal. For this plotline to work there had to be no sitting vice president, hence the requirement for Hoynes's rapid and sudden disappearance. The idea of a sex scandal may therefore have been the obvious solution that came to Sorkin and the writing team; however, this explanation appears somewhat tenuous as there had been few indications of such rash predilections prior to this. In other words, it was unlikely that such an astute politician as Hoynes would have made such elemental errors of judgment. Of course, there was never the slightest sense of a sexual scandal in Bartlet's own life; Josiah Bartlet, like the real-life Jimmy Carter, seems to have been one of the few presidents not to have seen power as the ultimate aphrodisiac. In a similar sense there was also little if any suggestion that Bartlet's administration was corrupt, at least not in a monetary sense. There were some insinuations, throughout the drama, admitting to the fact that money was the only way in which politics worked in America, but this was only portrayed to the extent one might have expected, given the inherent level of the practice within American political life. Hence, in an overarching sense, corruption was not an issue in the Bartlet administration; a somewhat reductive element in terms of potentially dramatic and polemical plotlines. To paraphrase Michael Herr, one of the most difficult stories to tell was the one about the man who loved his wife.[14]

* * *

In essence, there was an overarching contradiction running throughout the series: on the one hand, one of the most eloquent qualities of the show related to the aspirational way in which it could present America at its best—the idealism of the series was consistently reaching for the idea that America *was* the greatest country in the world. On the other hand, the series was unable to avoid accepting the unpalatable reality that America was seldom perceived in this way by the rest of the world. Hence, to respond to the issue posed at the start of this chapter: although the diverse political discourses within American society were often portrayed in a realistic fashion, there was, nonetheless, a sense of holding to the idea of America being a nation state that somehow rose above all other nation states. In *The West Wing* America *was* the land of the free and the home of the brave; and moreover, all the main protagonists seemed to genuinely believe this to be so. This was surely the underlying appeal of *The West Wing*, one of the significant reasons for its success and for its longevity. Thus, within the scope of its beguiling narrative *The West Wing* provided a space in which one could believe and accept the premise of this chapter: that America was the greatest country in the world. In *The West Wing* one could at least put forward an argument that this may have been so, with President Bartlet, his staff and we, the audience, at least holding to the tenuous aspiration that this might indeed be so.

11

"It's turtles all the way down"
The West Wing *and Religion*

Stephen Hawking began his acclaimed book, *A Brief History of Time*, with the following anecdote:

> A well-known scientist (some say it was Bertrand Russell) once gave a public lecture on astronomy. He described how the earth orbits around the sun and how the sun, in turn, orbits around the center of a vast collection of stars called our galaxy. At the end of the lecture, a little old lady at the back of the room got up and said: "What you have told us is rubbish. The world is really a flat plate supported on the back of a giant tortoise." The scientist gave a superior smile before replying, "What is the tortoise standing on?" "You're very clever, young man, very clever," said the old lady. "But it's turtles all the way down!"[1]

This anecdote could be interpreted as offering a metaphor for the possession of a religious belief, a belief that explained the universe, but a belief that was ultimately illogical, at least when considered within the context of a scientific discourse. In *The West Wing*, religious belief was a constant trope; and while relatively few of President Bartlet's staff exhibited specific faith-group traits,[2] Bartlet himself was a devout Roman Catholic who appeared to believe in a literal God; a literal God who had sent his only son, Jesus Christ, to redeem mankind by dying on the cross. To argue that religious faiths are as irrational as imagining the world being balanced on a giant tortoise may appear to be a somewhat disproportionate point-of-view; however, the argument put forward in this chapter will go some distance to present this as one potential way of positioning religious belief within *The West Wing*.

In the episode "Two Cathedrals" (2/22), in the famous scene wherein Bartlet berated God as a "feckless thug," Bartlet appeared to be addressing God directly, as if "He" had an actual existence. In the episode, Bartlet quoted Grahame Greene's well-known comment from *Brighton Rock*: "You can't conceive ... nor can I ... the appalling strangeness of the mercy of God."[3] However, Bartlet may have been better off quoting a near contemporary of Greene's, George Orwell, who said: "One cannot really be a Catholic and [a] grown-up."[4] Orwell's comment might be seen as apposite, insomuch as, from a pragmatic and rational perspective, to make a direct address to a supposed supreme being, of whom there is no evidence, could be seen as, at best, a grown-up version of having an imaginary friend, or, at worst, evidence of a psychosis—a mental health disorder so severe as to cause a loss of awareness of external reality.[5] In this way, a skeptical approach might see this as undermining Bartlet's competence as a politician and as a president. However, as noted, religion was a constant presence in the show; and President Bartlet, like President John F. Kennedy, was "a devout, practicing and thinking Catholic."[6] Of course, we are dealing here with a president of a nation state wherein a literal belief in God was hardly unusual. Nonetheless, this could not help but diminish, albeit from an outsider's point-of-view,[7] the level of intelligence and rational authority the president appeared to possess.

In such a context, it should be noted that intelligence was one of the most significant qualities extolled within *The West Wing*'s utopian vision of political discourse. Spencer Downing commented: "Sorkin fetishizes intelligence."[8] Trevor and Shawn J. Parry-Giles noted: "*TWW* offers a romantic hero who achieves heroic status not from military accomplishment or exemplary physical deeds but from a powerful—indeed, Nobel Prize—winning—intellect."[9] To Simon Philpott and David Mutimer, "Josh Lyman and Sam Seaborn are tertiary educated men whose masculinity is defined by sharp intelligence."[10] In this way, while intelligence was revered and upheld in the series, in contrast, a fundamental religious belief in a literal God (as portrayed by Bartlet), might be seen as signaling a curtailment of intellectual thought, a means of preventing one from thinking, of disallowing intelligence the scope to question and to interrogate. For example, such statements as: "The soul survives after death," or "God is all knowing" or even "God is great" are neither true nor false. They are simply meaningless within a discourse of rational and humanist thought; the use of the word "God" simply acting as a means of precluding analytical debate. The greatest danger to both society and the individual, as we learn from Socrates, is the suspension of critical thought; and in *The West Wing* this was to become one of the most interesting disparities, one of the most interesting dichotomies.

As intimated, America is a much more religiously inclined nation state than most other nation states in the Western world. As Melissa Crawley commented: "Americans rank among the most religious people worldwide in terms of a belief in a supreme being, membership in religious organizations and attendance at religious services."[11] In most nation states it would seem as if culture might be expected to eventually assemble a valid alternative to religion; but in the case of America this does not seem to have progressed very far. In this context, the impact of Puritanism on American culture should not be underestimated. In a sense America was a nation state founded upon a Puritan ethic, especially in the sense of the centrality of the Bible and a literal belief in scripture.[12] In *The West Wing* it was not uncommon—in fact it was ubiquitous—for Bartlet to finish his speeches with a comment in the manner of: "May God bless the United States of America." This was representative of American presidents in the real world; but this would not be, for example, representative of speeches made by the heads of government in the United Kingdom, in the rest of Europe or in other Western nation states. It is important to acknowledge the significance of this in terms of political government in America, as Melissa Crawley has again commented:

> Accordingly, the president becomes the representative of the nation's civil religion.... He affirms that God exists and that America's destiny of national policies must be interpreted in the light of the Almighty's will.[13]

In terms of culture eventually assembling an alternative to religion, Terry Eagleton put forward the argument that "in most stretches of the globe, including much of the United States, culture never ousted religion in the first place."[14] Eagleton went on to conclude, somewhat pessimistically: "The age in which culture sought to play surrogate to religion is perhaps drawing to a close. Perhaps culture, in this respect at least, has finally admitted defeat."[15] In *The West Wing*, this proposition seemed to be reinforced: religion was a constant element in the series, especially in terms of Bartlet's Catholicism. There was rarely any sense of criticism for the Catholic Church in America, and no mention of the scandals that were occurring at the time the series was being aired; for example, the infamous Cardinal Law case of 2002.[16] The Roman Catholic Church, in the era of *The West Wing*, would seem to have been in some trouble: the pedophile scandals, the diminishing membership of the laity in the developed world, the shortage of priests, the vast numbers of Catholics who ignored the Church's teaching on birth control and so on. However, all of this was scarcely alluded to in *The West Wing*; instead, Bartlet's faith merely added to the feel-good bearing of the series, the continual sense of a sentimentalized discourse at play. Thus, the makers of the series may have been aware of the tensions between religion and the wider culture within American society, but they seldom seemed inclined to allow a discussion of this issue.

The West Wing was more inclined to allow a critique of other religious faiths, Islam being the obvious example. This was seen most pertinently in the episode "Isaac and Ishmael" (3/1), *The West Wing*'s fictitious but narratively beguiling response to the 9/11 attacks. A similar stance was adopted elsewhere in the series; for example, the episode "Enemies Foreign and Domestic" (3/19) dealt, in a barely fabricated fashion, with the notorious incident of March 11, 2002—the fire at the Girls' Intermediate School No. 31 in Mecca. During the incident the religious police are said to have forced fleeing schoolgirls back into the burning school because they were not wearing their robes and headdresses. According to Terry Eagleton, "fourteen girls died and dozens of others suffered terrible injuries," suggesting this occurred because the girls were improperly dressed.[17] In the fictionalized world of *The West Wing*, CJ informed the press room that there had been a fire at the King Fatah Middle School in Medea and that seventeen girls died because they had been prevented from leaving the burning building because they were not "dressed properly." CJ was asked by a reporter if she was outraged, to which she replied: "Outraged? I'm barely surprised. This is a country where women aren't allowed to drive a car. They're not allowed to be in the company of any man other than a close relative, they're required to adhere to a dress-code that would make the Maryknoll Nun look like Malibu Barbie." CJ went on to allude to the number of people beheaded for criminal offences; how there was no free press, no elected government, no political parties; how religious police, carrying nightsticks, were free to publicly beat women not adhering to the appropriate dress code—and finished by saying: "Seventeen schoolgirls were forced to burn alive because they weren't wearing the proper clothing. Am I outraged? No, that is Saudi Arabia, our partners in peace."

It may have appeared as if such criticisms were being made of the political system in Saudi Arabia; however, the underlying criticism would seem to have been aimed at Islam itself. The incident at the school has become notorious, perhaps compounded, to some extent at least, by its fictionalized usage in *The West Wing*. However, more recent accounts have suggested that the original reports may have been distorted. Fifteen young girls did die in the March 11 fire at the school; however, the majority of the deaths seem to have occurred when a staircase collapsed as the girls were fleeing the building, rather than because they were forced back into the building because of being improperly dressed. The true sequence of events may never be known, but it is possible to argue that *The West Wing*, albeit within a fictionalized discourse, may have distorted (knowingly or unknowingly) the actual events at the school.

* * *

Islam and Christianity have always had an underlying concern with death and what waits beyond. Within the overarching discourse of religious belief in *The West Wing*, one of the key issues was that of eschatology, another of the grandest of grand narratives.[18] This is most relevant to Islam, but as intimated above, it has also impacted upon Christianity and Judaism. The implication is that within a religious society, cultural and scientific progress may be less likely if the individual is more concerned with his or her personal salvation, more concerned with a future life in heaven—more concerned, that is, with any hope of salvation in the real world.[19] Fundamentalist religions, such as Islam, Christianity and Judaism, require believers to accept—on faith alone—the absolute belief in a prescribed list of written beliefs that derive from so-called sacred texts. This creates a problem that is seldom addressed. Any text—whether it be sacred or not—is ruled by two constants: when it was written and when it was read. In terms of sacred books such as the Quran, the Bible and the Torah, literal-mindedness thus encounters difficulties because of the changing context of the sacred text. As Eagleton has pointed out, the term "sacred text" is a contradiction in terms, insomuch as all texts are "profaned by a plurality of meanings."[20]

Such a predicament occurred in *The West Wing*, in the aptly titled episode "In God We Trust" (6/20). Bartlet and Arnold Vinick (the Republican nominee for the fictional 2006 election, played by Alan Alda) were discussing religion and whether a presidential candidate could publically state whether or not he (or she) was a churchgoer. Vinick intimated that he had previously been a Catholic, that he had gone to mass every Sunday and had followed the tenets of his faith. Vinick then recounted the following story: "One Christmas my wife gave me a very old edition of the King James Bible—17th century. It was a real find for a book collector. It was a thrill just to hold it. Then I read it." Vinick's phrase, "Then I read it," was a crucial comment, perhaps one of the most crucial comments on religion in the series. Bartlet suggested Vinick should "not take it literally." Vinick responded by saying: "That's what my friends in the priesthood have been telling me." However, it is possible that Vinick's comment, "Then I read it," may have meant he read it critically, especially as he went on to say: "The more I read it the less I could believe." It is certainly true to say that many Christians, many Muslims and many Jews read the Bible, the Quran and the Torah, but whether they read it in a critical fashion is less certain.[21]

* * *

From a different perspective, the French biologist and philosopher Jacques Monod has argued that mythic discourses were survival devices, and that the survival value of myths (he avoided the use of the term religion) were useful, but that they would, in time, be replaced.[22] However, it would seem—disregarding the advances in science, psychology and all the many diverse ways we now have of understanding ourselves—that religion still holds sway. The Greek playwright Euripides, over 400 years before the birth of Christ, put forward the question: "Do we, holding that the gods exist, deceive ourselves with unsubstantial dreams and lies, while random careless chance and change alone control the world?"[23] From a rational point-of-view, and from all the available evidence, this would appear to be a convincing argument. Yet a significant percentage of the world is reported to believe in a religious faith: there are 2.2 billion Christians, 1.6 billion Muslims, 1 billion Hindus, 500 million Buddhists and 14 million Jews. If one adds these numbers together, over a half of the world appears to adhere to a religious belief, while no less than 95 percent of Americans are said to have a literal belief in God. As Theodore Roszak put it: "If God has at last died in our culture, he has not been buried."[24] In *The West Wing*, Roszak's comment was played out to continuous effect; however, there was an underlying acceptance that religion—especially in the case of Bartlet's Catholicism—had gone far beyond its original value as a survival device; religion was a core element of Bartlet's character.

Bartlet was an intelligent man; nonetheless, the underlying religious discourses within the series continually appeared to possess a significance as great, if not greater, than Bartlet's unquestioned intelligence. An alternative point-of-view—for example, the concept of Occam's Razor—was seldom put forward. While it is seldom used to critique religion, this concept would seem to be a valid argument against a literal religious belief. In other words, there may be a simpler explanation for the Christian belief that Jesus of Nazareth was the Son of God, a spiritual being who preached in Palestine 2,000 years ago and was born in a stable in Bethlehem[25]; was conceived of a virgin[26]; was sent into the world by his Father to redeem mankind of Adam's sin; and who, after being crucified, rose from the dead and ascended into heaven, so that all who believe in "Him" shall never die. This is a synopsis of Roman Catholic doctrine; however, a more likely explanation might be to perceive of an ordinary man with something close to a perfect, if unlivable, message that was ultimately translated into the Roman Catholic Church—with its vast material wealth and its long history of condoning holy wars—disregarding the teaching of a man who preached unconditional poverty and unconditional pacifism. However, these contradictions seldom entered into Bartlet's way of thinking; a literal faith in God was all consuming.

Yet, there is another way of looking at this issue, for if a religious explanation is rejected, then what chance of making sense of the world? A religious explanation, no matter how simplistic it may be, would at least appear to offer one means of answering the big questions. Take, for example, the question of how life came about: it seems statistically unlikely that life would have emerged by pure chance; it has been estimated that for nucleotides, the basic units of DNA, to have come about through pure chance would require something like 140 different operations, taking place at the same time and in the correct sequence—and that the likelihood of this happening would be 10 to the power of 109. Since the number of electrons in the known universe is only 10 to the power of 80, then there would seem to have been little chance of this occurring via a random event. The universe is neither big enough, nor old enough for such mechanisms to have occurred by chance.²⁷ It could be that there are mechanisms we are presently not aware of, mechanisms we may eventually discover, but it is more likely that we will never have an answer. There are some things we do not know, and some things we will most likely never know—hence the simplistic recourse to a creator, to a God who made the universe. Such a simplistic recourse may prevent rational enquiry and may prevent the argument going any further but, it has to be admitted, it at least offers a way of answering such questions.²⁸

Nonetheless, all human societies have attempted to come to terms with life and death, to create beauty, to gain knowledge and, as Peter Watson has argued, to get at "the truth," whatever it may be.²⁹ One of the potential failings the human subject has consistently demonstrated has been the inability to accept the prospect that life may be meaningless, or at least meaningless insomuch as we will never be able to fully understand it. We live, we die, and there is no means with which to explain the experience; thus the idea that there may be something beyond such a wholly ambiguous experience has been at the core of most if not all religions.³⁰ Indeed, there were few voices raised in *The West Wing* to suggest an alternative argument: that we will never understand our lives and our environments. In other words, an existentialist discourse was seldom represented within the overarching discourse of *The West Wing*.³¹ This was perhaps a loss, but perhaps not unsurprising within a mainstream American television series. However, a recourse to Sartre, or Camus, or even Kierkegaard might have provided an alternative to the relentless array of religious discourses in play within the show's seven seasons.

The philosophical arguments of such thinkers might have afforded an antidote to the feel-good, over-sentimentalized discourses found so often within the series. Take, for example, Albert Camus's famous comment on the issue of the absurd: "I don't want to die and I don't want anyone I love to die. I am going to die and everyone I love is going to die. This is what makes life absurd." Similarly, Jean Paul Sartre put forward the view that man exists without purpose and the only meaning to life is the one we create. However, Sartre did not rely on an atheistic perspective; a belief in God, according to Sartre, was a personal choice, yet, for Sartre, we cannot defer responsibility to a deity deriving ultimately from our own minds.³² In a similar sense, Soren Kierkegaard, the so-called father of existentialism, argued that religious belief was a matter of passion, not of thought, and that reason can only undermine faith—never justify it. Finally, Bertrand Russell, while not strictly an existentialist, noted:

> All the labour of the ages, all the devotion, all the inspiration, all the noonday brightness of human genius, are destined to extinction in the vast death of the solar system, and the whole temple of man's achievement must inevitably be buried beneath the debris of a universe in ruins.³³

In this way, an engagement with such existentialist ways of thinking might have enriched the overarching demeanor of *The West Wing*, and—as suggested elsewhere—avoided the excessive degree of bathetic sentimentality found so consistently within the series as a whole.

Finally, there was the issue of scale: Why would a creator of a hundred billion stars have decided to redeem mankind by having his only "Son" crucified? If only in terms of the laws and mechanics of physics, this would seem unlikely, implausible and ultimately unconvincing.[34] As such, this would seem to echo the reductive scope of the turtle argument, as described at the beginning of this chapter. There is a sense in which such an argument had at least some merit, insomuch as it provided an answer, no matter how simplistic, to the question of who, or what, created the universe. Hence the turtle argument was at least a way of avoiding such questions; it prevented wasting time on a question whose answer may never be found. However, there was a further issue, even if it was turtles all the way down—as Terry Eagleton put it: "You can tough the question and claim that it's turtles all the way down, but all the way down to what?"[35] Hence even here, in this reductive discourse, the fundamental questions still remain unanswered. Nonetheless, in *The West Wing* there was a sense in which Bartlet's Catholic faith played to such a practice; Bartlet (perhaps with Martin Sheen behind him) would seem to have had a literal belief in a religious faith that, in a final summation, would seem to have had little more intellectual weight than the turtle solution.

Stephen Hawking, who began his book *A Brief History of Time* with the story of the turtles, ended the same book in this way:

> However, if we do discover a complete theory, it should in time be understandable in broad principle by everyone, not just a few scientists. Then we shall all, philosophers, scientists, and just ordinary people, be able to take part in the discussion of the question of why it is that we and the universe exist. If we find the answer to that, it would be the ultimate triumph of human reason—for then we would know the mind of God.[36]

Hawking most probably did not believe in a literal God—a so-called sky God; however, in *The West Wing*, Bartlet (along with the general milieu of American society) would appear to have believed in such a literal deity. This was a situation that was apparent throughout the show, so far as *The West Wing* went; it really was turtles all the way down.

12

Playing in the Dark
Racist Discourses

Was *The West Wing* a racist text, or at least was it a racist text within a certain specific context? In response to such a question, perhaps the first area to consider would be the issue of "whiteness" as depicted within the series. On a literal level *The West Wing* was white because it took place in the White House, a building so-called because of the Aquia Creek sandstone used in its construction. However, it was also a "white house" because it has always been predominantly inhabited by white people,[1] and it was certainly a "white house" in terms of its fictitious representation in *The West Wing*. As Trevor and Shawn J. Parry-Giles noted: "At base, *TWW* is a predominantly white show that features mostly white characters that perpetuates an ideology of whiteness."[2] Hence it is perhaps ironic to note that the White House was largely built by black slaves—a detail *The West Wing* did allude to in the episode "Night Five" (3/14). Here Stanley Keyworth, the psychiatrist helping Bartlet with insomnia, was given a tour of the White House by Josh Lyman. During the tour Keyworth posed an innocent, if significant question: "Who built the White House?" Josh replied, "It was designed by an Irish architect named James Hoban, who won the job in open competition. It was built largely by slaves; they just found the pay receipts a few months ago." This was as far as the discussion of slaves and the White House went; there was no follow-up, and the conversation moved on to other matters. However, the ironic point was well made: the White House was built by black slaves.

There were some exceptions to the whiteness of the characters in the White House; in other words, there were a small number of characters within the cast who were not white. The most notable examples were Dulé Hill as Charlie Young, the president's "bodyman," John Amos as Admiral Percy Fitzwallace, the Chairman of the Joint Chiefs of Staff, and Anna Deavere Smith as National Security Advisor Nancy McNally; however, these were the only African American characters of significance in the series. It would seem that

12. Playing in the Dark   101

Sorkin might have initially imagined what amounted to an all-white cast and only introduced black characters after criticisms of implied racism, as Paul Challen put it:

> After Aaron Sorkin was criticized for the lack of minority characters in the pilot episode, he made assurances there would soon be people of color in important positions in subsequent episodes.[3]

In terms of a consideration of the issue of race in *The West Wing*, Charlie Young was perhaps one of the most thought-provoking characters. While the motives behind the creation of such a character were no doubt well intentioned, there were, nonetheless, some problematical issues, which were often so clichéd and stereotyped that they inhabited, at times, an unintended racist discourse. In Charlie's first scenes, in the episode "A Proportional Response" (1/3), his innocent demeanor, as a young, naive African American man under intense pressure, seemed to lampoon racist expectations. In addition, there was some apprehension by some of the protagonists in the drama about hiring a young black man to be a "bodyman" to an older white president.[4] Admiral Fitzwallace, when asked by Leo about the racial implications of hiring Charlie in this role, commented: "I've got some real honest to God battles to fight, Leo, I don't have time for the cosmetic ones." Of course, in a literal sense, these were cosmetic issues—or at least issues of complexion, both in the narrative discourse of the series and in the commercial considerations for the makers of the series.[5]

There was also the issue of blackness and its association with violence. Insomuch, it seemed significant that a number of black characters in the series were subject to extreme forms of violence; for example, Admiral Fitzwallace would be killed in a terrorist attack in Season 5[6]; similarly, the president's doctor, Michael Tolliver, would die in a terrorist attack at the start of Season 1. In terms of Charlie, we would subsequently learn that his mother, a police officer, had been shot "in the line of duty," and Charlie, himself would be the object of an attempted "lynching" at the end of Season 1—because of his "miscegenic relationship" with Zoey.[7] Of course, there was no explicit racism toward Charlie in the White House; however, there were subtle suggestions of implied racial anxieties. This would be witnessed, for example, in the scene wherein Leo and Bartlet discussed Charlie's request to date Zoey. Leo asked: "You got a racial problem?"[8] Bartlet claimed he did not, but the fact that Leo raised the question was, in itself, significant. Simon Philpott and David Mutimer summed up the issue in this way:

> Charlie fulfils the ethnic fantasies of many liberals: a young, self-possessed, sober, drug free black man taking charge of his battered family and all the while bettering himself. This is the kind of black man that liberals like Josh and Sam know they can whiten and integrate into their world.[9]

One way of attempting to articulate the implied racism present in *The West Wing* might be to go back to America's beginnings—back to the Declaration of Independence. In the course of the series Bartlet referred directly to the Declaration of Independence on just two occasions. The first instance occurred in the episode "What Kind of Day Has It Been" (1/22), where Bartlet noted how his great-grandfather's great-grandfather had been the New Hampshire delegate to the second Continental Congress: "The one that sat in session in Philadelphia in the summer of 1776 and announced to the world that we were no longer subjects of King George III, but rather a self-governing people." The second instance occurred in the episode "The Two Bartlets" (3/13), wherein Bartlet told Toby: "My family signed the Declaration of Independence. You think I've got an ethnicity problem?" In neither of the two instances was there any sense of satirical quality to the comments; in fact, in the latter comment Bartlet would appear to assume that the Declaration of Independence did not have an ethnicity problem, which—from an impartial perspective—would appear to have been inaccurate. Of course, all nations states, if one goes back far enough, are built upon violence and brutality of some kind, but what would appear to be different in the case of the United States of America was that it began by compounding this with a sense of hypocrisy. The second sentence of the Declaration of Independence proclaimed:

> We hold these truths to be self-evident, that all men are created equal, that they are endowed by their Creator with certain unalienable Rights, that among these are Life, Liberty and the pursuit of Happiness.

The "we" in question at the start of the sentence were white free people; in other words, only certain people had certain unalienable rights to life, liberty and the pursuit of happiness. As Toni Morrison would note, there were "inherent contradictions in a free republic committed to slavery."[10]

This was hardly a palatable proposition, especially within the idealistic discourse of *The West Wing*. However, albeit from a cynical point-of-view, America was a slave republic built on genocide, something *The West Wing* continually had difficulty in presenting. To paraphrase Leslie Fiedler: America was a culture with a collective unconscious desire to shed its guilt via a retreat into a lost childhood it never possessed.[11] It was such a sense of both innocence and arrogance that arguably set America apart from other nations states: all nation states have committed acts that could be questioned in a moral sense, but few have also claimed such a level of moral superiority while in the task of committing those acts. Such a degree of hubris, one could argue, still prevails in America in recent decades, this being played out to full measure within *The West Wing*. One strategy of avoiding such a reality was not to even think about it, as Toni Morrison (talking of slavery in America) argued: "In matters of race, silence and evasion have historically ruled the literary dis-

12. Playing in the Dark   103

course."[12] This would seem to be exactly the strategy *The West Wing* adopted; the ideological practices of race were seldom acknowledged anywhere in the show. For example, a cursory online search reveals that slavery—in terms of the slavery of African American peoples—was only referred to in eight episodes, with most cases being of only a perfunctory nature.[13]

The one instance where *The West Wing* was able to approach the subject in any depth occurred in the episode "Six Meetings Before Lunch" (1/18). The episode included a conversation between Josh and Jeff Breckenridge, a potential candidate for the post of assistant attorney general for civil rights. Breckenridge, an African American, had suggested he might be in favor of slavery reparations; in other words, in favor of offering financial compensation to the descendants of Africans who were enslaved and sent to the Americas. A figure of $1.7 trillion was suggested, which Josh dismissed—claiming the United States would have to sell Texas and the U.S. Navy to pay for it. Yet, in the year 2000, the year in which the episode took place, there were 34.7 million African Americans living in the United States, 12.3 percent of the population. Simple division suggests $1.7 trillion would equate to approximately $38,000 for each descendent. This would seem a risible amount of compensation, and would only begin to repair the injury inflicted, not just to the individuals concerned, but also to the African cultures from which the slaves were taken. If the total material damage was to be repaid, then the actual amount might well bankrupt America. However, monetary concerns would seem to miss the point, as Breckenridge commented at the end of the scene: "You can't kidnap a civilization and sell them into slavery. No amount of money will make up for it."

The argument was well made; Josh attempted to counter by making the point that "six hundred thousand white men died over the issue of slavery."[14] However, this appeared as mere rhetoric; it could not counter the reality of American history.[15] In a specific sense, America could be envisaged as a nation flawed from its beginning, a nation proclaiming, at its birth, that all men were created equal, seemingly unaware of the hypocrisy so transparently at play within such a claim. However, it was not merely the damage done to the slaves and their descendants—it was also the damage done to slavers and their descendants. The consequences of this damage are arguably still felt today; one might note that lynchings were still occurring within the early lifespans of some of the characters in the series. Within living memory, white Americans would go to "see the show," the lynching of black Americans, as if it were part of a day out: white men, women and children would witness the barbaric torture and murder of black men, black women and black children. This was a legacy of American life that *The West Wing* seldom acknowledged.

* * *

Elsewhere in the series it was possible to identify other racist discourses, however innocent their origins may have been. These included attitudes toward Native Americans, toward followers of Islam, toward the British, toward the French and so on. In the case of Native Americans, there is a story, albeit possibly apocryphal, that the country singer Johnny Cash was once asked why he always wore black, "as if he were going to a funeral." Cash gave the laconic reply: "Well, maybe I am." Cash, who claimed to have Native American ancestry, was most likely thinking of the genocides inflicted upon the Native American peoples; hence his reply could be seen as evidence that he had a clearer understanding of America than the discursive practices at play within *The West Wing*. In a similar vein, the deliberately contentious British journalist Julie Burchill, describing the American experience in Vietnam as less a war and more one long atrocity, commented: "I realize that our American friends, living in a country built on genocide, may not appreciate the difference." The issue of the treatment of Native Americans was alluded to only rarely in the series itself, one example being the episode "The State Dinner" (1/7). Here the somewhat risibly named Mr. Bambang, an assistant of the Indonesian president, admonished Toby after Bartlet had made a speech criticizing Indonesia's attitude to human rights: "Mr. Ziegler, does it strike you at all hypocritical that a people who systematically wiped out a century's worth of Native Americans should lecture the world so earnestly on human rights?" It was a remark Toby was unable to rebut—a remark America itself would seemingly be unable to rebut.

There was also the issue of simple nomenclature; in other words, the linguistic appellations employed when referring to the original inhabitants of the Americas. This was seen to most obvious effect in the episode "The Indians in the Lobby" (3/8). In using such a title there would seem to have been no sense of irony, but to a non–American ear the title sounded at best blatantly politically incorrect, and at worst blatantly racist. The worst instance occurred at the beginning of the episode, when Josh was heard to shout: "There are two Indians in the lobby"—this being compounded by Leo responding: "One of them wants to become a rabbi"—almost as if it were the start of a joke.[16] The American academic response did not appear to be more palatable; in an essay published as late as 2005, Nathan A. Paxton, in his article "Virtue from Vice: Duty, Power, and *The West Wing*," was able to refer to Native Americans as "Indians" and "these Indians" on numerous occasions.[17] The correct term for the original people living on the continent that would come to be called North America was not the somewhat insensitive soubriquet "Red Indians." It has been estimated that, in the United States alone, there were over 500 Native American nations—and in none of these nations were people either red or Indian.[18]

However, in the imaginary reality of *The West Wing*, the "Indians" are presumably still waiting in the lobby. The president, of course, never came close to meeting the "Indians" in the aforementioned lobby; he was too busy, for most of the episode, obsessing about the correct way to cook a Thanksgiving turkey—even to the extent of personally calling the "Butterball Hotline." A cynical reading of this decidedly unfunny burlesque would be to say it was intended to deliberately undermine the cause of the "Indians" in the lobby—while the two Native Americans patiently waited for their grievances to be heard, the president was dealing with the niceties of Thanksgiving cuisine. As such, a satirical reading of the scene would be to observe how Bartlet was not "talking turkey" in the American parlance; he was—again as American parlance would have it—a "turkey."

CJ was the one character in the episode who seemed sympathetic to the two Native Americans (in the lobby)—Jack Lone Feather and Maggie Morningstar-Charles—but even she did not appear to take the situation wholly seriously, commenting almost flippantly: "This is going to have something to do with us screwing you out of all your land, isn't it? Indians on the day before Thanksgiving. Wow. Ironic. How do you keep fighting these smaller injustices when they're all from the Mother of Injustices?" Maggie replied: "What's the alternative?" Keith Topping praised this episode, giving it "full marks for the courage of *not* taking easy options over the Indian storyline."[19] However, the opposite would appear to have been the case. The episode did take easy options—even racist options. Or at least one could argue this, given the response Maggie Morningstar-Charles made—a response so incisive that CJ could not offer an answer. Maggie's question was perhaps one of the most relevant questions pertaining to race in the series.

In a later episode, "The Two Bartlets" (3/13), CJ's implicit racist views were seen more clearly; this occurred in a comment she made relating to why her father had not had a more successful career as a teacher: "After my father fought in Korea, he became a teacher, and he raised a family on a teacher's salary [but] anytime there was an opportunity for career advancement, it took an extra five years because invariably there was a less-qualified black woman in the picture." Trevor and Shawn J. Parry-Giles were astute in commenting on this:

> CJ's statement reaffirms the popular conception of white male victimization as an outgrowth of affirmative action and ignores the historical conditions of racism and the data on career advancement and college admissions for groups targeted by affirmative action.[20]

CJ appeared to believe her father might not have developed dementia if he had received the promotion he deserved; however, the near-ancestors of "the less qualified black woman," would likely have been slaves—and this was perhaps one reason why she was less qualified. CJ's implied ignorance as to the background of the "less qualified black woman" did not excuse her blatant racist views.

In terms of the aforementioned bias against other racial groups, the issue of Islamic bias was readily apparent in the "Isaac and Ishmael" (3/1) episode and elsewhere in the series, where there was "a consistent and underlying message that the Arabs simply cannot be trusted."[21] In another context, the show's attitude to the United Kingdom was as clichéd and stereotyped as might have been expected: the British were pompous, superior and eccentric. This was exemplified in the character of Lord John Marbury and also, albeit on a lesser scale, Bernard Thatch, another clichéd British protagonist. There was one memorable scene that went beyond the clichéd discourse. In a conversation between Marbury and Toby, the discussion unexpectedly became more serious. Marbury noted "the darkness in our sunshine, the shadow in our souls, the biblical sins of the fathers. For Americans, it's slavery. Slavery is your original sin. That and your unfortunate history with your aborigines."[22]

One of the most aggravating examples of nonchalant racism was arguably *The West Wing*'s attitude to the French. This was apparent throughout the entire run of the series; there were too many examples to note in full, but the following instances might be noted. In the episode "Manchester Part 2" (3/3), referring to France's help in diplomatic talks with Haiti, Bartlet cast this deliberate slur: "The State Department's suggesting that we praise the French government for their help in resolving this matter. I would, but I'm worried they'd surrender." Likewise, in the episode "Full Disclosure" (5/15), CJ commented, "The President has no intention of starting a worldwide bra war. I really don't think the President would ever start a war that the French might actually win." There were other such comments, all somewhat arid and dismissively racist, but perhaps the most interesting aspect to the anti–French discourse concerned the subplot of Jean-Paul, Zoey's new boyfriend, or to give him his full name: Jean-Paul Pierre Claude Vicomte de Condé de Bourbon. Jean-Paul was something of a cliché: conceited and superior, a smug, youthful, and aristocratic dilettante who seemed to personify the French nation,[23] a comic villain with his risible hairstyle only rivaled by his risible accent. Jean-Paul also used narcotics and would subsequently be responsible for "spiking" Zoey's drink at her graduation party—which would inadvertently lead to her kidnapping. After this Jean-Paul conveniently disappeared from the narrative—presumably to return to his clichéd way of life in France. However, the most egregious racist slur to the French would occur in the episode "Abu el Banat" (5/9), wherein Bartlet flippantly referred to Jean-Paul as "the frog"—hardly a comment in the rhetorical style of the great statesman Bartlet purported to be.

* * *

In summary, *The West Wing* would seem to be arguing against the fact that America was, and remains, a racist country.[24] In the actual world America may have had a black president from 2008 to 2016, while in the alternative universe of *The West Wing* it had a Hispanic president from 2006 to either 2010 or 2014, but beneath this advancement remained a deeply racist society. It was in such a context that *The West Wing* seemed to avoid dealing overtly with racism in American society, it being either unwilling or unable to do so. This is not to say this was not possible; for example, Paul Haggis's film *Crash* (2005), made toward the end of *The West Wing*'s initial broadcast, demonstrated it was possible to depict a realistic picture of racial attitudes in American life. Or at least this film (and others) was able to portray a more realistic picture than the idealistic view presented in *The West Wing*. All the main characters in the show were Americans, and, to a man and woman, they all appeared to be proud to be Americans. Yet, to an outsider's point-of-view, there would seem to be less to be proud of within this specific context of race in American life.

The series was able to allude to terrorism, on numerous occasions, with a clarity of vision missing from its representation of racism; the irony being that for a significant section of American society—for millions of African Americans—terror has been a constant facet of their lives for several hundred years. *The West Wing* was not able to delineate this reality of American life, and in this sense, it could be argued that the fabric of American values may have been flawed from its idealistic beginnings. As Ta-Nehisi Coates, in an article in *The Atlantic* in 2014 analyzing slave reparations, put it:

> The laments about "black pathology," the criticism of black family structures by pundits and intellectuals, ring hollow in a country whose existence was predicated on the torture of black fathers, on the rape of black mothers, on the sale of black children. An honest assessment of America's relationship to the black family reveals the country to be not its nurturer but its destroyer.[25]

From a similar perspective, Trevor and Shawn J. Parry-Giles noted how "African Americans always perform race and are subject to the white gaze"[26]—and that *The West Wing* "accentuates presidential whiteness."[27] The authors also commented: "Rather than take the opportunity for the president to address the historical legacies of racism in the United States, *TWW* accentuates the logic of whiteness and reverse racism."[28] In this sense, what was ultimately troubling was the inability of the show to confront its own past in terms of slavery; as Leslie Fiedler put it: "The ultimate horror, the unmitigated terror of conscienceless and brutal slavery."[29] In the episode "Inauguration Part 1" (4/14), Bartlet asked Will Bailey—in a discussion of genocide in the fictitious African state of Kundu—"Why is a Kundunese life worth less to me than an American life?" Will spoke truth to power: "I don't know, sir, but it is." In such a context *The West Wing* rarely allowed for the possibility that a black American life might be worth less than a white American's—but this could be seen as being the clear corollary of the argument. What *The West Wing* inadvertently succeeded in accomplishing was to put forward the idea that although all nation states are racist, not all began by claiming the opposite, and not all sought to dissemble the truth in such a sentimental and hypocritical way.

13

Potus Interruptus
Gender and Queer Theory

The West Wing was decidedly reticent in terms of sexuality. In a sense this could be explained via the show's position on prime-time U.S. network television; in other words, as with the proscription of explicit language, scenes of explicit sexual content could not be depicted on American network television. However, such a sense of reticence went much further, at times almost to the point of prudishness; for example, in the episode "Take Out the Trash Day" (1/13), Bartlet, while reading a sex education paper, declared: "I won't say *that* word." Similarly, in the episode "Ellie" (2/15), Mrs. Landingham scolded Charlie: "Charlie, please don't say the word 'erotic' in the Oval Office."[1] As such, the Oval Office would seem to have been a somewhat different place than it was for the previous real-life incumbent. As Clive James put it: "Bartlet's administration, in at least one crucial respect, is nothing like Bill Clinton's. There is no sex."[2] There were some attempts at portraying sexual desire, albeit within the safe surroundings of a monogamous relationship; for example the scenes between Bartlet and Abbey in the episode "And It's Surely to Their Credit" (2/5)—wherein the president and first lady sought, unsuccessfully, to find time for a romantic tryst, even to the extent of the first lady wearing an oft-mentioned: "special garment." However, any sense of actual sexual tension seemed unconvincing; and there were few genuinely explicit sexual scenes anywhere within the series.[3] If the word "erotic" could not be uttered in Bartlet's White House then the chance of any genuine eroticism seemed unlikely.

In this way, a hedonic calculator might suggest a decidedly depleted level of *jouissance* within the drama. However, when one looks more carefully at the personal lives of the staff in the drama, then it becomes clear that "most of *The West Wing*'s characters don't have a life outside the office,"[4] that "no one on *The West Wing* has time for a relationship,"[5] and that "the vigor and vitality generated by intense sexual attraction"[6] was sublimated elsewhere—

in other words, sublimated into the demands of the working environment. Insomuch, there were numerous instances of how work affected the personal lives of the characters in the drama. For example, in "Five Votes Down" (1/4), in one of the more extreme cases, Leo's marriage incurred mortal injury when he told his wife that his job was "more important" than his marriage. There were numerous less extreme examples: in "Take Out the Trash Day" (1/13), CJ commented: "I can't remember the last time I got home before midnight." In "Take This Sabbath Day" (1/14), Sam was forced to forgo his sailing weekend; in "The Stackhouse Filibuster" (2/17) all the staff had Easter holiday plans, but these were all curtailed because of events in the episode; in "The Fall's Gonna Kill You" (2/20), CJ was in the White House Counsel's office at 5.30 in the morning; similarly, in "H Con 172" (3/11), the working day had already started at 7.00 a.m., but Donna was still in the office at 10.45 p.m.—and so on throughout other diverse examples. In other words, given the excessive demands of work in the White House, the obvious question to ask was how any of the characters found time to forge meaningful personal relationships.

If one were to discount Bartlet and Abbey, together with the other exception of Charlie and Zoey, then it would seem none of the main characters in the series succeeded in generating stable and viable relationships. As intimated above, Leo's wife left him early in the series; Toby could not persuade his ex-wife, Andy, to live with him, even after the birth of their twins; CJ only consummated her affair with Danny at the very end of the series[7]; Sam was unable to get "beyond debating school vouchers"[8] with Mallory, and fared no better with Ainsley[9]; Josh broke up with Amy and his seemingly endless non-affair with Donna represented the series' most extended *coitus interruptus*—only achieving a half-hearted resolution near the very end of the series. In the case of Bartlet himself, there appeared to be little sense of power being the ultimate aphrodisiac; once again contrary to his real-life avatar in the White House, Bartlet appeared almost asexual. In fact, at times Bartlet seemed to go out of his way to curtail sexual pleasure. This was apparent in the way he sought to pursue a repressive attitude toward his daughters, together with embarking (with Leo) upon an almost sadistic ploy to prevent Sam going out with Mallory. All of this contributed to a sense of anhedonia—a deliberate ban on pleasure derived from sexual pursuit and gratification.

As if by way of compensating for this, there was a sense of Bartlet having an extended family, with his staff co-opted into a quasi-family unit. If this was the case then there were obvious implications, as Trevor and Shawn J. Parry-Giles put it: "*TWW* depicts its characters as part of a metaphorical family, most men and women on the show avoid the suggestion of 'incest' by becoming sexually engaged with those outside of the 'family's' inner circle."[10] This was an apt point; however, as suggested above, there was little evidence of much "engagement" outside of the "family circle." What was apparent was

13. Potus Interruptus

Bartlet acting as a kind of surrogate father, whom his staff served "at his pleasure." This phrase: "I serve at the pleasure of the president," was a significant aspect of the show and one cannot help but perceive of a sublimated sexual inference. It was a phrase consistently repeated throughout the series; for example, as previously intimated, at the end of the episode "Let Bartlet be Bartlet" (1/19), where Josh, CJ, Sam and Toby, without any sense of satire, intoned the same solemn message: "I serve at the pleasure of the President."

In the following episode, "Mandatory Minimums" (1/20), there was a scene in which the underlying implications of such an outpouring of "pleasuring" was played out in almost risible form. For reasons not entirely clear, most of Bartlet's senior staff assembled in his bedroom late at night, anxious to talk over the events of the day.[11] Heather Richardson Hayton, alluding to the odd (not to say queer) components of the scene, commented: "At 11 p.m., Bartlet is awakened to have a staff meeting in his bedroom—and this is no Clintonesque bad joke."[12] There was a somewhat absurdist notion to the scene, with the intimacy of the staff seemingly dedicated to forming a "perfect union" with the president. The one character who appeared to see through this bizarre charade was Amy Gardener[13]; in a later episode, "Constituency of One" (5/5), Amy resigned, telling the president, "I wasn't made to serve at someone else's pleasure."

* * *

If there was a relative paucity of heterosexual relationships in *The West Wing*, there was an even greater paucity of homosexual relationships—in fact, there was an almost total lack of any same-sex relationships in the series. The episodes "Twenty Hours in L.A." (1/16) and "The Portland Trip" (2/7) were arguably the only ones to deal directly with "gay" issues in anything like a significant way. In the former episode, Ted Marcus, a Hollywood mogul described as a "gay activist," was concerned about the issue of "banning gays in the military." The latter episode included a plotline in which a Republican senator, Matt Skinner, one of the few openly "gay" characters in the series, was permitted to at least begin to explain his sexuality. Skinner told Josh: "My life doesn't have to be about being a homosexual—it doesn't have to be entirely about that."[14] Josh at least appeared to understand, but then, exasperated by the attitude of many Republicans to homosexuality, Josh suddenly told Matt: "You're gay!" It was a key line, within a key scene, and one that delineated the attitude to different sexualities within the series.[15] As such, although *The West Wing* was considered to be a liberal show, it was a show that often leaned to a more conservative way of thinking—as here, in terms of sexuality.[16]

To once again draw upon a comparison to *The Wire*, in this corresponding drama at least three main characters had same-sex inclinations,[17] not that this had any actual significance to their presence within the drama. This was not the case in *The West Wing*, on the rare occasions when "gay" characters were featured their "gayness" was the reason for them being featured. This could be witnessed in the instances cited above and also elsewhere within the drama. For example, the murdered high school student Lowell Lydell in the episode "In Excelsis Deo" (1/10) appeared to have been based on Matthew Shepard in Wyoming. Shepard had been a student at the University of Wyoming, but on the night of October 6, 1998, he was tied to a fence—to be beaten, tortured and left to die. In *The West Wing*'s fictional version, Leo told CJ how a "gay" high school senior had been attacked: "They stripped him naked, tied him to a tree and threw rocks and bottles at his head." This plot element featured in a number of succeeding episodes concerning the White House's attempt to deal with the murder. In the episode "Take Out the Trash Day" (1/13), both Leo and Bartlet made wrong assumptions about Mr. Lydell, the dead boy's father, assuming a man who had a low-level job and lived in Minnesota would not have progressive views about sexuality. Similarly, CJ wholly misunderstood the attitude of Lydell to his murdered son's sexuality; the key scene occurred when Lydell eloquently denounced Bartlet's cowardice: "I don't understand how this President, who I voted for, I don't understand how he can take such a completely weak-ass position on gay rights [on] gays in the military.... I want to know from this President, who has served not one day in uniform.... I want to know what qualities necessary to being a soldier this President feels my son lacked? Lady, I'm not embarrassed my son was gay. My government is."

* * *

It has been argued that attitudes toward sexuality "have always been more repressive in the USA" than in most other Western countries.[18] One reason for the greater and more pervasive sense of repression in America is said to have been the influence of religion, particularly fundamentalist Christianity. Such a prevailing view would seem to espouse the idea that sexual activity should be reserved for the sole purpose of procreation; hence limiting sexual activity to the enablement of reproduction via heterosexual coitus—in other words, a penis penetrating a vagina with the object of conception being the only legitimate form of sexual activity. In reality, human beings have always indulged in a diverse range of sexual activities, extending far beyond such a proscriptive choice of options.[19] However, the repressive discourses of religion have continually sought to create an arena in which to conform and to be "normal." Perhaps the most damaging of such repressive discourses was the condemnation of homosexuality, as found in the Old Testament.[20] In terms of sexuality, one thing *The West Wing* succeeded in doing was to offer a linkage between homophobia and fundamentalist Christianity, with the underlying sense that this may have had more to do with repressed desire than with genuine religious conviction.

Hence it might be said religion has played a significant role in making something that is highly desirable wholly forbidden; many religious faiths (especially Christianity and Islam) have attempted to proscribe as iniquitous what every human instinct says is intensely pleasurable. In other words, as Roger Horrocks has argued, religion's concept that sex was sinful has created "a stark dualism between body and soul [that] has dominated Western culture up to the present day."[21] Horrocks added: "It is striking how often in fiction characters cry out 'Oh God' at the moment of sexual climax, the intensity of the experience seems to make people seek religious words to express the ineffable."[22] To put this another way, the bliss of sexual orgasm is not unlike the experience of religious ecstasy, taking us to a place that "seems like the source of being itself."[23] To express this in Jungian terms, sex allows the individual to reach for the center of the psyche, a way of feeling at one with our material existence.[24] However, this sense of looking at human sexuality with a degree of existential clarity was seldom apparent in *The West Wing*. In contrast, a religious discourse consistently held sway; once again resulting in a disparity with the supposedly liberal point-of-view that purportedly prevailed within the series.

* * *

One way of more fully understanding the repressive attitudes toward sexuality in *The West Wing* might be achieved via a consideration of sexuality from a theoretical perspective. Since the 1980s, university students studying humanities in the United Kingdom, in the United States, in Europe and especially in France, have formed a new academic generation; in Terry Eagleton's words, such students were: "fascinated by sexuality but bored by social class ... enthused by popular culture but ignorant of labour history ... enthralled by exotic otherness but only dimly acquainted with the workings of imperialism."[25] As Eagleton suggests, there would appear to have been a change in theory's main arenas of concern; as Jane Gallop put it: "Around 1985, feminism began to give way to what has come to be called gender studies."[26] Gender theory, or what subsequently came to be known as queer theory, has been influential in academic studies since the 1990s. Notwithstanding its name, queer theory was not primarily concerned with "gay" men and lesbian women; the name (rescued from its derogatory and homophobic connotations)[27] instead looked at all that was "queer" in culture as a whole, all that seemed to go against the normal, the standard, the customary, the conventional and the accepted.

The philosopher who had most influence on queer theory was Michel Foucault; although he died in 1984, Foucault's work has retained a lasting significance within this area of study. In Foucauldian terms, the simplistic idea that sexuality was a natural occurrence has been deconstructed; in Foucauldian terms sexuality became a historical construction, with Foucault arguing that "sexuality represents a powerful archaic force that will always threaten authority," so much so that a history of sexuality "will also be a history of repression."[28] In this way, Foucault's overarching argument focused on the idea that sexuality has become a core component of our sense of identity—a fundamental "truth" of who we are. Or as Tamsin Spargo put it: "A vital feature of Foucault's argument is that sexuality is not a natural feature of human life but a constructed category of experience that has historical, social and cultural, rather than biological origins."[29] In a Foucauldian sense sexuality is therefore fluid in more ways than one; it is about the exchange of intimate bodily fluids—but it is also fluid in the ways in which individuals feel and think about each other.[30]

As such, Foucault's ideas were pointing to the sense that all human beings have a fluid constitution when it comes to sexual inclinations. As Freud had claimed, we are all polymorphously perverse. In other words, sexuality was a much more diverse arena than might be assumed; as Marjorie Garber put it: "The world is flat. The sun revolves around the earth. Human beings are either heterosexual or homosexual."[31] Garber went on to ask why everyone was not bisexual; she provided this response:

> The answers are not far to seek: repression, religion, repugnance, denial, laziness, shyness, lack of opportunity, premature specialization, a failure of the imagination, a life already full to the brim with erotic experiences, albeit with only one person, or only one gender.[32]

In a more theorized arena, and in drawing upon structuralist and poststructuralist thought to deconstruct previously established binary oppositions, one can demonstrate that recognized pairings were not absolute.[33] One of the questions queer theory posed was whether there was any authentic meaning in oppositions such as masculine/feminine, heterosexual/homosexual, or active/passive. Queer theorists argued that such oppositions must be deconstructed in order to demonstrate the inherent bias within the dominant culture—most specifically within the skewed dynamics of a phallocentric discourse.

As such, queer theory would come to perceive heterosexuality not as a biological imperative, but as a socially constructed edifice, with sexual behavior no longer genetically determined, but learned within a socio-cultural context. Within such a theoretical model, sexual orientation could be questioned, with heterosexuality becoming a more ambiguous concept—not the natural and unchanging structure as had been previously thought. So much so, that even the procreative argument seemed less convincing; in other words, even

13. Potus Interruptus

in the most conventional of heterosexual relationships, sexual activity has always been more about pair bonding, the maintenance of a relationship via intimacy, rather than procreation. One of the key arguments here was to clarify the distinction between sex and gender; sex being the biological referent, the chromosomal differences within the body, and gender being the parallel cultural term, the differentiations of bodies that occur within a social and cultural space. The significant issue resided within the argument that gender was a social and cultural category imposed on a sexed body; with the key argument revolving around the question of what was biologically determined and what was socially constructed.

The critic of most importance here, and arguably the most important critic within queer theory as a whole, was Judith Butler. Butler's book *Gender Trouble*, first published in 1990, is now accepted as being one of the most influential texts within the field. Butler's work cast doubt on the very idea that "sex" should be designated as a phenomenon grounded in nature. Butler argued that the entire cultural construction built upon the anatomical oppositions of the genital organs to designate gender identity was false. Butler's theoretical goal was to "denaturalize" the "heterosexual matrix" and, in an overarching sense, to put forward the argument that gender may not proceed from sex; this was the "gender trouble" Butler had in mind.[34] In addition, Butler conceived of gender as an improvised performance, a space where differing sexual identities could be adopted and explored, a space where one's sexuality had nothing to do with heterosexual and homosexual acts; in essence, gender was a "performative act." Within such an argument Butler perceived of conventional heterosexuality as a mere imitation, as a pastiche, a masquerade of an original form that, in fact, had no real existence. In other words, men dressed up to look like men, women dressed up to look like women, but all was mere performance.[35]

Another significant theorist within gender studies, Eve Kosofsky Sedgwick, argued that male-to-male desire, within western culture, was legitimated on a homosocial basis. Homosociality referred to the way men, working in a patriarchal league with one another, were regulated by two forms of oppression: "homophobia and misogyny."[36] In a specific sense, Sedgwick's argument alluded to the idea that the privileges granted to such male-to-male relationships stood in "dangerous proximity to the very homosexuality" patriarchy was required to condemn.[37] In *The West Wing* homosocial couples were readily apparent, this being personified by Ed and Larry. This male couple, "these two guys" as they were often called, played roles of little significance in the series, and yet they were present in all seven seasons, from the first episode to the last. As Josh said to Ed and Larry in the episode "100,000 Airplanes" (3/12): "Do the two of you ever go anywhere separately?" Ed: "It's weird, isn't it?" Josh: "A little weird. Yeah." It was a little weird; with the repetition seeming to almost suggest it was a little queer as well. As an ambiguous male couple, Ed and Larry seemed almost to be reminiscent of Rosencrantz and Guildenstern in *Hamlet*,[38] replete with at least a suggestion of deliberate homosocial or even homoerotic implications.

Elsewhere in the series there were a number of other male couples: Bartlet and Leo and Sam and Josh being two of the obvious examples. For example, in the episode "Enemies" (1/8), Bartlet comforted Leo on hearing he had separated from his wife, telling him, "I'm right next door, all night." In the episode "The Stackhouse Filibuster" (2/17), Bartlet and Leo took a late-night dinner together in the president's private dining room, a romantic meal originally planned for the president and his wife. On seeing the layout of the dining room the male couple decided to go ahead. "We'll just pretend there's no candlelight," said Bartlet, to which Leo responded: "And that we're not paranoid homophobes." There were similar scenes in other episodes: Bartlet and Leo sitting alongside each other outside the Oval Office, watching the snow fall in "H. Con 172" (3/11); or the intimate scene at the end of the episode "Third Day Story" (6/3) wherein Bartlet took Leo's hand after his heart attack.[39] In the case of Sam and Josh, there were a number of other homosocial references: for example, in the episode "The State Dinner" (1/7), Josh and Sam were so enamored with each other's tuxedos (Josh going so far as to straighten Sam's bow tie) that Mandy had to ask: "Do you guys want to be alone?" There was a similar scene in "Somebody's Going to Emergency, Somebody's Going to Jail" (2/16), where admiration of male apparel was again to the fore. Josh asked if Sam was wearing a new shirt; Sam said he was, and then said: "Guys like you—I'm one of them."[40] There were numerous other instances between other men in the series; for example, in the episode "Things Fall Apart" (6/21), there was a humorous exchange between Josh and Matt Santos. Late at night Santos had gone to Josh's hotel room to discuss an aspect of the campaign strategy; Josh made a vaguely amusing joke that he and the visiting congressman should have "three feet on the floor"—however, Santos's line, "Shall we toss for it?" was funnier still.

Leslie Fiedler's analysis of American culture and literature offered a potential explanation for such homosocial relationships. Fiedler was writing primarily of the American novel, although his argument worked for American culture as a whole. Fiedler noted the inability of the American male to deal with mature heterosexual love and the responsibilities it entailed; instead he saw a consistent obsession with death, incest and an "innocent homosexuality." Fiedler saw America as a place without a significant history, without class structures: "A world which left behind the terror of Europe not for the innocence it dreamed of, but for new and special guilts associated with the rape of nature and the exploitation of dark skinned people; a world doomed to play out the imaginary childhood of Europe."[41] In his book *Love and Death in the American Novel*, first published in 1961 and one of the first major studies "to treat gender as an issue in American literature,"[42] Fiedler famously spoke of "the holy marriage of males."[43] In other words, American men, including those in *The West Wing*, sought male companionship to free themselves of the "entanglements of heterosexual passion, marriage and domestic obligations."[44]

Such a concept was seldom explicitly explored in *The West Wing*; however, a careful reading of the series reveals a number of slippages that seemed to betray recurring anxieties around this concept. For example, in the episode "Post Hoc, Ergo Propter Hoc" (1/2), Josh posed the following question to Toby and Sam: "Who among us hasn't known forbidden love?" Josh was seemingly talking about Sam's affair with a prostitute; but there were other potential readings available. In the episode "Bartlet's Third State of the Union" (2/13), Josh appeared to be transparently homophobic, or least he betrayed an anxiety that other men might find him sexually attractive. Kenny (Joey Lucas's male translator) said: "Joshua Lyman, you have the cutest little butt in professional politics." Josh replied: "Kenny, really, that had better been her talking."[45] In Charlie's first scene, in the episode "A Proportional Response" (1/3), Josh asked Charlie a number of personal questions, such as: "I wonder if you could tell me about your social life. Your friends, what you like to do." Sam interrupted: "He's asking if you're gay." A number of issues were raised here: Why would Sam assume this, and even if he was correct why would Josh be interested in Charlie's sexuality? In the episode "Mr. Willis of Ohio" (1/6), Josh still seemed beset with sexual anxiety, so much so that when he and Charlie went out for a drink, Charlie joked, "What kind of bar is this, Josh?" with the obvious inference it might have been a "gay" bar. Finally, there was Josh's homophobic statement in the opening episode of the series, "Pilot" (1/1): the comment that he thought Lloyd Russell (the congressman Mandy was working for) "was gay" because "he always seemed effeminate to me." Josh's comment was significant not only because it linked same-sex inclinations with effeminacy, but also because it raised the question as to why Josh would have formed such an opinion in the first place.

The implied relationships between men in the drama were echoed within the implied relationships between women. A close reading and a careful analysis of female-to-female relationships suggested there were a number of instances of implied homosexual attraction. The first significant instance occurred in the episode "The Leadership Breakfast" (2/11). One element of the episode's plot concerned an attempt to placate a *New York Times* columnist, an unperformed character named Karen Cahill. As all the male staff members were unwilling to meet the columnist, Donna was sent instead; at an off-stage meeting between the two women Donna found a way to lose an item of her underwear, this subsequently being mailed back to the White House. How

Donna had come to misplace her underwear was never explained, but there were some ambiguous references. Sam told Donna, "I hear the two of you made a connection." Donna replied, "I had a most stimulating conversation with her." However, the idea that Donna somehow lost her underwear during this "connection," during this "stimulating" meeting, was almost as implausible as the detail that Donna would sew a name-tag into her underwear.

A more explicit reference came later in the series, in the episode "The Hubbert Peak" (6/5), this time in a scene between Donna and Kate Harper. The scene began with small talk, with Donna assuming Kate had come to see Josh, but Kate told her: "Actually, I came by to see you.... How soon before you're out of that cast?" Donna responded: "Soon, I can't wait." Kate went on: "Look, we don't know each other that well, but if you ever wanted to talk. I just thought if you ever wanted someone, another woman." Donna seemed uncertain, Kate asked: "Is this completely inappropriate?" Donna said it was fine, and the conversation ended with Kate saying: "Well, if you ever want to." In one way, at a literal level of discussion, this could have been read simply as a discussion of PTSD, insomuch as Donna had recently been injured in a terrorist attack and Kate, as a former CIA operative, would likely have had similar experiences. However, and at a different level of interpretation, it could have been read as a subtle attempt at flirtation.

A similar scene occurred in the episode, "The Wedding" (7/9), this time between Kate and CJ. Both women complimented each other on their clothes and make-up. Kate joked: "Nothing says 'International Crisis' like a pair of black stilettos." CJ repeated the compliment: "Yeah. You really look nice." Kate replied: "Okay, now I'm starting to think you're hitting on me." CJ changed the topic: "Who's the guy?" "What makes you think there's a guy?" Kate ambiguously replied—and there the scene ended. Once again, a potential reading would be to see Kate (who often favored a quasi-masculine attire of grey flannel trouser suits) and CJ indulging in a faux-lesbian tryst. Such a reading would be strengthened via previous questions about CJ's sexuality; in the episode "Faith Based Initiative" (6/10), CJ had been faced with internet rumors that she was pursuing "a radical homosexual agenda." It was clear that this was not a serious issue and CJ did not respond publicly, however, she told Leo: "I'm a heterosexual, except, as of today, I'm the most famous, the most powerful lesbian on the planet. And the fact of the matter is, I'm absolutely crazy about this man I just met and had two fabulous dinners with in the space of one week." Finally in this context, after close to 150 episodes, a same-sex relationship for a regular cast member *was* revealed, this occurring in the episode "Election Day Part 1" (7/16). Herein Ronna Beckman, played by Karis Campbell, was explicitly shown as being in a relationship with a young woman called Cindy, a campaign worker. It was made clear they had been having an affair on the election campaign. Ronna would eventually become President Santos's press secretary, fulfilling the same role as CJ to President Bartlet, hence providing an additional echo to the veiled rumors surrounding CJ's sexuality.

Such ambiguously veiled same-sex allusions between female characters perhaps allowed for the construction of an answer to one of *The West Wing*'s most famous unsolved mysteries: What was the cause of Mandy's unexplained disappearance at the end of Season 1? Mandy Hampton was arguably one of the most intriguing characters of the show—albeit only appearing for one season. At first, Mandy featured as one of the most significant characters; however, as the season progressed Mandy's importance appeared to lessen. By the episode "Six Meetings Before Lunch" (1/18) she was reduced to arguing the fate of a dead panda bear—as if to deliberately demean her character's importance. Two episodes later, in "Mandatory Minimums" (1/20), Mandy was literally led out of the Oval Office, perhaps in a deliberately symbolic way. Finally, in the end-of-season finale "What Kind of Day Has It Been" (1/22), Mandy did not appear to be present at the fateful town hall meeting in Rosslyn, her last line in the series taking place earlier in the same episode—the unremarkable comment: "How do you feel about him [the President] taking off his jacket?" After this Mandy seemed to simply disappear; she was not mentioned again and her absence was not commented on within the drama.

One potential explanation might have been that Mandy may have developed as a character with same-sex inclinations. There were a number of implicit suggestions of this; for example, although Mandy had previously had a romantic liaison with Josh, she also had a business partner, a character named Daisy Reese. Daisy was a young African American woman and there were suggestions that she and Mandy may have been having a relationship of a more personal kind. The indications were subtle and understated, but were nonetheless discernible if one looked for them. They were perhaps simply the way in which the two characters interacted together, the way they shared the space they inhabited, and the way they spoke to one another.[46] In addition, Mandy was often shown dressed in quasi-masculine attire (a pants suit), she had very short hair, and her opening scene showed her driving aggressively in an almost clichéd powerful car. These were clumsy yet potential signifiers of a deliberately constructed ambiguous identity. Also, in an interview included within the Special Features in the DVD of the series, Moira Kelly stated that Mandy was "sexy in her own way"—which could be read in a number of ways, but one obvious way would have been as an indicator of bisexuality. As such, if Mandy had prevailed as a major player in the drama this would not only have allowed for a potentially bisexual character, but Mandy might also have contributed a strong feminist presence—her intelligence and her independence might likely have provided this. However, Mandy progressed no further than the first season; she departed the show—banished to the so-called world of "Mandyville."

In summary, it could thus be argued that *The West Wing* chose to adopt a conventional attitude toward sexuality. In other words, it was a decidedly "straight" world, and it was not afraid to admit to this. To take just one random example, in the episode "Here Today" (7/5), it was intimated that Abbey had had doubts about the sexuality of her daughter, Ellie; however, on hearing Ellie was planning to get married, Abbey stated: "I am not unhappy that my daughter is straight after all." There were numerous other examples throughout the series, some of which have been alluded to in this chapter; but of course the world is not a "straight" world, and never has been. The Kinsey Report of 1948, *Sexual Behavior in the Human Male*, hardly conducted within a progressive era or place, suggested that 38 percent of the adult male population in America had admitted to same-sex contact to the point of orgasm. However, in the world of *The West Wing* this was hardly evident; for the majority of the time it was a heterosexual world. Yet, if sexuality is infantile in origin, as Freud suggested, and performative in adulthood, as Butler suggested; then such binary oppositions as heterosexuality and homosexuality begin to make less and less sense. It may be that society, culture and religion have all made continued efforts to support such structures, but, within the theoretical concepts of queer theory, they begin to seem less and less convincing. As Marjorie Garber argued, by the turn of the 19th century homosexuality stopped being what people did and became who they were, and the same could easily be said of heterosexuality.[47] CJ, in the quote above, may have claimed she was a heterosexual, but she was not—at least CJ was not a heterosexual in the sense that none of us are. The human subject merely indulges in certain sexual practices, be it with a member of the opposite sex, the same sex, or otherwise. In essence, *The West Wing* had little regard as to the way theory has challenged the status quo; in the real world heterosexuality and homosexuality were much more fluid and diverse than convention would allow, but this was not the case in the conformist world of *The West Wing*.

14

Hollywood MS
The Portrayal of Disabilities

If *The West Wing* was reticent in looking at the vagaries of human sexuality, it was not reticent when considering the vagaries of disability in its various characters. In fact, the show's approach to disability was arguably one of its most engaging elements. The most obvious example of disability—and the one most crucial to the development of the show's narrative—was Bartlet's multiple sclerosis (MS), or to put it more precisely, Bartlet's relapsing-remitting multiple sclerosis (RRMS). However, there were a number of other examples worthy of mention; for example, there was Joey Lucas, the hearing impaired political pollster played by Marlee Matlin[1]; in addition, there was Josh's post-traumatic stress disorder, a facet of the drama that while arguably less convincing, nonetheless provided an exploration into the condition; there was also CJ's father who had a form of dementia. This arguably had little relevance to the overarching plotline of the series, but it once again presented a relevant condition. In the case of the autism of Senator Howard Stackhouse's grandson, while this did not occur on-screen, it nonetheless brought forward a condition seldom discussed in mainstream television drama. Finally, there were a number of different disabilities within a number of different characters. These included CJ, who would appear to have had many of the facets of a person with dyspraxia, and CJ's assistant, Carol Fitzpatrick, who would appear to have been an undiagnosed dyslexic—or at least she was highly intelligent but had difficulty with the most basic elements of literacy.[2] There were also other potential conditions: Ainsley Hayes exhibited some of the signs of mild Asperger's Syndrome, while both Margaret Hooper (Leo's secretary) and Arnold Vinick demonstrated suggestions of having obsessive compulsive disorder. There were other instances too numerous to detail here.

As suggested above, the most significant example of disability in the series, and the main focus of this chapter, was Bartlet's MS. However, before undertaking a consideration of this facet of the drama, it may be relevant to consider another issue: CJ's potential special learning disability. As far as can be ascertained (from a search of the published literature and from disparate online sources) it would appear that no one has yet suggested CJ may have been dyspraxic—that CJ may have had what is now more commonly known as Development Coordination Disorder (DCD). This lack of comment would seem to disregard numerous references throughout the series; for example, in her opening scene in the opening episode of the series, "Pilot" (1/1), CJ was shown exercising in the gym and then inadvertently falling off a treadmill. It was a humorous scene—almost slapstick in its range, but significant nonetheless in the context of a dyspraxic disability. In the episode "In the Shadow of Two Gunmen Part 2" (2/2), CJ was shown falling into a swimming pool—her own swimming pool in Los Angeles—again demonstrating a lack of coordination. There was also an incident in the episode "Bartlet for America," where CJ would demonstrate her sporting finesse by accidently hurling a basketball through a campaign office window. In a further slapstick scene, in the episode "We Killed Yamamoto" (3/21), CJ was made to appear both foolish and clumsy in the scene on the target range, falling backward at the recoil of a powerful handgun. Also, there was the scene in the episode "Game On" (4/6), where CJ, in pure delight, fell over after hearing Bartlet's response to Governor Richie's expected "ten word" comment. Finally, there was the scene in "The Long Goodbye" (4/13) where CJ and her father were shown fishing, with CJ demonstrating repeated signs of clumsiness in her attempt to cast a line—something that even CJ's father, with the disadvantage of Alzheimer's Disease, was able to successfully accomplish.[3]

The question of whether it was a conscious design on the part of the writers to make CJ dyspraxic would not seem of great significance. What *was* significant was the subtlety and the finesse in the way a character such as CJ existed within her own narrative discourse. This sense of verisimilitude was one of the beguiling attributes of the series, one of the reasons it has prevailed as a cultural text, and one of the reasons why so many viewers—in the age of box sets and online streaming—continue to follow the drama. In terms of CJ's implied condition, such an interpretation arguably enhances an appreciation of her character; it obviously explained her clumsiness, but it also provided an additional reading of her character, enhancing and strengthening our appreciation, and hence going some way to further illuminating her place in the drama.

In terms of Bartlet's disability, one of the questions to ask would be at what stage Aaron Sorkin and the show's other writers determined that Bartlet actually had MS. It has been suggested that this was only decided some way into the first season and that the choice was "very last minute"[4]—a number of sources, including Sorkin himself, would seem to support this claim. However, in adopting the theoretical designs of a reader response approach, the first intimations of MS affecting the president could, in fact, be read within the first episode, "Pilot" (1/1). As discussed briefly in Chapter 7, Bartlet made a grand entrance into the series as a kind of "wounded king," walking with a cane, having injured himself by falling from a bicycle. However, it could be questioned whether Bartlet had really fallen off a bicycle, or whether this was a false story to cover up the use of a walking stick after an MS attack. As intimated above, there is no requirement to speculate whether this was the intent of the creators of the show or not. In other words, we as readers of *The West Wing* can conduct whatever hermeneutical response we wish, to locate such a reading within the fictitious discourse of the drama in whatever way we choose, outside of any authorial intent.

There were a number of other instances during the first season that were arguably indicative of Bartlett's MS before it was made public to viewers. One example was the scene in the episode "Five Votes Down" (1/4) of Bartlet acting in what seemed like an inebriated way, after mixing his medication for what was said to be back pain; this would seem to have had little narrative relevance—other than offering a mildly amusing interlude. However, in retrospect, and from a different perspective, Bartlet's inability to understand that the two medications, Vicodin and Percocet, should not be taken together could have been viewed as another facet of MS, an example of a brief incident of mental confusion. In a similar way, in the episode "The State Dinner" (1/7), Abbey told Bartlet: "You don't have the power to fix everything." Abbey was referring to Bartlet's inability to deal with all the political issues he had to confront; but the comment could just as easily have been read as an early coded allusion to MS. In a later episode, "Celestial Navigation" (1/15), the moderator at the college lecture Josh was delivering was shown walking with crutches, in a manner that could have suggested he had MS; this was not commented on in the episode—but could have been read as a subtle indication of Bartlet's condition.[5]

In the series itself, MS was not intimated explicitly until the episode "He Shall from Time to Time" (1/12); however, the backstory would later reveal that Bartlet had begun to feel ill with pain in his legs in 1991; two years later the symptoms returned and a medical examination eventually diagnosed him with MS.[6] In addition, even though he possessed significant personal wealth, Bartlet did not have medical insurance—this would have presumably been to avoid having to disclose MS in an authorized sense—in other words, a written declaration on paper.[7] At this time, in the alternative universe of *The West Wing*, Bartlet would have been the U.S. congressman for New Hampshire, either ending his first or beginning his second of three terms in office; hence it was clear that even at this early stage a "cover-up" was in operation. In other words, a decision was made not to disclose the medical condition, but not to lie about it either. This was not unusual, according to journalist and medical doctor Lawrence K. Altman, citing a Harris Poll for the National Multiple Sclerosis Society: some 40 percent of patients with MS elect to hide their diagnosis.[8] Thus, Bartlet's deception—or his decision not to disclose information—could be seen as a cumulative series of events, a sequence of circumstances that eventually forced him into a network of subterfuge. Bartlet had not previously disclosed his illness, hence when he ran for the presidency he was not able to disclose this medical condition. There was also the issue that, as Bartlet himself would later admit, he ran for the presidency believing he had little chance of winning; however, Bartlet *did* win, and was then placed in a position of engendering a conscious deception upon the American public, eventually being seen as a president who had perpetrated a "massive fraud on the American public."

Of course, this was not an unknown occurrence. As Staci Beavers has noted, Bartlet's deception was not so different than the extent to which the American public were "kept in the dark" in regards to the health of President Franklin Roosevelt, Roosevelt's polio being an obvious comparison to Bartlet's MS.[9] In addition, Woodrow Wilson had a series of debilitating strokes, while John F. Kennedy had a number of health issues, including Addison's Disease, all of which were seldom discussed in public. In other words, none of these conditions were fully declared while the incumbent presidents were in office.[10] However, in *The West Wing*, this was a scandal—or at least it was as close as Bartlet's administration came to a scandal. In a sense, a Bartlet scandal had to be of another kind. A scandal in Bartlet's administration could not have involved sexual infidelity; nor could it have involved corruption—either political or financial. Bartlet was simply too honest; he possessed too high a moral character to permit such behavior.[11] Yet for all of this, the scandal did not last; in the episodes at the beginning of Season 3 it seemed, for a short time, that the MS issue would develop into something approaching the Watergate affair, but this did not progress much further. Bartlet simply accepted a censure for not declaring his illness and the drama moved on, with Bartlet being re-elected in Season 4, and MS scarcely proving to be of relevance.

* * *

In a more specific context, Heather A. Zoller and Tracy Worrell, in their 2009 article "Television Illness Depictions, Identity, and Social Experience: Responses to Multiple Sclerosis on *The West Wing*," explored the validity of Bartlet's MS, seeing it as an important depiction of the condition on network television, insomuch as—as the authors put it—"long-term attention of illness on television remains rare."[12] In the article, MS was cited as being a disease that affects approximately 350,000 Americans, its primary symptoms including: "weakness, fatigue, vertigo, numbness, impairment of memory and concentration, visual disturbances and possible mood swings."[13] However, while Zoller and Worrell commended *The West Wing* for portraying MS as a chronic disease, given that it was such a high profile show, they concluded: "For the most part, audience members felt the show failed to depict significant elements of the disease."[14] Zoller and Worrell's research employed focus groups, interviews and electronic message boards to ascertain the opinions of people with MS, reporting that the respondents

> referred to the President's illness as "Hollywood MS" ... the symptoms of most concern for many viewers were stress and fatigue.... One focus group participant said, "We've got a man who apparently works from the early morning and he's always walking home in the dark at night unaffected by the day's activities, seemingly, and that's unbelievable."[15]

In addition, Zoller and Worrell noted how there was a suggestion that the medication Bartlet used, Betaseron, both overstated its effectiveness and understated its side-effects, and that—in an overall sense—the series significantly underplayed the actual effects of the debilitating disease.

In defense of the portrayal of the condition in the show, it might be noted that Bartlet had RRMS,[16] and hence had long periods of remission. In addition, there were some instances when the worst aspects of the disease *were* stated. This occurred most pertinently in the episode "The War at Home" (2/14), wherein Abbey told Bartlet: "Do you get that your immune system is shredding your brain?" Abbey went on to relate, in graphic detail, what was to come: "Fatigue, an inability to get through the day, memory lapses, a loss of cognitive functions, failure to reason, failure to think clearly." In the event, most probably due to both artistic license and commercial concerns, little of this came to pass, or at least it did not occur within the fictional timeline of the series. There was a suggestion of what was to come during a scene in the episode "Abu el Banat" (5/9), wherein Bartlet and Abbey—somewhat poignantly—faced up to Bartlet's probable death, the possibility of "a syringe on the night-stand."[17] In a less harrowing context, the episode "A Change Is Gonna Come" (6/7) was devoted to Bartlet's recurring difficulties with the disease, although this was not made clear until the ending of the episode. Bartlet had had difficulties with both his vision and his mobility; he had not seen the Taiwanese flag, one of the supposed plotlines of the episode. However this, together with a rare number of other instances, was the exception; in general terms MS did not appear to seriously impede Bartlet.

This would seem to have been the case even beyond the conventional timeline of the series: the episode "The Ticket" (7/1) began with a proleptic scene three years into the future, wherein Bartlet was shown on the day that appeared to commemorate the opening of his presidential library. It was an intriguing scene insomuch as it allowed a rare glimpse into the future of the drama's fictitious discourse; most of the main characters were present and it was therefore possible to glimpse their continuing stories.[18] However, of more significance was the physical demeanor of Bartlet: here he was, now some 20 years after a diagnosis of MS, and now he was walking with a cane. Hence, in the fairytale discourse of *The West Wing*, unpleasant realities did not occur; Bartlet's MS was working its way forward, but only gradually, and was not seriously impairing the ex-president. This was as far as the fictitious discourse of *The West Wing* proceeded; mercifully, there would be no access to the scene of a syringe on the nightstand, narrative closure preventing any further narrative illustration.

In the context of its approach to disabilities—and specifically in relation to Bartlet's MS—*The West Wing* appeared to live up to its reputation of having a ubiquitous sense of sentimentality. This comment might be supported via a comparison to other depictions of MS on screen, the film *Hilary and Jackie* (1998), directed by Anand Tucker, being an apposite example.[19] Tucker's film told the story of the cellist Jacqueline du Prez and her sister, Hilary, and arguably offered a more accurate depiction of the way MS affects the life of an individual. Of course, it must be accepted that MS affects different people in different ways, some more severely than others; however, the almost brutal depiction of du Prez degenerating under the effects of her illness convinced in a way *The West Wing* could not. The devastating effects of MS, as it attacked du Prez's body, appeared to have a greater sense of verisimilitude: the destruction of her nervous system, the resultant paralysis, the loss of hearing and finally her death. All of this was depicted—albeit with a dark and satiric sense of humor—with a remarkable display of honesty. This was portrayed, most tellingly, in the scene wherein du Prez attempted to play the cello at a time when MS had robbed her of the physical dexterity to do so. At no point in the entire run of *The West Wing* was such an authentic representation of the realities of MS shown; as intimated above, this was perhaps because the series had to abide to commercial concerns. Nonetheless, there remained the impression that a sense of authenticity had been lost—and that Bartlet (as a fictional individual with MS) had "got off" very lightly.

In summary, the way in which *The West Wing* approached the issue of disability, albeit rarely commented upon, could nonetheless be seen as one of the most engaging subtextual elements of the series. This was seen to some effect within personal relationships; for example, between CJ and her father, and to a greater extent in terms of the dynamics between Bartlet and Abbey. What was of most interest in the latter relationship was the sense of a genuine closeness between the two characters, seldom seen elsewhere in the series, and in the way such a closeness helped them face the prospect of Bartlet's death. In other words, Bartlet's MS allowed *The West Wing* to reflect upon the ultimate human condition, and to reflect upon the issue of mortality, an issue rarely dealt with in the show. In another sense, disability was of interest insomuch as the series seldom dealt with healthcare issues,[20] but at least it was open to such issues in terms of its approach to disability as an ideological concern. In a further sense, while the series seldom featured minorities center stage—in other words, ethnic minorities, or minorities in terms of sexual identity—it did succeed in placing characters with disabilities at the center of the stage. In addition, while the series did not quite put forward a Social Model of Disability—the idea that disability is mainly experienced by the way society and culture are organized, rather than by the individual's impairment—it did at least provide a space to offer examples of a minority voice— and in so doing presented a noteworthy contrast to the usual mainstream discursive practices at play within the series. By way of a final appraisal, even if Bartlet's medical condition was "Hollywood MS," it nonetheless succeeded in putting forward a minority voice: a voice that would rarely be put forward on a mainstream network television drama.

15

The Politics of Maryland
The Wire *and* The West Wing

As previously ascertained, sentimentality was not an unknown attribute of *The West Wing*; in fact, it was arguably both one of its most telling strengths and most telling weaknesses. In an attempt to explain such an apparently paradoxical facet of the show, a comparison to another television drama of the same time may perhaps be constructive. The comparison in question is a discussion of the linkage to the celebrated crime drama *The Wire*. While both shows shared a similar time and space—*The West Wing* ran for seven seasons on NBC, from September 22, 1999 to May 14, 2006; *The Wire* ran for five seasons on HBO, from June 2, 2002 to March 9, 2008—there were a number of disparities. It is perhaps fair to say that *The West Wing* and *The Wire*, each in their own individual and particular ways, represent an embodiment, a personification, and even an epitome of American television drama on the cusp of the 20th and 21st centuries; however, they achieved such accolades via very different aesthetic choices and via markedly dissimilar ways of presenting contemporary American society and culture.

The Wire was created and primarily written by author and former police reporter David Simon[1]; it was set in Baltimore, Maryland, a city only 40 miles from Washington, D.C., but a world away from the world of *The West Wing*.[2] In many ways *The Wire* could be seen as an antidote to the sentimentality of *The West Wing*, a remedy for the relentless optimism and for what was arguably an unrealistically idealized version of modern-day America. In contrast to *The West Wing*, the narrative discourse of *The Wire* generally eschewed rhetorical and optimistic utterances and, indeed, sentimentality of any kind. In fact, the series seemed to eschew any semblance of a principled ethical debate; instead it merely strived for a constant sense of authenticity. As David Simon noted: "Nobody wins, because the game of inner city Baltimore is not winnable.... *The Wire* is not interested in good and evil; it's interested in economics and sociology and politics."[3] In *The West Wing* there *was* an interest in good and evil. There appeared to be an honest belief that such concepts actually prevailed within the politics of American life; as Aaron Sorkin admitted, he believed in writing within a "romantic idealistic style."[4] Herein was the key difference between the two shows: resigned pragmatism as against hopeful idealism.

There seemed to be a consistent sense of moral ambiguity throughout the narrative discourse of *The Wire*; in a colloquial idiom, the game was rigged— in fact, everything was rigged, and corruption seemed to be inherent in every facet and aspect of life. In contrast, *The West Wing* seemed to be imbued with the naive belief that the problems within American society could be solved, or if not solved, could at least be alleviated. In *The Wire* the level of corruption within all aspects of American life was simply taken as a given; however, in *The West Wing* President Bartlet was not corrupt, neither was his staff, and it appeared as if they believed that corruption in the outside world could at least be countered. Hence, while *The Wire* extolled a pragmatic acceptance that corrupt institutions will never change, in the alternative universe of *The West Wing* the main protagonists seemed to be continuously bent on the path of righteousness. In Melissa Crawley's words: "The overriding narrative of the Bartlet administration is about pursuing a course of action for a noble cause."[5] Not so within the narrative discourse of *The Wire*. Within its matter-of-fact approach, there were no noble causes, all institutions seemed to inherently lack nobility, corruption was all-pervasive, and there was an unabashed acceptance that there was no way to resolve it.

This predicament was perhaps seen to most telling effect in terms of the issue of race. The literary critic Frederic Jameson, in an essay entitled "Realism and Utopia in *The Wire*," noted that unlike in the vast majority of American television dramas, in *The Wire* "the majority of its actors are black'"[6] and that "*The Wire* is in that sense what is now called *post-racial*."[7] In a literal sense, Jameson was correct: it has been estimated that some 70 percent of the cast of *The Wire* were African Americans, a ratio seldom approached within American television drama. However, Jameson's comment had a further resonance, insomuch as race within *The Wire* was presented so convincingly, so authentically, as to "utterly dissolve the category."[8] In *The West Wing* this was hardly the case. As discussed in Chapter 12, the world of *The West Wing* was a decidedly white world; there were token African Americans, but it was hardly the post-racial world Frederic Jameson had in mind. The closest *The West Wing* came to the racial discourse of *The Wire* was a conversation early in the first season between Leo and Congressman Mark Richardson. Leo commented: "An entire generation of African American men are being eaten alive by drugs and poverty."[9] However, Richardson, who was black, was dismissive—he was aware that Leo, even as chief of staff to the president, had no power to effect any significant change. In this way the scene was one of the rare instances in which the worlds of *The Wire* and *The West Wing* seemed to meet.

As intimated, there was an overarching sense of verisimilitude within *The Wire*, a consistent intent to offer an authentic version of reality. The point at issue was realism, "the high case of realism," as Slajov Žižek, in his discussion of the show put it.[10] There was an authentic sense of reality in *The Wire*, insomuch as characters died as people often die in real life—without meaning, without warning. One might think of Stringer Bell, shot to death in Season 3, an event few viewers might have seen coming; in a similar sense, there was the way in which Omar Little was shot to death in Season 5, without any prior forewarning—going against any sense of conventional plotting.[11] There were deaths in *The West Wing*, but these were usually signaled in a narratively conventional way; for example, the death of Leo McGarry did not come as a complete shock to the audience. Other than Mrs. Landingham, together with two secret service agents Molly O'Connor and Simon Donovan, perhaps the only unexpected death of a recurring character was that of the Admiral Fitzwallace, but even here this did not come as a complete surprise.

In a similar context, Nathan A. Paxton, in his essay "Virtue from Vice: Duty, Power and *The West Wing*," noted that "the forces of narrative convention, stories following certain patterns, [let] us know that we will not have to worry at the end of the day because everything has to work out all right."[12] This was certainly true of much of the narrative discourse of *The West Wing*, but not so in *The Wire*. In other words, *The Wire* offered an accurate representation of modern-day America—without the maudlin hope that everything will eventually work out right. In contrast, *The West Wing* consistently offered a somewhat contrived representation of what Americans would like America to be. In *The Wire* there was seldom anything approaching an idealized view; the political systems seemed to work, but the level of corrupt practice was so all-pervasive as to extinguish any form of idealism. One might think here of Tommy Carcetti's political maneuvers to become mayor in Season 4, these arguably being far more believable than any example of political maneuvering in *The West Wing*.[13] In this way, *The Wire* presented in its five seasons a convincing portrayal of life in inner city Baltimore, whether it be illicit drug dealing, the unions on the waterfront, city politics, the school system, or the print media—all adding up to present an unapologetic look at the underside of life in America at the start of the 21st century.

* * *

In his essay on *The Wire*, Frederic Jameson commented on the lack of generic expectations within the drama; in other words, while the series may have been positioned within the genre of the crime thriller, there were few instances of conventional motifs from that genre. For example, there were

15. The Politics of Maryland

"few chase scenes" and there were "no cliff-hangers."[14] Instead, as Jameson noted, in place of a conventional crime story, the series could better be read as "a struggle between two collectives: the police and the crime gangs."[15] The dramatic discourse was sufficiently nuanced as to preclude good and evil. Heroes were not heroes and villains were not villains, this being an ethical scenario somewhat different from the one found in *The West Wing*. In this sense, and from a Marxist perspective, *The Wire* could be read as a series about class struggle between two opposing cultures—the police and the drug dealers. Slajov Žižek, lecturing on the series, noted that capitalism's primary aim was to reproduce itself, to preserve itself, and that capitalism had no interest in advancing society—in progressing to a more equitable way of life.[16] Hence Žižek posed the rhetorical question: Who is the culprit in the world of *The Wire*? He reached for a conclusion that it may have been the capitalist system, itself. By way of Michel Foucault's *Discipline and Punish*, Žižek noted that the police and the criminals needed each other, with the implication that one side was no better than the other.[17] Once again, this was a state of affairs somewhat removed from the world of *The West Wing*.

* * *

In terms of an intertextual arena, *The Wire* has often been described as resembling a Greek tragedy: Žižek, for example, noted this a number of times,[18] while David Simon himself noted that "*The Wire* is a Greek tragedy in which the postmodern institutions are the Olympian forces."[19] Simon went on to state:

> In much of television, and in a good deal of our stage drama, individuals are often portrayed as rising above institutions to achieve catharsis. In this drama, the institutions always prove larger, and those characters with hubris enough to challenge the postmodern construct of American empire are invariably mocked, marginalized, or crushed. Greek tragedy for the new millennium, so to speak.[20]

In *The Wire*, in the episode "Dead Soldiers" (3/3), Acting Commissioner Ervin Burrell would tell his subordinates: "If the gods are fucking you, you find a way to fuck them back. It's Baltimore, gentlemen, the gods will not save you!"[21] However, while this may have been a deliberate ploy on the part of the show's writers, *The Wire*'s actual intertextual resonance may have resided within another contextual arena. As Frederic Jameson noted, *The Wire* was akin to a great novel that was almost Dickensian in nature. Jameson noted: "There are at least a hundred characters deployed in each season, many of whom carry their own independent plotlines ... this is a series, or serial, like those by Dickens."[22] Thus, *The Wire* might be positioned as a great novel similar in length and scope to Dickens; while accepting the fact that *The Wire* was a 60-episode television series, it could, nonetheless, be looked upon as one of "the great American novels."[23] It would perhaps be more difficult to convincingly maintain that this was true of *The West Wing*—that the show resembled one of "the great American novels."

* * *

There were other clearly apparent differences between the two shows. One example was the use of music: in *The West Wing*, non-diegetic music was used in a conventional way, in order to create a range of emotive moods; in *The Wire* little if any non-diegetic music was used—music was only included if it occurred within the action of the drama.[24] In addition, *The Wire* seldom employed narrative tropes such as time slippages; there were no flashbacks—no analeptic scenes.[25] In contrast, *The West Wing* continuously used subtle and sophisticated time slippages—both back and (albeit less commonly) forward.[26] In a further context, *The Wire* was more relaxed in dealing with different sexualities; as alluded in Chapter 13, Detective Kima Greggs was an African American who was also a lesbian; Omar Little had male lovers; and even Bill Rawls, commanding officer and Detective Jimmy McNulty's nemesis, frequented gay bars. However, such sexual preferences were not significant to the overarching discourse of the drama. Instead there was a casual acceptance of fluid sexualities, a discourse decidedly absent from *The West Wing*. There was also the issue of authentic language. While there were few uses of expletives in *The West Wing*, in *The Wire* accurate street language was constantly employed without censure, such as a consistent use of the so-called "n word"—together with the ubiquitous oedipal epithet and a full range of other four-letter words. As such, the use of linguistic invective in *The Wire* was arguably more authentic than that found in *The West Wing*.[27]

As intimated in Chapter 7, one obvious explanation for some of these differences related to the different channel platforms upon which each series was originally aired. In America *The West Wing* was shown on network television (on NBC), while *The Wire* was shown on the cable channel HBO. The former was subject to much greater constraints in terms of sexual content, violence and explicit language, while the latter had much greater scope and much less censorship in terms of "adult" content.[28] Janet McCabe, in a discussion of HBO "pushing the envelope" in terms of program content, noted: "Without advertising pressures or strict limits on content, HBO made a virtue of its autonomy from that which constrained network television."[29] However, McCabe also noted: "Sorkin's *West Wing* proves it's possible to do incisive adult drama while staying within traditional network standards."[30] In such a sense, disregarding the means of broadcast and the differing degrees of artistic freedom, both of the shows could be said to have earned the reputation of being *zeitgeist* dramas—of encapsulating the essence of their times, albeit in differing ways.[31] Both shows were decidedly situated within their own timeframes in the first decade of the 21st century. Hence both have rapidly dated—but both have arguably come to be seen as historical objects—historical accounts of their own times.

In terms of its positioning within a contemporary setting, *The Wire* would seem to have been more relaxed in grounding itself within the historical reality of its own timeframe. The most important event that occurred during or near the transmission of both shows was 9/11. *The West Wing* took great care in both reacting and not reacting to the events of 9/11; the episode "Isaac and Ishmael" (3/1) was written and transmitted within weeks of the attack. It was clearly a reaction to the attack—but at the same time it was clear that 9/11 was not a reality in the alternative universe of *The West Wing*. This was not the case in *The Wire*; herein the 9/11 attacks were a reality. In the opening episode of the series (filmed just weeks after 9/11) McNulty was shown talking to an FBI agent, attempting to get help in the police's attempt to bring down Avon Barksdale's drug domain. "We just don't have the manpower to stay big," the FBI agent told McNulty, "Not since those Towers fell." McNulty replied: "What, we don't have enough love in our hearts for two wars?" The script did not elaborate further, but it was clear that the towers were the twin towers of the World Trade Centre and the two wars were the war on drugs and the war on terror. This was one example of the different ways in which the two series told their stories, one seeming to inhabit the real world, and one seeming to inhabit a world that was not quite the real one.

Finally, there was the issue of casting; this was of interest insomuch as a number of minor characters in *The West Wing* were played by actors who played major characters in *The Wire*. In other words, a number of regular players in *The Wire* made guest appearances in *The West Wing*, but this was not reciprocated; none of the main players in *The West Wing* would appear in *The Wire*. For example, Michael Hyatt, Brianna Barksdale in *The Wire*, would appear in *The West Wing* as Angela Blake, Senior Aide in the Department of Labor. Lance Reddick, who played the ongoing character Cedric Daniels in *The Wire*, appeared in a one-off performance as an unnamed Washington, D.C., police officer in *The West Wing* episode "In Excelsis Deo" (1/10).[32] Deirdre Lovejoy, who appeared in all 60 episodes of *The Wire* as the assistant district attorney Rhonda Pearlman, guest starred in two episodes of *The West Wing*, "Eppur Si Muove" (5/16) and "The Supremes" (5/17), as Lisa Wolfe—a sympathetic Republican. Michael Kostroff, who played Maurice Levy, Avon Barksdale's lawyer in *The Wire*, appeared as Charlie Young's legal counsel in the episode "A Change Is Gonna Come" (6/7); in *The Wire* Kostroff played a corresponding role, a white lawyer for a black man, but whether this was a deliberate narrative echo remains open to speculation. Lastly, Maria Broom, who had appeared as Maria Daniels (wife of Cedric Daniels) in sixteen episodes of *The Wire*, played Cathy Holland, the head-teacher of the public school Matt and Helen Santos visit in the episode "The Last Hurrah" (7/20).[33]

All of this would suggest one cultural text was appropriating the discursive practices of another, as if *The Wire* was insidiously infringing upon the narrative discourse of *The West Wing* via a covert and clandestine approach.

In summary, a comparison of the two seemingly similar but very different shows offers a sense of how diverse television drama can be. According to David Simon, "Most smart people cannot watch most TV, because it has generally been a condescending medium, explaining everything immediately, offering no ambiguities, and using dialogue that simplifies and mitigates against the idiosyncratic ways in which people in different worlds actually communicate."[34] Simon was referring to *The Wire*, but the same might be said of *The West Wing*. It is true to say that *The Wire* achieved more critical plaudits; for example, in the opinion of some critics *The Wire* has come to be regarded almost as if it were the *Citizen Kane* of the television world.[35] But in contrast to this, *The West Wing* was more commercially successful, more well known and more lauded with entertainment industry accolades and awards. While the main tone of *The Wire* was "a kind of resigned wisdom,"[36] the main tone of *The West Wing* was arguably that of unrestrained optimism, this likely being one of the reasons for the latter's greater commercial success. *The West Wing* and *The Wire* were unquestionably some of the most strikingly impressive American television programs of recent times. However, in a final summation, what might be said, in essence, was that *The West Wing* was how America would like to be, and *The Wire* was how America actually is—this perhaps being as accurate a representation of both shows as it is possible to make.

16

Nostalgia for the Present
Postmodern Readings

It would seem accurate to say that *The West Wing* would not readily be described as a postmodern text; wholly conventional in the way it told its story, it did not exhibit many facets of postmodernity. However, a postmodern reading *of* the text would appear to be of relevance, and, furthermore, the use of postmodern concepts to advance an interpretation of the series may be both informative and rewarding. As such, the ideological framework of the drama would seem (either consciously or unconsciously) to have been resistant to the fundamental tenets of postmodernism: *The West Wing* still appeared to believe in tales of human progress, to believe reality was a taken-for-granted quality and to believe capitalism and consumerism should remain unchallenged. Thus a postmodern reading of a postmodern-resistant text might be seen as embracing a hermeneutic approach worthy of some consideration—as will now follow.[1]

Postmodernism has been much misunderstood by some, and much derided by others. Nonetheless, it remains a significant arena of thought, one that helps to explain the seemingly absurd social and cultural environment we currently appear to inhabit. In other words, postmodern ideas at least allow a way of attempting to deal with the complexities and contradictions of contemporary life. However, one should perhaps first pose the following question: What is postmodernism? Yet even to attempt to pose such a question would seem to be problematic, insomuch as one of the most essential aspects of postmodernism lies in its diversity, in its opacity, in the way we cannot easily define what the term means. In such a sense there are perhaps as many answers to the question "What is postmodernism?" as there are those who would attempt to answer it. However, one attempt at a definition might be phrased as follows: postmodernism represents a response (evident since the 1960s) to changes in society and culture, such as technological advances; shifting political concerns; the rise of social movements; differing work and social patterns; the loss of faith in religion in the West; and—in essence—all the differing ways in which we now see ourselves within the postmodern environment we inhabit.[2]

A further way of achieving a better understanding of postmodernism might be gained by looking toward its predecessor: modernism. Postmodernism is, in a literal sense, simply "post" modernism—the cultural movement that came after modernism. Modernism, as a cultural movement, is relatively easy to define: it was the movement that dominated the arts and culture in the first half of the 20th century. Within an artistic and cultural setting modernism challenged the fundamental elements of the past. As the name suggests, it wanted to be new; it wanted to look at the world from perspectives different than those of the past. Thus melody and harmony were put aside in music, perspective and direct pictorial representation were rejected in painting, traditional forms were abandoned in architecture, and in literature there was a renouncement of a range of previously accepted notions: traditional narratives, chronological plotting, omniscient narrators, closed endings and so on. In this way, modernism emphasized subjectivity; there was a tendency toward turning inward, having more interest in the production of cultural artifacts than in the world itself.

While some of the qualities found in modernism could also be seen in postmodernism, there was a fundamental difference in the way the two movements looked at the world. One could say that modernism looked back to the past with a degree of nostalgia, to an earlier age when faith and authority were more certain; postmodernism, on the other hand, appeared to celebrate a sense of fragmentation. While modernism offered a tone of lament, a sense of pessimism and almost a sense of despair about the world, postmodernism in contrast offered a feeling of exhilaration, an escape from the claustrophobic embrace of fixed systems of belief. In addition to this, there was a further unambiguous differentiation. Modernism possessed an asceticism, a certain sense of moderation and discipline: the square concrete buildings of its architecture, the minimalist poetry of William Carlos Williams, the blank drama of Samuel Beckett, the experimental novels of James Joyce and Virginia Woolf and so on. By contrast, postmodernism disdained any idea of asceticism; it believed in excess, in gaudiness, in diversity, in eclecticism and, at times, in sheer bad taste.

However, the two movements shared a commonality in terms of their different origins, or at least a similar rationale in terms of their historical beginnings. It has often been said that modernism was a response to the immense changes World War I inflicted upon Western culture; and, in a similar way, postmodernism has been seen as a response to the still greater changes wrought by World War II. The fact that postmodernism did not begin to make itself felt until sometime in the 1960s, some 20 years after the end of

16. Nostalgia for the Present 137

World War II, perhaps suggested some sense of the damage those changes had wrought—a sense of a society and a culture sleepwalking for two decades before it had the awareness to make a response. In terms of postmodern theory, three key theorists have come to prominence: Jean François Lyotard, Jean Baudrillard and Frederic Jameson. All three theorists offered different but valid descriptions of postmodernism, and all, in some way at least, can be seen in the context of an interpretation of *The West Wing*.

Jean François Lyotard's book *The Postmodern Condition*, first published in France in 1979 and translated into English in 1984, more fully established the term "postmodernism" into both academic and general usage. In the book, Lyotard famously defined postmodernism as "incredulity towards meta-narratives." In essence, Lyotard was arguing that the big stories, the "grand narratives," no longer had relevance in terms of the way we perceive of our society, our culture and ourselves. The grand narratives, the great tales of human progress, were no longer tenable in a postmodern world; the best we could hope for were a series of mini-narratives, which were always provisional, always contingent and always relative. Hence, if the grand narratives were no longer relevant, then the idea that there was an aim to history and human development began to fail and our hopes, most specifically the idea that history was the story of man's evolution toward enlightenment, ceased to have meaning. At its core, the real intention of Lyotard's argument pointed directly toward an attack upon the ideals of the Enlightenment. Lyotard saw the Enlightenment as simply a part of the authoritative, overarching, totalizing explanations of human affairs. These narratives, which purported to explain and reassure, were really only illusions fostered in order to repress difference and plurality.

In terms of *The West Wing*, there was an overarching sense of there being an attempt to refute Lyotard's argument, albeit in an unconscious way. *The West Wing* was far too optimistic to embrace Lyotard's ideas; in *The West Wing* the grand narratives remained very much in operation. There was no doubting this; tales of human progress, embedded within the American Dream, proliferated throughout the course of *The West Wing*. While in a certain sense it could be argued that a postmodernist view, with its acceptance of the loss of any sense of the grand narratives, may have been the only viable way of explaining the world, within *The West Wing* there were no such concerns. The series continually embraced the grand narratives—they were present throughout the series, from the first to the last episode. From a postmodern perspective the signifier was continuously threatening to break loose from the signified: as David Lyon put it, the late 20th century was "witness to [an] unprecedented destruction of meaning."[3] In *The West Wing*, on the other hand, life went on oblivious to this predicament; Bartlet's presidency prevailed via a romantically idealized and optimistic belief in the American way.

In Philip Cass's words, "*The West Wing* [was] a linear descendant of Frank Capra's films about the perfectibility of the American political system by the good will and understanding of decent men and women."[4] One of the great attractions of *The West Wing* was the way in which it could create a world in which this was believable, convincingly oblivious to the anxieties of postmodern theoretical concerns.

Jean Baudrillard was another significant figure in the field of postmodern thought, specifically for his concept of the "loss of the real." This was the view that the perverse influence of images from film, television, advertising, the internet and so on had led to a loss of distinction between the real and the imagined within the contemporary world. In a postmodern milieu, there was a sense in which almost everything we experience was in some way filtered through the media, and that it therefore becomes more and more difficult to evaluate illusion and reality. On a screen, where all is surface with no depth, this therefore produces a malign influence on our perceptions of the real world. The result is a culture in which these distinctions have been eroded, where it is difficult to be sure what is real and what is not. To take one of Baudrillard's examples: Disneyland has become a mythologized misrepresentation of the United States, a place where all the values of American society and culture are exalted, but in miniature, in idealized and in comic-strip form; in other words, a self-contradictory reality that had no actual reality.

In the past a sign was a surface indication of an underlying depth or reality; today a sign would seem to have become merely an indicator of another sign. Hence within postmodernism, the distinction between what is real and what is simulated begins to dissolve and threatens to collapse completely. In this context, everything has the potential of becoming merely a model or an image: the "hyper-real," as Baudrillard called it. Furthermore, in a world of simulation there is a sense of cultural productions not merely being copies of an original, but being copies of a copy that had no existence in the first place.[5] In a different setting, but within a similar argument, a further example of the "loss of the real" can be seen in the way CGI (computer generated imagery) within contemporary cinema has changed our reception and our appreciation of the feature film, to the extent that the average viewer can no longer be sure if they are watching real images or computer generated "real" images.

How seriously we should take Baudrillard's ideas remains open to question. In their extreme form the "loss of the real" presented potentially sinister consequences, seeming to legitimize a callous regard for human suffering; not so far away from claiming, for example, that the Holocaust had not happened.[6] On the other hand, the concept at least allowed for one explanation for the way in which culture has developed in the contemporary era. In terms of hyper-reality in *The West Wing* itself, the idea that the show put forward a hyper-real representation of the U.S. presidency, if only within its idealistic media representation, would seem to have had some credence.[7] As has been intimated, there was a sense that the alternative reality of *The West Wing* was preferable to the actuality of American politics. In other words, the series took a kind of sentimentalized solace in a fictional world, what Baudrillard would have seen as a "Disney-fication" of the real world.[8] In a sense this would perhaps represent an accurate appraisal of the series; *The West Wing* may have seemed to possess a sense of authenticity, but this was arguably mere pretense. In a Baudrillard reading the drama had little to do with reality—it was merely a copy of a reality that had never existed.

Frederic Jameson is a Marxist theorist who has had a significant influence on postmodern theory. Jameson famously defined postmodernism as "the inevitable cultural logic of late capitalism." By this, Jameson argued that postmodern culture had lost connection with history, and was therefore left with only a shallow interest in the material present. Whereas we might previously have possessed a faith in God, or in art and culture, or even in ourselves—now we merely believed in the marketplace. Religion no longer had relevance, political doctrines such as Marxism no longer had relevance, scientific discourse no longer had relevance, and even self-analysis within a Freudian context no longer had relevance. All we were left with was consumerism; within an environment of late capitalism "shopping" appeared to be all that mattered. Hence the consumer has become *the* key figure in our social, cultural and moral focus, defined via an incestuous relationship with the media, with society populated not by workers, but by consumers. As David Lyon put it, "Our fetishism of commodities hides the real nature of capitalist exchange and exploitation."[9] In *The West Wing* consumerism, in itself, was not markedly significant—few if any of the main characters had time to resort to this, so occupied were they with their work in Bartlet's service. As such, almost no one appeared to exhibit excessive consumerist behavior. There were exceptions—for example, CJ shopping for her Vera Wang dress—but generally work was all-important. However, as discussed in Chapter 9, the majority of the main characters (Sam, Josh, Toby, Leo, CJ) appeared to possess wealth; they dressed well and they lived in comfortable homes. Once again, the only poor person who appeared to struggle within a consumerist society was Charlie—the stereotypical poor African American.

Jameson's work was also relevant in terms of the way the media operated in society. The media (the press, television, radio, the internet, social media and so on) became a "monster" no one could control, a "monster" that was driving our culture as never before. In a historical sense, television was perhaps the most pernicious influence, it being no coincidence that television, consumerism and postmodernism all appeared to emerge within the same cultural epoch. Television was the inevitable juncture of our junk culture, "the cradle of the best of the worst," and here one might recall, once again,

Theodore Sturgeon's oft-quoted epigram that 90 percent of everything is crap. In the malign world of television this proved correct: all was surface—there was no depth, there was nothing behind the rapid movement of pixels upon a flat screen. The remote control, the multiplicity of channels, the increasing difficulty of differentiating commercials and programs, made this an even more typical example of postmodern culture, and made Sturgeon's phrase one of the most telling oxymorons of our present age. In terms of *The West Wing*, it is perhaps somewhat ironic that it at least attempted to defend against this charge. As one of the most significant television dramas of recent times, offering television of a rare level of artistic integrity, it merely demonstrated that the exception does not prove the rule.

Hence the three descriptions of postmodernism—incredulity toward meta-narratives, the loss of the real, and the inevitable cultural logic of late capitalism—allow one to at least consider *The West Wing* within the framework of a postmodern reading. In addition, each of the three descriptions comes together in a wider context when one considers the sense in which postmodernism challenged and repudiated the ideals behind the Enlightenment. The Enlightenment was a time of profound faith in human reason, a time when we believed we had a clear idea of who we were, of what we were doing, of where we were going; a time of clarity of thought, a time of harmony, balance and proportion, wherein we embraced our role in the universe with a sense of confidence and clarity. As intimated previously in this chapter, Lyotard saw the Enlightenment simply as one of the many discursive practices that seek to control the way we live our lives. In a sense the Enlightenment was the grandest of the grand narratives, an essential paradigm that purported to explain the human condition; however, if one looks at the contemporary state of human affairs then one might well concur with postmodernism's attacks upon the ideals of reason, truth and progress. In *The West Wing*, Bartlet (for one) would no doubt have been cognizant of the ideals of the Enlightenment and was perhaps in agreement with those ideals. In addition, given the general tenor of the drama, Bartlet may well have believed in such an optimistic philosophical stance. Once again, it was a facet of the idealistic discourse of the drama that it chose to avoid embracing any alternative positions, or any sense of the more marginalized discourses of postmodern thought.

* * *

In a wider perspective, if one considers the historical events that arguably brought about postmodern ideologies, primarily that of World War II, then one can begin to appreciate the reasons why postmodernism caused such a fundamental shift within the human psyche. In the light of such cataclysmic events as the Holocaust and the use of atomic bombs, together with the sheer carnage and loss of life the war caused,[10] this brought about a change in how

16. Nostalgia for the Present

we viewed ourselves, arguably reducing belief and confidence in old traditional values. Hence ideas of truth and progress became harder to uphold—and the idea that history was the story of man's evolution toward a central objective began to have less and less relevance. However, while postmodernism may have derived from the cataclysmic and devastating events of World War II, it is possible to trace the antecedents of such ideas as far back as the 19th century, to a number of attacks on conventional and taken-for-granted beliefs. Four key thinkers, all working either in the mid-to-late 19th century, or into the cusp of the 20th century, can be seen as contributing toward this change in the way we view ourselves. The four thinkers: Charles Darwin, Karl Marx, Sigmund Freud and Albert Einstein, all argued (albeit sometimes inadvertently) against the need for a belief in a deity, in a divine being, or in a creator of the universe—a key facet of postmodernist thought.

Charles Darwin's theories suggested that man had not been "made" in God's image, but instead had evolved, via natural selection, from simpler and more primitive forms of life. Hence there was no need for a Garden of Eden, because life had evolved on Earth via natural processes; there was no need for a creator or a designer, natural selection providing most of the answers to the questions we may wish to ask. While Darwin's ideas did not explain how life had been created in the first place, as soon as one accepted Darwin's thesis then at least part of the reason for believing in God had a tendency to dissipate; a single entity did not create the natural world, and instead it happened via at least partially explainable reasons. Karl Marx, working at around the same time as Darwin, famously argued that religion was the opiate of the masses; in other words, religion was simply something the great mass of humanity used to make themselves feel better. In a wider context one could read Marx as suggesting religion was a way of controlling the masses, of offering illusory hopes that would divert the masses from realizing their actual plight within a capitalist system. Sigmund Freud, writing a couple of decades later, would dismiss religion by arguing that it was simply a "universal neurosis." In Freud's view, religious belief was simply a matter of a great mass of people who were all suffering from the delusion that God existed. In Freudian terms there was no need for God to exist, the widespread occurrence of such a belief being explained by human frailty; in other words, by an inability to accept the world as it was. In Freudian analysis we would be better advised to seek a solution to our neurotic impulses than to retreat into the delusional state of the religious believer. Finally, while Albert Einstein famously claimed: "God does not play dice with the universe" (by which he presumably meant that life could not have come about by chance and that the odds of life arising spontaneously were simply too risible), his work nonetheless offered a sense of understanding the universe without the necessity of a recourse to an omniscient God.

These assaults on the need for a religious belief could be seen as creating something of a moral vacuum, for if we did not believe in God where was a sense of a moral code to be found? One potential solution came from the poet and cultural critic Matthew Arnold; Arnold believed we could achieve a moral outlook to life by striving to become more cultured individuals. Arnold famously claimed that if we were to attend to "the best that is thought and known in the world," then this, to put it somewhat simplistically, would make one a "good" person. In other words, if one read the great literature of the world, listened to the great music, and looked at the great paintings then this would make one a "good" person. Hence we might not believe in a God any longer, but nonetheless we could still find some moral character within the highest of artistic and cultural pursuits. However, this line of reasoning, which was arguably flawed from its beginning, appeared to lose all credibility when placed alongside the events of the Holocaust, when it was compared to what happened in Germany during the 1930s and 1940s. Germany lay at the heart of Western culture, within the very cradle of Western civilization, insomuch as it was arguably *the* most cultured place on earth, the home to some of the greatest writers, philosophers, composers and artists of our culture. Yet it committed a monumental crime, the genocide of the majority of European Jewry, a crime so vast as to be beyond linguistic accountability.

In relating this issue to postmodernism, it has been said, albeit in a clichéd way, that God died in Auschwitz. However, while God may not have literally "died" in Auschwitz, the extent of the damage wrought by the Holocaust must give one pause for thought; in other words, pause to consider the extent of the damage the Holocaust inflicted upon the values of Western culture. While Western culture might still seem to be "alive and kicking" over seven decades from the end of World War II, there is, nonetheless, the sense of something having died without the people quite realizing it. Herein lies a possible explanation of the way in which postmodern theory has attempted to explain our culture, no matter how unpalatable the explanation might be. In a postmodern context, in an open consideration of our civilization, it would seem clearly apparent that the great ideals of Western culture are "dead." All the great hopes of the Classical World, of the Renaissance, of the Enlightenment, of Romanticism, of Realism, and even Modernism, dissipate and come to nothing when we enter the unremittingly honest world of the postmodern.

In other words, with history now seen as a mere narrative, and with humanity no longer seen as a logical or rational species progressing toward an evolutionary goal, we are therefore left with an indifferent or—worse—a meaningless universe. This universe needs no moral character, requires no God, and is unimaginably violent, a universe crammed end to end with "exploding stars" and "bloodied jaws."[11] However, in what would appear to be a willful disregard of this gruesome predicament, postmodern culture goes on happily mixing genres, playfully foregrounding intertextuality, celebrating parody, acknowledging the past must always be revisited with irony, rejoicing in the fact that all hierarchies are suspect, and so on throughout the diversity of other postmodern tenets. Hence we seem to inhabit a degraded landscape of kitsch and pastiche, a TV series and *Reader's Digest* culture of advertising, B-movies and pulp fiction[12]; a degraded landscape in which the distinction between high and low culture has become so blurred that there is now little distinction between a Shakespearian sonnet and a soap opera. As we are dealing with television, for proof of this claim, a random journey through the myriad available television channels will offer all the evidence required. This is our culture; and the human subject, instead of being perceived as a rational entity, now turns out to be merely a mélange of conscious and unconscious desires with no specific aspirations, no specific objectives, our experience consisting of only a disconnected, rudimentary and instinctive way of dealing with our existence.[13]

* * *

In looking toward a way of encompassing postmodern theory within a reading of *The West Wing*, it is worth noting that although, as intimated at the start of this chapter, the series was far from being a postmodern text, there were, nonetheless, a number of instances where a postmodern reading appeared to have relevance. As Trevor and Shawn J. Parry-Giles commented: "In its mimetic portrayal of presidential politics, *TWW* offers a romantic narrative reflective of the postmodern condition in U.S. culture."[14] In a mimetic sense *The West Wing* was self-evidently a cultural text grounded within the medium of television; and, as such, it could not help but be immersed within the postmodern traits found within that medium. As discussed above, television, in a general sense, epitomizes some of the worst aspects of postmodern culture; hence *The West Wing* struggled in preventing itself from descending into such sullied depths, because of the very medium it inhabited. As such, *The West Wing* was one of the rare exceptions to the rule: a television drama that consistently upheld cultural principles of a high aesthetic bearing; and, furthermore, it succeeded in doing so throughout its seven-year run—so much so that now, 20 years after its initial broadcast, it still prevails as a cultural object of the highest standards.

There were a number of examples of postmodern techniques that are worthy of commenting upon. For example, in the episode "Let Bartlet Be Bartlet" (1/19), Leo, while undertaking a re-evaluation of Bartlet's presidency, stated: "We're gonna raise the level of public debate in this country, and let this be our legacy." It would seem self-evident that one potential reading of the line would be to interpret it as a "grander" story; in other words, as a story outside of a fictitious discourse, Leo's line was a clear delineation of one of the core aspirations of *The West Wing*. In making a drama about a fictitious American president, Aaron Sorkin and the other writers on the show were attempting to raise the level of public debate in the real world.[15] A similar example occurred in the episode "Two Cathedrals" (2/22), wherein Leo uttered a decidedly significant line. It occurred as Bartlet was about to answer a crucial question at the press conference held shortly after the president's MS had been revealed. The question revolved around whether Bartlet would be seeking a second term. The question was put, Bartlet asked for it to be repeated, and he appeared as if he was about to answer when the scene cut to Leo, as he and the other staff were anxiously awaiting the President's response. "Watch this," said Leo with some gravity, and here the episode reached its closure—these were the last words of the episode and of the season. On one level Leo's phrase was indicative of an innate knowledge of how the president was about to answer; however, on another level it was a self-referential comment. In such an interpretation Leo was speaking directly to the viewing audience of the drama, who were doing just what he had said—but the audience would have to wait until the start of the third season to discover why Leo was telling them to "watch this."

A further example of a postmodernist approach occurred in the episode "Access" (5/18). The episode, written by Lauren Schmidt and directed by Alex Graves, was dissimilar from all other episodes of the series. The format was atypical, the way in which the episode was photographed was different,[16] it was one of the few episodes to begin without the "Previously on *The West Wing*" teaser, and it was an episode outside the timeline of all the other plotlines of the drama.[17] The episode inhabited the "faux documentary genre,"[18] somewhat reminiscent of Tim Robbins's film *Bob Roberts* (1992), which, in turn, was influenced by the *cinéma vérité* style of D.A. Pennebaker's *Dont Look Back* (1967).[19] The episode revolved around what appeared to be a PBS film crew making a documentary of a day in the life of the White House press secretary, CJ Cregg; however of most interest in terms of a postmodern approach was the sense of hyper-reality. The episode was a television program about a television program, a fictional documentary about a fictional television drama; and, in terms of postmodern theory, what was interesting was the presentation of varied registers of reality—for example, significant parts of the story were told via characters looking at TV monitors. As such, there were complex but ultimately transparent techniques to give the episode a sense of reality. All of these techniques contributed to the idea of reality's noticeable resemblance to itself; in other words, there were levels of simulation in numerous scenes throughout the episode, fragments of reality that played to the ideas of Baudrillard's concept of television as one of the ultimate postmodern forums.

In an overall sense, Frederic Jameson's idea of a "nostalgia for the present" perhaps best sums up the appeal of *The West Wing* in the context of a postmodern reading. The drama was set in "the present" but it reached back to an earlier time; its values, together with its hopes and dreams, seemed to derive from a point further back in time, a point that may never, in fact, have existed. In this way there was a sense that *The West Wing*, with its dogged optimism and its relentless sentimental aspirations, continually refuted the postmodern paradigm. In reality it would seem that we *do* prevail in a world that has little actual meaning, whether a postmodern approach is adopted or not; as Lawrence M. Krauss put it "we continue to marshal the courage to live meaningful lives in a universe that likely came into existence, and may fade out of existence, without purpose, and certainly without us at its centre."[20] Within such a purposeless universe, wherein the paradigm of progress has collapsed, wherein we seem to merely live in a world of simulation, wherein even "consumerism cannot deliver what it promises,"[21] only a recourse to postmodern thinking would seem to prevail. A world characterized by a loss of faith in meaningfulness and originality, a world with only a celebration of fragmentation, a sense of surface without depth, a sense that everything, including our culture, is a commodity—this is the world of the postmodern.

17

Cellmates in The Hague
Bartlet Flouts International Law

In the episode "Bad Moon Rising" (2/19), the White House counsel, Oliver Babish, told Bartlet: "They want to drag you to The Hague and charge you with war crimes, do as they say." Babish was talking about Bartlet's disclosure of multiple sclerosis, but in the following season, beginning with the episode "We Killed Yamamoto" (3/21), it seemed as if this scenario might become a reality. In a number of episodes toward the end of Season 3 and the beginning of Season 4, one of the main plotlines concerned the discovery that Abdul Shareef, the defense minister of the fictitious gulf state of Qumar, might have been responsible for a number of terrorist attacks against the United States, including a foiled plot to blow up the Golden Gate Bridge. Insomuch as the evidence against Shareef would not be admissible in court, Bartlet was eventually persuaded to have Shareef assassinated. Bartlet being Bartlet, this only occurred after much persuasion, after much soul-searching, after Bartlet had been convinced that there was no other option, and after Bartlet's moral scruples had been finally placated.

A number of critics have commented on this storyline; for example, Rachel Gans-Boriskin and Russ Tisinger argued that "in the course of leading, presidents must make decisions outside the scope of ordinary morality, and indeed, it is incumbent upon them to do so."[1] Gans-Boriskin and Tisinger were referring to the scene between Leo and Bartlet wherein Bartlet finally relented and ordered the political murder, saying: "It's just wrong, it's absolutely wrong," to which Leo responded: "I know, but you have to do it anyway." Bartlet asked why, to which Leo offered the terse reply, "Because you won." "Take him," Bartlet eventually stated.[2] In a similar vein, Young Hoon Kim argued that Bartlet, as president of the United States, had "the privilege and even the duty to transgress the law in order to protect the country from the threats of terrorism."[3] Trevor and Shawn J. Parry-Giles continued this line of argument, putting forward the proposition that a commander-in-chief was required "to embody the rational intelligence necessary to discern when the realities of war must take precedence over subjective moral tenets for the sake of national security."[4]

Such arguments might seem to have credence; however, there were other readings to be made. For example, a casual viewer of the show might have been persuaded of the overarching argument that Shareef was guilty, but a more discerning viewer might have considered other interpretations; a closer reading of the episodes in question arguably allowed for a different appraisal. A series of intelligence reports suggested Shareef was guilty; however, as intimated above, much of this would have been inadmissible in court, this primarily being because the evidence linking Shareef to terrorist attacks "was obtained by coercion."[5] For coercion read torture, as Trevor and Shawn J. Parry-Giles put it: "[Such evidence would be] thrown out of court because it originated from a Chechnya prisoner after 'prolonged physical abuse by Russian soldiers.'"[6] To reiterate: it would most likely have been thrown out of court for good reason, not merely on a technicality, insomuch as it is generally accepted that someone being tortured will eventually make *any* statement to prevent further torture—hence there must be at least some doubt as to the veracity of this evidence.

In addition (and this was perhaps an issue often overlooked), Bartlet ordered the killing of Shareef *and* his party. In other words, Bartlet ordered the deaths of human beings other than Shareef himself. These individuals were presumably Shareef's bodyguards, but we cannot be sure if there were also other people on the private jet who were killed—unstated collateral damage so to speak.[7] It is uncertain from the way the scene was filmed how many people were shot and killed, but it is clear there *was* collateral damage. To put this specifically: other human beings were killed by Bartlet's hired assassins, on Bartlet's explicit orders. In addition, this was an act of premeditated brutality, as Leo says: "We put fourteen bullets in his chest on an airstrip in Bermuda."[8] Leo would go on to tell the president: "He's killed innocent people. He'll kill more, so we have to end him." The counter-argument would be to say there may have been little viable evidence to support this statement, and that if they did "end him" then all that might happen would be that others might replace him and kill more innocent people. In addition, Leo's phrase, "he's killed innocent people," could equally have been applied to Bartlet—albeit not in an altogether deliberate fashion.[9]

* * *

Admiral Percy Fitzwallace, the Chairman of the Joint Chiefs of Staff, talking of terrorism and international law, had this to say in the episode "We Killed Yamamoto" (3/21): "We measure the success of a mission by two things: was it successful and how few civilians did we hurt? They measure success by how many civilians are killed. Pregnant women are delivering bombs. You're talking to me about international laws? The laws of nature don't even apply here."[10] The key issue would appear to have been the matter of intent. It is possible to argue that the United States has consistently attempted to avoid excessive collateral damage; however, if one considers either of the two Gulf Wars, in 1991 and 2003, American ordinance was responsible for killing many hundreds of thousands of civilians—and among these would have been, for example, pregnant women.[11] This may not have occurred in a deliberate and intentional way, but the significant issue was the willingness to put large numbers of civilians in mortal danger via a decision to pursue a strategic military campaign. From a Western viewpoint, one could reasonably argue that America's actions were different from those of terrorists, but from the point-of-view of the civilians being killed and maimed by American bombing, this distinction may not have been so noticeable.

In such a context, Trevor and Shawn J. Parry-Giles defined terrorism as signifying "acts that are intentionally designed to kill undeniably innocent individuals in order to achieve political goals."[12] However, it might be mentioned that some of the actions of America in the Vietnam War would, by this definition, also be classed as terrorism. This is not to mention the deliberate bombing of civilians in Germany and Japan during the Second World War, and, of course, the two atomic bombs exploded over the Japanese cities of Hiroshima and Nagasaki. This would seem to be getting to the core of the argument; in other words, Bartlet ordered the murder of Shareef, a character linguistically defined as a terrorist, when he himself could arguably have deserved a similar appellation. In Bartlet's defense, it could be argued that his action might have been morally sanctioned because the nation's security was threatened, and because there was no legal way of bringing the supposed perpetrator to justice. Yet the pretext of "national security" could be seen as supplying a "catch-all" excuse for almost any action taken. The context here is somewhat different, but one might recall Richard Nixon's comment to David Frost: "When the President does it, that means that it is not illegal."[13]

Whether Bartlet's actions, in this specific case, were legal or illegal, he was consistently been portrayed in *The West Wing* as both an intellectual and a moral president.[14] However, in this particular plotline—the case of a premeditated murder of another high-ranking politician—both of these attributes would seem to have been contradicted. One might think here of the story of the books in Hitler's office: when he came to power Hitler had a library of the world's great works of literature, philosophy, political science and so on; however, Hitler did not read any of the books on the many shelves, insomuch as he had already made up his mind about the world. Hitler was not unintelligent, but he was almost entirely self-taught, and hence had few teachers to offer him an objective perspective on the world, or to interrogate the judgments that became his core beliefs.[15] Bartlet may have read a cross-section of the same "great books" that resided on Hitler's bookcases, but some of his actions could be seen as being just as narrow-minded and dogmatic as Hitler's, at least in this particular instance. This is not to compare Bartlet to Hitler, but merely to point to the argument, originally expressed by Plato, that philosophers should take the role of politicians, or at least politicians should be familiar with philosophy. Bartlet was an intellectual, but in this instance it would appear he was swayed by advisors with a far narrower view of the world. Bartlet may have been an educated and erudite individual, but his political decisions, at times, fell far short of his education and his erudition.

Plato also believed that "politicians know the truth—but must not tell it."[16] This maxim was Plato's so-called "noble fable," a scenario that was played out repeatedly in *The West Wing*, albeit perhaps often outside the consciousness of the main players—if not sometimes outside the consciousness of the scriptwriters as well. In a sense the intent of the noble fable could be used to excuse Bartlet's actions in ordering the assassination of Shareef. As Trevor and Shawn J. Parry-Giles put it: "Although the assassination is perhaps unjust, *TWW* suggests no other alternative in the war America is now forced to fight."[17] However as the section of the drama wherein Bartlet actually gave the order to kill was played out, the viewer was presented with a *mise-en-scène* that seemed to deliberately evoke the world of the gangster film, with Leo as the quasi-*consigliore* and Bartlet as the quasi-godfather. In a specific sense, the scene of Bartlet giving the order to kill Shareef, which took place in a theater, seemed to deliberately recall the scene in Brian De Palma's film *The Untouchables* (1987), wherein Al Capone, played by Robert De Niro, was told of the successful murder of Jimmy Malone (Sean Connery's character), while watching the performance of another play in another theater. Such a seemingly deliberate intertextual allusion seemed to suggest that the world of the politician and the world of the gangster may not have been so far removed,[18] or at least that powerful men must sometimes resort to extreme violence in order to successfully accomplish their work.

While Bartlet's actions might be compared to the concept of politician as gangster, there was, nonetheless, the question of Bartlet's personal morality; for example, Melissa Crawley has argued that Shareef's murder depicted "the most obvious challenge to the notion of Bartlet as a moral leader."[19] It is clear that Bartlet was fully aware that his action was wrong, that he was committing an amoral act, a mortal sin. Bartlet's Catholicism was of interest here; for example, one might question how could Bartlet, a committed Catholic, have deliberately broken the sixth commandment, "Thou shalt not kill," or, as Exodus actually puts it: "You shall not murder"— the deliberate taking of another human life arguably being the worst commandment to break and the worst crime to commit. In such a sense it has to be admitted Bartlet was a criminal, a criminal guilty of premeditated murder. As president he may not have wanted to commit such an act, but nonetheless this was an act he eventually chose to undertake. One wonders if Bartlet absolved himself of guilt via the sacrament of confession; this was not shown in the narrative of the series, but it would seem possible that such an instance occurred.

However, whether or not Bartlet received absolution for his sins, it was self-evident that there were few "dire consequences for breaking international law in the world of *The West Wing*."[20] In fact, the term international law might almost be seen as an oxymoron, insomuch as world leaders on the winning side—no matter their actions—seldom, if ever, seem to face charges. One might think here of some of the actual politicians during *The West Wing*'s run, for example, politicians such as George W. Bush and Tony Blair. The legality of their actions were at least questionable, but the prospect of either of them ever being brought before a court was never a realistic possibility.[21] Olivier Corten in his paper "*A la maison blanche*: le président des Etats-Unis se soucie-t-il du droit international lorsqu'il décide d'une intervention militaire?"[22] argued that the approach and attitudes within *The West Wing* can only "make us think that international law is absent—or at least neglected."[23] In addition, Corten's paper concluded that the representation of the UN Charter in *The West Wing* followed that in other recent examples in American film and television, as in *Zero Dark Thirty* (2013), *24* (2001–2010) and *Homeland* (2011–2019); insomuch as "the President's powers cannot be restrained by the existing rules; those rules must simply be interpreted as allowing any military action necessary to protect the interests of the United States."[24]

In this sense it might be of interest to compare Bartlet's actions to the corresponding actions of an actual president; for example, Barack Obama's role in the killing of Osama bin Laden. It is unclear if Obama's intention was to kill or to capture bin Laden; however, in the fictional discourse of *The West Wing*, Bartlet directly ordered the killing of Shareef, who may be seen as a cipher (albeit an inaccurate one) for bin Laden. Of course Obama was locked into the events of post–9/11: George W. Bush's so-called "War on Terror," the invasion of Iraq, the orange-suited detainees in Guantanamo Bay, the use of so-called "enhanced interrogation techniques," the scandal of Abu Ghraib and the other so-called "horrors" of the Bush administration.[25] One might speculate what Al Gore's reaction might have been to 9/11, had he won the 2000 election[26]; whether he might have adopted a different, more morally sanctioned response to the terrorist attacks upon mainland America.

* * *

This discussion once again illuminates one of the traits of *The West Wing*: the show's all-embracing optimism, its life-affirming viewpoint and its feel-good sentimentalism, often resulting in what seemed, at times, to be an overarching sense of hypocrisy. As intimated above, at the time the relevant episodes were originally broadcast (May 2002), the Bush administration was sanctioning actions much worse than the assassination of a suspected terrorist. This was a reaction to the 9/11 attacks, but arguably a reaction that went beyond any sense of retaining a moral authority over the so-called terrorists the United States was attempting to defeat. In the fictional discourse of *The West Wing*, President Bartlet may have been viewed as a tolerant and benevolent president; however, in this part of the series, he too would seem to have lost his moral authority. In the most charitable light, Bartlet was a liberal president forced into making difficult decisions for the greater good. In a bleaker light, Bartlet became a self-identified murderer, morally corrupted by the power he had to wield in defense of the republic he headed. In essence it would appear that politicians might therefore be viewed as sanctioned sinners, sanctioned criminals, and, in the worst-case scenario, sanctioned murderers. From one point-of-view, Bartlet committed premeditated murder; hence an argument could be made that he should have been sentenced in The Hague to a long prison sentence by the International Court of Justice.[27] Of course, this was never going to happen. Bartlet would continue his presidency for two full terms, seemingly beyond the remit of international law; he would not be made to answer for his actions.[28]

18

The Crackpots and These Women
Misogynist Discourses

The fictitious administration of President Bartlet has consistently been seen as one committed to a representation of minorities,[1] an administration that purported to extol the rights of the misplaced and to strive to offer equality for all. However, the series would seem to have had few such inclinations when it came to the equality of women; in other words, when it came to confronting the issue of feminism. One obvious defense against this charge would be to say Aaron Sorkin and the other writers of the show were simply creating storylines that represented the real world. In other words, the show merely reflected the chauvinistic world of American political life, offering an authentic mirror-image and likeness; it was thus a sexist show that embodied a sexist world. Nonetheless, the charge remains; *The West Wing* was indubitably a sexist and chauvinistic television drama. It may have possessed high standards in other areas of supposed equality, but in its depiction of women it routinely affected a masculine bias; it could not, in any sense, be viewed as a feminist text.

In looking toward a feminist reading of *The West Wing*, it might first be expedient to attempt to offer an answer to the question: What is feminism? A dictionary definition would suggest feminism to be a belief in women's rights on the grounds of the equality of the sexes. In the space of a more academic forum, feminism might be defined as follows:

> A conscious movement to resist patriarchy, to disturb the complacent certainties of a patriarchal culture, to assert a belief in sexual equality between male and female subjects and to eradicate sexist domination in society.[2]

However, it would be a mistake to think of feminism as a single unified artifact, insomuch as there are, in fact, a diversity of feminisms. It would also be a mistake to believe feminism began in the 1960s; it would be more accurate to see the rise of women's rights in the 1960s as merely the latest cycle of feminist thought. Nonetheless, this latest wave of feminism rapidly found its way into the academic forum—arguably becoming one of the key approaches within cultural theory—while also finding resonance and currency outside of academia. One of the reasons for this may have been that feminism was so logically grounded. Men, being physically more powerful than women, would have originally assumed dominance because of this brute fact—and women, who would previously have tended to have been either pregnant or caring for children, would have needed the protection offered from their male hunter-gatherer mates.

To some extent, this somewhat unsophisticated scenario would seem to prevail today, although upheld by a series of more subtle strategies and discursive practices. Men continue to be made to believe that bigger is better: their physique, the money they earn, the car they drive. They are persuaded to believe hardness is better: their muscles, the facts they believe in, their country's foreign policy. They are made to believe that up is better than down: their stocks and shares, their attitudes to life's problems, their mobility in the job market and so on. Hence what is clear in this scenario is that it is better to be big, hard and up, rather than small, soft and down; all pointing, of course, to indicators of virility. Lynne Segal, in her influential book of the 1990s, *Straight Sex*, noted the almost transparent way in which ideals of masculinity were, in fact, built upon anxieties over sexual prowess. Segal also noted how right-wing ideologies mobilize against women via their sexuality: "Against women's sexual autonomy, against abortion, against homosexuality, against divorce, against sex education, indeed against everything that has helped undermine men's control over women's sexuality."[3] An awareness of such an argument might be seen to illuminate many of the gender conflicts in *The West Wing*; as feminism, often unsuccessfully, attempted to disrupt the androcentric hegemony prevailing within the narrative of the drama.

This would not be to neglect the fact that there were a number of significant female characters in *The West Wing*; one thinks, for example, of Mandy Hampton, Amy Gardner,[4] Abigail Bartlet, Nancy McNally, Joey Lucas—and, of course, CJ Cregg, arguably the most significant female presence on the show. However, although such female presences inhabited the drama, there was a habitual sense in which they were compromised because of their gender identity. For example, while CJ held a significant post in the Bartlet administration (as White House press secretary and then as the president's chief of staff), there were nonetheless constant instances of CJ being undermined because of her gender—in other words, for specifically acting as a woman in a predominantly masculine world. A case in point occurred in the episode "The Women of Qumar" (3/9). Here CJ's "emotional outburst" over the administration's decision to sell arms to the fictitious state of Qumar was an apt instance of how her judgments were compromised because of her femininity. This was seen to some effect in the following exchange between CJ and National Security Advisor Nancy McNally. McNally explained the United States needed the airbase in Qumar for strategic reasons. CJ countered by suggesting it was merely convenient and that they had alternative bases, going on to say: "They beat women, Nancy. They hate women. The only reason they keep Qumari women alive is to make more Qumari men." McNally was pragmatic: "This is the real world, and we can't isolate our enemies.... It's a big world, CJ. And everybody has guns, and I'm doing the best I can." CJ merely restated: "They're beating the women, Nancy!"[5] It was a well-written and well-acted scene, one that enabled a genuinely emotive content to develop. However, it was, nonetheless, overly clichéd from a feminist perspective, with one critic describing CJ in the scene as being "highly emotional in a stereotypical manner,"[6] and this would certainly appear to have had some degree of truth. If the scene had been played with a male actor in the role—Sam Seaborn would have made an apt choice—then the inherent gender bias might not have been so formulaic.[7]

* * *

As discussed in Chapter 13, it was apparent that a number of available female characters in the series remained single and unattached: CJ, Mandy, Donna, Ainsley, Amy, Joey and so on. This raised the implication that if women held office, or had demanding professions, this diminished their hopes of personal relationships. Such a state of affairs also applied to the men in the series, the apparent explanation being the same: that work surpassed any hopes of secure and long-lasting relationships. However, the women were often little more than accessories to men: secretaries, assistants, associates, and subordinates of various kinds. In other words, they often did not even have the compensation of a working life that was sufficiently important to make up for such a sacrifice.[8] This has been commented upon by a number of critics. For example, Trevor and Shawn J. Parry-Giles noted:

> All of the women are valued and praised, but in gendered ways. C J. is noticed for her energy and appearance, and Mrs. Landingham for her motherhood and her faithful dedication. Even when Mandy is admired for her perseverance and commitment, this trait is contextualized as a gender role reversal. The episode ["The Crackpots and These Women"] separates male from female by positioning the females as an object of gaze and comment.[9]

In a similar context, Simon Philpott and David Mutimer commented:

> The women serve as protectors and nurturers of their men. This applies to Mrs. Landingham—whose sometime matronly tone with the President reflects a relationship that dates back to Bartlet's youth—Donna, with respect to Josh, and Margaret, Leo's secretary. Interestingly, it is the female characters that do not work in the immediate

orbit of the men of the inner circle—Mandy Hampton, Amy Gardner, Ainsley Hayes, and Joey Lucas—that most ruffle and challenge.[10]

Finally, Samuel Chambers and Patrick Finn noted:

> Sorkin seems simply to reduce the female characters on his show to the oldest of stereotypes, to confine them to the subject positions that they sometimes seek to resist.[11]

As suggested above, the character of CJ Cregg was arguably the female role that went the furthest in striving to deny such a subordinate position. This may have been partly due to the strength Alison Janney's acting brought to the role. It is possible Janney may have been considered for her role as CJ because of her appearance in the film *Primary Colors* (1998). In the film, Janney played the role of Miss Walsh, an adult literacy teacher, who was "visited" by presidential candidate Jack Stanton (John Travolta). In her opening scene Janney somehow managed to clumsily fall *up* the stairs—this arguably forging the idea of CJ falling off the exercise machine in her opening scene of *The West Wing*. As discussed in Chapter 14, CJ's clumsiness may have had a dyspraxic element; however, there was also the sense of Allison Janney, as an actress, being held back because of her height and general appearance. As Paul Challen put it: "Casting directors seemed to think that the six foot actress was too tall for the small screen" and that the only roles she could play were "lesbians and aliens."[12] In this way there was a sense in which CJ's/Janney's lack of a conventional sexual appeal may have contributed to her ability to prevail more successfully in the masculine world in which she worked. This premise was delineated in the episode "Gone Quiet" (3/7). Here CJ was heard singing Right Said Fred's song "I'm Too Sexy."[13] However, within such an argument it could be said that CJ was not too sexy; she was not too sexy for her shirt—or for anything else for that matter. The French phrase *jolie laide*[14] perhaps summed up such a proposition, CJ/Janney was unconventionally attractive—in a literal sense, she was pretty/ugly, hence one potential explanation for her success throughout the entire run of the drama. The specific issue here was the proposal that CJ was able to be such a significant female protagonist, one that rose to a less than subordinate position, because her sexuality did not challenge the dominant patriarchal structures at play within the drama.

In terms of a feminist approach toward sexuality itself, and, in one particular sense, prostitution, here *The West Wing* was of some interest. As discussed in Chapter 13, there was little explicit sexual content in the show; hence it was not surprising that the series seldom alluded to prostitution. However, there was one significant exception, this occurring at the very beginning of the drama, wherein Sam unwittingly spent a night with Laurie Rollins, a character who was described variously as a prostitute, a call girl and a hooker.[15] Laurie was something of a stereotype: she was merely "moonlighting as a prostitute,"[16] while attending Georgetown University with the aim of becoming a lawyer. Throughout the first season, the relationship between Sam and Laurie was revisited, with Sam attempting to help whenever he could. The idea of helping a "fallen woman" was burlesqued in the drama, but there was still the sense this was what Sam was, in fact, attempting to do. However, Laurie's doubtful moral character enabled her to be manipulated when it was necessary, as Simon Philpott and David Mutimer noted:

> Laurie is fair game in the mind of Josh and Sam because ultimately her relationship with Sam falls outside of liberal norms and so is stripped of legitimacy and privacy. The inability of Sam and Josh to accord the woman dignity and respect enables them to trample upon Laurie's private life in the quest for political advantage over their Republican opponents.[17]

Nonetheless, this situation was not restricted to Laurie. It was evidenced in the "casual sexism of many central male characters"[18] who "routinely sexualized" women.[19] In addition, as Trevor and Shawn J. Parry-Giles noted: "The messages that emanate from female characters routinely confirm powerful gender ideologies that are the bedrock of U.S. national identity."[20]

If one considers the representation of women in *The West Wing* in more general terms then further indications of blatant chauvinism become apparent. For example, in the episode "The Crackpots and These Women" (1/5), Bartlet and Leo somewhat blatantly "gazed"[21] at the women on their staff, almost as if they were deliberately engaging within a discourse of scopophilia, with the two men discussing the women in their employ in a supposedly complimentary way—but, in reality, within a decidedly sexist treatise. Bartlet stated: "We were talking about these women." Leo agreed: "We can't get over these women." Bartlet continued: "Look at CJ. She's like a fifties movie star, so capable, so loving and energetic." Leo added: "Look at Mandy over there. Going punch for punch with Toby in a world that tells women to sit down and shut up." Bartlet finished by saying: "Mrs. Landingham. Did you know she lost two sons in Vietnam? What would make her want to serve her country is beyond me, but in fourteen years, she's not missed a day's work, not one." The scene was so unknowingly patronizing as to be almost grotesquely condescending, presenting a paradigm for the disparaging attitude to sexual politics in the show.[22]

This was an exaggerated instance; however, there were numerous others. For example, the episode "Take Out the Trash Day" (1/13) included a scene in which Donna, Carol, Cathy, Ginger and Margaret—mostly assistants to powerful men—were seen talking together in the outer Oval Office. The conversation seemed to be intentionally flippant—almost to the level of gossip—to the extent that it was difficult to know what they were actually talking about. However, this stopped with the entrance of Mrs. Landingham, who asked: "What are you girls doing?" Margaret replied: "We're just talking, Mrs. Landingham." Mrs. Landingham was dismissive: "You all work for very important people. This is not a place for gossip. You understand me?" All five women replied: "Yes, Ma'am." Once again, the scene was so stereotypically clichéd as if to be deliberately sexist: women were described as girls, they were gossiping, they worked for *very* important people, who were, of course, predominantly men, and they were subservient to a dominant woman—Mrs. Landingham—who was unequivocal in letting them know their place.

In the episode "The White House Pro-Am" (1/17), the title referred to the president and his staff (predominantly men) being the professionals and to Abbey and her staff (predominantly women) being the amateurs—suggesting the supposition that men were superior to women. "You are prone to amateur mistakes," Sam would tell Abbey in the episode; in addition, CJ was made to appear "stupid"—being told by three men that she needed to "learn" to "read the signs." In this way, CJ, in general, was susceptible to male criticisms. In the episode "Mandatory Minimums" (1/20), CJ was told of her "dumb mistake" and her "amateur mistakes"; while in "Galileo" (2/9) CJ would comment: "That's the fourth time I've been called dumb." Elsewhere, other female protagonists were subject to the view that women were inferior; for example, Margaret forwarded an email that disrupted the entire White House system, the email concerning the calorie count in raisin muffins.[23] Mrs. Landingham was made to look foolish because she did not buy her new car at "below sticker" price.[24] Likewise, Ainsley inadvertently drank too much and, after sitting in wet paint, met the president in a bathrobe while singing "Blame It on the Bossa Nova." In such a way, Laura K. Garrett was correct in concluding:

> While *The West Wing* offers a glimpse of political women, it does not reflect an accurate portrayal of modern women in politics, and instead it comes close to perpetuating the stereotypes created by the media.[25]

Such a stereotyping was perhaps most appositely seen in Donna's character. Donna was consistently represented as lacking intelligence and sophistication; often her presence seemed to be merely that of an "idiotic exposition vehicle"[26]—wherein a male character, usually Josh, would then be enabled to discuss the intricate details of the plotline in question. In the episode "Let Bartlet be Bartlet" (1/19), there was a blatant example of this, with Donna asking: "How does the FEC work?" after which Josh gave the relevant explanation. A number of critics have commented upon this; for example, Philip Cass, discussing the episode "Gaza" (5/21), noted:

> Having Donna along on the fact-finding mission allows her—the sweet, blonde, slightly goofy girl from the Mid-West—to ask questions and receive highly simplified answers about the situation in the Occupied Territories.[27]

Similarly, Clive James, talking about the first seasons of the show, noted:

> Donna, played by Janel Moloney, has a double function: everything has to be explained to her, which makes her useful for purposes of exposition, but she also has a gift for asking the awkward question that stops the hot-shots in their tracks.[28]

Elsewhere Donna was often depicted in a less than complimentary way. For example, in the opening to the "Isaac and Ishmael" (3/1) episode, Donna's only line was: "And I get a boyfriend!" While the male characters were expressing profound thoughts on the implications of the 9/11 event, Donna was only commenting on her personal life. Similarly, in the episode "Inauguration Part 1" (4/14), Donna seemed more interested in the fact that tickets to the inauguration ball had arrived than in the news that 15,000 people had just been killed in Kundu. There was also the sense that Donna was simply not as clever as the men surrounding her[29]; to cite just one example, in the episode "Disaster Relief" (5/6), Donna did not know the meaning of the word "schadenfreude," while in the same episode Josh seemed concerned that she might have mistaken the word "philately" for "fellatio."

At other points in the series there was a similar sense of women being made to appear more frivolous than men. For example, in the episode "The Cold" (7/13), Donna and Ronna (already replete with risible sounding names) discussed the prospect of U2's singer, Bono, joining the Santos campaign. There followed a somewhat predictable and clichéd response, with the two women either feigning or portraying excitement at meeting the singer. In the end Bono was not to appear, the closest the series got to a bona-fide rock legend joining the campaign was Jon Bon Jovi, several episodes later. A similar trope would be seen in the differences between Matt Santos and his wife Helen. At the end of the Christmas episode "Impact Winter" (6/9), Josh and Santos were shown discussing the prospect of running for the presidency, while Helen asked: "Matt, where's the box for the tinsel, honey? Have you seen it anywhere?" Another instance occurred in the episode "The Last Hurrah" (7/20), wherein Santos—now as president-elect—was dealing with important issues of state, while Helen was meeting with the White House decorator to decide on their children's bedrooms: "Here's what I've sketched for Peter's room, a cowboy theme. And here's what I came up for Miranda's room. A place a princess would love." Finally, in the closing episode of the series, "Tomorrow" (7/22), the now President Santos talked, albeit in clichéd terms, about foreign affairs: "This Kazakhstan thing is a mess. We've got thousands of our soldiers in the middle of Central Asia. They haven't a clue as to what's next." Helen interrupted, saying: "Nine inaugural balls. You think I'm supposed to wear nine gowns?"

There was also the issue of sexist vocabulary, of inappropriate gender nomenclature. For example, women were routinely described as "girls," while men were routinely described simply as men. In terms of specific examples of sexist vocabulary toward women, there were too many instances to cite in detail. However, to reference just one character, there are numerous examples of other characters using sexist vocabulary about Ainsley Hayes. In her opening scene in the episode "In This White House" (2/4), Ainsley was introduced by Josh saying to Toby: "Sam's getting his ass kicked by a girl." Ainsley was a woman—but her age, or gender for that matter, would have seem to have been of little relevance in terms of her debating skills. In the following episode, "And It's Surely to Their Credit" (2/5), Ainsley was referred to as a "kitten," while in the next episode Ainsley was called "a blonde and leggy fascist" and "a baton twirler."[30] Ainsley's attitude to feminism was highlighted in a scene in the episode "Night Five" (3/14); the scene began with Ainsley returning to work after attending a social function and wearing an evening gown. When Sam saw her he commented: "Hayes, you could make a good dog break his leash." Later in the episode, Celia Walton, a temporary member of staff, challenged Sam for his comment: "Do you mind if I say something to you.... The way you talked to that woman before.... I don't know her name. The 'dog on a leash' ... It was rude, it was inappropriate, and it was offensive.... You demeaned her." Sam denied this: "No, we're friends. It's completely mature.... I wasn't demeaning her. I was complimenting her." However, Celia countered: "She's an Associate White House Counsel and you're complimenting her on her sexuality?" All Sam could say was: "She looked good in that dress." Later, when Ainsley herself returned, Sam said: "Celia, I asked Ainsley and she said she didn't mind at all. I think it's important to make clear I am not sexist." Ainsley supported Sam, "He's not sexist." Celia responded: "I'm surprised you're willing to let your sexuality diminish your power." Ainsley disingenuously countered: "I don't even know what that means"—with Celia telling her: "I think you do." All Ainsley could say was: "And I think you think I'm made out of candy glass, Celia. If somebody says something that offends you, tell them, but all women don't have to think alike.... I like it when the guys tease me. It's an inadvertent show of respect that I'm on the team and I don't mind when it gets sexual. And you know why? I like sex. I don't think that whatever sexuality I may have diminishes my power. I think it enhances it." In response to this Celia then finally used the "f" word: "What kind of feminism do you call that?" All Ainsley could say was: "My kind"—after which the scene ended.

There were a number of issues to note here; the first being that the scene was written by a man (Aaron Sorkin), and hence it was a masculine voice that was ultimately speaking the lines. Whether an actual woman in Ainsley's position would have made such comments is open to question: Would a woman really claim she enjoyed being "teased" because a work colleague had made a comment about her sexual appeal? Whether she would have considered this a show of respect, a way of becoming "part of the team," is again open to question. Although the scene was written in such a way as to undermine Celia's argument, within a feminist reading it would seem that Celia had, nonetheless, made her point. When Celia asked Ainsley what kind of feminism she called this, all Ainsley could respond was: "My kind"—an unconvincing definition at best. By any contemporary understanding of sexual politics Sam's comment was offensive and demeaning; to demonstrate this all that needs to be done would be to reverse the scenario; to imagine how Sam would have responded to such a sexual remark made about his body. From a feminist point-of-view the scene was perhaps one of the most revealing of the drama—insomuch as it demonstrated the simplistic and often crude approach to sexual politics within the series. Yet a voice, Celia's, was heard and succeeded in putting forth a feminist view, albeit positioned within a biased and androcentric discourse.

As such, the scene could be seen as a clear case of sexual harassment. It may have been a minor harassment—compared to other more serious cases in the workplace—but it was a harassment nonetheless.[31] Sam's behavior was not appropriate to his position; and the fact that Celia, a temporary member of staff, should have been the person to complain was significant. In other words, this suggested that such behavior was commonplace in the workplace, and that Celia had a higher expectation of professional conduct in such an environment. Ainsley, whatever she may have claimed, was a woman holding a responsible job, a woman who was verbally abused by a man who had power over her, a man who could, for example, have had her dismissed. Finally, Sam's claim that "she started it" suggested something even more damaging. In the context suggested by Sam, Ainsley "started it" by wearing a dress that Sam found sexually appealing, thus producing the dog on the leash comment.[32] Such behavior would not seem to be so far away from men who defend sexual assault because the woman had been wearing provocative clothing.

* * *

As intimated previously, at numerous instances in the series women would be routinely demeaned via the ways in which men referred to them: as girls, kittens, hookers and so on. This continued throughout the series. For example, in the episode "The California 47th" (4/16), Will Bailey—the president's new speech writer—referred somewhat disparagingly to his team of assistants, four young female interns, calling them "the Robert Palmer girls"; in the next episode, "Red Haven's on Fire" (4/17), Will would call them "the Ronettes," as if to draw attention to their ages, to their gender and to the idea that they were not overly intelligent. Similarly, there was Arnold Vinick's comment in the episode "The Al Smith Dinner" (7/6), in a reference to Donna, who had criticized his position on abortion. Vinick said: "Since I don't have a functioning uterus, like Tippi Hedren here, of course I'm not qualified to talk about it." While such demeaning and sexualized statements might have been excused as merely representing the way society operated, there was nonetheless a sense that the high moral values, as espoused by Bartlet's White House, were not being upheld. There may have been rare instances of male characters being the subject of sexually based insults, but these were difficult to locate—none can be cited here.

By way of approaching a summary, one might begin by confirming the series was as conventionally sexist as might have been expected. The show might have feigned to be putting forward a liberal and tolerant view of society in 21st century America, but this was prime-time network television, and hence it was not going to veer far from the status quo. In the episode "Bartlet for America" (3/10), Bartlet absentmindedly mused upon the subject of gender. "The things we do to women," Bartlet mused, referring to his wife, Abbey, and how she was to be professionally reprimanded for her participation in concealing Bartlet's multiple sclerosis. However, there was a sense that Bartlet's phrase was merely an indifferent and ultimately insincere appraisal of the plight of women. In an overarching sense *The West Wing* rarely ventured far from the dominant discourse of patriarchal authority, anchored, as it was, within the society within which it took place. As such this was much as might have been expected, the fictional drama merely mirroring the reality it sought to represent. In this way it has to be accepted that little new ground was broken in the drama, at least in terms of the injustices perpetrated upon women.

One of the few instances wherein Bartlet was confronted directly with the reality of feminism came in the episode "Abu el Banat" (5/9). In this element of the drama, Bartlet was attempting to convince his oldest daughter, Elizabeth, that she could run for Congress. Elizabeth's husband, Doug, was seen by Bartlet as not being as capable of running for political office, hence his advice to his daughter that she should run in his place. This was in spite of the fact she had two relatively young children. Bartlet told his daughter, "You can handle it." Elizabeth demurred, "I can't. Forgive me, Ms. Steinem and Ms. Friedan, you cannot do it all." Bartlet countered: "Your mother did." Elizabeth seemed to know better: "No, Daddy. She didn't." The inherent detail to note here was that Bartlet was able to achieve the presidency because he was supported by his wife, who was the primary caregiver for their three daughters. Herein was the gender inequality that Bartlet seems to have failed to understand. As such, in this scene and in numerous others, the underlying patriarchal discourse of *The West Wing* revealed itself as being decidedly chauvinistic; whatever its supposedly liberal qualities, it was illiberal in its attitudes toward the equality of men and women in the society and culture it portrayed.

19

Cultural Differences
Postcolonial Readings

The West Wing was very much an American drama, and for the majority of its seven seasons it seldom concerned itself with issues outside of the United States. There were exceptions; for example, the recurring instances of Islamic terrorism, seen to most significant effect in the "Isaac and Ishmael" (3/1) episode and in the recurring storyline of Bartlet's decision to assassinate Abdul Shareef, the defense minister of the fictitious gulf state Qumar, a narrative strand that occupied the closing episodes of Season 3 and the opening episodes of Season 4. As discussed in Chapters 8 and 17, these were notable aspects in the ways in which the storyline of Bartlet's presidency was told; however, other than this there was relatively little attention paid to issues outside of America—the only other relevant example occurring in the episode "Gaza" (5/21). However, even here this concerned only minor characters: Donna, Admiral Percy Fitzwallace and others. This sense of insularity, in a prime-time American television drama, was perhaps not wholly surprising, echoing the sense of insularity in America itself. It has often been said that Americans are not as interested in the rest of the world as, for example, people in Europe and other parts of the developed world. One thinks of the cliché that only 10 percent of Americans have passports; this may not be wholly accurate,[1] but nonetheless the point is made. As such, and from a certain perspective, this could be seen as mirroring—and to some extent explaining—*The West Wing*'s inherent lack of interest in events outside of America's borders.

The aspect of cultural theory most applicable in this context would be that of postcolonialism. This was a theoretical school of thought that only emerged as a distinct category in the late 1980s and early 1990s, although its early ancestry can be traced back to Edward Said's book of 1978, *Orientalism*.[2] One of the most significant effects of postcolonialist theory has been to undermine the universalist assumptions made by Western culture. As such, postcolonialism rejects the universalism of white, Eurocentric discourse; of marginalizing everything that is not Western—the taken-for-granted idea that Western culture is, in some way, superior to all other traditions. Postcolonial criticism discards such universalist thinking, replacing it with the idea that white, Eurocentric[3] norms were being promoted by a sleight-of-hand, to elevate the concept of Western culture as being all-important, while at the same time marginalizing all others. In other words, postcolonialist theory rejects the overarching notion that Western civilization, arts, culture and society were of greater significance than other traditions.[4]

In 1969, the art historian Kenneth Clarke wrote and presented a series of thirteen programs on BBC television, a series that outlined the history of Western art and culture from the so-called Dark Ages to the present day. The series proved to be a significant success, being seen as one of the landmark events in television history. The title of the series was *Civilisation*; and this title, in itself, spoke eloquently of the biased, narrow-minded and dogmatic assumptions that postcolonialism sought to expose.[5] In other words, the sense in which cultural and artistic productions were blithely seen from a Western perspective, demonstrated the inherent prejudices at play. To take the example of television alone: in the United Kingdom there are few non–Western programs; other than home productions, most programming consists of American productions and some European productions, together with programming from other Western countries such as Australia, New Zealand and so on. Otherwise, television from other parts of the world is rarely shown. Such a Western bias would transparently appear to extend into film, into literature and into the cultural arts in general. If we make the unconscious claim that great art and literature has a timeless and universal significance, but only within a Western perspective, we thereby demote and disregard social, regional and national differences, preferring instead to judge all the cultural arts by a single, supposedly "universal" standard.[6]

One of the most interesting scenes in *The West Wing*, from a postcolonialist perspective, occurred in the episode "Somebody's Going to Emergency, Somebody's Going to Jail" (2/16). In the episode CJ met with three academics, geographers from the Organization of Cartographers for Social Equality: Dr. John Fallow, Dr. Cynthia Sayles and Professor Donald Huke. The geographers explained that they would like the Bartlet administration to "aggressively support legislation" that would make it mandatory for every public school in America to teach the "Peters Projection Map instead of the traditional Mercator." Dr. Sayles then went on to add: "The Mercator Projection has fostered European imperialist attitudes for centuries and created an ethnic bias against a Third World." CJ appeared skeptical; Fallow explained that in 1569 the German cartographer Geradus Mercator had designed a map of the world as "a navigational tool for European sailors." Mercator's projection—essentially a means of representing a globe in a rectangular presentation—succeeded in allowing accurate means of crossing the oceans; however, it also acted to distort the relative size of nations and continents. Land masses nearer the poles appeared larger; for example, Greenland appeared to be roughly the same size as Africa, whereas, in reality, Africa was fourteen times larger. In a similar way, Europe appeared to be larger than South America, whereas, in reality, it was half its size—and so on throughout other examples. The cartographers then presented a new map, the Peters Projection, a map of the world with a "fidelity of axis" and a "fidelity of position"; in other words, a map with a sense of "social equality" where countries were shown in their true sizes. Professor Huke, seemingly oblivious of the sexual innuendo, summed up the significance of accurate projection by stating: "In our society we unconsciously equate size with importance, and even power." Finally, Dr. Fallow went some way in successfully encapsulating the core of the postcolonial argument: "When Third World countries are misrepresented they're likely to be valued less. When Mercator maps exaggerate the importance of Western civilization, when the top of the map is given to the northern hemisphere and the bottom is given to the southern, then people will tend to adopt top and bottom attitudes."[7]

The scene in the episode was portrayed within the context of a facetious discourse, but the intent of the argument was serious. The three academics presented a significant postcolonialist argument, although the term "postcolonialist" was not used. However, within a postcolonialist approach such a bias toward the way the world is projected geographically, via maps or charts or atlases, poses a valid argument. This can be seen within a diverse range of other geographical factors; for example, the term "Middle East" in itself suggests a certain bias—the East—be it Near, Middle or Far—could just as easily have been visualized as the center. One might ask: The East of where? Perhaps somewhere that was not the West? Such a use of nomenclature would seem relevant to the idea of the East, or the Orient, as a repository of those aspects of culture the West would abhor; aspects such as cruelty, decadence, laziness and so on.[8] As Edward Said has argued, the non–European was the exotic "other," and people outside of the Western tradition were positioned as anonymous masses rather than individuals, their actions determined by instinctive and clichéd emotions, such as lust and fury, rather than by conscious choices and rational decisions.[9] Hence the East was seen as a place of the exotic, the mystical, the seductive; a part of the developing world (a term, in itself, something of a cynical euphemism) wherein all of its actual properties were distorted through the lens of a Western point-of-view—this acting as a further distortion, just as the Mercator projection distorted the map of the world.

* * *

Another significant aspect of *The West Wing*, from a postcolonialist point-of-view, was the representation of Palestine. One of the plotlines at the end of Season 5 and the beginning of Season 6 followed Bartlet's attempt to solve the Israeli/Palestinian conflict[10]; it represented one of the few instances wherein actual foreign states were used in a major storyline, or at least foreign states outside of the Western nations. Otherwise, as will be seen later in this chapter, major storylines outside of America were often placed within a discourse of fictitious nation states. However, there were complications insomuch as the leaders of the two sides were fictitious. Hence there were obvious difficulties in representing a political situation—grounded in reality—within a fictitious drama.[11] Nonetheless, the depiction of the Palestinians and Israelis at the peace talks was of interest, provoking a range of pertinent issues in terms of a postcolonial reading. To cite just one example, both parties arrived at Camp David, the location for the talks, on a Friday, on the Muslim holy day and the eve of the Jewish holy day; hence, both delegations were shown praying. The members of the Israeli contingent were shown sitting comfortably around a table, in the light, looking relaxed and civilized. In contrast, the members of the Palestinian contingent were shown praying outside, in the gathering dark, against a background of tangled undergrowth. The ideological dichotomy could not have been clearer; as Philip Cass put it: "Here are the civilized Israelis, ready, however reluctantly, to talk and out there in the wild woods are the Palestinians, afraid to come in to the light."[12]

* * *

As suggested above, Edward Said, himself a Palestinian-American, is generally agreed to have been one of the most influential of figures in the postcolonial debate. In making use of Foucauldian ideas within a postcolonial context, Said suggested that the "truth" of a statement (within a discourse) depended less on what was being said than on who was saying it, when they were saying it and where they were saying it from.[13] In terms of a postcolonialist approach to *The West Wing* such a concept could often be seen; in other words, Bartlet's America consistently appeared to be right simply because it had the power and the means to confirm the validity and the "rightness" of its various pronouncements and statements. This was seen to specific effect in the Bartlet administration's dealing with the Middle East and with Islamic nations—both real and fictitious. A number of critics have commented on this; for example, Steven Aoun argued that *The West Wing* was unable "to conceive [of] the complexities of the Middle East in anything other than Western terms."[14] Lynn Spigel, citing Edward Said's description of the Arab as the "other," argued that *The West Wing* depicted Islamic countries as the antithesis of Western culture and progress:

When Josh details the cultural wasteland of Islamic fundamentalism, he enacts one of the central rhetorical principles of Orientalism, for as Said argues, the "net effect" of contemporary Orientalism is to erase any American awareness of the Arab world's culture and humanity.[15]

In a similar vein, Trevor and Shawn J. Parry-Giles argued:

TWW relegates people of color and their concerns to the margins, [it] manifests "weak multiculturalism" in which canons are expanded to include minority voices, ... the watchwords are "tolerance, sensitivity and openness," creating an outlook that "flirts with the idea of group rights without wholly embracing it."[16]

In terms of the Islamic world itself, the overarching attitude of *The West Wing* was seen to most exaggerated effect in the episode "Isaac and Ishmael" (3/1). This was discussed in some depth in Chapter 9; however, within a postcolonial approach and in looking at the drama as a whole, the Islamic world was rarely seen in a developed and rounded way. To put this another way, it would seem to be a fairly secure wager that Aaron Sorkin had not read *Orientalism* before he wrote the "Isaac and Ishmael" episode. Here the Islamic world was definitively seen as the "other"—with the West in *The West Wing* decidedly representing the mean, the standard, the norm.

* * *

There is, of course, much to criticize in the way religion has affected those countries that follow the Islamic faith. It would seem valid to argue that, in a predominantly fundamentalist society, social and cultural progress may be less likely; that is, if the individuals within such a society are more concerned with their hopes of an afterlife—rather than their hopes in the real world. In other words, one of the results of religious fundamentalism is intellectual repression—leading to cultural and scientific stagnation. To take one example, the subjugation of women in many Islamic societies has resulted in half of the population having a lesser chance of being educated. In such a context, it is not difficult to answer the question: Why has Western culture produced so many important philosophers, writers, scientists—those thinkers and artists who would seem to have proved significant in the dominant intellectual history of the world?[17] In his book *A Terrible Beauty: A History of the People and Ideas That Shaped the Modern Mind*, Peter Watson questioned why Islamic technological innovation was so much slower than that the West. Watson suggested one potential response would be to say the Islamic world turned its back on many technological inventions because of a fear of sacrilegious intent. In the West there was a coming to terms with the modern world, not overly influenced by religion, aided by a democratic system, with an openness to the sciences and the humanities and a sufficiently advanced economic system to allow this.[18] As Damian Thompson has noted, "No Muslim country—not one—has a viable educational system or a university of international stature."[19] Such a lack of education will eventually have practical implications—backward nation states facing more advanced nation states will always come off worst. For example, America has the bomb, but no Middle Eastern countries (apart from Israel) currently have nuclear weapons. However, they might have had them—had it not been for the way in which religious fundamentalism curtailed scientific development. In the end this scenario may come down to unadorned military power and technology—who has the bomb and who does not.

In the episode "The Red Mass" (4/4), there was a possible reference to such a scenario. The reference was carefully concealed and has been little commented upon, but nonetheless it was perhaps one of the most interesting exchanges in *The West Wing*, at least within such a specific context. In the episode Leo and Sam were discussing a foiled attempt by terrorists to blow up the Golden Gate Bridge. Leo commented: "I don't know what winning looks like. What does it look like? Is it the US flag flying over Mecca? Is that what's going to straighten this out? And if that's the case, why are we postponing that? What are we hoping is going to happen in the meantime?" Sam replied: "That somebody will think of something before we have to do the unthinkable." The scene finished at this point, but "the unthinkable" that Sam would seem to have been referring to may have been a scenario in which the United States made a widespread nuclear strike on the Middle East. The language here was subtle, but the intent and the fear that this might happen was present in the way Sam delivered the line.[20]

* * *

As discussed in Chapter 3, *The West Wing* appeared to exist in a parallel universe, similar to but different to our own, to the extent that some foreign states were grounded in reality, as in Israel or France, while others were imaginary, as in Qumar and Equatorial Kundu. Such a technique had a variable sense of plausibility, to the extent that such a practice sometimes served to lessen the sense of realism within the narrative structures at play. At times this so significantly reduced the drama's ability to offer a valid representation of the world that there was an almost comic book approach. For example, in DC comics Kahndaq and Kasnia were fictitious countries in the Middle East and Eastern Europe, in the Tintin comics Borduria was a mythic totalitarian state in the Balkans, Wonder Woman came from the wholly invented island nation of Themyscira, and so on. While there were understandable reasons for creating fictional characters, to create fictional countries would seem to have been more problematical—especially when the fictional countries were such obvious ciphers for actual nation states. The overall impression—of using such fictional places as a narrative device—was to allow *The West Wing* an uncomplicated way of running storylines similar to real events, while at the same time offering a way of creating happier endings in the idealized world of President Bartlet. Hence, a great terrorist attack—to blow up the Golden Gate Bridge—was averted, while the 9/11 terrorist attacks were not. Similarly, Bartlet's administration was able to prevent the fictional genocide in Kundu, while the Clinton administration, in the real world, had been unable to prevent the actual Rwandan genocide. All of this appeared to add weight to the feel-good political fantasy that was *The West Wing*. In addition, from a postcolonialist perspective, all that resulted was to allow some foreign states—behind their fictitious avatars—to be still further satirized; to be presented in a more exaggerated way as the "other" to America's dominant position in the world.

In summary, a postcolonialist approach to *The West Wing* would seem to confirm the prejudices America has adopted toward the rest of the world, especially the non-Western world. The cultural differences between the Americans in the show and the non–Americans were clearly discernible; such characters were routinely seen as the "other," and they were seldom seen as fully rendered characters in the way American characters were. For example, the Kundu ambassador seemed like a mere cipher with little sense of an interior personality; this was also seen in the soon-to-be-assassinated Abdul ibn Shareef, the Qumari minister of defense. A postcolonialist approach would therefore observe the way in which America was presented in the series as *the* world power, a world power without noticeable flaws. In reality the reputation of America, as actually envisaged by much of the rest of the world—especially the non-Western world—was that of a bully at best; and, at worst, that of a nation state lacking a rational sense of the world.[21] Of course, the America presented in the series was anchored within the idealized world of Bartlet's liberal and well-meaning administration, but whether this was convincing remains open to question. In this way *The West Wing* merely served to disguise the actual reality, to placate the liberal pieties of its audience and to insidiously misrepresent all that opposed the so-called American way. By way of a final observation, two comments by Toby Ziegler, the supposed liberal conscience of *The West Wing*, might serve to display such liberal pieties. First, in the episode "Enemies Foreign and Domestic" (3/19), Toby appeared to adopt a megalomaniacal role, commenting: "If we were able to enforce US law around the world, I'd retire and go scuba-diving." In the episode "Night Five" (3/14), Toby made this simplistic claim: "They'll like us when we win." Toby was talking about the Islamic world and its attitude to America; the line was repeated four times in the episode—aptly expressing the authentic opinion of a character even as tolerant and liberal as Toby. Hence this arguably presented an estimation of the way in which Toby—and the show as a whole—actually viewed the world outside of America.

20

"Education is the silver bullet"
Pedagogy in The West Wing

In the episode "Six Meetings Before Lunch" (1/18), Sam Seaborn spoke lyrically of the importance of education in America. In a conversation with his forever-unrequited love interest Mallory O'Brien, he placed the subject of education within an almost evangelical discourse: "Education is the silver bullet. Education is everything. We don't need little changes. We need gigantic monumental changes. Schools should be palaces. The competition for the best teachers should be fierce. They should be making six-figure salaries. School should be incredibly expensive for government and absolutely free of charge to its citizens." In the episode "Hartsfield's Landing" (3/15), Bartlet repeated this idea, telling Toby that education could be a "silver bullet" for "crime, poverty, unemployment, drugs, hate." The same idea was repeated in the episode "Process Stories" (4/8), when a character called Chris Whittaker, a pollster hired by Bruno Gianelli, repeated the same line to CJ: "I said education is the silver bullet. That's what this election is about." However, in the event, the Bartlet administration never quite succeeded in putting such noble aspirations into practice; and, aside from a few minor plotlines, there seems to have been no attempt to actually aspire to such a noble task, silver bullet or no silver bullet.

Nonetheless, in a different context, the show succeeded in using another kind of silver bullet. In other words, *The West Wing* succeeded in acting as a pedagogical tool in itself; to teach its audience, predominantly its American audience, some of the more subtle aspects of the American political system. This has often been observed in the literature on the show: for Lynn Spigel *The West Wing* was "an earnest attempt to use television as a form of political and historical pedagogy."[1] Trudy L. Hanson argued that a viewing of the show offered "a strong possibility that young people will learn more about the political process."[2] For Julie Levin Russo the show succeeded "educationally" by "offering a realistic, behind-the-scenes peek into the inner workings of government."[3] Michael Dumlao saw the show as "offering a seamless blend of education and entertainment."[4] Kay Richardson argued that a consideration of the show's "contribution to popular culture" was not "via a mass audience, but via an educational one."[5] Other critics argued that the show reached "more Americans than any regularly scheduled news broadcast"[6] and that "for one hour a week, Americans [could] overcome political malaise and feel connected to the presidency in ways that formal journalism [could not] facilitate."[7]

The range of pedagogic material dispensed throughout the seven seasons of the show is too wide and diverse to evaluate in any depth; however, a small sample might suffice to offer a sense of the ubiquity of such aspects of the show. As intimated in Chapter 18, it was often Donna to whom such educational wisdom was bestowed; in other words, it was often Donna who became the blank exposition sheet for Josh to impart didactic material. For example, in the episode "Mr. Willis of Ohio" (1/6), the didactic discourse dwelt upon the importance and the workings of the U.S. census; while in the episode "Bad Moon Rising" (2/19), Josh extolled the Mexican bailout, with Donna once again the willing student. However, whether seven years of pedagogical programming had any actual influence is uncertain; Staci Beavers was one critic to consider this issue, concluding that, as yet, there was "no evidence whether *The West Wing* has had any measurable impact on viewers' political opinions."[8]

Nonetheless, there would seem to be at least some evidence from what might be described as the most extreme example of blatant pedagogy in *The West Wing*, that of the episode "Isaac and Ishmael" (3/1). As discussed in Chapter 8, this was an episode so didactic that the White House mess was literally transformed into a classroom, "a racially and gender-plural space"[9] wherein the main cast members proceeded to teach America a lesson. A number of critics commented on this aspect of the episode, for example, Cory Baker: "*The West Wing* is always didactic, but this episode takes it to new levels."[10] Philip Cass concurred: "The episode's intention is to teach, not entertain."[11] For Rachel Gans-Boriskin and Russ Tisinger the episode was

> an example of the didactic nature of the show run amok ... as he [Sorkin] delivers through the mouths of his characters a lecture on terrorism, Islamic fundamentalism and tolerance.[12]

Lynn Spigel noted how the episode placed viewers

> in the position of high school students—and particularly naïve ones at that. The program [spoke] to viewers as if they were children or, at best, the innocent objects of historical events beyond their control.[13]

For Trevor and Shawn J. Parry-Giles, "the students [were] presented as frightened and anxious, capturing the public anxiety that existed after 9/11."[14] And finally, Jack Holland noted how the episode adopted

> an explicitly pedagogical theme to *teach* viewers how to think about the event of 9/11, to capitalise on the show's cast in their positions as authorised experts, capable of articulating and explaining events which had thus far left America's "brightest and best" baffled ... the episode thus confirms that the role of the public is to listen to those government officials who are "experts" who have the knowledge of, and the capability to respond to terror that they themselves lack.[15]

As such, the children in the episode could be seen as ciphers for an immature American public, a public that required teaching from experts—such experts as found on *The West Wing*.[16]

Bartlet and his "tireless staff of wunderkinds"[17] were highly intelligent, sometimes to the point of having a grating sense of intellectual superiority, with the sense of disdainfully looking down on others who did not possess the same acumen. An apposite example of this could be seen in Toby's bravura conversation with an unnamed and seemingly unintelligent congressman, as featured in the episode "He Shall from Time to Time" (1/12). The congressman was arguing against the need for the N.E.A., commenting "Rogers and Hart didn't need the N.E.A. to write *Oklahoma*, and Arthur Murray didn't need the N.E.A. to write *Death of a Salesman*." Toby was adroit in responding: "I'd start by telling them that Rodgers and Hammerstein wrote *Oklahoma*, and Arthur Murray taught ballroom dance, and Arthur Miller did need the N.E.A. to write *Death of a Salesman*."[18] In a similar way, Robert ("Bingo Bob") Russell, the Colorado congressman who succeeded John Hoynes as vice president, was often ridiculed for lacking the same level of intelligence as the other staff in Bartlet's administration. In the episode "Disaster Relief" (5/6), Russell was derided for seemingly using a nonexistent word, propulgate: "Excuse me, Toby ... the Speaker is trying to propulgate a tax bill onto an appropriations package. We start allowing that, we're never going to get budgets passed." After the meeting, Leo commented: "I'm pretty sure there's no such word as propulgate. Maybe he meant propagate, or promulgate." The word Russell was reaching for was probably "propagate," meaning to cause an increase or to promote an idea; with the word "promulgate" meaning to put something, usually a law, into action. In fact, Russell's composite word has, since its appearance in the show, entered into the *Urban Dictionary*—a "crowdsourced" online dictionary—the meaning given there being as follows:

> To attach something (frequently something unwelcome and done maliciously) to something desirable. Commonly used in politics when an unwelcome amendment is added to a bill.

The derivation of the word, as cited in the *Urban Dictionary*, referenced *The West Wing* as the original usage. Hence, in a circulatory fashion, Russell may have had the last laugh, insomuch as his use of the word—no matter how disparaged—has now become recognized, at least in terms of one dictionary. This was especially relevant as Leo often seemed to have linguistic problems of his own; for example, his inability to pronounce "Eritrea" on one occasion and "antipode" on another. In addition, "Bingo Bob" may not have been quite as "stupid" as Bartlet's staff seem to have believed; in a later episode, "Faith Based Initiative" (6/10), Russell delivered what was arguably one of the show's more amusing lines, saying during a "budget glitch" meeting: "So no one here is troubled that the Paper Reduction Act is more than 500 pages long?"

Although the series often appeared to pride itself on the high level of intellect of its main characters, essentially those in Bartlet's inner circle, there were—at times—slippages in the intellectual quotient such characters possessed. An example of this occurred in the episode "Evidence of Things Not Seen" (4/20); in the episode there was a repeated trope concerning whether an egg could be balanced on its end at the time of the vernal equinox. Much discussion was made of this throughout the episode, with the idea of such an event only being possible at the time of the equinox adding a superstitious quality to it, an idea few if any of the intellectual "wunderkinds" on the staff seriously challenged.[19] CJ persisted with the concept, succeeding, at the end of the episode, in balancing an egg on its end; however, by this time there was no one present to witness such a "miracle"—presumably a reference to the episode's title. Nonetheless, disregarding the supposed level of intelligence of the characters in question, nobody made the simple point that one can balance an egg on its end at any time one wants—the vernal equinox being irrelevant—because this is entirely dependent on the surface on which the egg is balanced—on how it is cushioned. To take an extreme example, one could easily balance an egg on modeling clay. In the closing moments of the episode CJ, appropriately sitting in a room just outside the Oval Office, appeared to balance the egg on the thick green baize of a card table—a not too impossible task, but this was a task that no one concerned appeared to have any understanding of, or at least no one in the assembled cast appeared to express any sense of this idea.

In an earlier episode, "The Fall's Gonna Kill You" (2/20), a similar situation occurred; in the episode Donna, as well as being placed (once again) in the position of providing a landscape for plotline exposition, was also placed (once again) in the position of misconstruing a complicated situation she did not fully understand. In this case, the situation concerned a satellite that was about to fall from the sky and crash to the earth. Donna, unaware that such an event occurred on a regular basis, with little risk of causing actual damage,

20. "Education is the silver bullet"

sought to attempt to avert this impending "disaster." However, neither Donna nor the writers of the episode seem to have been aware of the so-called Kessler Effect, which may have a significant effect in the future. The Kessler Effect was a theory proposed by Donald J. Kessler in 1978, a theory that described the risk of cumulative low-earth orbit collisions resulting in a self-sustaining and cascading collision of space debris. In this scenario, one satellite collides with another, creating more debris until, at an exponential rate, the Earth is surrounded by a cloud of debris—which may eventually preclude the use of satellite technology. Hence Donna's concern for the planet may not—in the long run—have been so misplaced.

In terms of a pedagogic reading, the question as to what degree the series could be said to have participated in the construction of an authentic political discourse, and hence one which could be cited as an authentic educational tool, would seem relevant. There have been a number of attempts in the academic literature on the show to evaluate the accuracy of such a claim,[20] but it remains problematic to be sure of the value of it. There was a sense of verisimilitude within *The West Wing*, but the overarching sense was that the drama—as presented throughout its seven-year run—was simply an antidote to an unpalatable reality. The series began during the last years of Bill Clinton's administration, and prevailed throughout the first years of George W. Bush's administration, but there was a sense that Bartlet's administration was the one the American public may have wanted, or at least the American public of a certain liberal persuasion—in other words, the section of the American public who actually watched the show. In fact, there have been suggestions that the next administration, that of Barack Obama, may have been influenced by *The West Wing*. For example, David Sims observed how the show had "often bled into," or even "influenced, reality," how it was "now old enough [to have] surely inspired some of the younger staffers in the Obama administration to get into politics" and that it was easy to understand why "Obama White House officials are looking backward [to the] hard-charging, lovable do-gooders of *The West Wing*."[21] Clive James made a similar point, noting:

> *The West Wing* reminded the world that America had intellectual capacity behind economic muscle, and surely helped prepare the way for Barack Obama's election.[22]

Hence, although we cannot be wholly sure of *The West Wing* as an authentic pedagogical tool, it would seem fair to suggest that the show may have had at least some influence on future politicians, and thus at least some effect on America and on American politics.

However, there still remains the issue of the idealized discourse at play within the drama. The romanticized ambience presented within the *mise-en-scène* of *The West Wing* was seldom able to admit to the reality of

American politics; in other words, the sense that it was embedded within a corrupt system. It could be argued that an avoidance of such a construct of reality prevented *The West Wing* from looking in any real depth at the social conditions present in American life; in terms of education, for example, there was rarely any serious attempt to consider what was actually going on within the schools of America. If one were to once again compare *The West Wing* to *The Wire*, in *The Wire* an entire season, Season 4, was devoted to the state of the education system in America, while in *The West Wing* there were rarely any actual schoolroom scenes. There was the visit of Mallory's class to the White House, and there were brief scenes of the Santos family looking for schools in Washington, D.C., but this aside—whatever the declaratory rhetoric of the silver bullet—education was not an issue, or at least not a direct issue in terms of the schoolroom environment. It may seem a cynical point-of-view, but *The West Wing* would appear to have had the naive and even credulous sense that there *were* noble causes, that it was possible to solve the problems inherent within American society—in this case, the education of its children. In reality education was merely a part of a corrupt system, wherein such problems may be insolvable. From a skeptical and pragmatic point-of-view one might conclude that there were no noble causes, all institutions were inherently corrupt, and that there was no way to resolve such a society—a point-of-view the dramatic discourse of the show would obviously disavow.

By way of summing up the argument: *The West Wing* succeeded—albeit in only a partial way—in putting forward the importance of education; it also succeeded—once again to a limited extent—in acting as a pedagogical tool to inform its viewers as to specific elements of American political institutions. According to Aaron Sorkin, this latter issue was not the deliberate intent of the program makers:

> We're all very flattered when we hear that the show illuminates certain things. We hear it from high school history and social studies teachers ... but that's not our goal.... We are storytellers first and last. If we do something else, well then, that just speaks to the power of storytelling.[23]

This may have been Sorkin's official stance; however, the evidence from numerous examples on the show would seem to belie this claim. The primary aim of the show was that of telling a good story, but it would seem clearly apparent that there was a conscious aim of "illuminating certain things," as Sorkin put it; in other words, there was a direct didactic intent consistently present throughout the series. This would seem to have been confirmed at various instances via deliberately imparted self-referential contexts. For example, in the episode "Manchester Part 2" (3/3), Doug Wegland, one of Bruno Gianelli's campaign assistants, told Toby: "You couldn't stop educating the public. You guys are never happier than when you're educating the public!" In the narrative context of the episode, the remark concerned a way of educating the American public that multiple sclerosis was not a fatal disease; however, the remark also pointed to the much wider sense in which the program itself was never happier than when *it* was educating the public. This was most probably a deliberate intent; in other words, Aaron Sorkin, the writer of the episode, was most probably implying a conscious, self-referential connotation to the line.

Finally, in terms of the drama putting education itself at the forefront of the political debate, here it was more difficult to make such a decisive claim. As with so many other issues, *The West Wing* simply did not have the means or the scope to demonstrate how it might have enacted its political agenda. As Pete Davis put it:

> The Bartlet Administration had few bold ideas. What was the Bartlet plan to ensure universal access to healthcare? Or the Bartlet plan to combat global warming? What did President Bartlet do to close the education gap between poor and rich children? Or to ensure that every child who succeeds in high school will be able to pay for college?[24]

A silver bullet, in the mythology of the horror genre, was a way of killing a werewolf or another similar supernatural being; as such it has come to allude to a way of cutting through the complexities of a problem and offering a solution. Often, *The West Wing* appeared to invent a magic wand to solve many of its problems, and here—in the case of education—it seemed to do just this, which was perhaps, in a final consideration, as realistic as the idea of slaying a supernatural being with a silver bullet.

21

A Valentine to Washington
Narrative Authenticity

The question of how believable, how authentic, how plausible were the stories being told in *The West Wing*, would seem to have some relevance within a critical and analytical discussion of the show. Aaron Sorkin may have claimed that he—together with the other writers on the series—were "storytellers first and last," but the question that then arises was just how credible were the stories being told. It is certainly true that there was a clear sense of surface verisimilitude to the show; perhaps incurred, in part at least, by the sense of routine the series was able to instill over its 155 episodes. This was partly achieved by the show's high production values: by the way it was filmed, by the convincing sets and by the quality of the acting. However, good as this may have been, there was still a sense that the show never quite appeared to wholly convince; as Peter de Jonge put it, *The West Wing* presented a "kinder, gentler, nobler White House" but possessed a sense of reality that seemed only "tantalizingly possible."[1]

The authenticity of the staff in Bartlet's administration would perhaps be a good place to begin a discussion of the narrative authenticity of the show. The first observation to make is that there seldom appeared to be any internal rivalry among staff members.[2] The only exception would seem to have been Vice President Hoynes; other than this everyone seemed to "get on," as John Podhoretz put it:

> There are no staff conflicts of any consequence in Sorkin's *West Wing*, no turf battles between these White House aides. They love each other, admire each other, and support each other ... [these] characters have come to save America and the world.[3]

Pamela Ezell made a similar point:

> Where was the self-interested jockeying for position, the rivalry between the young ambitious heirs apparent ... in Sorkin's vision of the White House, staff members are

selfless; their dedication to their own achievement is second to their commitment to a common cause.[4]

It is generally recognized that solipsism—the idea that only the self exists—is the default human condition; in other words, egotistical feelings, self-indulgence, and narcissism let free on a universal scale represent the underlying human pattern of behavior. In the real world of politics this was often played out; that is, real-life administrations found staff members indulging in a variety of duplicitous acts against each other. To put it mildly, this was not played out in *The West Wing*. Instead, these were noble individuals involved in acting out great and noble quests, as a number of critics have commented:

> These characters aren't human beings—they're noble soldiers in a noble cause, and they have been washed clean of every impurity because of it.[5]
> Bartlet and his cadre of loyal idealistic aides ... are noble: they serve with the zeal of missionaries.[6]
> [These are] heroic figures pursuing a noble quest for that which is right and just.[7]
> *The West Wing* presents a glorified and overly noble version of the life and work of the White House staff.[8]

These were clearly noble individuals—but there was more. Other critics noted the sense of "duty" the staff possessed; for example, Nathan A. Paxton argued that "duty motivates and rewards the people in the universe of *The West Wing* ... the call to duty occurs suddenly, often out of the blue ... it presents a moment of choice, between acceptable self-interest and sanctified service to others."[9] Janet McCabe commented upon the "duty and loyalty" of the staff, and how they were "honorable individuals fighting for higher principles, and a magic beauty."[10] In an overall sense it would seem clear, from the general consensus of critical responses, that the depiction of Bartlet's staff was almost "too good to be true." The members of Bartlet's staff were too idealistic, too ready to devote themselves to public service[11]; and, with their "Talmudic sense of right and wrong"[12] they appeared to have used "the Declaration of Independence as a credo and the Constitution as a sacred text."[13] These were articulate and heroic individuals intent on extolling the virtues of big government, they were "imbued with integrity, intelligence, and dedication" and they had "taken it upon themselves to make the United States and the world a better place."[14]

In addition to this, there was also the way in which the show appeared to fall victim to "the fallacy of personality-driven politics."[15] In other words, there was an overly developed concentration on Bartlet's immediate staff. For example, such crucial figures as the attorney general, or the secretary of state, or any other members of the cabinet, were seldom seen; instead the small coterie of Bartlet's staff was the main focal point of the drama. Perhaps even more implausible was the fact that nearly all of Bartlet's staff remained in their posts for the majority of the eight years of the presidency. Other than Mrs.

Landingham, who died at the end of Season 2, the only real exceptions were Sam and Leo, and in both cases the reason for leaving concerned real world events, rather than events within the fictional world of *The West Wing*.[16] In defense of such criticism, it might be noted that there was a need for dramatic economy and simplicity. It may have been difficult for the audience to identify, and even to remember, the multiplicity of characters that existed in a real-life administration; the reduction of characters to a few main players most likely enabled the narrative of the show to be more clearly understood.

* * *

In a wider perspective, the narrative authenticity of the show, in itself, was often questionable. *The West Wing* concerned itself with real issues; however, as intimated in previous chapters, the show simply did not have the means to fully interrogate the issues it raised. As Melissa Crawley put it, "Issues [were] debated but rarely resolved."[17] Similarly, Rachel Gans-Boriskin and Russ Tisinger commented: "*The West Wing* simultaneously asks difficult questions and supplies overly easy answers."[18] Likewise, Spencer Downing noted: "*The West Wing* never portrayed what might actually happen in a country led by an ideal president. One never saw the results of effective gun control legislation, better school funding, or more progressive taxation."[19] In addition, Nathan A. Paxton commented on how "the promise of programs and agendas that seem too good to be true are probably exactly that—too good to be true."[20] Finally, Yair Rosenberg argued:

> In Sorkin's fictional universe, a towering presidential figure—Josiah Bartlet—is able to tackle international and domestic crises through a mix of political dexterity and rhetorical finesse. There are few impasses an eloquent appeal cannot solve, and almost no foreign-policy conundrum for which a clever solution cannot be conceived.[21]

The West Wing appeared to build its fictional universe in a convincing way, episode-by-episode, season by season; however, this was only an illusion. In reality, a majority of those issues under discussion did not have to be accommodated within the universe in which they were created. The episodic structure of the series, with its narrative ellipsis between episodes, may appear to have allowed an authentic world; however, in a diverse range of instances the show simply sidestepped the consequence of real issues; the fade to black at the end of each episode was often just this—and we seldom fully achieved an awareness of the outcome of the particular plotline in question.

Hence, there were a significant number of episodes that—on closer examination—did not make complete logical sense. Thus, *The West Wing* seemed to succeed in having it both ways—repeatedly putting forward idealized solutions that would not work in practice. This was a situation that recurred numerous times in the series, often rendering almost risible narratives instead of realistic representations of American political life. Such dilemmas, such moral complexities were seemingly resolved—but seldom followed up. This has frequently been noted in the literature on the show; for example, Michelle Mouton commented that *The West Wing* raised "important issues but did not follow through satisfactorily."[22] Donnalyn Pompper noted that "debates are left fundamentally unresolved, giving audiences a sense of debates in progress."[23] Trevor and Shawn J. Parry-Giles argued that in the show, "disorder represents an integral theme rather than a plot device to be resolved quickly at the end of each hour's episode."[24]

There was therefore the overarching idea that *The West Wing* achieved the appearance of narrative progression by repeatedly failing to resolve narrative predicaments—via the simple strategy of proceeding to other plotlines. There were too many such inconclusive narrative patterns to detail in full; but the following examples might be offered. In "The State Dinner" (1/7), Bartlet seemed to succeed in achieving a deal with the Teamsters Union by threatening to nationalize the trucking industry and to draft the truckers into the military; this seemed an implausible threat, but it seemed to be taken seriously. In the episode "Shibboleth," (2/8), Bartlet apparently solved the problem of what to do with a boat containing several hundred persecuted Chinese Christians by requesting the governor to have the National Guard "look the other way," but here the episode reached a closure—with no attempt at an explanation of how this would happen.[25] In "The Women of Qumar" (3/9), during a plotline concerning so-called Mad Cow Disease (Bovine Spongiform Encephalopathy), Bartlet speculated: "We lose $3.6 billion in beef exports, fast food is deserted, supermarkets pull beef"—however, Mad Cow Disease was never heard of again. In Season 4, the Kundu crisis occurred, Bartlet ordered American troops to avert the genocide taking place, but the storyline was not returned to—the issue was not resolved. In Season 5, the budget crisis seems to have been solved via Bartlet's walk to Congress, which seemed to procure a fairytale-like ending that was never quite explained.[26] In Season 6, Bartlet and his staff appeared to solve the Israeli-Palestinian conflict—as well as later appearing to solve the North Korean nuclear capability issue—not to mention making attempts to improve relationships with Cuba—all of which were never fully explained. Finally, in Season 7, in the penultimate episode of the show, "Institutional Memory" (7/21), a character called Frank Hollis, a Bill Gates simulacrum, appeared to offer CJ a job, a job that was nothing less than a blank check for $10 billion, to enable C.J. to save the world—or at least to solve some of its problems.

Perhaps the most unconvincing plot element in *The West Wing* came in Season 4, with Bartlet's successful campaign against Governor Robert Richie to win a second term as president. The season was originally broadcast in 2002, just two years after George W. Bush's "victory" over Al Gore in the 2000 election. As intimated previously, in Chapter 1, this plotline might be interpreted as sheer wishful thinking; a way of defeating Bush within a fictional discourse—the way it should have been, not the way it was.²⁷ As such, it seemed a somewhat shallow and transparent exercise, mere self-congratulatory hyperbole, and hardly a credible plotline. In addition, there was the lack of any dramatic tension. Of course, the writers of the show were in a difficult position; everybody was cognizant that the season had another fifteen episodes to run, so how could Bartlet lose? As Matthew David Barber put it: "NBC isn't going to fire the entire cast in midseason and start over. This victory's a done deal."²⁸ It has been said that some staff writers, together with members of the cast, wanted Bartlet's second-term election to be closer.²⁹ However, this was not to be, and it was accepted that this aspect of the narrative would lack dramatic tension. As Aaron Sorkin commented: "Since the audience already knew who was going to win, we were going to have to dramatize something else."³⁰ But what this "something else" might have been was not made entirely clear. As such, this part of the drama was arguably as false as the oft-repeated idea, in the episode "Game On" (4/6), that Governor Richie was planning to use a simple ten-word response that—in its simplicity—would derail the more erudite Bartlet in the television debate. The "ten-word" response turned out to be: "The American people know how to spend their money better than the federal government." However, this supposed "ten-word" phrase was actually fourteen words in length. Whether this was deliberate or an oversight is uncertain—but it was arguably as false as the storyline of Bartlet's second presidential election.

In the episode "Shutdown" (5/8), Abbey had said to Bartlet: "Don't be so melodramatic"—this was apt advice, as many of the storylines of the drama, at times at least, threatened to descend into transparent melodrama. For example, the episode "The Long Goodbye" (4/13) might well have been part of an up-market soap-opera. It had little relevance to the overarching plotting of the show; at best it was a narrative *cul-de-sac*, with no bearing of any discernible kind on the political events taking place in the White House.³¹ Similarly, in the episode "Third Day Story" (6/3), while the political narrative of an Israeli-Palestinian peace deal was proceeding in the background, the episode moved toward more of a soap-opera mode than that of a political discourse: Leo's heart attack, Bartlet's guilt, Donna in a wheelchair and so on. Audun Engelstad was resourceful in commenting on this facet of the show, observing that "melodrama [was], no doubt, the dominating mode of popular television shows"—going on to argue "melodramatic narrative structures were dominant throughout the series."³² Melodrama might be defined as a type of drama that highlights suspense and romantic sentiment, with characters who are either good or bad.³³ Within such a context one could argue that *The West Wing* fell within such a category; and furthermore, in a wider sense, melodrama might be said (as Engelstad argued) to have defined the dramatic character of the series as a whole.

21. A Valentine to Washington

Alfred Hitchcock once noted that drama was life with the dull parts taken out; Aristotle suggested we enjoy literature because it was an "imitation of life," because life's rhythms could be relived, but wherein there was always a twist, "the biter bitten," "the tables turned" and so forth; while Terry Eagleton observed that something must be absent from any narrative—if everything was in place there would be no story to tell. In looking toward a summary on the topic of narrative authenticity within *The West Wing*, it would seem that all of these factors were in play. However, the consistently contrived plotting, found throughout all seven seasons of the show, played out another dictum about cultural narratives: that there was a difference between truth and fiction—fiction had to make sense. Perhaps one of the failings of *The West Wing* was that it held so closely to this latter idea. In other words, there were seldom any real surprises in the drama, as there were, for example, in such contemporary television dramas as *The Wire* and *The Sopranos*. As noted in Chapter 15, one might think of the capricious death of Omar in Season 5 of *The Wire*, or the wholly unsettling closing moments of the final episode of *The Sopranos*. In *The West Wing* there was seldom any sense of such jeopardy; the narrative held to a much more assured discourse. We knew Bartlet would survive the assassination attempt and we knew Zoey would be rescued from her kidnappers,[34] just as we knew Bartlet would win his re-election campaign—and so on throughout other examples within the narrative of the show.

In the episode "In the Shadow of Two Gunmen Part 1" (2/1), Leo said to Bartlet: "They say a good man can't get elected president. I don't believe that, do you?" Within the idealistic discourse of the series Leo and Bartlet may have believed a good man could be elected president; however, from all the evidence available, it would seem they were wrong. As Lesley Gayle, the founder of one of the first fan websites dedicated to the show, put it: "I'm not sure of course, but I doubt that such an honest and truly caring person would make it that far in politics."[35] It has been said that *The West Wing* offered "an idealization of the American system, not a critique of it"[36]—yet it would seem many people loved *The West Wing* because of its idealism. In reality, and albeit from a cynical perspective, the only thing such an audience received was a "Pollyanna fantasy," a fantasy of a Democratic president who "never abandon[ed] his principles."[37] This was *Mr. Smith Goes to Washington* revisited with some relish, "a Capra-like White House populated by people who serve[d] with [the] zeal of missionaries, the kindness of camp counselors, and the ethical fiber of Sunday School teachers."[38] In a final consideration, Sorkin may have claimed that *The West Wing* was a valentine to Washington, but—as noted in the introduction of this study—valentines are often unacknowledged, often unrequited and (perhaps most significantly) often unwanted. Hence a cynical appraisal of the show might find it about as credible as the average message found within the average valentine card.

22

"Your father was a prick"
Psychoanalytical Readings

As discussed in Chapter 7, the above phrase, "your father was a prick"—uttered with such aplomb by Mrs. Landingham in the episode "Two Cathedrals" (2/22)—was arguably the most explicit use of language in all seven seasons of *The West Wing*. However, in addition to the "shocking" quality of such an epithet, such a phrase might also be seen as acting as an apposite way to introduce a psychoanalytical reading to the drama. At a mundane level, this surprisingly vulgar expletive could be read at a reductive and literal level of signification; in other words, to simply confirm the generative abilities of the father to produce offspring. In such a context it was ironic that it was Lawrence O'Donnell who played the role of Bartlet's father, as O'Donnell, as one of the writers of the show, was also metaphorically a father, a creator, to Bartlet's character. In addition to this, and again as briefly referenced in Chapter 7, the curt epithet could also be seen as alluding to the idea that Bartlet's father possessed the "ultimate signifier"; in Jacques Lacan's psychoanalytical concept of the "Name of the Father" (*nom du père*), the idea was that the phallus was the ultimate signifier, an idea that will be discussed, in greater depth, later in this chapter.

Psychoanalytical theory investigates the interaction of the conscious and unconscious elements of the mind. All of Sigmund Freud's work depends on the notion that there is a part of the mind that is beyond the conscious, but which—nonetheless—has a profound influence on our lives and our actions. The classic method of exploring the unconscious mind would be by entering analysis; by talking with a psychoanalyst several times a week, talking without inhibition, and talking in such a way that repressed fears could be uncovered, instead of buried in the unconscious. In a parallel way, this is what cultural critics do when they interrogate texts from the point-of-view of a psychoanalytical perspective. The reason Freud's methods have been of such interest to cultural critics is that they seek the unconscious of the play, novel,

22. "Your father was a prick" 183

song, poem—or television drama—in the same way as the analyst seeks the unconscious of his or her patient. Thus, a psychoanalytical interpretation would always look toward the unconscious elements of the cultural text; the silences or absences, elements that are prevented from entering the dominant ideological discourse—such gaps and slippages betraying a diverse range of repressive forces. The text cannot speak directly, but can do so via symbol and metaphor; and, in the case of *The West Wing*, an analysis of the silences within its discourse can look toward revealing a diverse range of relevant issues—as will be considered in this chapter.

Freudian theories of psychoanalysis might be said to have one advantage, insomuch as psychoanalysis would appear to be one of the few aspects of cultural theory to have found its way into the discourse of ordinary life; in Terry Eagleton's words it has "seep[ed] down to street level."[1] It is certainly true to say that Freud has had a significant influence on Western thought and philosophy. It has been suggested that in the same way as Nicolaus Copernicus demonstrated the world was not the center of the universe, and Charles Darwin demonstrated man was not the center of the animal kingdom, so Freud "demonstrated that the conscious mind was not [the] master of its own house."[2] As Marjorie Garber put it:

> Freud is the intellectual forerunner of most modern and postmodern speculations on sexuality and bisexuality. Popularized, quoted out of context, dehistoricized, and rewritten by followers often less brilliant and more dogmatic than he, Freud ... has become a cultural monolith.[3]

It is certainly true to say that Freud is open to ridicule and vulnerable to skeptical criticism; if taken out of context some of Freud's ideas could be perceived as being almost risible. Yet Freud put forward an explanation of human behavior that arguably convinces more than any other school of thought. It has to be accepted that there is little hard evidence for many of Freud's claims; however, supported by evidence or not, many Freudian ideas have come to have a language, a narrative, and a rationalization that has found resonance in society. In a sense the tenets of psychoanalysis have become "true" insomuch as they have become so ingrained in the public consciousness that they appear to be true.[4]

Freud's influence on our ideas of sexuality, as Marjorie Garber argues, should not be underestimated. Freud famously defined human beings as being polymorphously perverse; in other words, Freud argued that the sexual instinct was heterogeneous, that it sought pleasure wherever it could find. Furthermore, Freud contended that much sexual activity mirrors infantile desires, that sex was infantile in origin if not in actuality, based on the mouth, the anus and the genitals. In this sense it was Freud's view that adult sexuality was always the result of repression of the early events in infancy, only coming under the control of the reproductive function during adulthood. Hence, to cite one example, infantile sexuality could be seen in the desire to suck, given that such activity was primitive and irrational and only explicable when seen as echoing infantile pleasure. In such a context Freud did not consider the heterosexual-homosexual argument of any real importance, with Freud seeing sexuality on a much wider basis, within a polymorphous context outside the scope of so-called conventional sexuality.

In more general terms, Freudian thought argued that the mind is incohesive, habitually duplicitous, always balanced between maturity and childishness, self-deluding, unable to understand itself, and hence endlessly caught between the base instinct of seeking pleasure and the attempt to adopt rational and socially sanctioned behavior. As Terry Eagleton put it, Freud suggests "that we never grow up anyway, and that maturity is a fantasy entertained only by the young."[5] A significant causal factor why the human mind seems so incohesive, why it seems continually balanced between maturity and childishness, was—of course—dependent upon Freud's insistence that we witness the unconscious at all levels of our existence. In other words, we are consciously aware of only a fraction of the ways in which we inhabit ourselves. Freud's theory of the unconscious was an innovation; if such a radical concept was accepted then there seemed at least the possibility of approaching an understanding to the human condition. In this way Freud has influenced significant aspects of current theory. Freud remains one of the most influential thinkers on philosophy and critical theory; he remains influential in terms of the way we interpret the human mind and the origins of mental illness, along with the unconscious influence of sexuality on psychic development.

Of all of Freud's followers, Jacques Lacan arguably proved to be the most significant—at least in terms of the application of psychoanalysis to critical theory. Lacan's work brought Freudian analysis into a linguistic arena of debate; it was Lacan who first argued that language was imprecise in terms of its meaning, consistently saying either more—or less—than what the speaker intended.[6] In such a way Lacanian psychoanalysis deconstructed the idea of the subject as a stable amalgam of consciousness. Instead Lacanian thought argued that the subject was a mere assemblage of signifiers clustering around a proper name.[7] In addition, Lacan suggested how it was inherently futile to attempt to cure human neurosis, since being neurotic, in a certain way at least, defined what it meant to be human. Lacan argued that we, as human subjects, constantly feel a sense of lack, a sense of a loss that can never be replaced—and that this can only be overcome fleetingly, at the moment of sexual union and orgasm. We spend our lives within the symbolic arena, in an endless process of deferred desire, moving from one signifier to another in a hopeless search for wholeness. As such, to exist as a human subject is to lack something; a concept that, when applied to the narrative discourses present within *The West Wing*, might be seen as going some way in explaining some of the ambiguities found within the text.

Perhaps one of Lacan's most significant concepts was that of the mirror stage. The mirror stage occurs when the young child gains an illusory sense of control over the world; the child identifies with its own image, as seen in the mirror, the "I" who watches and the "I" who is watched. The child realizes it can control the image but is not able to express the complexity of the relationship between the two concepts. It is only when the child leaves the "imaginary" world and enters the "symbolic" world of language that this becomes possible. The symbolic order constantly offers the promise of recapturing the sense of wholeness experienced within the imaginary—but this is illusory; just as the "I" in the mirror can never attain unity with the "I" who is watching, we can never fuse these concepts—instead all we possess is an endless and fruitless search to recapture what cannot be recaptured. Lacan was not referenced in the show, and seldom alluded to in the literature on the show[8]; however, Lacanian and Freudian concepts could be seen as acting throughout the series. In fact, psychoanalytical concepts could be seen from the very beginning, from the opening episode of the series. In "Pilot" (1/1), Bartlet was said to have sprained his ankle—and appeared walking with the aid of a cane. Hence here was the leader of the free world making his first entrance, but presented as a wounded and lamed king. This had obvious Oedipal allusions, insomuch as the literal meaning of Oedipus might be translated as "swollen foot." Such a portrayal seemed significant insomuch as Bartlet was also shown limping and walking with a cane in the last episode of the series, "Tomorrow" (7/22), as if completing a circle of sorts.[9]

In terms of the presence of Oedipal relationships in the drama, it was perhaps significant to note the way in which Bartlet consistently acted as a kind of symbolic father to his staff, and the way in which Bartlet adopted the role of metaphorical father to his surrogate family. A number of critics noticed this facet of the show; for example, Melissa Crawley commented:

> Through a narrative that consistently frames Bartlet as the patriarch of his family, his staff and his country, Sorkin encourages the viewer to connect the presidency to the language and imagery of fatherhood.[10]

Crawley's comment was apposite, for, as noted in Chapter 13, there seemed to be a significant lack of settled marital relationships in the show; in other words, it seemed as if most of the main characters lacked any familial lives of their own. Hence, as Crawley went on to note: "The lack of scenes depicting the characters' actual homes creates the impression of the White House as their literal home."[11] This could be seen, for example, in the episode "The Crackpots and These Women" (1/5), wherein Bartlet prepared a chili supper for his staff—in his own home, the White House. Here Bartlet acted out the role of the patriarchal figure, seated at the head of the table overseeing his "family." Another example occurred when Josh Lyman was shot in the assassination attempt at the end of Season 1, with Bartlet referring to Josh on several occasions as "my son." It might also be noted that Charlie, the president's "body man," also acted as a kind of surrogate son. In the episode "Shibboleth" (2/8), Bartlet presented Charlie with a carving knife (replete with the signature of its maker, Paul Revere), an instrument of power and authority, passed down from generation to generation—from father to son. It would not seem necessary to state the Freudian implications of such a bestowal, and, in Lacanian terms, the symbolic signifier was clearly present in terms of the language and imagery of fatherhood.[12]

In a psychoanalytical reading, Bartlet's relationship to his own father was also of significance. What was subtle and carefully nuanced was the fact that Bartlet's mother, although seemingly still alive within the timeline of the series, was barely a presence within the narrative.[13] Instead, the surrogate mother was Mrs. Landingham; this was shown throughout the first two seasons of the show in a number of episodes, but perhaps to greatest effect in the flashback sequences in "Two Cathedrals" (2/22). Here the young Bartlet—then a schoolboy—first meets the younger Dolores Landingham, who tells him, "What is it you're afraid of? Look at you. You're a Boy King." In a psychoanalytical reading this line was significant, as it allowed for a more persuasive and believable enactment of the Oedipal crisis. The young schoolboy Bartlet unconsciously desires the mother's body, and the mother substitute here—played to telling erotic effect by Kirsten Nelson—was therefore easier to accept as a repressed love object. In Freudian terms, when an individual is severed from the mother's body—at the time of the Oedipal crisis—that individual will unconsciously spend the rest of his life searching for something of which he has little conscious awareness: the original lost love object—the mother's body. In a universal sense, this is a quest that engenders the impetus of our narratives and our lives, pushing us on to pursue substitutes for this lost state. From a psychoanalytical perspective we spend the rest of our lives attempting to recover this "blissful state," sexual love being a mere proxy, a mere substitute.[14]

If Mrs. Landingham was the surrogate mother, for whom Bartlet had unconscious erotic desires, then Bartlet was also the "Boy King" who unconsciously wanted to kill his father, or at the very least wanted to defeat his father. There was a sense, throughout the series, that Bartlet was continually attempting to resolve his relationship with his abusive father. This was confirmed by his therapist, Stanley Keyworth, in the following exchange from the episode "Night Five" (3/14). Bartlet said: "I'm not trying to get my father to like me." Keyworth responded: "Good, because it's never, never going to happen." It was clear that Bartlet's childhood experiences with his father had

had a significant effect on his adult life; for example, Bartlet commented to his personal physician, Morris Tolliver: "I'm an accomplished man, Morris. I can sit comfortably with prime ministers and presidents, even the pope. Why is it every time I sit with the Joint Chiefs, I feel like I'm back at my father's dinner table?"[15] As such, it was clear that Bartlet was obsessed with his father and the physical and emotional abuse he had suffered at his father's hands. In the episode "Two Cathedrals" (2/22), Bartlet famously castigated God, his ultimate father, calling him a "feckless thug." However, in a sense it was also possible to read this line as a reference to Bartlet's actual father, the father who had abused him as a child, toward whom he still felt a bitter resentment.

In the ironically entitled episode "The Two Bartlets" (3/13), Toby appeared to go some way in psychoanalyzing Bartlet in terms of his relationship with his father. Toby began by noting there had always been a concern about the two Bartlets: "The absent-minded professor with the 'Aw, Dad' sense of humor, disarming and unthreatening—and the Nobel Laureate, still searching for salvation." Bartlet sarcastically dismissed this: "You're gonna sing a country western song?" Toby responded in kind: "The one whose father never liked him because he was too smart?" Bartlet commented the conversation was no longer any fun for him; but Toby reached further: "Your father used to hit you, didn't he, Mr. President.… Your father used to hit you … not like a spanking.… He punched you." Exasperated, Bartlet attempted to explain: "It was a complicated relationship.… Why are we talking about this?" Toby then completed his psychoanalytical questioning: "So maybe if you get enough votes, win one more election, maybe your father will…" But Bartlet had had enough: "You have stepped way over the line, and any other President would have your ass on the sidewalk right now. I don't know what the hell goes on in a Brooklyn shrink's office, but get the hell out of my house!" At this Toby politely thanked the president and withdrew.[16] It was perhaps one of the most heated and dramatic exchanges in the entire run of the series; one of the few instances wherein Bartlet was confronted with an accurate analysis of his character: "the abused child whose longing for his parent's approval [had] followed him into adulthood."[17] So affronted was Bartlet that he resorted to threats of dismissal, replete with anally abusive insults and anti–Semitic slurs.[18]

It is clear that Toby's analysis of Bartlet was both perceptive and accurate; as intimated above, the flashback scene in "Two Cathedrals" (2/22) made it clear that Bartlet loved his mother and hated his father. Hence Mrs. Landingham's atypical use of profanity was also correct: "Mr. President, your father was a prick." Bartlet's father was a "prick" in a literal sense insomuch as he possessed the ultimate signifier to sire his son, but within the vulgar metaphor he was also a bullying persecutor of his son. In "Hartfield's Landing" (3/15), Bartlet attempted to defend the "prickishness" of his father: "Can we please talk about my father with some respect; the man's gone, he's my father, he wasn't a Dickens character." As far as can be ascertained no one had suggested Bartlet's father was a Dickens character; and Freud would no doubt have observed a slippage in Bartlet's comment. In other words, his father was a prick and a dick(ens)—at least in the Freudian slip Bartlet appeared to make. It would seem clear that rid of inhibition, his ego and his superego, Bartlet's id would have liked nothing better—would have relished the opportunity—to metaphorically slay his father.[19]

* * *

In terms of Lacanian theory, the episode "The Fall's Gonna Kill You" (2/20) was of interest. In the episode—during another flashback sequence—Leo wrote Bartlet's name on a napkin: "Bartlet for America." It was the start of Bartlet's run for the presidency; however, over the passage of time the ink would seem to have become diffuse, to have dissolved into the tissue-like paper upon which it was written. It was as if Bartlet, as a man in possession of the ultimate signifier, was not quite in control of "the word."[20] In fact, the character most often in control of "the word" was a woman, CJ Cregg. Here CJ, in her role as press secretary to the president, was seemingly in control of the word—at least in terms of being Bartlet's conduit to the media, and hence to the outside world. Yet, for strategic reasons, CJ was often left uninformed of what was actually going on, to prevent her from having to directly deceive the press. Hence CJ did not always control "the word"—it was the men around her who ultimately controlled language. Another obvious Lacanian reference could be seen in the episode "Ellie" (2/15). In the episode, Bartlet told his daughter, Ellie, "It is the law." The reference was to a remark the Surgeon General had made about the use of cannabis; however, it could also have been read as a reference to Lacan's concept of the "Name of the Father": the symbolic father, the ultimate father in possession of the ultimate signifier, who ruled the symbolic order and governed the taboo on incest within the Oedipus complex.[21]

* * *

Elsewhere in the drama, a psychoanalytical reading revealed further, if somewhat obvious, symbolic references; for example, the establishing shots of Washington, D.C. often included the Washington monument—an overtly Freudian symbol of virility and power.[22] In a similar context, CJ's attraction to her bodyguard, Simon Donovan, was intensified when CJ witnessed his prowess on the firing range; CJ was not able to control the recoil of the handgun, while Donovan scored multiple hits on the target—this having obvious, if somewhat artless, Freudian references. In a more comedic setting, played out in a scene from the episode "Take Out the Trash Day" (1/13), Mrs. Landingham, as Bartlet's surrogate mother, seemed to first offer and then refuse what seemed to be a deliberate Freudian symbol: "Good morning Mr. President. Did you say you wanted a banana.... Nancy, run get the President a banana." But Bartlet demurred: "I really don't want a banana." "They've got lots of potassium," Mrs. Landingham told the president, but he was "done talking." However, later in the episode, Bartlet changed his mind: "Mrs. Landingham, you're not going to believe this but I think I'd actually like a banana." But the prize was withheld: "I'm afraid not sir. You were offered one earlier, sir, and you were snippy." In the context of a psychoanalytical reading, it was apparent that there were comic Freudian indicators at play in this scene.

At other times there were signs that Bartlet had an almost child-like reliance on Mrs. Landingham. For example, in the episode "A Proportional Response" (1/3), he asked for her help: "Mrs. Landingham, I can't seem to find my glasses anywhere. Can you please do whatever it is you do when I can't find my glasses?" This was repeated elsewhere in the drama, as in the episode "Shibboleth" (2/8) wherein Bartlet came out of the Oval Office to ask Mrs. Landingham for a copy of the Thanksgiving proclamation: "Sir, why don't you use the intercom ... you don't know how to use the intercom.... Maybe after the ceremony, you could get one of the fourth-graders to come in and show you how to use the intercom." At times Mrs. Landingham's concern for the president took on a further level of maternal concern, as in the episode "Let Bartlet be Bartlet" (1/19), where there was some anxiety about the president's diet: "You're not getting enough roughage ... you know I'm right about that." In other instances, the incest taboo appeared to be threatened, as in the sense of familiarity and even intimacy in the episode "He Shall, From Time to Time" (1/12). Bartlet asked Mrs. Landingham, "How do I look to you?" Mrs. Landingham responded: "You're a very handsome man, Mr. President."

In an overall sense, the application of a psychoanalytical reading of *The West Wing* might be seen to go some way in explaining some issues arising in a discussion of the series. A brief reading of some of the most obvious issues have been offered in this chapter, but one might also think, by way of a final example, of the way in which Bartlet's staff appeared to be imbued with a dedication toward the presidency, toward Bartlet and ultimately toward the "American Way." This might be explained by Freud's term "cathexis," cathexis being the process of investment of mental or emotional energy in a person, object or idea. Often this was a process of sublimation, in which a repressed emotion was promoted into something more noble; for example, the way sexual urges are sublimated and given expression in the form of intense religious experience.[23] Finally, and at a more profound level of discussion, Bartlet's staff's behavior could be explained using Jacques Lacan's concept that we can only enter the world as human subjects via the symbolic order of language;

that we can only position ourselves within language by adopting a "sexed" identity, wherein the phallus (or lack of it) becomes the privileged signifier of sovereign power.[24] Both of these concepts, in psychoanalytical terms, could be seen as illuminating some of the motivations possessed by the various protagonists within the series.

23

Unearned Emotion and the "Plaintive Oboe"
W.G. Snuffy Walden's Music to The West Wing

Perhaps one significant weakness of *The West Wing*, or at least the one aspect in which the show failed to excel, was the musical soundtrack by W.G. Snuffy Walden. The soundtrack, as composed by Walden, consistently failed to move far beyond the conventional television drama—and, in most other respects, *The West Wing* was certainly far beyond the range of the average television drama. Walden's music was standard fare, continually returning to the predictable and the routine. It has to be admitted that Walden was, and is, an accomplished and prolific writer of music for an impressive number of television series, including *thirtysomething, The Wonder Years, Rosanne*—and many others.[1] Yet there remains the sense that there was an error made, a chance missed; the decision to use Walden's skills as a composer arguably excluded the opportunity for the show to succeed and to express itself to a still greater extent. However, this was not to be; it is said that Walden originally "got a call from Aaron Sorkin to do *Sports Night*"[2]—apparently Sorkin approached Walden because "he loved *thirtysomething*."[3] Walden provided the music for both seasons of *Sports Night*, and this would subsequently lead to him composing the music for *The West Wing*.

It has been reported that Walden cannot read music—and a cynic might be tempted to say he could not write it either. However, this would be too caustic and inaccurate an appraisal; as intimated above, Walden was sufficiently accomplished to have written scores for a wide range of television work. However, his music—at least in the case of *The West Wing*—was seldom memorable; for example, it would seem doubtful—with the exception of the main title theme—that many people would be able to recall Walden's musical contributions to the series. Yet even here, in the case of the main theme of *The West Wing*, which opened each episode, there was a predicament. The scoring of the piece for full orchestra, with its soaring string section, the Copeland-like horns, tuned timpani and even the subtle use of xylophones, succeeded in creating a stirring sense of political grandeur and national pride; yet the theme continually failed to reach a resolution—rising and then falling but never seeming to reach a destination. Walden was not a Michael Nyman, a Hans Zimmer, a John Barry, a Wendy Carlos, or a Mica Levi; instead he was merely an accomplished composer of music for television drama, the master of "the plaintive oboe"—as Joshua Malina would often put it on *The West Wing Weekly* podcast. In essence, Walden was—more often than not—merely the master of the transparently manipulative emotional cue.

* * *

In a more specific sense one might argue that one of the most detrimental aspects of Walden's music was the way in which it exaggerated some of the more excessively sentimental elements of the show. This was particularly apparent in the scenes in which Walden's music accompanied Bartlet's early speeches. Within such speeches there was already a sense of descending into a maudlin discourse of gratuitous emotion; Aaron Sorkin's scripts—for it was Sorkin who was mainly responsible for such excessive levels of sentimentality—were already emotionally charged, but it was the overlay of Walden's music that seemed to exaggerate such excesses of emotion. Bartlet's speeches seemed to strive for poetry but often descended, no matter the supposed eloquence of Sorkin's writing, into unadorned bathos.[4] For example, consider "The Crackpots and These Women" (1/5), an episode that ended with this soliloquy by Bartlet: "You know, when smallpox was eradicated, it was considered the single greatest humanitarian achievement of this century. Surely, we can do it again. As we did in the time when our eyes looked towards the heavens, and with outstretched fingers, we touched the face of God." Keith Topping, the author of one of the most entertaining books on the show, *Inside Bartlet's White House: An Unofficial and Unauthorized Guide to The West Wing*, described this scene as being "One of the most beautiful pieces of TV ever made."[5] This was one point-of-view; however, another point-of-view might be to say the scene represented the zenith of uncalled for sentimentality, replete with the manipulatively clichéd music of W.G. Snuffy Walden. From this point-of-view such rhetorical utterances were simply too overblown to take seriously. There were other instances just as risible—for example, Bartlet's speech in the episode "20 Hours in America Part 2" (4/2), which began with the famous line: "The streets of heaven are too crowded with angels tonight," then moved toward a Kennedy-esque rhetoric: "We will do what is hard. We will achieve what is great," before ending with: "This is a

23. Unearned Emotion and the "Plaintive Oboe"   193

time for American heroes and we reach for the stars. God bless their memory, God bless the United States of America."[6] Janet McCabe, author of another laudable book on the show, *The West Wing: TV Milestones Series*, described this as an "electrifying sermon."[7] To many viewers in America this may have seemed a valid description, with the scene being viewed as if it were an example of inspirational rhetoric of the highest order. However, to others—perhaps from a more cynical European perspective—the scene, its writing and its performance merely seemed to descend into almost embarrassing bathos.

Other examples of Walden's music compromising the drama are many; in fact, too many to discuss in detail, but the following instances might be noted. The first example came in the first episode, "Pilot" (1/1), during Bartlet's speech about the Cuban asylum seekers: "With their clothes on their back, they came through a storm, and the ones that didn't die wanted a better life, and they want it here." An already sentimentally manipulative and implausible scene was exaggerated by Walden's music—the first instance of many to come. In the episode "The State Dinner" (1/7), in a scene concerning a siege in Idaho, Walden's music, cueing on Mandy's line—"there are children in there"—seemed to needlessly enhance the dramatic effect of the scene, damaging the dramatic impact of the line via hyperbole and overstatement. In one of the best episodes of the first season, "The Short List" (1/9), the final scene depicted Bartlet announcing Roberto Mendoza's nomination for the Supreme Court. The rigorous critique of the politics required to achieve this was undermined by the unnecessary use of Walden's music. In the second season, in the episode "In This White House" (2/4), Walden's music added unnecessary drama to the plotline concerning President Nimbala; Nimbala, the president of an "AIDS ravaged" African country, received news of the overthrow of his government, this being accompanied by the use of the aforementioned "plaintive oboe," two beats on a timpani and high strings in a minor key—all to needlessly emphasize the emotive significance of this news. In a similar way, the scene in the episode "The War at Home" (2/14) wherein Bartlet learned of the downing of a Blackhawk helicopter and the killing of nine commandos, demonstrated the intrusiveness of Walden's music; the scene was well played until the closing moments, when the music—both clichéd and nondescript—faded up on the soundtrack. Elsewhere in the series the same situation repeated itself; in Season 3, in the episode "On the Day Before" (3/5), Charlie refused the offer of immunity in the investigation into the cover-up surrounding the concealment of Bartlet's MS: "I'll stay with my team," Charlie declared. The scene was sufficiently sentimental to begin with, but Walden's music acted to needlessly enhance the setting. In Season 4, during the episode "Twenty-Five" (4/23), in the scene in which Toby announced the birth of his twins, a scene as sentimental as *The West Wing* could attain, once again Walden's music succeeded in overly embellishing a scene that needed no embellishment. Perhaps the most grievous example appeared in Season 6 in the episode "The Dover Test" (6/6); the closing scene, of Bartlet meeting injured troops in the hospital in Dover, approached a nadir in sentimentality, with a wounded soldier—with both legs missing—saying to his president: "I want to go back, sir." This scene, replete with CJ crying, with Bartlet looking presidential, with a prayer being intoned, and with W.G. Snuffy Walden's music, might well have been a candidate for one of the most overwrought scenes within the show.

* * *

As if by way of an antidote, there was also a significant amount of source music included in the series. The website *tunefind.com* lists a total of 154 songs used in the 155 episodes. The fact that so much extant music was included perhaps says something about the inherent qualities of Walden's music. In most instances the source music seemed well used; in fact, there were few exceptions, the worst instances arguably being the use of the song "Brothers in Arms" by Dire Straits in "Two Cathedrals" (2/22), and the use of Jeff Buckley's rendition of Leonard Cohen's song "Hallelujah" in the episode "Posse Comitatus" (3/22).[8] However, the source music elsewhere seemed more astutely chosen and more artistically valid; one thinks, for example, of Yo Yo Ma playing the prelude from Bach's "Cello Suite Number 1" with effortless precision in "Noël" (2/10); or Buffalo Springfield's "For What It's Worth" in "Isaac and Ishmael" (3/1); or Tori Amos's cover of "I Don't Like Mondays" in "20 Hours in America Parts 1 and 2" (4/1/2); or Richie Havens's stirring rendition of Bob Dylan's "The Times They Are a-Changin'" in "Election Night" (4/7).[9] Other notable examples included: "Angel" by Massive Attack, the source dance music in the nightclub where Zoey was kidnapped in the episode "Commencement" (4/22); and Lisa Gerrard's atmospheric composition "Sanvean," used over a montage of the Catholic mass in Washington and the bombings in Qumar in "7A WF 83429" (5/1); while Blind Willie Johnson's song "Dark Was the Night, Cold Was the Ground" eloquently closed the episode "The Warfare of Genghis Khan" (5/1). In the episode "A Change Is Gonna Come" (6/7), James Taylor offered a signature version of the Sam Cooke song that gave the episode its title, while the Steve Miller Band's "Jet Airliner" provided a sense of cinematic coverage in the episode "The Mommy Problem" (7/2). The adagio of Mozart's "Serenade No. 10 for Wind Instruments in B flat major" was used to almost Kubrickian perfection in the episode, "Mr. Frost" (7/4)—this was the piece with which Antonio Salieri was so enchanted in the film *Amadeus* (1984). In a similar way, the Handel aria "Lascia ch'io pianga" played well in the episode "The Wedding" (7/9), several years before its iconic use in Lars Von Trier's film *Antichrist* (2009). Finally, in the closing episode of the drama, "Tomorrow" (7/22), a blues rendition of "America the Beautiful," delivered impeccably on a National Steel guitar by Kevin Roosevelt Moore, aka "Keb Mo," completed the use of source music in the show.

* * *

James Joyce once described sentimentality as "unearned emotion,"[10] and *The West Wing* was indubitably replete with an abundance of unearned emotion—frequently sustained via the music of W.G. Snuffy Walden. As has been intimated, one of the most telling aesthetic properties of the show was that, while it was so unremittingly sentimental, it nonetheless was able to achieve a level of artistic discourse that overcame some of the more maudlin aspects of the drama. In other words, the fact that Aaron Sorkin could get away with such a level of sentimentality said much about the innate quality of his writing during the first four seasons of the series.[11] As Janet McCabe put it:

> Formulaic maybe, sentimental and schmaltzy at times, but with its adroit use of language and rhythmic cadence, crackling wit, and political savvy, *The West Wing* had its audience.[12]

Other critics commented in a similar way:

> The American capacity for forgetting is seen most clearly [in] *The West Wing*.... We need think only of the mawkishly sentimentalized moments of American patriotism: the gang on the Brownstone steps sequentially intoning God Bless America, or in the Oval Office, serving at the pleasure of the President of the United States.[13]
>
> The show suffers from a "split personality" where the show's realism and sardonic insights are undercut by the "emotional mushiness" and "inspirational uplift" of the scenes designed to cater to the viewing audience.[14]
>
> *The West Wing*'s depiction of President Bartlet's hard decisions often has some grave flaws. There is strong sentimentality covering an odd failure in basic literary technique.[15]

Michael Dumlao described W.G. Snuffy Walden's soundtrack as traversing "the soundscape of the American experience, deftly plucking the proverbial heartstrings as only a virtuoso can."[16] However, in looking toward a summary of the use of music on *The West Wing*, another point-of-view might be that Walden's intrusive and manipulative music was detrimental to the series, and that the show might—in a final consideration—have been better off without it. Or at least it might have been better off without it in those cases where the music was most invasive to the plot, in those cases where, as Joshua Malina would put it: "The words [were] good enough."[17] It would be interesting to consider how much better the series might have been without Walden's music, without the overt musical embellishments that consistently threatened to render the aesthetic discourse bathetic. But this was not to be: Walden's music prevails, an ever-present ally in augmenting the sentimental traffic at play.[18] As another critic put it, Walden's music, in an overarching sense, "offered an almost *Walton-esque* quality to the series ... such was the predominantly sentimentalized discourse at play within the formulaic musical soundtrack."[19] Stanley Kubrick once intimated something to the effect that the level of sentimentality in a film should diminish as the course of the narrative progresses, that a film should get "tougher" in sentiment as its narrative proceeded. Unfortunately, American films (and television dramas) have tended to be the opposite, a tendency played out with some force in the case of *The West Wing* and often exaggerated by the musical accompaniment to the drama.

24

Society Must Be Defended
Poststructuralist Readings

One final way of gaining an understanding of *The West Wing* might be found in one of the last images we see in the series, at the end of the final episode, "Tomorrow" (7/22). In this, the 155th of 155 episodes, as Bartlet's personal effects were being removed from the Oval Office, one of the last images seen—as the camera rested upon a bookshelf—was a copy of Michel Foucault's book *"Society Must Be Defended": Lectures at the Collége de France, 1975-76*. In the book Foucault presented a bleak view of human history, one in which social life was not a form of "benign cooperation,"[1] but instead a form of conflict, even a form of permanent war. Foucault argued that this extended into the modern-day world, with nation-states controlling their populations, even outside of times of actual war, in a decidedly proscriptive manner. Foucault argued: "The modern state wages war against its own by engaging in discourses and practices of purification and elimination." Why this book should have been on Bartlet's bookshelf remains something of a mystery; but placing it within the frame, in such a deliberately mannered way, would seem to suggest it represented a significant part of the story of *The West Wing*—especially as the scene came so close to the end of the story.

There was therefore a certain sense of irony present within the scene. President Bartlet's fictional administration would at least appear to have had a much more optimistic and liberal inclination than the modern state as described within Foucault's book; as an unnamed contributor to the website *Foucault TV* commented: "*The West Wing* holds out a dream of peaceful cooperation—a somewhat different position to Foucault's bleak view of society in discord." There has to be a certain reticence about reading too much into a single image, a few seconds of film, but the image of Foucault's book on Bartlet's bookshelf could not help but at least suggest we—the audience—might have been misreading Bartlet's actual intent about the modern state. As intimated above, Foucault's book chronicles a history in which "the modern state wages war against its own" by "engaging in discourses and practices" against its own people. However, little of this would seem to occur within the liberal space of *The West Wing's* fictional world; instead "bellicosity is directed outward—to terrorists, rogue states, failed empires. America is in no consequential way at war with itself." In the same way as Foucault carefully enveloped the book's title within quotation marks, the placement of the book gave the scene a certain irony: Was Bartlet simply an eclectic reader, or was the inclusion of a book by France's most famous philosopher a way of apologizing for the anti-French bias in the rest of the show? Whatever the answer, the inclusion of Foucault's book remains a beguiling piece of enigmatic plotting.

In terms of Michel Foucault's work in general and its significance to poststructuralist thought, one might attempt to paraphrase Foucault's overarching argument by distilling it to the following phrase: "What is true depends on who rules the discourse."[2] Foucault may not have used this exact phrase, but nonetheless it would seem to sum up a significant aspect of his work.[3] According to Foucault, the discourse of any discipline—medical, legal, military, scientific—governs the production of knowledge. In Foucauldian terms "truth" was therefore reduced to being a mere ideological maneuver of the discourse. In addition, another key element of Foucauldian thought was the issue of sexuality; Foucault consistently argued that the old order of political control had been replaced with a new regime of power, one exercised control through the stipulation of norms for human behavior,[4] that is, via sexual proscription. In other words, for Foucault sexuality was nothing more than the means through which power is organized within Western society; for Foucault the major concern was authority's need to regulate the sexual behavior of the individual. To consider, for a moment, such a concept in relation to *The West Wing*, the innate puritanism of the show might therefore be interpreted as a means of responding to such Foucauldian restrictions and disciplines. As discussed in Chapter 13, sexuality in *The West Wing* was seemingly prevented at every opportunity, almost as if it were following a Foucauldian model of restricted behavior.

* * *

It has often been said that structuralism gave way to poststructuralism in 1968, with the publication of Roland Barthes's essay "The Death of the Author." As discussed in Chapter 4, this was a rhetorical means of asserting the independence of a literary or cultural text, a way of asserting the text's immunity to the possibility of being limited to any notion of what the author might have intended. However, this was only one aspect of poststructuralist thought; within the discourse of poststructuralism we appear to enter a uni-

24. Society Must Be Defended 199

verse of uncertainty, a decentered, "deconstructed" universe. In this sense, deconstruction theory might be seen as a major part of poststructuralist theory, deconstruction theory being a highly skeptical school of thought that would seem to reject *all* previous claims made by *all* previous systems; deconstruction theory is nothing less than a fundamental critique of all the intellectual assumptions that underlie Western thinking. In terms of a reading of a cultural text—such as *The West Wing*—deconstruction theory would consider such a text on the assumption that it has not one meaning but many, that meaning itself is fragmentary, and that a detailed examination of a text releases a diversity of latent, fragmentary and contradictory meanings. While this may be seen as a task running retrograde to many critics and perhaps even more readers, this would be, nonetheless, the intent of a deconstructive reading of the text.

In Chapter 7 a structuralist reading was compared to seeing a cultural text as a jigsaw: individual pieces of a jigsaw were meaningless in themselves, only making sense when the entire puzzle was constructed and the "big picture" could be seen. In terms of poststructuralism, and specifically deconstruction theory, the intent was not so much to look at the ways in which the pieces of the jigsaw fitted together into a single coherent unit—instead, deconstruction theory was more concerned with exploring the gaps, the dislocations, the disjunctions among the individual elements in question. In other words, there was no intent to complete the jigsaw, to see the big picture. Deconstruction theory merely wanted to look at the ways in which it was put together—and the ways in which it could be taken apart. However, deconstruction theory need not necessarily be interpreted in a negative context; it was not "destructive," it was "deconstructive." As such, deconstruction theory could be seen as an affirmative concept, allowing an unbiased appreciation of the means of production, revealing the underlying hegemony at work, with "taken for granted" assumptions now being challenged instead of being blindly accepted. In this way, the text opens to reveal plural and diverse readings, as against the single, harmonious reading of authorial intent. Instead of being an object for passive consumption, the text now becomes an object for each reader to construct and deconstruct in order to produce meanings of their own.

In this way, deconstruction could be seen as an attack on so-called common sense, an attack putatively led by Jacques Derrida, one of the most original if least read of twentieth-century philosophers. Derrida, like Foucault and Jacques Lacan, was concerned with the inexactitude and the contradictions of language; for Derrida not only do words have unconscious elements, the words themselves have a greater history than any one person's experience, and hence the words have a greater meaning than the speaker can control.[5] For Derrida meaning was never complete, never fully realized; it was always postponed, always deferred. In this Derrida was making use of inherent concepts within structuralism wherein the meaning of any signifier was always deferred. The simple act of looking up a word in a dictionary would confirm this idea; words can only be defined by other words, which are, in turn, defined by still further words, never to be rendered with a full and complete meaning. Hence we inhabit an endless process of deferral, we never reach an end to the search, we merely move from one word to another, a relentless deferment of meaning with no respite. Thus, with meaning forever deferred, existence itself becomes a process of deferral; this would be a point to bear in mind if one were to adopt a Derridian reading of *The West Wing*.[6]

In a wide-ranging sense, within poststructuralist thought the subject enters a universe of uncertainty, a universe with no fixed landmarks, a universe beyond linguistic accountability.[7] In the deconstructive world of poststructuralism, all meaning is seen as socially and culturally constructed; no statement is seen as being entirely innocent. Thus in terms of a poststructuralist reading, no matter how perverse it might seem, a reading of the text would not attempt to perceive a unified whole, but instead to perceive fractured and contradictory readings. In the so-called "real world," there would appear to be a sense of continually striving to achieve a unity of interpretation, whereas a deconstructive approach would continually argue that this is forever beyond our grasp. For Derrida truth, in itself, was decidedly uncertain; truth had become plural; there were many truths. This situation was so deeply ingrained and widespread that we could never hope to fully grasp what we meant, and we could never hope to have the functioning power to fully understand what we were attempting to say.[8] In a reductive sense, this argument would assume that historical truth had little to do with actual events. Instead there was the sense of history being concerned with raw power, with what the dominant discourses of the time judged to have happened; leading, in a similarly reductive way, to such issues as Holocaust denial.[9] However, a poststructuralist reading would dismiss such a charge by arguing it had little relevance outside of the hegemonic discourse, and that hegemonic forces were far more complex than such a simplistic reading assumed.

As far as can be ascertained, the word "hegemony" was not used on *The West Wing*; as—it might be argued—was the complex intent of the word itself. Hegemony might be defined as the way in which a dominant class gains and maintains its power, not merely by force, but via cultural and ideological influences. In other words, such a sense of dominance was not based solely upon the coercive power of the state, but rather on the ability of the state to exercise sufficient moral influence over its population. Hegemony possesses the facility of making certain beliefs appear either natural or invisible, to such an extent that they hardly seem to be beliefs at all; we think we are conscious individuals, making conscious choices, but in fact we have few actual choices.

For example, a democratic form of government, portrayed with such respect in *The West Wing*, might persuade the electorate they have some influence via the choice of an elected administration. However, when this choice is so limited—between the Republican and Democratic parties, a right-wing party and a slightly less right-wing party—then it would seem questionable whether a real choice exists. We think we are free agents, but in reality we are strictly controlled by a variety of subtle power structures. In essence, we willingly maintain a system that concentrates wealth and power in the hands of the few[10]; this was one of the unspoken, but readily apparent aspects of *The West Wing*. Hence an awareness of such hegemonic structures—via a poststructuralist reading—could be said to add to an appreciation of the show.

* * *

One tangential element of poststructuralist and deconstruction theory worthy of consideration the way in which Heisenberg's Uncertainty Principle might be applied to an epistemological approach to cultural texts. To put it simply, Heisenberg's Uncertainty Principle states that the act of measurement, in itself, alters an experiment; hence, in a simple example, the act of measuring the temperature of a flask of water can never be wholly accurate because the temperature of the thermometer used, will, in itself, influence the temperature of the water in the flask. Within the context of a poststructuralist approach, it can therefore be argued that an act of interpretation, in itself, alters the way we might read (or view) the cultural text in question. Thus, for example, in the case of *The West Wing*, our view of the drama is changed, however inconsequentially, by the criticism and the commentary we may have read or otherwise have experienced. This would probably be most apparent in the case of the "Isaac and Ishmael" (3/1) episode; as discussed in Chapter 8, this episode has been the subject of more critical attention than any other episode, and consequently one could arguably conclude that such hermeneutic attention has altered the ways in which we now view that episode. Thus, a poststructuralist approach would at least allow for an understanding of such a predicament, a predicament that might otherwise have not been so apparent.

One way to acknowledge such an idea, albeit at a relatively simplistic level of debate, might be to anchor such a theoretical approach within a more secure philosophical debate by linking poststructuralist thought to phenomenology. The school of phenomenology perhaps has more in common with the school of poststructuralism than would generally be accepted. For example, phenomenology, as a philosophical discourse of experience, would contend that physical objects do not, in and of themselves, have an existence; as Edward Quinn put it, it is a "philosophical method that describes objects as they are registered in the consciousness of the observer."[11] In terms of *The West*

Wing, it would seem valid to assume that the majority of viewers experienced the show within the conceptual realm of a realist approach—in other words, a common-sense approach that would assume, almost without question, that the narrative presented had an existence that was clear and unqualified. However, epistemologically this would seem to be problematical—at least if one considers Edmund Husserl's premise, that the world does not have an independent existence, but only has meaning when filtered through the human imagination. Within this philosophical premise, the problematical aspects of the clichéd question about the proverbial tree falling in the forest become apparent: If no one was present to hear the sound, did the sound occur?[12]

Husserl, often cited as the founder of the school of phenomenology, raised the question of whether there was a linkage between consciousness and reality, as Peter Watson argued:

> Put simply, the basic question for him [Husserl] was this: did logic exist objectively, "out there" in the world, or was it in some fundamental sense dependent on the mind?[13]

It is clear that the falling tree, in the famous hypothetical forest, created vibrations in the air, but whether this was a "sound" if no one heard such vibrations was the question. In the same sense, without a perceiving mind do such concepts as, for example, colors or numbers exist? That is, were the leaves on the famous tree green without a light sensitive retina to perceive them, and was the number of branches relevant with no one to count them? Do such concepts have an existence outside of the means of human consciousness, and, to push the argument further, do more abstract concepts, such as justice and freedom—very much human constructs—have any existence outside of human conceptualization?[14] Finally, to push the argument close to its limit, what can be said of God? Does God exist outside of human conceptualization?

* * *

At a more subjective level of debate, it would seem fair to say that a poststructuralist reading of any cultural text, would be concerned with a sense of personal identity—with a sense of who we are. René Descartes may have stated, "I think; therefore, I am." However, within a poststructuralist reading this reputedly profound comment would seem close to being inconsequential—insomuch as Descartes refrained from troubling to attempt to define just what "I am" actually means. In this sense, both phenomenology and poststructuralism have a significant concern with "the meaning of being"— in other words, with what it means to say "I am." Within poststructuralist thought the concept of "self" has been of specific significance, with the term "self" giving way to the term "subject." In the arena of poststructuralist theory, the human subject—already constructed by language—was seen as merely a product of historical, social and cultural forces—with the implication that an independent and autonomous "self" was an illusion. Hence the following question might be posed: Do we—as readers, as individuals, as subjects—read with no other desire but to enjoy literary and cultural productions, or do we read in an attempt to understand ourselves? In an overarching sense, cultural theory might be seen as an attempt to understand a world that is ultimately impossible to understand. Thus when we read (or view) a narrative we are playing a game of which we have no knowledge of the rules; and narrative, as Roland Barthes pointed out, is an enigmatic code with a cluster of subtle and barely discernible conventions. Hence the inherent difficulties of fully understanding any narrative, even a narrative as conventional and realistic as *The West Wing*.

One particular element of narrative that might be seen as specifically pertaining to poststructuralist thought would arguably be the notion of character. The average reader or viewer may take it for granted that characters within a narrative have some degree of authenticity, but, as Jonathan Culler has noted: "The notion of character, structuralists would say, is a myth."[15] Poststructuralists would go still further and argue that any character, in any narrative, is a mere illusion, an illusion in which the reader acts as a creative accomplice. Within such narratives, the descriptions and the actions of a character—if sufficiently convincing—might lead a reader to create the sense of an actual individual. However, the "iceberg principle" would seem to be at play within this context. In other words, the reader might assume that the material they were offered was merely a limited account of what lay beneath, whereas—at least in terms of characters within cultural narratives—the extant fraction of the iceberg is, in fact, all there is.[16] In terms of *The West Wing*, the show was clearly character driven throughout; the characters, as written and performed, were a significant element of the show. Prior to cultural theory much literary criticism colluded in the delusion that cultural texts were primarily about people who, though often thought of as fictional, still led lives much like our own and were therefore considered in terms of their lifelike qualities. Cultural theory, to put it mildly, would disavow this idea, looking elsewhere—specifically, at the ideological maneuvers such non-existent fictional characters were espousing— to read what the text was actually saying.

In approaching a summary: a poststructuralist reading of *The West Wing* would have been more interested in what was absent from the discourse than what was present, accepting that a cultural text speaks less about the world than it does about itself. In addition, such an approach would have an awareness of many voices, of a heteroglossia, within the discourse of the text; and finally would have—as Derrida maintained—a sense that language is never fixed, that it is fluid and volatile. The word aporia is a ubiquitous term in poststructuralist criticism; it literally means an impasse, a kind of "knot" in a text that cannot be unraveled or solved. Often this is concerned with the self-contradiction of the unspoken, of an ambiguity, and of a hermeneutic conflict that would seem irreconcilable.[17] In the case of *The West Wing* a poststructuralist reading may conclude that there were numerous instances of this phenomenon, as Samuel Chambers and Patrick Finn commented:

> The secret to the presentation of voice on *The West Wing* lies in what is missing.... While the show clearly panders to familiar notions of Truth, Justice and The American Way, it avoids providing closure on specific issues.[18]

As intimated in Chapter 21, albeit within an un-theorized reading, the show often avoided a sense of closure; within a poststructuralist approach this becomes more apparent, with the show continually appearing to recognize there were no real answers to any of the questions it raised. For example, "Commencement" (4/22) was an episode wherein all the main players seemed insistent on refusing to answer any of the questions asked of them. For instance, the journalist Danny Concannon, who had finally found evidence of Bartlet's involvement in the political assassination of Abdul ibn Shareef, would not answer any of CJ's questions as to his sources. Likewise, CJ would not answer any of Danny's follow-up questions. In the same episode, at the end of Bartlet's meeting with his staff, wherein he confirmed his involvement in Shareef's murder, Will Bailey asked a pertinent question: "How did you get Shareef's plane to land?" The question was not so much unanswered as wholly ignored by Bartlet, and ultimately by the writers of the show—within the narrative discourse of the drama, no answer was given to Will, or to the audience. In the same episode, albeit on a more prosaic level, Toby's ex-wife, Andy, received no response when she asked her ex-husband how he could have afforded her dream house in Georgetown, the house Toby had haplessly bought to persuade Andy to re-marry him. How Toby could have afforded the house was a question worth asking—but a question decidedly unanswered.[19] Finally, and once again in the same episode, Amy asked Donna one of the central questions of the series, at least within the sphere of romantic relationships: "Are you in love with Josh?" It was a question many viewers of the show had been asking since the beginning of the drama; however, Donna simply ignored the question—again withholding narrative information in what might be read as a decidedly poststructuralist way. As such, within the narrative of *The West Wing* (although it is not known if any of the creative agents involved had an in-depth sense of poststructuralist thinking) there was a clearly defined poststructuralist discourse at play, at least if one was prepared to look for it. Thus, in conclusion, it could be suggested that such a reading would arguably allow for a more insightful interpretation of some of the more subtle elements at play within the text.

Conclusion

The West Wing ended its seven-year run on NBC at 9.00 p.m. on Sunday May 14, 2005; and, whatever its many compromises, the closing scenes and closing moments represented prime-time network television drama at its best. As has been discussed a number of times herein, the show had significant flaws that might have compromised the high aesthetic attributes of any other television drama. *The West Wing* showed a presidency as it should have been, with its gullible idealism rendering it mere political fantasy, "political pornography for liberals,"[1] as one critic unkindly put it. At the start of one of the early episodes, "Five Votes Down" (1/4), Bartlet was shown giving a rousing speech in front of a large poster: "Practical Idealism." In one sense this was humorous, an oxymoronic statement that might almost have summed up the beguiling aspirations of the show; yet in another sense it arguably revealed the blank, formulaic and implausible qualities of the drama.[2] Aaron Sorkin, whatever else he may be, is not a cynic, and there was certainly little cynicism within *The West Wing*. In an overall sense, given its unabashed sentimentalized discourse, it would seem difficult to argue against the charge that the show was, to some extent at least, culpable of being both idealistic and naive.[3]

The perceptive viewer of the show might then ask a reasonable question: Why do we like it so much? As intimated, there was much to suggest we should not; for example, Simon Philpott and David Mutimer described the show as a "liberal fantasy" that remained "willfully blind to issues of race, gender and class":

> It revels in the eternal turning of the hourglass, secure in the belief of its innocence and goodness, certain it is still that bright, shining light upon the hill that draws to its shores the poor and huddled masses of the world.[4]

It would seem difficult to argue with such criticism, and yet, for all its faults, *The West Wing* has been described as being "probably the most morally serious yet popularly engaging fictional text in contemporary American culture."⁵ This was Young Hoon Kim's discerning appraisal of the show; in addition, Janet McCabe commented:

> It [*The West Wing*] undoubtedly brought a new level of sophistication and creativity to primetime ... its unique contribution was in how it delved deep into America's finest political aspirations, interrogated core values embedded in the Constitution, plundered the best of U.S. cultural values and literary forms, and translated this into contemporary quality network television.⁶

For Spencer Downing, the show "re-inscribed liberalism into the political mainstream by encouraging audiences to see liberal values as plausible, pragmatic, and patriotic."⁷ The idea of the show extolling liberal values that were plausible, pragmatic and patriotic would seem relevant, especially in the case of the latter attribute: the show's patriotic virtues. This would perhaps offer one way of approaching a solution to the question of why we like the show so much. *The West Wing* was a patriotic drama; it depicted an ideal, albeit improbable, White House that enabled discerning viewers to suspend their cynical perspectives and to believe, at least while viewing each episode, that such idealism could be accepted. In other words, we were able to adjourn our pragmatic view of the world, and to allow whatever liberal principles we had to flourish within the discursive arena of the show. To a large extent the issue of a patriotic democracy was at the heart of *The West Wing*—and in this way it became possible to believe in such idealistic characters working in public service. In the service of their country, and in the service of democracy, they could retain their idealism outside of the tawdry reality of political life. In essence, this was a show that presented an imaginary world of political discourse, devoid of the corruptive forces of the real world—but a show that somehow managed to remain convincing at the same time.

One reason why the show's audience has been so forgiving might be associated with the expansiveness and the depth of the textual narrative. In fact, from a critical perspective, the sheer expanse of the show would seem to be an issue in itself. One of the challenges of watching and reading *The West Wing* is simply its size; here we have a text of some 155 episodes, each having an approximate duration of some 42 minutes, adding up to a total running time of some 109 hours of complex television drama. If *The West Wing* had been a novel, it would be longer than any yet published—for example, one can read *Ulysses* in less than 30 hours—a quarter of the time it would take to watch *The West Wing*. In this way the series resembled the ungainliness of an oil tanker—it took a long time to turn it around—and as such it is a significant endeavor to watch the text. In addition, because of its length it would appear to be beyond the abilities of most viewers to process and hold all the narrative information the show offered. That is, while it is possible to recall the general plot-lines and to remember scenes within certain key episodes, who can remember what occurs in all the episodes?⁸ This was not a feature film lasting a couple of hours or even a novel one could read over the course of a few days. To experience *The West Wing* required a much greater investment.

One way around such a predicament might be to adopt additional strategies of viewing with which to approach as extensive a text as *The West Wing*. As intimated at the start of this book, cultural theory has seldom been used within hermeneutic considerations of *The West Wing*; hence the main intent within this particular work has been to consider *The West Wing* within the interpretative context it arguably deserves. In other words, as one of the most significant of television dramas, *The West Wing* could arguably be said to deserve as expansive an analytical consideration as possible. In terms of cultural theory and *The West Wing*, a wide-ranging number of theoretical components have been considered, for example: the structuralist readings put forward in Chapter 7; the Marxist readings offered in Chapter 9; the way in which gender theory was discussed in Chapter 13; the postmodernist theories put forward in Chapter 16; the questioning of feminist approaches in Chapter 18; the acknowledgement of racist and postcolonial discourses in Chapters 12 and 19; and the psychoanalytical readings offered in Chapter 22. In addition, issues of intertextuality, as discussed in Chapters 2 and 15, complimented by a discussion of reader response theories in Chapter 4, culminated in a discussion of poststructuralist theories in Chapter 24.

In terms of the theoretical approaches adopted herein, it is hoped that an understanding of *The West Wing* has thus been enhanced, albeit with the outcome of such hermeneutic considerations residing within the frame of each individual reader. As intimated previously, although the critical response has been extensive, it has seldom attempted to interrogate the show via the prism of critical theory. To some extent this might be explained by the decline of theory's influence in academic circles; the beginning of the show, in 1999, coincided with that decline. As Terry Eagleton noted in the 25th anniversary edition of his celebrated book *Literary Theory: An Introduction*[9]: "Theory no longer occupies the commanding space it used to" and it was no longer the "outlandish affair that it once was."[10] Eagleton went on to comment that there was now "less talk of semiotics, hermeneutics, post-structuralism and phenomenology" and instead "postmodernism, postcolonialism and feminism" had come to the fore.[11] However, critical theory remains a significant element of intellectual thought. It is perhaps not as influential in academia as it was in the 1970s and 1980s, but the existent body of work still represents a considerable repository of materials. Theory questions the most basic assumptions of all facets of human experience. This is its great appeal; nearly everything we accept as common sense, as taken for granted, when put to any kind of theoretical analysis can be seen to have social, cultural and historical constraints. Theory is, as Jonathan Culler put it, "a pugnacious critique of common sense."[12]

In his modest but nonetheless significant book *Literary Theory: A Very Short Introduction*, first published in 1997, Culler was astute in assessing the reason why theory would appear to be resisted by the common readership:

> A good deal of the hostility to theory no doubt comes from the fact that to admit the importance of theory is to make an open-minded commitment, to leave yourself in a position where there are always important things you do not know. But this is the condition of life itself.[13]

As well as referring to the condition of life itself, theory might also be seen as referring to the condition of death itself. This might be argued insomuch as there would seem to be something essentially eschatological about theory. As David Lehman put it, with theory there was "an air of last things, a brooding sense of annihilation."[14] This was especially so within such schools of thought as deconstruction and postmodernism, each possessing a sense of looking toward "the end of human progress."[15] In this way it is possible to conclude that theory's unabashed preparedness to look at such a sense of an ending was one reason for a resistance against it.[16]

There was also the issue of theory's willingness to accept chaos. As Jonathan Culler observed, what drives theory is the desire "to see how far an idea or argument can go."[17] In other words, theory does not "give rise to harmonious solutions," something *The West Wing* so consistently attempted to do; instead theory merely offers "the prospect of further thought," of complex and challenging presumptions, with theory ultimately representing "an ongoing project of thinking which does not end."[18] Nonetheless, the application of theoretical approaches can, at times, prove rewarding. As Terry Eagleton put it: "Critics of theory sometimes complain that its devotees seem to find theory more exciting than the works of art it is meant to illuminate. But sometimes it is."[19] In such a sense, theory might be said to allow the reader to have a greater understanding of the cultural text in question; or at least to begin to comprehend the sense that we are subjects of immensely complex ideological forces, and that a dialectical approach—the act of arriving at the truth via serious and considered analytical debate—may be the only way of gaining an understanding of the cultural text in question. There is nothing outside of the text. This would seem to be self-evidently correct—and cultural theory, however out of fashion it may seem, would arguably appear to be the only way of fully embracing such a complex scenario.

In addition to approaches from cultural theory, the discussion has also looked toward a range of more empirical issues that were arguably more grounded in the everyday world, but nonetheless had a place within an analysis of the show. For example, the discussion in Chapter 1 of the manner in which the show was cast allowed for an analysis of the ways in which *The West Wing* was ultimately character driven, and how this was one of the show's most direct and immediate attractions. Also, the use of an alternate reality—the way in which the show was real but somehow seemed to exist in an almost parallel world to the real one—was discussed in Chapter 3, and thus allowed for a discussion of the "mythic" resonances present within the drama. In Chapter 6, the way in which *The West Wing* was filmed, and the way in which the high production values rendered the *mise-en-scène* of *The West Wing* as cinematic television were discussed as two of the most compelling aspects of the show. Chapter 10 focused on the question of how valid the show's representation of American society was (Was America the greatest country in the world?); while in Chapter 17 the question of whether Bartlet should ultimately be seen as a war criminal was posed. Here, and elsewhere in the book, there was an attempt to read the show outside of an American frame of reference—a sense of how the rest of the world perceives *The West Wing* and, by inference, perceives America itself. The issue of religion was discussed in Chapters 5 and 11, including the very real sense that a literal religious belief underpinned the show's values—or at least the character of President Bartlet. In Chapter 14, the issue of disability in *The West Wing* was considered; a subject seldom dealt with in such depth and with such subtlety by prime-time American television. In Chapter 20, another topic seldom featured in depth on American television drama, that of education, was discussed; once again the show merited some value for presenting this issue in such depth. In Chapter 23, perhaps the show's weakest element, the musical soundtrack, was discussed. This seemed to be the one aspect of *The West Wing* that did not move beyond the mundane quality of the average television drama, and it has influenced the way in which we appreciate the show. Finally, the issue of narrative authenticity was discussed in Chapters 8 and 21—the former chapter looking specifically at the famous (or perhaps infamous) episode "Isaac and Ishmael" (3/1), an episode of extremes, demonstrating the best and the worst of Aaron Sorkin's writing.

    The West Wing began its seven-year run during the final years of the Clinton administration; however, as Melissa Crawley noted, the "newly installed conservative Republican administration made the action seem especially fictional."[20] Since then, after George W. Bush's eight years in office, America had a more Bartlet-esque administration under Barack Obama, that was followed by an administration that has arguably made the show seem even more "especially fictional." This may be a significant element in the show's enduring popularity. Twenty years since it was first broadcast *The West Wing* still prevails, still has relevance, and still speaks of the American Dream.[21] At times the show faltered in its attempt to portray such a dream; at times the show seemed to descend to excessive sentimentalism and gauche melodrama.[22] Nonetheless, the show was consummately successful in most other ways; it succeeded effortlessly in ideologically presenting an ideal image of the White House for millions of viewers. In essence, the show reached beyond the usual Hollywood cliché, offering a depiction of the presidency far more convincing than popular culture's customary representation of the office. These qualities should not be overlooked. *The West Wing* was a didactic show of some significance, a show that suggested the American system was not corrupt and not wholly un-heroic either. Whether the show was consistently accurate is perhaps beside the point, for *The West Wing* remains one of the most engaging and thought provoking television dramas yet presented on network television. It has aged well. Repeated viewings do not disappoint; it is beset with contradictions, yet it would be difficult to name anything to match it, and, in a final appraisal, it remains vastly superior to the vast majority of other television dramas.

Appendix A.
Seasons 1–7: A Synopsis

Season One of *The West Wing* began part way through the first year of President Bartlet's administration, and climaxed, 22 episodes later, with an assassination attempt on the president. The opening episode, "Pilot" (1/1), introduced the main protagonists, Bartlet and his staff: Sam, Leo, CJ, Josh, Toby and Mandy; it also introduced some of the most compelling tropes within the series: sex, race and religion. Subsequent episodes would explore Bartlet's contrasting views on the use of military force ("A Proportional Response" [1/3]), alongside Bartlet's views on women ("The Crackpots and These Women" [1/5]). However, the most significant plotline in the middle of the season was the election of a new Supreme Court judge, beginning in "The Short List" (1/9) and culminating in "Six Meetings Before Lunch" (1/18). Perhaps the key scene was the one between Bartlet and the retiring judge, Justice Joseph Crouch, with their conversation providing as accurate a representation of Bartlet and his presidency as might be found in the whole seven seasons. As a further indicator of the actual nature of Bartlet's presidency, the episode "Take This Sabbath Day" (1/14) showed Bartlet struggling with his conscience as to whether to commute the death sentence of a prisoner on Death Row, with Bartlet eventually choosing political expediency and letting the execution go ahead. Other issues in the season included: a discussion of slave reparations; the importance of education to the nation-state; and the skewed sentencing for drug offences—before leading to the assassination attempt on Bartlet and the cliff-hanger ending to the season.

Season Two of *The West Wing* began with two "back to back" episodes returning to the events of the assassination attempt. After this the plotline meandered for several episodes. Perhaps the most notable dramatic scene occurred in the episode "The Midterms" (2/3), in which Bartlet deconstructed the Old Testament; while the episode "Shibboleth" (2/8) dealt deftly with the issue of what might now be called asylum seekers, with Bartlet resolving the problem by sleight of hand. The plotline moved some way into soapbox drama with the Christmas episode "Noel" (2/10) detailing Josh's post-traumatic stress disorder, a plotline that would recur through several further episodes. However, toward the end of the season a more compelling storyline would develop; in the episode "17 People" (2/18) it would finally become apparent that Bartlet had been hiding a "secret affliction," and that Bartlet had perpetrated a fraud against the American public, insomuch as he had not disclosed he had multiple sclerosis (MS). This, together with the sudden death of the president's secretary, Mrs. Landingham, would build toward another end of season cliffhanger. In the episode "Two Cathedrals" (2/22), which was arguably one of the best episodes of all seven seasons, an authentic sense of *denouement* was achieved, with Bartlet cursing God (albeit in Latin) and thus achieving a polemical discourse rarely found elsewhere in the series. At the end the viewer was left to speculate whether Bartlet would seek re-election or not, although the observant viewer might have read the indicators and hence had a good sense of what outcome was to occur.

Season Three of *The West Wing* began with the episode "Isaac and Ishmael" (3/1), one of the most famous episodes of the series, but also arguably one of worst, or at least one of the most rushed and ill-considered episodes. It was *The West Wing*'s response to 9/11. Something had occurred in the universe of *The West Wing*, something similar to but different from the events of 9/11, an event that caused the staff to present an impromptu history lesson about two of the sons of Abraham and the subsequent history of terrorism. The season continued with stories concerning Bartlet's MS and his concealment of it, the appointment of a special prosecutor and other allusions to the Watergate scandal; this was followed by an interesting episode, "The Indians in the Lobby" (3/8), which at least attempted to address the issue of Native American rights, albeit within an unknowingly racist discourse. The following episode, "The Women of Qumar" (3/9), allowed CJ to voice her views on the mistreatment of women in Islamic societies; after this the storyline of most significance concerned Bartlet's decision to order the murder of Abdul ibn Shareef, the Qumari minister of defense, in the episode "Posse Comitatus" (3/22). After much searching of his moral conscience, Bartlet gave the order and Shareef was murdered in a so-called "black-ops" action. Shareef had been suspected of plotting terrorist attacks against America. Whether this was the case was not proved in a court of law; however, this plotline provided the culmination of the season and one of the main stories at the start of the next season.

Season Four of *The West Wing* began with a two-part episode, "20 Hours in America Parts 1 and 2" (4/1, 4/2), one of the rare instances in the series of the location being outside of Washington, in this case Indiana, offering a differing point-of-view of life in middle America. The main storylines concerned Bartlet's seemingly effortless way of winning a second term—the re-election having almost no dramatic content over the final result—along with Bartlet's effortless escape from a possible war crimes charge, an element of the plot that was never fully explained. Elsewhere, the season seemed, at times, to drift into soap-opera territory. For example, the episode "The Long Goodbye" (4/13) depicted CJ's father and his worsening dementia. It appeared almost as a stand-alone play, with little bearing to the main plotline. In a similar sense the episode "Holy Night" (4/11) spent a significant part of its time detailing the criminal past of Toby's father, again with little relevance to the main storyline. The season ended with a 23rd episode, one more than the other six seasons, an episode confusingly entitled "Twenty-Five" (4/23), which ended with the kidnapping of Bartlet's daughter, Zoey, and Bartlet's subsequent recusal from office—another cliff-hanger episode, and Aaron Sorkin's last contribution as writer on the series.

Season Five of *The West Wing* began with a replacement president, President Walken, threatening to let loose the dogs of war, and also with the aftermath of

Zoey's kidnapping. Both would be resolved—somewhat conveniently—by the second episode of the season, with Zoey being rescued and Bartlet, the recused president, un-recusing himself. Further storylines followed, including the appointment of a new vice president, a process that would eventually result in the compromise choice of Robert "Bingo Bob" Russell; there was also the appointment of a new Chief Justice of the Supreme Court due to the physical and mental decline of the present incumbent. In addition, in the episode "Shutdown" (5/8), as intimated by its title, this was a storyline wherein Bartlet refused to compromise further on the budget with Congress, causing a shutdown in government and a degree of dramatic tension. Otherwise, there were relatively meager storylines: Toby perceived a way to save Social Security in "Slow News Day" (5/12); there was a narratively reductive episode, "An Khe" (5/14) in which a younger Leo escaped capture after his plane was shot down in Vietnam; there was a guest appearance by the cast of *Sesame Street* in the episode "Eppur Si Muove" (5/16); and there was a stand-alone episode, "Access" (5/18), which adopted a documentary approach—a day in the life of CJ Cregg. The season ended with the death of Admiral Fitzwallace in the episode, "Gaza" (5/21), and its aftermath, "Memorial Day" (5/22), wherein Bartlet contemplated his response, and baseball was used as a metaphor for foreign policy—it was a whole other "ball game."

Season Six of *The West Wing* began with Bartlet's decision on how to react to the events in Gaza. This would result in one of the least realistic storylines in the series: a Middle East peace summit, which would lead to an eventual agreement, subsequently allowing Bartlet to seemingly solve the Israeli-Palestinian conflict. Otherwise, there was little of substantial weight in the early part of the season. Leo had a heart attack in the episode "The Birnam Wood" (6/2); Bartlet's MS appeared to be intensifying in "A Change Is Gonna Come" (6/7); Penn and Teller appeared to burn the American flag in the episode "In the Room" (6/8); and so on. By the middle of the season, from the episode "Opposition Research" (6/11) onwards, the main storyline had transferred from the White House to the beginnings of the next campaign trail, enveloped in Josh's decision to "find his guy" and make Matt Santos the next president. The main area of interest throughout the rest of the season was thus concerned with Santos being nominated as the Democratic candidate. In addition, in the episode "Ninety Miles Away" (6/19), Leo made a covert journey to Cuba to negotiate with Fidel Castro; there was also the disclosure that a military space shuttle existed, with the somewhat misdirecting implication that CJ was going to leak the story. Finally, the season closed at the Democratic convention with Santos's rousing speech eventually resulting in his nomination as the presidential candidate.

Season Seven of *The West Wing* began within a proleptic *mise-en-scène*, the scene being set three years into the then future of the drama, enabling the viewer to almost see who the next president was going to be. The succeeding episodes of the last season followed two main storylines: the presidential race between Santos and Vinick, and the aftermath of Toby admitting he was the source of the leak that revealed the existence of a military space shuttle. The former plotline, while outside of the previous narrative design of the series, proved engaging and dramatic; the latter was less convincing, insomuch as it was scarcely credible that a man as intelligent as Toby would have committed such an act in the first place. The episode "The Debate" (7/7) was of significance in terms of its transmission method: it was broadcast live, without the use of pre-recording on film. The episode "Running Mates" (7/10) was of interest for Martin Sheen's somewhat perfunctory tribute to John Spencer—the actor had died of a heart attack in December 2005 and his character, Leo, was to be written out of the series. However, in the meantime, the scenes Spencer had already shot were to be used in subsequent episodes. The season (and the series) then concluded with the narrow victory of Santos over Vinick and the preparation for the transition of government. The final scene consisted of Bartlet and Abbey leaving the White House in the presidential helicopter, with Bartlet staring down through the clouds and pondering his future—tomorrow.

Appendix B.
Episodes 1–155:
Broadcast Credits

Season 1

Pilot 1/1. Broadcast: September 22, 1999. Written by Aaron Sorkin. Directed by Thomas Schlamme. 41.06 minutes.

Post Hoc, Ergo Propter Hoc 1/2. Broadcast: September 29, 1999. Written by Aaron Sorkin. Directed by Thomas Schlamme. 39.37 minutes

A Proportional Response 1/3. Broadcast: October 6, 1999. Written by Aaron Sorkin. Directed by Marc Buckland. 41.52 minutes.

Five Votes Down 1/4. Broadcast: October 13, 1999. Teleplay by Aaron Sorkin. Story by Lawrence O'Donnell, Jr., and Patrick H. Caddell. Directed by Michael Lehmann. 42.15 minutes.

The Crackpots and These Women 1/5. Broadcast: October 20, 1999. Written by Aaron Sorkin. Directed by Anthony Drazan. 42.24 minutes.

Mr. Willis of Ohio 1/6. Broadcast: November 3, 1999. Written by Aaron Sorkin. Directed by Christopher Misiano. 42.19 minutes.

The State Dinner 1/7. Broadcast: November 10, 1999. Written by Aaron Sorkin and Paul Redford. Directed by Thomas Schlamme. 42.17 minutes.

Enemies 1/8. Broadcast: November 17, 1999. Teleplay by Ron Osborn and Jeff Reno. Story by Rick Cleveland, Lawrence O'Donnell, Jr., and Patrick H. Caddell. Directed by Alan Taylor. 42.18 minutes.

The Short List 1/9. Broadcast: November 24, 1999. Teleplay by Aaron Sorkin and Patrick H. Caddell. Story by Aaron Sorkin and Dee Dee Myers. Directed by Bill D'Elia. 42.22 minutes.

In Excelsis Deo 1/10. Broadcast: December 15, 1999. Written by Aaron Sorkin and Rick Cleveland. Directed by Alex Graves. 42.20 minutes.

Lord John Marbury 1/11. Broadcast: January 5, 2000. Teleplay by Aaron Sorkin and Patrick H. Caddell. Story by Patrick H. Caddell and Lawrence O'Donnell, Jr. Directed by Kevin Rodney Sullivan. 41.42 minutes.

He Shall, From Time to Time 1/12. Broadcast: January 12, 2000. Written by Aaron Sorkin. Directed by Arlene Sanford. 41.53 minutes.

Take Out the Trash Day 1/13. Broadcast: January 26, 2000. Written by Aaron Sorkin. Directed by Ken Olin. 41.51 minutes.

Take This Sabbath Day 1/14. Broadcast: February 9, 2000. Teleplay by Aaron Sorkin. Story by Lawrence O'Donnell, Jr., Paul Redford and Aaron Sorkin. Directed by Thomas Schlamme. 41.56 minutes.

Celestial Navigation 1/15. Broadcast: February 16, 2000. Teleplay by Aaron Sorkin. Story by Dee Dee Myers and Lawrence O'Donnell, Jr. Directed by Christopher Misiano. 41.52 minutes.

20 Hours in L.A. 1/16. Broadcast: February 23, 2000. Written by Aaron Sorkin. Directed by Alan Taylor. 41.42 minutes.

The White House Pro-Am 1/17. Broadcast: March 22, 2000. Written by Lawrence O'Donnell, Jr., Paul Redford and Aaron Sorkin. Directed by Ken Olin. 41.50 minutes.

Six Meetings Before Lunch 1/18. Broadcast: April 5, 2000. Written by Aaron Sorkin. Directed by Clark Johnson. 41.37 minutes.

Let Bartlet Be Bartlet 1/19. Broadcast: April 26, 2000. Teleplay by Aaron Sorkin. Story by Peter Parnell and Patrick H. Caddell. Directed by Laura Innes. 41.22 minutes.

Mandatory Minimums 1/20. Broadcast: May 3, 2000. Written by Aaron Sorkin. Directed by Robert Berlinger. 41.48 minutes.

Lies, Damn Lies and Statistics 1/21. Broadcast: May 10, 2000. Teleplay by Aaron Sorkin. Story by Patrick H. Caddell. Directed by Don Scardino. 41.52 minutes.

What Kind of Day Has It Been 1/22. Broadcast: May 17, 2000. Written by Aaron Sorkin. Directed by Thomas Schlamme. 41.51 minutes.

Season 2

In the Shadow of Two Gunmen Part 1 2/1. Broadcast: October 4, 2000. Written by Aaron Sorkin. Directed by Thomas Schlamme. 42.11 minutes.

In the Shadow of Two Gunmen Part 2 2/2. Broadcast: October 4, 2000. Written by Aaron Sorkin. Directed by Thomas Schlamme. 40.54 minutes.

The Midterms 2/3. Broadcast: October 18, 2000. Written by Aaron Sorkin. Directed by Alex Graves. 41.50 minutes.

In This White House 2/4. Broadcast: October 25, 2000. Teleplay by Aaron Sorkin. Story by Peter Parnell and Allison Abner. Directed by Ken Olin. 41.54 minutes.

And It's Surely to Their Credit 2/5. Broadcast: November 1, 2000. Teleplay by Aaron Sorkin. Story by Kevin Falls and Laura Glasser. Directed by Christopher Misiano. 41.51 minutes.

The Lame Duck Congress 2/6. Broadcast: November 8, 2000. Teleplay by Aaron Sorkin. Story by Lawrence O'Donnell, Jr. Directed by Jeremy Kagan. 40.53 minutes.

The Portland Trip 2/7. Broadcast: November 15, 2000. Teleplay by Aaron Sorkin. Story by Paul Redford. Directed by Paris Barclay. 40.43 minutes.

Shibboleth 2/8. Broadcast: November 22, 2000. Teleplay by Aaron Sorkin. Story by Patrick H. Caddell. Directed by Laura Innes. 41.07 minutes.

Galileo 2/9. Broadcast: November 29, 2000. Written by Kevin Falls and Aaron Sorkin. Directed by Alex Graves. 41.27 minutes.

Noël 2/10. Broadcast: December 20, 2000. Teleplay by Aaron Sorkin. Story by Peter Parnell. Directed by Thomas Schlamme. 42.19 minutes.

The Leadership Breakfast 2/11. Broadcast: January 10, 2001. Teleplay by Aaron Sorkin. Story by Paul Redford. Directed by Scott Winant. 41.36 minutes.

The Drop-In 2/12. Broadcast: January 24, 2001. Teleplay by Aaron Sorkin. Story by Lawrence O'Donnell, Jr. Directed by Lou Antonio. 41.29 minutes.

Bartlet's Third State of the Union 2/13. Broadcast: February 7, 2001. Teleplay by Aaron Sorkin. Story by Allison Abner and Dee Dee Myers. Directed by Christopher Misiano. 41.52 minutes.

The War at Home 2/14. Broadcast: February 14, 2001. Written by Aaron Sorkin. Directed by Christopher Misiano. 41.51 minutes.

Ellie 2/15. Broadcast: February 21, 2001. Teleplay by Aaron Sorkin. Story by Kevin Falls and Laura Glasser. Directed by Michael Engler. 41.38 minutes.

Somebody's Going to Emergency, Somebody's Going to Jail 2/16. Broadcast: February 28, 2001. Written by Paul Redford and Aaron Sorkin. Directed by Jessica Yu. 41.50 minutes.

The Stackhouse Filibuster 2/17. Broadcast: March 14, 2001. Teleplay by Aaron Sorkin. Story by Pete McCabe. Directed by Bryan Gordon. 41.36 minutes.

17 People 2/18. Broadcast: April 4, 2001. Written by Aaron Sorkin. Directed by Alex Graves. 42.18 minutes.

Bad Moon Rising 2/19. Broadcast: April 25, 2001. Teleplay by Aaron Sorkin. Story by Felicia Willson. Directed by Bill Johnson. 41.15 minutes.

The Fall's Gonna Kill You 2/20. Broadcast: May 2, 2001. Teleplay by Aaron Sorkin. Story by Patrick H. Caddell. Directed by Christopher Misiano. 42.12 minutes.

18th and Potomac 2/21. Broadcast: May 9, 2001. Teleplay by Aaron Sorkin. Story by Lawrence O'Donnell, Jr. Directed by Robert Berlinger. 41.41 minutes.

Two Cathedrals 2/22. Broadcast: May 16, 2001. Written by Aaron Sorkin. Directed by Thomas Schlamme. 42.14 minutes.

Season 3

Isaac and Ishmael 3/1. Broadcast: October 3, 2001. Written by Aaron Sorkin. Directed by Christopher Misiano. 39.36 minutes.

Manchester Part 1 3/2. Broadcast: October 10, 2001. Written by Aaron Sorkin. Directed by Thomas Schlamme. 41.46 minutes.

Manchester Part 2 3/3. Broadcast: October 17, 2001. Written by Aaron Sorkin. Directed by Thomas Schlamme. 41.35 minutes.

Appendix B

Ways and Means 3/4. Broadcast: October 24, 2001. Teleplay by Aaron Sorkin. Story by Eli Attie and Gene Sperling. Directed by Alex Graves. 41.48 minutes.

On the Day Before 3/5. Broadcast: October 31, 2001. Teleplay by Aaron Sorkin. Story by Paul Redford and Nadna Chitre. Directed by Christopher Misiano. 41.48 minutes.

War Crimes 3/6. Broadcast: November 7, 2001. Teleplay by Aaron Sorkin. Story by Allison Abner. Directed by Alex Graves. 41.53 minutes.

Gone Quiet 3/7. Broadcast: November 14, 2001. Teleplay by Aaron Sorkin. Story by Julia Dahl and Laura Glasser. Directed by Jon Hutman. 40.45 minutes.

The Indians in the Lobby 3/8. Broadcast: November 21, 2001. Teleplay by Allison Abner, Kevin Falls and Aaron Sorkin. Story by Allison Abner. Directed by Paris Barclay. 41.25 minutes.

The Women of Qumar 3/9. Broadcast: November 28, 2001. Teleplay by Aaron Sorkin. Story by Felicia Wilson, Laura Glasser and Julia Dahl. Directed by Alex Graves. 41.46 minutes.

Bartlet for America 3/10. Broadcast: December 12, 2001. Written by Aaron Sorkin. Directed by Thomas Schlamme. 42.38 minutes.

H. Con—172 3/11. Broadcast: January 9, 2002. Teleplay by Aaron Sorkin. Story by Eli Attie. Directed by Vincent Misiano. 41.35 minutes.

100,000 Airplanes 3/12. Broadcast: January 16, 2002. Written by Aaron Sorkin. Directed by David Nutter. 41.16 minutes.

The Two Bartlets 3/13. Broadcast: January 30, 2002. Teleplay by Kevin Falls and Aaron Sorkin. Story by Gene Sperling. Directed by Alex Graves. 41.30 minutes.

Night Five 3/14. Broadcast: February 6, 2002. Written by Aaron Sorkin. Directed by Christopher Misiano. 41.37 minutes.

Hartsfield's Landing 3/15. Broadcast: February 27, 2002. Written by Aaron Sorkin. Directed by Vincent Misiano. 41.45 minutes.

Dead Irish Writers 3/16. Broadcast: March 6, 2002. Teleplay by Aaron Sorkin. Story by Paul Redford. Directed by Alex Graves. 40.19 minutes.

The U.S. Poet Laureate 3/17. Broadcast: March 27, 2002. Teleplay by Aaron Sorkin. Story by Laura Glasser. Directed by Christopher Misiano. 41.47 minutes.

Stirred 3/18. Broadcast: April 3, 2002. Teleplay by Aaron Sorkin and Eli Attie. Story by Dee Dee Myers. Directed by Jeremy Kagan. 40.04 minutes.

Enemies Foreign and Domestic 3/19. Broadcast: May 1, 2002. Written by Paul Redford and Aaron Sorkin. Directed by Alex Graves. 41.46 minutes.

The Black Vera Wang 3/20. Broadcast: May 8, 2002. Written by Aaron Sorkin. Directed by Christopher Misiano. 40.45 minutes.

We Killed Yamamoto 3/21. Broadcast: May 15, 2002. Written by Aaron Sorkin. Directed by Thomas Schlamme. 41.44 minutes.

Posse Comitatus 3/22. Broadcast: May 22, 2002. Written by Aaron Sorkin. Directed by Alex Graves. 41.33 minutes.

Season 4

20 Hours in America Parts 1 and 2 4/1 and 4/2. Broadcast: September 25, 2002. Written by Aaron Sorkin. Directed by Christopher Misiano. 42.19 minutes and 41.55 minutes.

College Kids 4/3. Broadcast: October 2, 2002. Teleplay by Aaron Sorkin. Story by Debora Cahn and Mark Goffman. Directed by Alex Graves. 42.34 minutes.

The Red Mass 4/4. Broadcast: October 16, 2002. Teleplay by Aaron Sorkin. Story by Eli Attie. Directed by Vincent Misiano. 42.06 minutes.

Debate Camp 4/5. Broadcast: October 16, 2002. Teleplay by Aaron Sorkin. Story by William Sind and Michael Oates Palmer. Directed by Paris Barclay. 41.46 minutes.

Game On 4/6. Broadcast: October 30, 2002. Written by Aaron Sorkin and Paul Redford. Directed by Alex Graves. 41.50 minutes.

Election Night 4/7. Broadcast: November 6, 2002. Teleplay by Aaron Sorkin. Story by David Gerken and David Handleman. Directed by Lesli Linka Glatter. 42.00 minutes.

Process Stories 4/8. Broadcast: November 13, 2002. Teleplay by Aaron Sorkin. Story by Paula Yoo and Lauren Schmidt. Directed by Christopher Misiano. 41.49 minutes.

Swiss Diplomacy 4/9. Broadcast: November 20, 2002. Written by Eli Attie and Kevin Falls. Directed by Christopher Misiano. 39.50 minutes.

Arctic Radar 4/10. Broadcast: November 27, 2002. Written by Aaron Sorkin. Story by Gene Sperling. Directed by John David Coles. 41.34 minutes.

Holy Night 4/11. Broadcast: December 11, 2002. Written by Aaron Sorkin. Directed by Thomas Schlamme. 44.16 minutes.

Guns Not Butter 4/12. Broadcast: January 8, 2003. Written by Eli Attie, Kevin Falls and Aaron Sorkin. Directed by Bill D'Elia. 41.26 minutes.

The Long Goodbye 4/13. Broadcast: January 15, 2003. Written by Jon Robin Baitz. Directed by Alex Graves. 40.42 minutes.

Inauguration Part 1 4/14. Broadcast: February 5, 2003. Teleplay by Aaron Sorkin. Story by Michael Oates Palmer and William Sind. Directed by Christopher Misiano. 1.30 minutes.

Inauguration Part 2: Over There 4/15. Broadcast: February 12, 2003. Teleplay by Aaron Sorkin. Story by David Gerken and Gene Sperling. Directed by Lesli Linka Glatter. 42.07 minutes.

The California 47th 4/16. Broadcast: February 19, 2003. Teleplay by Aaron Sorkin. Story by Lauren Schmidt and Paula Yoo. Directed by Vincent Misiano. 41.35 minutes.

Red Haven's on Fire 4/17. Broadcast: February 26, 2003. Teleplay by Aaron Sorkin. Story by Mark Goffman and Debora Cahn. Directed by Alex Graves. 40.35 minutes.

Privateers 4/18. Broadcast: March 26, 2003. Teleplay by Paul Redford, Deborah Cahn and Aaron Sorkin. Story by Paul Redford and Deborah Cahn. Directed by Alex Graves. 40.39 minutes.

Angel Maintenance 4/19. Broadcast: April 2, 2003. Teleplay by Eli Attie and Aaron Sorkin. Story by Eli Attie and Kevin Falls. Directed by Jessica Yu. 40.23 minutes.

Evidence of Things Not Seen 4/20. Broadcast: April 23, 2003. Teleplay by Aaron Sorkin. Story by Eli Attie and David Handleman. Directed by Christopher Misiano. 41.51 minutes.

Life on Mars 4/21. Broadcast: April 30, 2003. Teleplay by Aaron Sorkin. Story by Paul Redford and Dee Dee Myer. Directed by John David Coles. 41.38 minutes.

Commencement 4/22. Broadcast: May 7, 2003. Written by Aaron Sorkin. Directed by Alex Graves. 42.15 minutes.

Twenty-Five 4/23. Broadcast: May 14, 2003. Written by Aaron Sorkin. Directed by Christopher Misiano. 42.48 minutes.

SEASON 5

7A WF 83429 5/1. Broadcast: September 24, 2003. Written by John Wells. Directed by Alex Graves. 40.34 minutes.

The Dogs of War 5/2. Broadcast: October 1, 2003. Written by John Wells. Directed by Christopher Misiano. 40.37 minutes.

Jefferson Lives 5/3. Broadcast: October 8, 2003. Teleplay by Carol Flint. Story by Carol Flint and Debora Cahn. Directed by Alex Graves. 41.30 minutes.

Han 5/4. Broadcast: October 22, 2003. Teleplay by Peter Noah. Story by Peter Noah, Mark Goffman and Paula Yoo. Directed by Christopher Misiano. 41.42 minutes.

Constituency of One 5/5. Broadcast: October 29, 2003. Teleplay by Eli Attie. Story by Eli Attie and Michael Oates Palmer. Directed by Laura Innes. 41.23 minutes.

Disaster Relief 5/6. Broadcast: November 5, 2003. Teleplay by Alexa Junge. Story by Alexa Junge and Lauren Schmidt. Directed by Lesli Linka Glatter. 41.17 minutes.

Separation of Powers 5/7. Broadcast: November 12, 2003. Written by Paul Redford. Directed by Alex Graves. 41.24 minutes.

Shutdown 5/8. Broadcast: November 19, 2003. Written by Mark Goffman. Directed by Christopher Misiano. 41.23 minutes.

Abu el Banat 5/9. Broadcast: December 3, 2003. Written by Deborah Cahn. Directed by Lesli Linka Glatter. 41.44 minutes.

The Stormy Present 5/10. Broadcast: January 7, 2004. Teleplay by John Sacret Young. Story by John Sacret Young and Josh Singer. Directed by Alex Graves. 41.02 minutes.

The Benign Prerogative 5/11. Broadcast: January 14, 2004. Written by Carol Flint. Directed by Christopher Misiano. 41.16 minutes.

Slow News Day 5/12. Broadcast: February 4, 2004. Written by Eli Attie. Directed by Julie Hebert. 41.52 minutes.

The Warfare of Genghis Khan 5/13. Broadcast: February 11, 2004. Written by Peter Noah. Directed by Bill D'Elia. 41.04 minutes.

An Khe 5/14. Broadcast: February 18, 2004. Written by John Wells. Directed by Alex Graves. 41.30 minutes.

Full Disclosure 5/15. Broadcast: February 25, 2004. Written by Lawrence O'Donnell, Jr. Directed by Lesli Linka Glatter. 41.05 minutes.

Eppur Si Muove 5/16. Broadcast: March 3, 2004. Written by Alexa Junge. Directed by Llewellyn Wells. 41.15 minutes.

The Supremes 5/17. Broadcast: March 24, 2004. Written by Debora Cahn. Directed by Jessica Yu. 40.31 minutes.

Access 5/18. Broadcast: March 31, 2004. Written by Lauren Schmidt. Directed by Alex Graves. 40.55 minutes.

Talking Points 5/19. Broadcast: April 21, 2004. Written by Eli Attie. Directed by Richard Schiff. 41.52 minutes.

No Exit 5/20. Broadcast: April 28, 2004. Teleplay by Carol Flint and Debora Cahn. Story by Carol Flint and Mark Goffman. Directed by Julie Hebert. 41.35 minutes.

Gaza 5/21. Broadcast: May 12, 2004. Written by Peter Noah. Directed by Christopher Misiano. 41.06 minutes.

Memorial Day 5/22. Broadcast: May 19, 2004. Written by John Sacret Young and Josh Singer. Directed by Christopher Misiano. 41.37 minutes.

SEASON 6

NSF Thurmont 6/1. Broadcast: October 20, 2004. Written by John Wells. Directed by Alex Graves. 41.14 minutes.

The Birnam Wood 6/2. Broadcast: October 27, 2004. Written by John Wells. Directed by Alex Graves. 41.20 minutes.

Third Day Story 6/3. Broadcast: November 3, 2004. Written by Eli Attie. Directed by Christopher Misiano. 41.34 minutes.

Liftoff 6/4. Broadcast: November 10, 2004. Written by Debora Cahn. Directed by Alex Graves. 41.46 minutes.

The Hubbert Peak 6/5. Broadcast: November 17, 2004. Written by Peter Noah. Directed by Julie Hebert. 40.57 minutes.

The Dover Test 6/6. Broadcast: November 24, 2004. Written by Carol Flint. Directed by Laura Innes. 41.05 minutes.

A Change Is Gonna Come 6/7. Broadcast: December 1, 2004. Teleplay by John Sacret Young and Josh Singer. Story by John Sacret Young. Directed by Vincent Misiano. 41.30 minutes.

In the Room 6/8. Broadcast: December 8, 2004. Written by Lawrence O'Donnell, Jr. Directed by Alex Graves. 41.17 minutes.

Impact Winter 6/9. Broadcast: December 15, 2004. Written by Debora Cahn. Directed by Lesli Linka Glatter. 41.12 minutes.

Faith Based Initiative 6/10. Broadcast: January 5, 2005. Written by Bradley Whitford. Directed by Christopher Misiano. 41.47 minutes.

Opposition Research 6/11. Broadcast: January 12, 2005. Written by Eli Attie. Directed by Christopher Misiano. 41.43 minutes.

365 Days 6/12. Broadcast: January 19, 2005. Written by Mark Goffman. Directed by Andrew Bernstein. 41.40 minutes.

King Corn 6/13. Broadcast: January 26, 2005. Written by John Wells. Directed by Alex Graves. 41.52 minutes.

The Wake-Up Call 6/14. Broadcast: February 9, 2005. Written by Josh Singer. Directed by Laura Innes. 41.41 minutes.

Freedonia 6/15. Broadcast: February 16, 2005. Written by Eli Attie. Directed by Christopher Misiano. 41.44 minutes.

Drought Conditions 6/16. Broadcast: February 23, 2005. Written by Debora Cahn. Directed by Alex Graves. 41.08 minutes.

A Good Day 6/17. Broadcast: March 2, 2005. Written by Carol Flint. Directed by Richard Schiff. 41.44 minutes.

La Palabra 6/18. Broadcast: March 9, 2005. Written by Eli Attie. Directed by Jason Ensler. 41.44 minutes.

Ninety Miles Away 6/19. Broadcast: March 16, 2005. Written by John Sacret Young. Directed by Rod Holcomb. 41.46 minutes.

In God We Trust 6/20. Broadcast: March 23, 2005. Written by Lawrence O'Donnell, Jr. Directed by Christopher Misiano. 41.47 minutes.

Things Fall Apart 6/21. Broadcast: March 30, 2005. Written by Peter Noah. Directed by Nelson McCorrmick. 41.47 minutes.

2162 Votes 6/22. Broadcast: April 6, 2005. Written by John Wells. Directed by Alex Graves. 40.55 minutes.

Season 7

The Ticket 7/1. Broadcast: September 25, 2005. Written by Debora Cahn. Directed by Christopher Misiano. 41.43 minutes.

The Mommy Problem 7/2. Broadcast: October 2, 2005. Written by Eli Attie. Directed by Alex Graves. 41.46 minutes.

Message of the Week 7/3. Broadcast: October 9, 2005. Written by Lawrence O'Donnell, Jr. Directed by Christopher Misiano. 41.25 minutes.

Mr. Frost 7/4. Broadcast: October 16, 2005. Written by Alex Graves. Directed by Andrew Bernstein. 40.28 minutes.

Here Today 7/5. Broadcast: October 23, 2005. Written by Peter Noah. Directed by Alex Graves. 41.46 minutes.

The Al Smith Dinner 7/6. Broadcast: October 30, 2005. Written by Eli Attie. Directed by Lesli Linka Glatter. 41.33 minutes.

The Debate 7/7. Broadcast: November 6, 2005. Written by Lawrence O'Donnell, Jr. Directed by Alex Graves. 50.45 minutes.

Undecideds 7/8. Broadcast: December 4, 2005. Written by Debora Cahn. Directed by Christopher Misiano. 41.32 minutes.

The Wedding 7/9. Broadcast: December 11, 2005. Written by Josh Singer. Directed by Max Mayer. 41.45 minutes.

Running Mates 7/10. Broadcast: January 8, 2006. Written by Peter Noah. Directed by Paul McCrane. 41.54 minutes.

Internal Displacement 7/11. Broadcast: January 15, 2006. Written by Bradley Whitford. Directed by Andrew Bernstein. 41.23 minutes.

Duck and Cover 7/12. Broadcast: January 22, 2006. Written by Eli Attie. Directed by Christopher Misiano. 41.20 minutes.

The Cold 7/13. Broadcast: March 12, 2006. Teleplay by Debora Cahn. Story by Debora Cahn and Lauren Schmidt. Directed by Alex Graves. 41.03 minutes.

Two Weeks Out 7/14. Broadcast: March 19, 2006. Written by Lawrence O'Donnell, Jr. Directed by Laura Innes. 41.49 minutes.

Welcome to Wherever You Are 7/15. Broadcast: March 26, 2006. Written by Josh Singer. Directed by Matia Karrell. 41.36 minutes.

Election Day Part 1 7/16. Broadcast: April 2, 2006. Written by Lauren Schmidt. Directed by Mimi Leder. 41.25 minutes.

Election Day Part 2 7/17. Broadcast: April 9, 2006. Written by Eli Attie and John Wells. Directed by Christopher Misiano. 40.58 minutes.

Requiem 7/18. Broadcast: April 16, 2006. Written by Eli Attie, Debora Cahn and John Wells. Directed by Steve Shill. 41.37 minutes.

Transition 7/19. Broadcast: April 23, 2006. Written by Peter Noah. Directed by Nelson McCormick. 41.51 minutes.

The Last Hurrah 7/20. Broadcast: April 30, 2006. Written by Lawrence O'Donnell, Jr. Directed by Tim Matheson. 41.36 minutes.

Institutional Memory 7/21. Broadcast: May 7, 2006. Written by Debora Cahn. Directed by Lesli Linka Glatter. 41.44 minutes.

Tomorrow 7/22. Broadcast: May 14, 2006. Written by John Wells. Directed by Christopher Misiano. 41.32 minutes.

Appendix C.
Directors and Writers

DIRECTORS

1. Alex Graves — 34 Episodes
2. Christopher Misiano — 34
3. Thomas Schlamme — 14
4. Lesli Linka Glatter — 8
5. Laura Innes — 6
6. Vincent Misiano — 5
7. Jessica Yu — 3
8. Bill D'Elia — 3
9. Ken Olin — 3
10. Paris Barclay — 3
11. Julie Hebert — 3
12. Andrew Bernstein — 3
13. Alan Taylor — 2
14. Robert Berlinger — 2
15. Jeremy Kagan — 2
16. John David Coles — 2
17. Richard Schiff — 2
18. Nelson McCorrmick — 2
19. Marc Buckland — 1
20. Michael Lehmann — 1
21. Anthony Drazan — 1
22. Kevin Rodney Sullivan — 1
23. Arlene Sanford — 1
24. Clark Johnson — 1
25. Don Scardino — 1
26. Scott Winant — 1
27. Lou Antonio — 1
28. Michael Engler — 1
29. Bryan Gordon — 1
30. Bill Johnson — 1
31. Jon Hutman — 1
32. David Nutter — 1
33. Llewellyn Wells — 1
34. Jason Ensler — 1
35. Rod Holcomb — 1
36. Max Mayer — 1
37. Paul McCrane — 1
38. Matia Karrell — 1
39. Mimi Leder — 1
40. Steve Shill — 1
41. Tim Matheson — 1

WRITERS

1. Aaron Sorkin — 85
   (31 sole credits/54 joint credits)
2. Eli Attie — 19 (9/10)
3. Lawrence O'Donnell, Jr. — 17 (7/10)
4. Debora Cahn — 14 (8/6)
5. Paul Redford — 13 (1/12)
6. John Wells — 11 (9/2)
7. Peter Noah — 8 (7/1)
8. Patrick H. Caddell — 8 (0/8)
9. Kevin Falls — 8 (0/8)
10. Lauren Schmidt — 7 (2/5)
11. Mark Goffman — 6 (2/4)
12. Josh Singer — 6 (3/3)
13. Carol Flint — 5 (3/2)

14. Laura Glasser	5 (0/5)	
15. Dee Dee Myers	5 (0/5)	
16. John Sacret Young	4 (1/3)	
17. Allison Abner	4 (0/4)	
18. Gene Sperling	4 (0/4)	
19. Michael Oates Palmer	3 (0/3)	
20. Paula Yoo	3 (0/3)	
21. Peter Parnell	3 (0/3)	
22. Bradley Whitford	2 (2/0)	
23. Alexa Junge	2 (1/1)	
24. Julia Dahl	2 (0/2)	
25. David Gerken	2 (0/2)	
26. David Handleman	2 (0/2)	
27. William Sind	2 (0/2)	
28. Felicia Willson	2 (0/2)	
29. Alex Graves	1 (1/0)	
30. Jon Robin Baitz	1 (1/0)	
31. Jeff Reno	1 (0/1)	
32. Nadna Chitre	1 (0/1)	
33. Pete McCabe	1 (0/1)	
34. Rick Cleveland	1 (0/1)	
35. Ron Osborn	1 (0/1)	

Chapter Notes

Introduction

1. The ending to the episode "The Midterms" (2/3), wherein several members of the cast (CJ, Josh, Toby and Sam) sat on a "stoop" somewhere in the suburbs of Washington D.C., and solemnly intoned, one by one, "God bless America," offers an apt sense of the degree of sentimentality at play within the series. A culturally distanced observer might have been forgiven in speculating whether this was to be taken seriously, whether this was, in fact, a knowingly subversive and satiric scene—it was not—and, as such, it represented both the charm and the naivety of *The West Wing*.

2. In terms of commercial success, this can be measured, albeit in a basic way, via a consideration of the viewing figures the show attained. However, perhaps surprisingly, *The West Wing* was not a huge commercial success, at least in terms of the raw viewing figures. According to the Nielsen Ratings, the first season attracted an average audience of 9.1 million viewers in the U.S. This increased to 17 million viewers in the second and third seasons, reducing to 13.5 million in the fourth season, and dipping just slightly after Sorkin's departure to 11.8 and 11.1 million in seasons five and six. There was then a significant drop to 8.1 million viewers for the seventh and final season. However, as Janet McCabe has pointed out, the show was astutely "aimed at a viewership the network could sell to sponsors at higher rates" (McCabe 2013, 23). In other words, the show "delivered a disproportionately high number of affluent, upwardly mobile, better educated, urban-minded professionals, ranking first among primetime shows in the percentage of eighteen to forty-nine-year-olds boasting a median income of $75,000 and above" (McCabe 2013, 24).

3. According to Janet McCabe, "Episodes were priced at around $2.7 million to produce" (McCabe 2013, 20). As each episode of the series had such a high budget, each episode appeared to possess the high production standards of a feature film, rather than that of a television drama. As Michael Mayers, the show's director of photography from 2004 to 2006, commented: "We work under the same production standards as the best Hollywood features'" (cited in McCabe 2013, 60).

4. The academic responses to the show were as follows: Janet's McCabe's *The West Wing*, a detailed analysis of the show from the perspective of its place in the history of television; Melissa Crawley's *Mr. Sorkin Goes to Washington*, an insightful and resourceful account of the show's didactic potential; Thomas Fahy's *Considering Aaron Sorkin*, a collection of essays on Sorkin's work, including a number of informative pieces on *The West Wing*; Peter C. Rollins and John E. Connor's *The West Wing: The American Presidency as Television Drama*, another collection of essays, this time solely on *The West Wing*, with a balanced set of responses from a diverse range of critical perspectives; and finally, Trevor and Shawn J. Parry-Giles' *The Prime-Time Presidency: The West Wing and U.S. Nationalism*, perhaps the most interesting, or at least the most theoretically focused book yet published on the series. It should be noted that the five academically positioned books were published in 2003, 2005, 2006, 2006 and 2013; hence only one (Janet McCabe's) was able to consider the series as a whole, with most of the other books looking to Seasons 1–4.

5. However, for a useful overview of such sources see Challen 2001, pp. 27–50. Challen offers a carefully selected and helpful overview of the contemporary press reaction to the series.

6. Some of the most useful websites are as follows: thewestswingweekly.com; www.westwingguide.com; www.westwing.beware.com; www.westwing.wikia.com; www.seventeenpeople.com.

7. There is also the issue of social media (scarcely recognized at the time of *The West Wing* itself). For example, there are subcultures on *Twitter* wherein fan activity can be witnessed—with individuals "tweeting" as avatars of characters within the original television series. See Bore and Hickman 2013.

8. As intimated, this would seem to be true even in the case of responses to the show from academic journals. A literature search in 2015 revealed some 72 published articles; however, there was relatively little use of cultural theory to explore the discursive practices inherent in the series. The majority of this material derived from American sources. It is possible that academic responses in other languages—in French, for example—may have looked at the show in a different way; but for reasons of practicality the literature review for this book has only encompassed materials available in English.

9. As will be seen, a seemingly innocuous detail at the very end of the final episode of *The West Wing* could potentially be interpreted as pointing to such a claim, almost as if the writer of the final episode, in this case John Wells, had deliberately placed such a detail within the closing moments of the show.

10. See Sontag 2001.

11. In adopting a theoretical approach, a number of intellectual dead ends will be avoided; for example, the issue of authorship. Aaron Sorkin, as the putative creator of the show, has been the object of much critical attention; however, the approach taken here will be to sidestep the issue of authorship using Roland Barthes's argument "The Death of the Author," which sought to dispense with such mundane preoccupations.

12. This quotation has been cited in a number of diverse sources, but it would seem to have originally derived from an interview with Terrence Smith on PBS's *The News Hour With Jim Lehrer* on September 27, 2000. See Fahy 2005, 63.

Chapter 1

1. Other actors had been considered for some of the main roles; for example, the casting of Toby Ziegler was a "two-man race" (Lacey, O'Connell and Bernardin 2014) between Richard Schiff and Eugene Levy. Levy as a comedian/actor might have brought a less morose sense to the role. In addition, Judd Hirsch is said to have been a potential actor for the role of Leo and CCH Pounder is said to have been a potential actor to play CJ Cregg. If the latter is true it would have strengthened the culturally diverse element of the show. Finally, other potential actors to play the president included Alan Alda, Jason Robards and Sidney Poitier. Alan Alda would later feature in the series as Arnold Vinick; Jason Robards had previously played Richard M. Monckton, a cipher for Richard M. Nixon in the 1977 television series *Washington behind Close Doors*—and may therefore have carried too much of a Republican slant to play such a determined Democrat as Bartlet; finally, Sidney Poitier would have made for an interesting choice as Bartlet, in other words, as a black president some time before Obama, enabling a still further searching interrogation of the issue of race in the show. However, Poitier may have been considered too old for the role. He would have been 72 when the series began and 79 when it concluded.

2. See, for example, David Barber's comment on the acting antecedents of some of the cast members: "John Spencer who plays Leo McGarry, Bradley Whitford who plays Josh Lyman, Richard Schiff who plays Toby Ziegler and Allison Janney who plays CJ Cregg, all have backgrounds as minor or supporting characters in television and films, often favoring the stage over the screen" (Barber 2009, 210).

3. The maid was only seen in long shot, but it would seem that she was black; hence this would appear to have been a conscious if minor element of the plot, and one with a relevance to the overarching discourse of race at play within the show.

4. To this might be added, albeit from a fictional discourse, just the slightest suggestion of President Merkin Muffley from Stanley Kubrick's film *Dr. Strangelove* (1964).

5. It would seem that a number of individuals working on *The West Wing* had a low opinion of President Bush. For example, Martin Sheen stated: "I think he's a bully. I don't think he has any heart … I think he's full of shit, frankly" (cited in Challen 2001, 35). In a similar way, Bradley Whitford, at a rally for Al Gore, during the 2000 election campaign, commented: "I'm not a politician, I just play one on TV—kind of like George Bush" (cited in Crawley 2006, 203n).

6. Barber 2009, 232.

7. Barber 2009, 232, 233.

8. See Nathan A. Paxton: "The parallels between the campaigns of Bartlet's competitor and the George W. Bush campaign of 2000 are not subtle, and they do not seem to be designed as such"(cited in Fahy 2005, 175n).

9. Rollins and O'Connor 2003, 77. Perhaps the only winner in this affair was Josh Brolin, the actor who played Governor Richie; Brolin would eventually go on to play George W. Bush himself in Oliver Stone's film *W* (2008).

10. One presumes Leo's wealth had derived from past business dealings—this being obliquely suggested in the episode "An Khe" (4/14).

11. See Chapter 7 for a fuller discussion speculating on this question.

12. Note, for example, Leo's irritation with the *New York Times* crossword in the opening episode, "Pilot" (1/1), the issue in question being Leo's annoyance with the misspelling of Muammar Gaddafi's name.

13. The episode in question had begun with a short and somewhat perfunctory tribute to John Spencer by Martin Sheen: "Good evening. On December 16th, we lost our dear friend and colleague, John Spencer. Through our shock and grief, we can think of no more fitting memorial to this wonderful man, this extraordinary actor, than to share with you, beginning tonight, the last few months of his work here on *The West Wing*. Johnny, it seems we hardly knew you. We love you and we miss you."

14. However, note there was no Mandy—her reappearance, had it occurred, has been described as a potential act of near genius, but there was to be no reprise of Mandy's first season appearance.

15. See, for example, Michelle Mouton's estimation of Toby as the "administration's Jewish, liberal, intellectual conscience" (cited in Rollins and O'Connor 2003, 192).

16. Crawley 2006, 84.

17. This short line was seen by one anonymous reviewer as being the greatest in the whole series (*TV Tropes.* n.d. "Series: The West Wing").

18. Transcribed from the DVD of the episode "The Crackpots and These Women" (1/5). It might also be noted how this line demonstrated how unrealistic Sorkin's writing could sometimes be; for example, it was somewhat implausible that, in the middle of a basketball game with the president of the United States (which in itself would seem to have been somewhat unlikely), Toby would have been able to come up with (and to deliver) such a carefully constructed and considered line as this.

19. In addition to the casting of the main actors, some of the other players in the series might be mentioned: Charles Young (Dulé Hill), the president's personal aide, and something of a token black character, but played throughout the series with some conviction; Abbey Bartlet (Stockard Channing), the first lady, a powerful female presence if often under-used; Admiral Fitzwallace (John Amos), the Chairman of the Joint Chiefs of Staff—another token black character, but one played to convincing effect; Zoey Bartlet (Elizabeth Moss), Bartlet's youngest and only fully realized daughter; John Hoynes (Tim Matheson), Bartlet's first vice-president—an engaging if conventional villain; Will Bailey (Joshua Malina), the replacement for Sam Seaborn—a role he never seemed to quite manage to fulfill; Matt Santos (Jimmy Smits), the Democratic candidate who would eventually succeed Bartlet; and finally, Arnold Vinick (Alan Alda), the Republican candidate for the presidency in the final season—a liberal and even likable Republican.

20. (*TV Tropes.* n.d. "Series: The West Wing").

21. John Podhoretz cited in Rollins and O'Connor 2003, 224.

22. Michelle Mouton cited in Rollins and O'Connor 2003, 193.

23. The last cluster of quotations derives from McCabe 2013, 92.

24. Transcribed from the DVD of the episode "The Indians in the Lobby" (3/8).

25. In terms of the idea of a censure, it would perhaps be relevant to acknowledge the censure Bartlet accepted from Congress for his non-disclosure of having multiple sclerosis. This occurred in the episode "H. Con—172" (3/11). The censure was read out only in the background at the very end of the episode, but it is worth reading in full: "Whereas, in his conduct of the Office of the President of the United States, Josiah Bartlet has engaged in a course of deceitful and dishonest conduct designed to impede and deny the disclosure of vital matters of public concern, the United States Congress hereby condemns him for acting in a manner contrary to his trust as President to the great prejudice of the cause of justice and to the manifest injury of the American people."

26. Transcribed from the DVD of the episode "Bartlet's Third State of the Union" (2/13).

27. See Chapter 17 for a more detailed discussion of this aspect of the series.

28. "I don't like the death penalty," Bartlet commented in the episode, the word "like" being relevant—Bartlet was not against the

death penalty, although his Catholic faith might have told him he should have been. Once again there was the suggestion that Bartlet lacked the courage of his conviction, that he cared more for political expediency. Bartlet's priest, Father Cavanaugh (played in a consummate cameo by Karl Malden), told Bartlet he was "like the kid in right field who doesn't want the ball to get hit to him." This would seem to aptly sum up Bartlet's position: when a difficult moral decision was to be made he would "duck" it if he could.

29. Note: there was a personal element that contributed to Bartlet's rash threat—Morris Tolliver, the president's personal physician, had been one of the passengers on the flight that had been shot down, allegedly by Syrian forces.

30. Transcribed from the DVD of the episode "Night Five" (3/14).

31. Transcribed from the DVD of the episode "Enemies" (1/8).

32. See Chapter 5 for an analysis of this episode, including the exchange between Bartlet and Jacobs.

33. At the end of this scene, there was almost a sense of vindictiveness to Bartlet's actions: before firing Toby he did not bother to mention Toby's previous service; instead Bartlet seemed still obsessed with Toby's supposed moral superiority:

BARTLET: That self-righteous superiority; not that you were smarter than everyone; that you were purer, morally superior.
TOBY: Due respect, sir, I don't think I'm morally superior to everyone.
BARTLET: No, just to me.

Note that after this final comment from Bartlet, for once Toby did not say, "Thank you, Mr. President." He merely walked out of the Oval Office without speaking, as if responding to a lack of respect on the president's part.

34. It might be noted that Crouch got much of this wrong, Bartlet would nominate Mendoza, he would be re-elected in three years time—but there was a sense (in terms of Crouch's argument, at least) that he would not deserve such a victory. Note also the fact that Bartlet revealed here an intention to run for a second term, even though, as it will later become evident in the narrative—and as discussed earlier in this chapter—he had made a promise to Abbey to serve only one term.

35. Cited in Crawley 2006, 138.

36. Cited in Crawley 2006, 139. Other examples included L. Anthony Sutin, who commented: "Bartlet's farfetched persona aggregated Ronald Reagan's charisma, Woodrow Wilson's intellect and the libido of Socks, the Clintons' neutered cat" (Sutin 2001, 560). Janet McCabe noted: "Several media watchers ... declared that this fictional Democrat president was smug, sanctimonious and self-congratulatory ... nothing more than a 'two-dimension glyph of implausible virtue' ... that the president is 'played for maximum hokiness and cracker-barrel wisdom' ... and 'with such windbag bluster it's a wonder he ever got a vote'" (McCabe 2013, 94).

37. The *National Review* was, of course, not a liberal publication. It was founded in 1955 by William F. Buckley, Jr., to extol the virtues of a conservative view of the world; hence Stuttaford's take on Bartlet and *The West Wing* not unsurprisingly adopted a somewhat skeptical and partial approach.

38. Stuttaford 2003, 1/5.

39. Stuttaford 2003, 3/5.

Chapter 2

1. Cited in Cuddon 1992, 454. Roland Barthes, in his famous essay "The Death of the Author," would use a slightly different phrase, "a tissue of quotations," seeming to add the implication that literary and cultural texts might also blur, merge and be absorbed into one another. Barthes' essay will be considered in more depth in Chapter 4 of this study.

2. Quinn 2004, 173. See Chapter 24 for a discussion of other aspects of a poststructuralist reading of the show.

3. Webster 1990, 96.

4. Webster 1990, 96.

5. The original draft of *The American President* screenplay is said to have run to 385 pages—about three times the length of a conventional two hour film—hence it is likely that a number of plot ideas for *The West Wing* derived from this original source. See Rollins and O'Connor 2003, 139).

6. For example, the scene of Shepherd attempting to order flowers on the phone was similar to Bartlet attempting to gain help on the Butterball Hotline in the episode "The Indians in the Lobby" (3/8).

7. Sheen played Shepherd's chief of staff in *The American President*. In fact, over the course of his acting career Martin Sheen has inhabited a number of Oval Offices, some six versions at the last count:

- *The Missiles of October* (1974) as Robert F. Kennedy
- *Blind Ambition* (1979) as John Dean

- *Kennedy* (1983) as President John F. Kennedy
- *The Dead Zone* (1983) as the fictional President Greg Stillson
- *The American President* (1995) as A.J. MacInerney
- *The West Wing* (1999–2006) as President Josiah Bartlet

8. The play ran on Broadway during 1960 and 1961 for some 520 performances, and has had a number of revivals since.

9. Vidal, as a "scion of Washington's political aristocracy" who consistently maintained "an amused superiority to everything, in particular the orthodoxies of the middle-brow," might have been particularly vitriolic in his opinions on *The West Wing* (See Park 1991, 438–439).

10. It was suggested, in Chapter 1 of this study, that *The West Wing* was astutely cast; nonetheless, there were some instances where other choices may have provided for a better outcome. For example, it has been said that John Spencer, although a consummate actor, did not have a sufficient sense of menace to warrant the role of chief of staff. As intimated, one might think of Robert Vaughn as Frank Flaherty, the Haldeman-esque chief of staff in *Washington behind Closed Doors*. Here such a sense of menace might have provided some degree of respite from the ubiquitous bonhomie so often found in *The West Wing*. An actor who might have played such a role was William Devane; Devane who played the minor role of Secretary of State Lewis Berryhill in *The West Wing*, had a convincing sense of cynical knowingness and ingrained ruthlessness, albeit wrapped in a kind of sub–Jack Nicholson persona. Other roles could—in retrospect—have also been recast; to take just one other example, consider Jessica Chastain in the role of Donna. Chastain would have been only 22 when the series began, but would arguably have served the role to greater effect than Janel Moloney. Moloney played Donna with a degree of flair, but she was a performer with a limited acting persona—another actress might have brought much more to the role.

11. Clive James has also noted the possible influence of both these sources: "*Tanner* might even have been Sorkin's direct inspiration for *The West Wing*, if it wasn't the movie *Thirteen Days*" (James 2016, 65).

12. It was somewhat ironic that the West Wing—the building itself—was seldom shown in *The West Wing*. The building has been shown to some effect in other dramatic representations, an apt example being seen in *Thirteen Days*; however, the establishing shots of the White House in *The West Wing* routinely showed either the North Portico or the South Lawn—seldom (if ever) the West Wing itself.

13. Other examples of recent political television dramas, such as *Veep* (2014–2019) and *Madam Secretary* (2014–), might also be mentioned.

14. In the scene, after spitting in the face of the crucified Christ, Underwood had second thoughts, attempting to remove the sacrilegious spittle; however, this only resulted in the plaster body of Christ falling to the ground and breaking into numerous pieces. The scene ended with Underwood picking up one of the pieces, a broken piece of Christ's earlobe, commenting with his habitual caustic wit: "Well, I've got God's ear now."

15. Incidentally, it might be noted that The Big Lebowski himself appeared in one of the early episodes of the show, an engaging cameo by David Huddleston as Senator Max Lobell in "Lies, Damn Lies and Statistics" (1/21).

16. The direct references included: the episode "The U.S. Poet Laureate" (3/17), wherein Laura Dern, as the eponymous U.S. poet laureate, told Toby she couldn't find a rhyme for Ziegler, before adding: "Dylan could do it"; and the episode "Things Fall Apart" (6/21), when Josh and Santos discussed whether a song with the line "if wishes were horses" was written by Dylan. In the same episode Santos would be asked by a journalist what his favorite Dylan album was, to which he replied: "I guess I should say *Highway 61 Revisited* and then we could just ease into transportation policy, but really, it's *Blonde on Blonde*."

17. The Steadicam scene of Josh walking, flanked by Mallory and Zoey, in "Mr. Willis of Ohio" (1/6), appeared to mirror the famous scene in *Eyes Wide Shut* of Tom Cruise flanked by two "flirtatious" models. However, the episode was broadcast in November 1999 and *Eyes Wide Shut* had only been released in September 1999—hence there was little time for this to have been a conscious allusion.

18. The diminishing chronological quality of both sets of captions was similar, as was the use of font and background color.

19. Leo was testifying before a Congressional hearing investigating Bartlett's lack of public disclosure of having a serious health issue (multiple sclerosis); Michael Corleone was testifying before a Senate committee looking into his role as the head of organized crime—two somewhat different scenarios. Nonetheless, there would seem to have been

obvious intertextual allusions being made in this scene.
  20. See, for example, Abbey's comment in the episode "Separation of Powers" (5/7): "She [Zoey] was always Jed's little girl."
  21. *Economist*. July 4, 2002. "Unreality TV: Irreverent Television Is Good for Politicians."
  22. Cited in Rollins and O'Connor 2003, 195.
  23. Crawley 2006, 10.
  24. Crawley 2006, 153.
  25. *King Lear* Act 1, Scene 1, 47–50. Unfortunately, Sorkin's script (with additional help from Kevin Falls and Laura Glasser) then went on to over embellish the subtle allusion, with the script subsequently having Bartlet say, "*King Lear* is a good play."
  26. See Ruditis and Jackman 2002, 266, one of the few instances in the literature drawing attention to this scene and its intertextual reference to *King Lear*.
  27. The use of episode titles in the show was linguistically eclectic; eight of the 155 episodes were entitled in languages other than English. The following were in Latin: "Post Hoc, Ergo Propter Hoc" (1/2) (literally "after this, therefore because of this"); "In Excelsis Deo" (1/10) ("glory be to God in the highest"); "Posse Comitatus" (3/22) (literally "the power of the county"); and "Eppur Si Muove (5/16)" ("and yet it moves"). In Hebrew: Shibboleth (2/8), literally "the part of a plant containing grains," in a colloquial sense a word that is problematic to pronounce for non-native speakers. In Korean, there was "Han" (5/4) ("a sadness so deep no tears will come"); in Bedouin "Abu el Banat" (5/9) (a phrase meaning "father of daughters"); in Vietnamese "An Khe" (5/14) (the name of a district in the Central Highland region of Vietnam); and in Spanish "La Palabra" (6/18) ("the word").
  28. This particular plotline was very much a re-reading of *King Lear*—with Elizabeth taking on the role of either Regan or Goneril.

Chapter 3

  1. However, a number of critics seem to have been in denial about the actual historical provenance of the series. For example, David Barber stated: "The choice of Eisenhower as a cut-of-point [sic] is interesting in itself. This policy effectively exorcises not only Clinton, but also Kennedy, Johnson, Nixon, Ford, Carter, Reagan and Bush from the series. The most obvious effect this has on the series is to prevent Bartlet being directly compared with these recent Presidents" (Barber 2009, 215). As will be seen in this chapter, this was factually incorrect, insomuch as there were numerous references to Kennedy, Johnson and Nixon in the series. Barber went on to claim: "Sorkin also eliminates the scandal of Watergate and the slow defeat in Vietnam, together with the subsequent political cynicism that they caused throughout America" (Barber 2009, 215). This was also incorrect. A close reading of the series would demonstrate that Watergate and certainly Vietnam—Leo was a fighter pilot in that war—were existent in the universe *The West Wing* inhabited. Barber (whose research was otherwise accurate) may have been using an article by Peter de Jonge first published in October 2001: "As a rule, the scripts avoid references to any president since Eisenhower ... and according to a co-executive producer, Kevin Falls, who runs the writers' room, 'When we talk about the Kennedy Center in *West Wing*, we're referring to George Kennedy'" (de Jonge 2001). This, in turn, may have derived from a comment made by Aaron Sorkin to the Writers' Guild of America early in the show's run: "Eisenhower is the most recent president I'll mention" (cited in Topping 2002, 269).
  2. The relevant part of Roedecker's post is as follows:

> The 25th Amendment, that was passed in 1967 in OTL [our time line] wasn't passed in the West Wing Universe. So after President Richard Nixon resigned on noon of August 9, 1974, as there was no current Vice-President in office as Spiro Agnew had resigned in 1973, the presidency passed to the Speaker of the House Democrat Carl Albert of Oklahoma. President Albert refused to effectively reverse the mandate of the Republican landslide victory of 1972, and announced he would request for Congress to pass a bill to hold a special presidential election on Tuesday November 5, 1974. A bill was passed just weeks later, and a presidential election was set for that date. Both the Democrats and the Republicans held conventions in early September. The Republicans chose the Minority Leader in the House of Representatives, Congressman Gerald Ford of Michigan as their candidate. The Democrats chose Acting-President Albert as their candidate, however in the election various other Democrats also chose to run for president. This fractured the Democrat vote and enabled Congressman Ford to not only win a plu-

rality in the popular vote, but a majority in the Electoral College and therefore the presidency. As a result of the 1974 Presidential Election, the four-year cycle of presidential elections was shifted. During the presidency of Gerald Ford, an amendment eventually was passed that clarified provisions regarding succession to the Presidency, and established procedures both for filling a vacancy in the office of the Vice President as well as responding to Presidential disabilities. As a result of this amendment in 2003, President Bartlet had to pick a new Vice-President following the resignation of John Hoynes. President Ford chose to only serve one term and in 1978, Ronald Reagan won the Republican nomination. He defeated Jimmy Carter in the presidential election and went on to serve from 1979 to 1987. In '86, Democrat D. Wire Newman defeated Vice-President Bush. However, President Newman was defeated in his bid for re-election in 1990 by Republican Owen Lassiter. President Lassiter served from 1991 to 1999. His Vice-President was defeated in the Electoral College by Democrat Governor Josiah "Jed" Bartlet. So then, this is the history of presidential politics in the West Wing Universe from 1969:

Richard Nixon (Republican)—1969–1974
Carl Albert (Democrat)—1974–1975
Gerald Ford (Republican)—1975–1979
Ronald Reagan (Republican)—1979–1987
D. Wire Newman (Democrat)—1987–1991
Owen Lassiter (Republican)—1991–1999
Josiah Bartlet (Democrat)—1999–2007
(Roedecker 2005)

3. It is perhaps more likely that Albert, in the national interest, would simply have resigned as soon as the House of Representatives and the Senate had confirmed a Republican vice president, who would then immediately have become president—this may likely have been Gerald Ford. However, the idea of calling a presidential election instead is not wholly implausible.

4. CJ was addressing the press within a discussion of the Bartlet administration's attitude to drug policy; her comments were as follows: "How surprising that in the midst of an important debate the President would be accused of being soft on drugs. Steve Onorato has a memo written by the Assistant Surgeon General. I'd be happy to produce similar memos written for every President in the last 30 years, including four Republicans."

5. There were a number of other examples of current day celebrities appearing in the series; for example, Penn and Teller in the episode "In the Room" (6/8), Jon Bon Jovi in the episode "Welcome to Wherever You Are" (7/15), and so on, which again tended to lessen the relationship between the real world and the fictitious world of *The West Wing*.

6. Critics have offered differing ideas as to the way Qumar resembled actual nation states. For example, Andrew Davison argued: "Qumar is a fictitious state that strongly resembles real world Saudi Arabia" (Davison 2010, 471); by contrast, Rachel Gans-Boriskin and Russ Tisinger stated; "Qumar ... seems to be an amalgamation of Iraq, Afghanistan and Saudi Arabia" (Gans-Boriskin and Tisinger 2005, 104).

7. This plotline seems, in retrospect, somewhat awkward, lacking the finesse of the usual plotting within the series. To begin with, Rwanda had been specifically referenced numerous times in Season 4 (in episodes five, seven, ten and fifteen) before the plotline about Kundu was developed. In an overarching sense, it may have been decided that a further foreign policy storyline was required, and that the one chosen, genocide in Kundu, would serve to act as another form of wish fulfilment; in other words, a way of making up for President Clinton's lack of action in Rwanda—via a retelling of the same story some ten years later.

8. Cass 2007, 36.

9. Transcribed from the DVD of the episode "The Dogs of War" (5/2).

10. However, note that Arafat would later be written out of the historical timeline of the series—and replaced by a fictitious Palestinian leader, Chairman Farad.

11. Gaddafi came to power in 1969 and was referenced in the opening episode, "Pilot" (1/1); Queen Elizabeth succeeded to the British throne in 1952 and was referenced in the series on a number of occasions; Fidel Castro came to power in Cuba in 1959 and appeared briefly in the episode "Ninety Miles Away" (6/19), albeit in a non-speaking role—literally in the shadows.

12. Lyndon Johnson was mentioned in the episode "Five Votes Down" (1/4). Josh remarked: "LBJ never would've taken this kind of crap from Democrats in Congress." However, the most interesting allusion to Johnson (although not by name) occurred in the episode "The War at Home" (2/14). Here Bartlet was considering—albeit briefly—the prospect of a "jungle war" in Columbia, to which Leo responded: "I fought a jungle war.

I'm not doing it again. If I could put myself anywhere in time it would be the Cabinet room on August 4, 1964, when our ships were attacked by North Vietnam in the Tonkin Gulf. I'd say, Mr. President, don't do it." President Johnson was the president in question at this meeting, and Leo would seem to be suggesting that this was the start of another jungle war, in other words, another Vietnam War.

13. At this point Mandy's dialogue trailed off, as if any further talk of Nixon was to be avoided. Note that after his visit to China in 1972, President Nixon had been given two giant pandas: Ling-Ling and Hsing-Hsing. The pandas lived in the National Zoo in Washington, D.C. into the 1990s, but did not produce any viable offspring.

14. Note that, once again, the dialogue appeared to trail off at the mention of Nixon's name.

15. There were numerous other Watergate references scattered throughout the series. For example, Donna was referred to as Deep Throat in the episode "H. Con—172" (3/11); likewise, in the episode "Full Disclosure" (5/15), CJ would imagine herself as Bob Woodward meeting Deep Throat, commenting: "So call me, or tell me what dark parking garage to meet you in and I'll be right there." There were other potentially deliberate Watergate allusions. For example, the special prosecutor Clement Rollins in the episode "Ways and Means" (3/4) was played by Nicholas Pryor; in 1977, Pryor had played Hank Ferris, one of Richard Moncton's aides in the television drama *Washington behind Closed Doors*. In a similar sense, in the episode "Take Out the Trash Day" (1/13), it was revealed that the vice president had an assistant called Chad Magrudian. This could be seen as having acted as a reference, albeit a somewhat tenuous one, to Jeb Magruder—one of Nixon's aides who was jailed for his part in the Watergate scandal. In addition, in the episode "The War at Home" (2/14), Bob Woodward was clearly referenced—as a guest on the fictitious television show *Capitol Beat*. Finally, the fact that the head of Bartlet's secret service detail was named Ron Butterfield may not have been a coincidence; the name resonated with Alexander Butterfield—the Nixon aide who inadvertently revealed to the Senate Watergate Committee and to the world the existence of a White House taping system, an action that arguably led to Nixon's ultimate fall from power.

16. Paul Ruditis and Ian Jackman, in *The West Wing: The Official Companion*, offered additional and supplementary dialogue to the scene in question—the following lines by Admiral Fitzwallace: "Kennedy once said, after he got to the White House, that the thing that made him sad was that he realized he was never gonna make a new friend. That's why presidents hold on to their old ones" (cited in Ruditis and Jackman 2002, 21). The published script (see Sorkin 2003a, 122), unofficial online sources and the DVD of the episode all omitted the reference to Kennedy. It is difficult to account for this incongruity; it is uncertain, for example, whether Ruditis and Jackman were pointing to the earlier broadcast version of the episode, or—more likely—whether they had access to a version of the script that was ultimately changed. However, for whatever reason, it is clear that the reference to Kennedy was deliberately deleted.

17. The episodes were "Enemies" (1/8), "Galileo" (2/9), "Enemies Foreign and Domestic" (3/19), "Abu El Banat" (5/9), "Full Disclosure" (5/15) and "Mr. Frost" (7/4).

18. The reference to Kennedy came during a discussion of whether to send troops to protect black churches that were being targeted and attacked, wherein Bartlet asked: "Was Eisenhower wrong in '57? Kennedy in '61?" Transcribed from the DVD of the episode "Bartlet for America" (3/10).

19. There were a number of other references. For example, there were specific references to Kennedy by name in the episodes "7A WF 83429" (5/1) and "Running Mates" (7/10), while in the episode "Message of the Week" (7/3) Bruno Gianelli (at this point in the drama Arnold Vinick's campaign manager) commented: "No senator has won the Presidency since 1960. There is a reason for that." Frustratingly, Bruno did not explain what his reason might have been; however his reference to a senator winning in 1960, other than confirming that the four-year election cycle had previously been held within the conventional time frame, was also a clear and obvious reference to Kennedy. Kennedy, prior to his election as president, had been the senator for Massachusetts from 1953 to 1960.

20. Crawley 2006, 74.

21. In the published script the term Camelot was not italicized, a possible indication that it did not refer to the musical.

22. The interview was published in the December 6, 1963 issue of *Life* magazine.

23. See (http://www.jfklibrary.org/Research/Research-Aids/JFK-Speeches/San-Antonio-TX_19631121.aspx).

24. See Topping 2002, 144, who also mentions this similarity.

25. For example, in the episode "The Dogs of War" (5/2), in a conversation about the importance of putting aside conspiracy theories surrounding the temporary incoming administration of President Walken, Leo told Josh: "This isn't the grassy knoll."
26. One reason the assassination of President Kennedy may never be resolved might lie in the hesitancy of historians to fully explore the subject area; it has been said that professional historians are wary of looking too closely at the assassination because of the risk of being labeled "conspiracy nuts."
27. For a fuller analysis and discussion of the use of time slippages within the series, see Chapter 15.
28. For example, the Christmas episodes of the show (which occurred in six of the seven seasons) were all originally broadcast in December, just before the Christmas holiday.
29. In addition, the episode "The Wake-Up Call" (6/14)) took place on a specific date (February 14, 2005); and the final episode of the series, "Tomorrow" (7/22), took place on January 20, 2007.
30. Of the 155 episodes, there were only two stand-alone episodes—episodes that were outside of the continuity of the series as a whole: "Isaac and Ishmael" (3/1) and "Access" (5/18).
31. Wodak 2010, 44.
32. Wodak 2010, 44.

Chapter 4

1. Crawley 2006, 8.
2. Belek 2010, 41.
3. Barber 2009, 237.
4. Challen 2001, 49. However, note that it could be argued that this may not have been an entirely valid comment; for example, the average viewer of *The Sopranos* might well have been aware that David Chase was seen as its originator, or that David Simon was often seen as the originator of *The Wire*.
5. Crawley 2006, 7.
6. Rollins and O'Connor 2003, 136.
7. Cited in Rollins and O'Connor 2003, 137. Likewise, even a critic as erudite as Clive James could mistakenly claim that Sorkin had "written, on his own, every episode of the first four seasons" (James 2016, 61).
8. Parry-Giles and Parry-Giles 2006, 10. In a work of otherwise high academic scholarship, the authors listed incomplete and inaccurate writing credits; a significant number of episodes had incomplete writer credits—being routinely credited to Sorkin, when a significant number were co-written with other authors. The book was published in 2006, but apparently went to press around January 2003—hence it is possible that the authors did not have access to officially released recordings of the series and may even have been relying on home recordings—hence offering a possible explanation for this discrepancy.
9. See Appendices for details of the writing and directing credits for each episode, together with running times and the original broadcast dates.
10. In terms of the issue of co-writing contributions, there were a number of different formats of writing credits at the end of various episodes. These included the following variations:

Written by Aaron Sorkin
Teleplay by Aaron Sorkin, Story by Lawrence O'Donnell, Jr., and Patrick H. Caddell
Written by Aaron Sorkin and Paul Redford
Written by Paul Redford and Aaron Sorkin
Teleplay by Allison Abner & Kevin Falls and Aaron Sorkin, Story by Allison Abner
Written by Eli Attie and Kevin Falls and Aaron Sorkin
Teleplay by Paul Redford and Deborah Cahn and Aaron Sorkin, Story by Paul Redford and Deborah Cahn

11. In addition, it might be noted that as Sorkin only worked on the first four seasons, the ratio of his writing credits as sole author was still further reduced—a total of only one fifth of the 155 episodes.
12. Crawley 2006, 202n.
13. Cited in McCabe 2013, 35.
14. Cited in McCabe 2013, 35.
15. Cited in McCabe 2013, 35.
16. de Jonge 2001.
17. See Topping 2002, 92–94 for further details of this incident.
18. Cited at http://www.imdb.com/title/tt0745635/trivia (Accessed August 20, 2016.)
19. de Jonge 2001.
20. Cited in Rollins and O'Connor 2003, 173.
21. Fahy 2005, 2.
22. However, it might be noted that even in cases of Sorkin being given a sole "written by" credit, other writing credits would be included. For instance, for the last episode listed above (and the last episode to include Sorkin as a scriptwriter on *The West Wing*),

"Twenty-Five" (4/23), some seven other staff writers were listed: Debora Cahn, David Gerken, Mark Goffman, David Handleman, William Sind, Paula Yoo and Michael Oates Palmer.

23. As far as can be ascertained, original scripts (other than the fourteen examples published by Sorkin) are not available in manuscript form. There was one exception: "Pilot" (1/1), available online, at: http://www.dailyscript.com/scripts/West_Wing_Pilot.pdf. The script, dated February 6, 1998, had some significant differences to the final version of the script as filmed. The script, which would appear to be authentic, was of interest for a number of reasons. For example, Leo was called Leo Jacobi in this version, perhaps indicative of a change in ethnicity. In addition, a scene of Mandy moving into her office was deleted entirely from the episode—the scene being substantial, over three pages long in the original draft. Also, there were numerous minor changes apparent from the original script to the extant dialogue in the broadcast episode.

24. In an overall sense it should be noted that a screenplay—or in this case, a teleplay—is not a completed text. It is "merely a handbook detailing dialogue and action to be used and shaped by the director and actors and editor and so on. In other words, a mere diagram of the finished article" (Tiffin 2013, 289). At best a screenplay might thus be seen as being akin to a musical score, or at worst to an instructional manual; in other words, it is merely a guide as to how to perform, and it is not a fully considered cultural text.

25. Sorkin 2003b, 501.

26. In fact, the "various reasons" for Sorkin leaving would seem to have come down to monetary issues: an increase in the budget due to Sorkin's late delivery of scripts, coupled with a fall in the viewing figures—reputedly due to Sorkin's apparent dissatisfaction with Rob Lowe's portrayal of Sam Seaborn and the subsequent departure of Lowe from the show. At a meeting with NBC—toward the end of the fourth season—Sorkin refused to make any changes in his writing of the show, thus unknowingly quitting without realizing he was doing so.

27. Barber 2009, 239.

28. Ruditis and Jackman 2002, 33.

29. Wolff 2000.

30. Fahy 2005, 115.

31. It is an obvious point, but one worth making: in *The West Wing*—as in other television dramas, and in feature films—the director credit routinely came last, after the writing credits, as if to imply importance and significance.

32. The whole concept of *auteur* theory, in itself, has always been a somewhat dubious subject area. There have been *auteurs*, but only in rare instances, Stanley Kubrick perhaps being one of the most convincing examples. Kubrick had a writing credit on nearly all his films; in addition, almost every artistic decision was either made by Kubrick or had a significant contribution by him. Kubrick influenced all the creative and all non-creative aspects of the work: the initial financing, the casting, the scripting process, the design of the sets, the camera angles and movement, the editing, and the use of music, together with the diverse other aspects that go into the making of a film.

33. Schlamme directed fourteen episodes of the show—see Appendices for a complete list of directorial credits.

34. Graves directed 34 episodes.

35. Misiano directed 34 episodes.

36. See Lodge 1992, 166–172.

37. Cited in Lodge 1992, 171.

38. Paraphrased from Barthes S/Z, cited in Green and Le Bihan 1996, 184

39. Cited in Lodge 1992, 170.

40. Cited in Lodge 1992, 172. Barthes's ideas were revolutionary if only because of their anti-theological implications. To proclaim the Death of the Author would eventually lead to a proclamation against a belief in the ultimate author—in other words, a belief in a deity, in God.

41. Cited in Green and Le Bihan 1996, 185. See also Green and Bihan's own comment: "The act of reading is a concretization of the consciousness of the author: like a musical score, it has intention and form, but is only realized in the act of performance" (Green and Le Bihan 1996, 188).

42. The term "horizon of expectations" derives from the work of Hans Robert Jauss. It refers to the criteria with which readers judge literary texts in a particular given period. See Cuddon 1992, 415.

43. Parry-Giles and Parry-Giles 2006, 52.

44. Cass 2007, 34.

45. See Williams 2011, 277.

46. Limerence refers to the obsessive infatuation some fans of the show appear to have had with various main characters.

47. See Williams 2011, 278.

48. According to Sorkin, Akiva Goldman, the television and film writer, was the actual originator of the series, or at least the originator of the idea behind the series. According to the story, Sorkin's agent had set up a meeting

with John Wells, who was then currently the producer of *ER* and had significant influence with NBC; the night before the scheduled meeting Sorkin had invited some friends to his house—including Akiva Goldman. At one point during the evening Sorkin and Goldman left the main party and went downstairs to the basement. Goldman, who knew about the meeting, asked Sorkin what he was going to pitch, Sorkin said he wasn't sure. Goldman, pointing to a poster for *The American President*, said: "Hey, you know that would make a good series ... but this time you'd focus on the staffers." The following day Sorkin met with John Wells, and when asked what he wanted to do, Sorkin replied: "I'd like to do a series about staffers at the White House," and the deal—so the story goes—was made. See Lacey, O'Connell and Bernardin 2014; Sorkin 2003a.

Chapter 5

1. See, for example, Nelson and Longfellow 1994.
2. We learn this in the opening episode of the series, "Pilot" (1/1).
3. Bartlet's abusive language came at the end of the scene, when he suggested Jacobs belonged to the "Ignorant Tight Ass Club." This scatological insult corresponded to a similar insult Bartlet had made in the opening episode, "Pilot" (1/1), suggesting three individuals of the Christian right should get their "fat asses" out of his White House.
4. Jacobs committed the *faux pas* of remaining seated when the president entered the room, but this could be put down to nervousness or a lack of knowledge of etiquette, rather than a deliberate act of discourtesy.
5. The scene has been criticized as being an "unrealistic broadside" (cited in Rollins and O'Connor 2003, 46), a "pure Hollywood fantasyland. No real life president would be so self-indulgent as to launch such a tirade and dress down a White House guest at a social event" (47), and even a president might "feel the need for manners" (48).
6. This was a fictional discourse; however, it could be argued that Jacobs's doctoral research might have been just as significant as Bartlet's doctorate in economics; furthermore, one might note in this context how, in the episode "The Short List" (1/9), Bartlet insisted on being allocated his academic title by way of a formal address, which would seem to have been all that Jacobs was doing on her radio show. One way of judging the value of a doctorate would be to note the prestige of the university that made the award, but as Jenna Jacobs was a fictional character we cannot make this kind of judgment. However, it might be noted that (in the real world) Laura Schlessinger's PhD was in physiology from Columbia University's College of Physicians and Surgeons, which Bartlet may have found more relevant and more valid.
7. It should perhaps be noted that Jacobs was not permitted to make any further comment. She was not permitted to reply to the scriptural quotations, being silenced both by Bartlet and by Sorkin's script.
8. Bartlet and Jacobs could have cited a more severe mandate from Leviticus: "If a man also lie with mankind as he lieth with a woman both of them have committed an abomination, they shall surely be put to death" (*KJB* Leviticus 20.13).
9. Hanegraaff 2001.
10. Hanegraaff 2001.
11. Hanegraaff 2001.
12. Hanegraaff 2001.
13. The issue of abortion itself was covered in a number of other episodes, but only in passing. These episodes were the following:

> "The Short List" (1/9)—Justice Roberto Mendoza's attitude to abortion was briefly discussed.
> "Take this Sabbath Day" (1/14)—the Catholic Church's unimpeachable attitude to life—no abortion, no death penalty—was mentioned in passing.
> "The Stackhouse Filibuster" (2/17)—CJ mentioned that women seeking abortions should not be lectured at.
> "Manchester Part 1" (3/2)—Leo joked that the press was going to write a story about Bartlet performing an abortion in the Rose Garden.
> "100,000 Airplanes" (3/12)—Amy Gardner mentioned abortion clinics in passing.
> "The Two Bartlets" (3/13)—Amy Gardner mentioned late-term abortions in passing.
> "Privateers" (4/18)—Abbey Bartlet alluded to the difficulty of talking about abortion.
> "The Supremes" (5/17)—Evelyn Baker Lang, a potential candidate for the Supreme Court, admitted she had had an abortion when she was in law school.
> "Third Day Story" (6/3)—it was suggested that a disincentive to have children was not far away from government-ordered abortion.

"Message of the Week" (7/3)—Vinick noted that Santos had previously voted for partial-birth abortion. "Here Today" (7/5)—there were two distant references to abortion made by members of Santos's staff.

14. Transcribed from the DVD of the episode "Pilot" (1/1). Incidentally, there was an inherent bias in one particular detail of Leo's comment: Why would Bartlet only discourage *young* women from having abortions? Although this would seem almost risible, one might ask whether Bartlet was also concerned with older women having abortions.

15. Transcribed from the DVD of the episode "Pilot" (1/1).

16. Transcribed from the DVD of the episode "The Al Smith Dinner" (7/6).

17. Hanegraaff 2001.

18. Hanegraaff 2001.

19. Hanegraaff 2001. The point that HIV/AIDS has killed far more people via heterosexual encounters than homosexual encounters is an obvious one, but one that should perhaps be restated.

20. However, it should be accepted that men taking part in same-sex activity may have more partners and may indulge in multiple sexual couplings, hence leading to a greater risk of contracting a number of sexually transmitted diseases, including HIV/AIDS.

21. Hanegraaff 2001.

22. Jacobs was obviously nervous and at a distinct disadvantage during her conversation with the president, but an analysis of her brief remarks showed that, when she was allowed to speak, she managed to offer a creditable account of herself.

23. The sexual pretensions were clearly apparent. As Cruise's character somewhat archly put it: "I put the bat in the closet."

24. Bush 2009. Such an issue would reoccur, with some exaggeration, in the episode "Isaac and Ishmael" (3/1). See Chapter 8 for a discussion of this episode in relation to racial and religious stereotyping.

Chapter 6

1. This could be seen in the cost of each episode. As intimated in the introduction, each episode had a reputed budget of around $2.7 million (McCabe 2013, 20). Also, as Michael Mayers, another of the show's directors of photography, commented: "We work under the same production standards as the best Hollywood features" (cited in McCabe 2013, 60).

2. It should be noted that Thomas Del Ruth rarely worked on feature films, before or after *The West Wing*; nonetheless, he was able to bring a cinematic style to his prolific work on television.

3. David Barber noted how this (the quality of the set design) demonstrated "the fact that the series is made using a large, lavish set rather than a sequence of isolated rooms that cutting between shots would suggest. This gives the series a feeling of place and permanence from the beginning and is equally an important first step in the construction of presidentiality" (Barber 2009, 206).

4. It should be noted that this particular shot was not wholly continuous. There were a number of short inserts cut into the main shot, but nonetheless it remains a consummate piece of camera work.

5. In fact, according to one source, some 20 to 30 takes were required to successfully film this shot (Ruditis and Jackman 2002, 26).

6. McCabe 2013, 64.

7. The Steadicam was a handheld camera that was able to produce secure images via the use of a system of stabilizers. It had previously been used in Hal Ashby's film *Bound for Glory* (1976), in John Schlesinger's *Marathon Man* (1976) and in *Rocky* (1976), directed by John G. Avildsen; however, *The Shining* was the first film to use the camera to an authentically innovative extent.

8. Kubrick died on March 7, 1999; *The West Wing* began broadcasting six months later, on September 22, 1999.

9. Dumlao 2005.

10. McCabe 2013, 60.

11. Cited in Barber 2009, 249.

12. In terms of further technical details, it would appear that almost the entire series was shot on film in 35mm, apart from the pilot episode which, according to Thomas Del Ruth, "was shot in 16mm, a cost-saving measure in case the show didn't get picked up." (Available at: https://theasc.com/magazine/oct00/power/pg3.htm.)

13. The term "dissolve" refers to the ways a transition between two different scenes can be made. In *The West Wing* scene changes were generally conventional; in other words, without significant variation from a straight cut between scenes.

14. The use of a freeze frame was common in the last shot of many episodes of *The West Wing*; however, these were not exactly freeze frames—rather jump cuts to a still image from earlier in the episode. The use of an actual freeze frame was rare in the series.

15. These were commonly either aerial or long shots of the White House, and on a number of occasions such shots appear to have been used more than once. In fact, some of the establishing shots, mostly of the White House, seemed to be of poorer technical quality and, in some cases at least, there was the suggestion that stock footage, rather than original footage, may have been used.

16. Cited in Rollins and O'Connor 2003, 146.

17. In a specific sense, this only included 154 episodes, the opening episode, "Pilot" (1/1), had no "previously" to allude to—the disembodied voice, heard in other episodes, was not heard here.

18. Otherwise, voice-over in general was rarely used in the series, the only exceptions being in the following episodes: "100,000 Airplanes" (3/12), "Access" (5/18), and an extensive use of voice-over in the episode "The Stackhouse Filibuster" (2/17), wherein CJ, Sam and Josh each dictated an email to their parents, this being rendered in voice-over form, an efficient if somewhat unimaginative way in which to advance the story.

19. The precise quotation as cited might turn out to have been apocryphal. The first written reference to it, by Sturgeon himself, has been traced to the March 1958 issue of the magazine *Venture Science Fiction*, wherein Sturgeon concluded, albeit in a slightly different form, that "ninety percent of SF is crud."

20. Storey 2001.

21. Lyon 1995.

22. Baudrillard also commented: "There is nothing more mysterious than a TV set left on in an empty room. It is even stranger than a man talking to himself or a woman standing dreaming at her stove. It is as if another planet is communicating with you" (Baudrillard 1999, 50).

23. Lyon 1995, 57.

24. However, as intimated previously, it should be noted that, with commercial breaks, the show totaled an average time of only 42 minutes an episode, which equated to some 108 hours of dramatic presentation—still an impressive figure.

Chapter 7

1. Eagleton 1983.
2. Eagleton 1983, 113.
3. Watson 2000.
4. Green and Le Bihan 1996, 184.
5. This was one of the themes inherent within one of Barthes's most influential books: *Mythologies*, first published in 1957.

6. Barry 1995, 49.

7. The series can be seen as beginning within a structuralist discourse and ending (perhaps deliberately) within the range of a poststructuralist discourse, as will be discussed in Chapter 24.

8. This dialogue was not entirely audible on the broadcast and in recorded formats, but published sources confirm this. See Sorkin 2003a, 9.

9. Incidentally, it might be noted that this exchange between Bartlet and Mrs. Landingham included the first use of the only real catch-phrase of the series, Bartlet's oft-repeated: "What's next?"

10. In terms of a specific use of language; there was also the point that the first word of the series, "two," was enclosed within the last word of the series, "tomorrow."

11. All of this might be seen to gain more relevance when one considers that in the final episode of the series, "Tomorrow" (7/22), Bartlet intimated that he would like to ride a bicycle again.

12. For example, if one were to adopt the concept of a world in which there were only one gender, there would be no need for such terms as man and woman, or male and female; or imagine a planet with two suns, where a sun was always in the sky: here there would be no such concept as day or night.

13. See Chapter 13 for a discussion of the sexual relationships (or the lack of them) of the main protagonists in the series.

14. The actual quotation was as follows: "A proper name should always be carefully questioned, for the proper name is, if I can put it like this, the prince of signifiers: its connotations are rich, social and symbolic." The quotation came from an essay entitled "Textual Analysis: Poe's 'Valdemar'" (Lodge 1992, 176).

15. Janet McCabe makes a similar point: "The Bartlets, whose names Josiah and Abigail [were reminiscent] of America's Puritan past" (McCabe 2013, 93).

16. Note that Toby temporarily served as press secretary, a stand-in for CJ, in the episode "Liftoff" (6/4).

17. Only one minor example has been identified, this being the abrasive chat show host, Taylor Reid, who briefly acted as a foil for CJ in Season 5.

18. Ronna Beckman, played by Karis Campbell, was an interesting character, insomuch as she was the only mainstream protagonist on the show to be in a same-sex

relationship. This will be discussed further in Chapter 13.

19. The name was arguably a reference to Sir Thomas Malory, the author of the 15th century text *La Morte d'Arthur*; other than being one of the first major written works in the English language, it was a major source for all subsequent texts on Arthurian legend, up to and including the Broadway musical *Camelot*.

20. This trait was also apparent in other black characters; for example, CCH Pounder played a character called Deborah O'Leary in the episode "Celestial Navigation" (1/15), another Gaelic-sounding name for a character played by an African-American actor.

21. As Clive James, talking of the use of expletives in the series, put it: "Network rules prevail and we never hear a dirty word" (James 2016, 70).

22. The scatological quota seldom reached a higher level, but there were some exceptions. For example, in the episode "The Ticket" (7/1) Josh referred to a Democratic representative from Colorado as "a little turd," and in the episode "Running Mates" (7/10), Josh commented to Toby, "Last time you were more than usually assholic."

23. The only other authentic expletive occurred in the episode "Ninety Miles Away" (6/19), wherein Leo was heard to say, "Que mierdra," this being Spanish for "What the shit!"

24. See Sorkin 2003a, 380.

25. See Ruditis and Jackman 2002, 344.

26. Bartlet was telling God to "go to hell," a novel idea; however, this translation contained a high element of artistic license. Bartlet did not mention any of the accustomed Latin words for hell: *infernum, gehenna, abyssus*.

27. Valerie Cunningham, "Filthy Britten." January 5, 2002. Available at: https://www.theguardian.com/education/2002/jan/05/arts.highereducation (Accessed November 3, 2016)

28. A search of the transcripts of the show suggests that 32 of the 155 episodes specifically alluded, in some way, to the necktie; hence this would not seem to be without significance.

29. Cited in Kirkham 1996, 166.

30. Such a sense of transgression can be seen in such cultural arenas as the schoolgirls at *St Trinians*, Hermione Granger in the Harry Potter films, Madonna in a number of stage and music video guises, Diane Keaton in *Annie Hall* and so on.

31. There were a number of other examples wherein the necktie represented power. For example, in the episode "The Benign Prerogative" (5/11), Bartlet was shown selecting a tie and then asking: "Which one screams dominance?"

32. A further homosocial exchange could be seen in the episode "Game On" (4/6), wherein Sam gave Will Bailey his tie. This could be seen as a symbolic act—Will would subsequently replace Sam, with the necktie thus acting to confer authority from one man to another.

33. "Goldfish" are an American confectionary, fish shaped crackers marketed by the Campbell Soup Company.

34. One might recall here Josh's comment in the episode, "Guns Not Butter" (4/12), quoting Winston Churchill: "The best argument against demcracy is a five minute conversation with the average voter." See Chapter 10 for a fuller discussion of this issue.

35. For example, in one of the last scenes of the final episode, "Tomorrow" (7/22), Bartlet's motorcade was shown leaving the inauguration ceremony, and his car was shown approaching a street sign proclaiming: "No Left Turn." This appeared to offer a final semiotic gesture and a clear indicator of political leanings; in other words, just how liberal a politician had Bartlet been? Had he always avoided left turns?

Chapter 8

1. Sorkin 2003b, 11.

2. Sorkin: "What I really wanted to do was postpone our premiere ... I didn't want the show to go on the air. I felt it was in bad taste" (cited in Fahy 2005, 14).

3. Sorkin's initial idea to postpone the show's new season may have been well founded. As Peter de Jonge put it: "Sorkin became convinced that his show's subtle connection to reality had been severed and that unless he could find a way to let viewers know that his characters had suffered the same trauma as everyone else, the show would forever clink hollow" (de Jonge 2001).

4. Sorkin 2003b, 15.

5. Cited in Fahy 2005, 14.

6. Sorkin 2003b, 15.

7. Cited in Holland 2010, 7. Jaap Kooijman has argued how a number of American dramas of the time, including *The West Wing*, could not ignore 9/11 without losing their credibility. For example, the crime series *Third Watch*, which was set in New York, responded by "replacing its new season opener with a

special nonfiction episode entitled "In Their Own Words," featuring real-life New York police officers, fire-fighters, and paramedics telling about their experiences" (Kooijman 2008, 53).
    8. As Sorkin put it: "We couldn't just do a regular *West Wing* ... the show had to bow its head somehow before it moved forward" (cited in Holland 2010, 19).
    9. See Sorkin 2003b, 19. According to Robert Jones and George Dionisopoulos, "First drafts of the script were a 'hate-filled diatribe against Islam,' but with each revision it settled down a little bit'" (Jones and Dionisopoulos 2004, 36).
    10. Trevor and Shawn J. Parry-Giles reported: "The episode scored a 16.3 rating with more than 25 million viewers tuned in, ranking the show as the third-most watched for the week in which it aired" (Parry-Giles and Parry-Giles 2006, 159).
    11. In terms of the academic response to the episode, the following journal articles and monographs might be noted: Barber 2009, Cass 2007, Chambers and Finn 2001, Crawley 2006, Fahy 2005, Gans-Boriskin and Tisinger 2005, Gillan 2006, Holland 2010, Jones and Dionisopoulos 2004, Kim 2009, Kooijman 2008, Parry-Giles and Parry-Giles 2006, Philpott and Mutimer 2006, Puar and Rai 2002, Rollins and O'Connor 2003, Spigel 2004, Wodak 2010.
    12. All cited in Fahy 2005, 70.
    13. Cited in Cass 2007, 37.
    14. Barker 2011, no page number.
    15. Gans-Boriskin and Tisinger 2005, 106.
    16. Cass 2007, 37.
    17. Crawley 2006, 134.
    18. Jones and Dionisopoulos 2004, 21, 22. The two authors also quoted George Stephanopoulos, who described the episode as "a prime-time town meeting on a lot of the issues raised by the attacks.... You'd be hard pressed to find this sophisticated a debate on most news shows."
    19. Parry-Giles and Parry-Giles 2006, 18.
    20. Parry-Giles and Parry-Giles 2006, 163.
    21. Barber 2009, 225.
    22. Sorkin 2003b, 21–22.
    23. Barker 2011, no page number.
    24. Wodak 2010, 47.
    25. In terms of a potential fracture to the narrative, there have been a number of uncanny coincidences surrounding the 9/11 attacks, for example: the cover illustration of Don Delillo's 1997 novel *Underworld*; the opening of Arthur C. Clarke's 1972 novel *Rendezvous with Rama*; and Laurie Anderson's 1981 song "O Superman." In addition, Robert Jones and George Dionisopoulos alluded to "a chillingly prophetic bit of dialogue from *Nosebleed*, a Jackie Chan terrorist–action film under production at the time. One character in the film noted that the World Trade Center 'represents capitalism. It represents freedom. It represents everything America is about. And to bring those two buildings down would bring America to its knees'" (Jones and Dionisopoulos 2004, 21).
    26. For further information relating to imaginary stories in DC Comics of the time, see the following online source: http://dc.wikia.com/wiki/Category:Imaginary_Stories
    27. Holland 2010, 3.
    28. Philip Cass, in response to this question, provided another: "And what do you call a country where Israeli tanks arrive at 4 a.m. to blow up your house? It was not a question anybody asked, or answered" (Cass 2007, 38).
    29. Gillan 2006, 16. Gillan added: "The Cold War having ended a decade prior to 2001, Americans were forced to find a new 'other,' the terrorist espousing Islamic fundamentalist extremism, onto whom they could project their fears" (Gillan 2006, 17). Lynn Spigel made a similar point, noting that "the episode uses historical pedagogy to solidify American national unity *against* the 'enemy' rather than to encourage any real engagement with Islam" (Spigel 2004, 244).
    30. See Jones and Dionisopoulos 2004, who make a similar point.
    31. Cass 2007, 38. See also Samuel Chambers and Patrick Finn, who put forward a convincing argument that the episode confined "terrorism to an attack on pluralism" whereas terrorism was "an attack on colonialism" (Chambers and Finn 2001, 5).
    32. Gans-Boriskin and Tisinger 2005, 105.
    33. Philpott and Mutimer 2006, 352.
    34. Holland 2010, 6.
    35. See Chapter 10 for a more in-depth discussion of America's supposed position as the "greatest country in the world."
    36. Young Hoon Kim made a similar point: "Instead of delving into the underlying reasons of why America was attacked on September 11 2001, and currently faces terrorism, the show, in fact, creates a terror mastermind like bin Laden and executes him" (Kim 2009, 6/16).
    37. Mao's actual slogan was: "Political power grows out of the barrel of a gun." However, the intent behind the statement remains the same.
    38. As Bob Dylan put it in his song "Union Sundown" from the 1983 album, *Infidels*:

"This world is ruled by violence, but I guess that's better left unsaid."

39. Incoherent insomuch as a significant part of the population of Northern Ireland already consider themselves to be British.

40. The argument perhaps depends on what is meant by terrorism, and, for that matter, what is meant by failure. For example, the Suffragettes could be described as having been a terrorist movement. They did not set out to deliberately maim or to kill, but were prepared to commit violent acts to achieve their aims—aims that were successfully accomplished.

41. Topping 2002, 266. Toby Ziegler was often seen as the conscience of the Bartlet administration, as the most liberal and even most moral individual on Bartlet's staff. However, in this episode even Toby seemed to have lost his liberal conscience and to be caught up in the patriotic fervor of the moment. In an episode from the same season, "Night Five" (3/4), Toby made two comments that exemplified his actual views on the Muslim world. Toby claimed Muslim children were being taught nothing but the Koran and how to hate America; he then went on to comment that America should respect all religions and cultures, but only "to a point." This rejoinder, "to a point," was significant in terms of the show's overarching political discourse, hence leaving the viewer to ponder whether Toby was the liberal voice he was often assumed to be.

42. Cass 2007, 39.

43. As in Woody Allen's *Annie Hall* (1977), where Allen's character, Alvy Singer, magically conjured up Marshall McLuhan from behind a film poster to confound an irritating university professor.

44. Trombley 2012, 330.

45. Cited in Trombley 2012, 334.

46. Holland 2010, 3.

47. Holland 2010, 10.

48. Holland 2010, 11.

49. Holland 2010, 16.

50. Gans-Boriskin and Tisinger 2005, 110.

51. Gans-Boriskin and Tisinger 2005, 100.

52. Holland 2010, 15.

53. As Holland put it: "[In] juxtaposing American heroes and cowardly martyrs, 'Isaac and Ishmael' closed ... by reinforcing and amplifying one of the key themes of the official response to 9/11" (Holland 2010, 15).

54. Note that other characters also seemed to suddenly change their political and moral views; for example, CJ now seemed to fervently believe in the CIA and that certain elements in society needed to be shot in the street.

55. Robert Jones and George Dionisopoulos noted how "Sorkin contrasts these scenes [Josh's seminar] with Leo acting irrationally and very much as a racist, which is completely out of his normally cool-headed character" (Jones and Dionisopoulos 2004, 31).

56. Cited in Kooijman 2008, 57. Puar and Rai, for reasons—it must be said—not entirely clear, perceived of the character of Raqim as a "sexually ambiguous figure" (Puar and Rai 2002, 134). This line of thought was predicated on the argument that "gender and sexuality [are] central to the current 'war on terrorism'" (117). The authors went on to note that "sexuality is central to the creation of a certain knowledge of terrorism" and that "the image of the modern terrorist" is tied to "a much older figure, the racial and sexual monster of the eighteenth and nineteenth centuries" (117).

57. Jones and Dionisopoulos noted: "Rakeem's [sic] dialogue is also the only point at which the episode makes reference to its fictional history of the series" (Jones and Dionisopoulos 2004, 35). In other words, it is difficult for the episode to claim to be "non-canonical," a "narrative aberration," if it deliberately places itself within its own historical context.

58. It will later turn out that the actual terrorist had been captured coming across the border "from Ontario to Vermont." As Ontario and Vermont do not share a border, it is possible this was a deliberate inaccuracy, one that pointed to a general lack of verisimilitude in the episode as a whole.

59. Gillan 2006, 18. It is conceivable that there was a subliminal message in the remark: that Americans should get over the trauma of 9/11 and get back to work.

60. Holland 2010, 5. According to the generally accepted story, Isaac was the child of Abraham and Sarah, from whom the Jewish peoples descended, while the Arab people forged their descent via Ishmael—the child of Abraham and Hagar—with the resultant conflict arising from the differences between these two half-brothers.

61. Holland 2010, 5.

62. As Rachel Gans-Boriskin and Russ Tisinger commented: "In many instances, Sorkin and the other writers of the program avoid substantive discussions of issues by constructing scenarios that ignore fundamental aspects of the 'real situation,' thereby providing the audiences with easier answers than the real situations merit" (Gans-Boriskin and Tisinger 2005, 111).

63. At times the episode appeared to

almost resemble a vaudeville show, with Toby saying, at one point: "CJ Cregg, ladies and gentlemen"—as if she was about to do "a turn" in a burlesque show.
  64. Kooijman 2008, 57–58.

Chapter 9

  1. A search of online sources suggests that the Marx brothers *were* mentioned in the series, in some three different episodes: "Lies, Damn Lies and Statistics" (1/21), "Debate Camp" (4/5) and "Freedonia" (6/15). However, unless it has been overlooked, Karl Marx was not mentioned by name in any of the show's episodes.
  2. In the extreme sense, such an economic system may become one close to that of slave labor, and thus a system so inherently unfair—as well as markedly inefficient—that it will be challenged, undermined and eventually overthrown.
  3. Again, in an extreme sense such an economic system will seldom work, insomuch as human nature seldom extends far beyond one's immediate family and friends, at least in terms of cooperation and sharing for the greater good. Hence it is a system easily exploited, a system vulnerable to misuse, and a system ultimately open to corruption.
  4. In the episode "Guns Not Butter" (4/12).
  5. The aristocracy may not exist in the free republic of the American state; however, the exaggerated differences between the very rich and the very poor act to compensate for this omission.
  6. For a further discussion of Marxist elements in *The Wire*, see Jenkin 2012.
  7. The United Kingdom of course, still has a monarchy, along with an established class system, which—from a Marxist perspective—would be seen as almost absurd. Note that the United Kingdom itself was seldom referenced in *The West Wing*; the only significant British character in the series was Lord John Marbury, played to great effect by the Welsh actor Roger Rees. On the one hand, this was an apt example of stereotyping within the series. Marbury was an eccentric British diplomat who might have been playing a mixture of Bertie Wooster and Sherlock Holmes on an off day. On the other hand, the character was played with such conviction as to contradict such a judgment.
  8. See Barry 1995, 156–171.
  9. As Anindita Biswas commented: "The show is focused singularly on upper middle class elites … with only … a handful of characters belonging to the lower middle class … these only represented within peripheral roles—in other words, not a representation of a composite society" (Biswas 2008, 94).
  10. As Bartlet says in the episode "Bad Moon Rising" (2/19), "Were I to die, my family would not miss my government salary."
  11. In terms of class factions on the show, see Debora Cahn's comments on *The West Wing Weekly* podcast for the episode "The Supremes" (5/17). Cahn, the writer of the episode, made the point that two of the characters new to the show, Ryan Pierce and Marina (no given surname), were deliberately cast to show the differences in social class in American life.
  12. See Eagleton 1983, 19.
  13. As Adam Phillips once commented: "Everybody knows that you can only make a profit if somebody else's labor has been exploited; it's not a mystery, it's absolutely clear, what is shocking is that those excesses are entirely acceptable."
  14. Eagleton 2004, 184.
  15. Cited in Rollins and O'Connor 2003, 40.
  16. Crawley 2006, 70.
  17. Douglas 2002.
  18. Douglas 2002.
  19. Douglas 2002.
  20. For example, in Christianity the relationship thus became a three-fold arrangement: you and I and Christ. By contrast, in Martin Buber's argument (although Buber could hardly have been called a Marxist), when human beings care for each other they enter a perfect relationship, what Buber called "I and Thou."
  21. See Chapter 11 for a fuller discussion of the issue of religion in the series, in particular the influence of religion on Bartlet's presidency.
  22. See Parry-Giles and Parry-Giles 2006, 126–129, for a further discussion of this aspect of the episode.

Chapter 10

  1. How accurate such statistics were is open to question—certainly this last instance on infant mortality would seem to have been deliberately erroneous.
  2. Cass 2007, 33.
  3. Crawley 2006, 103. It would seem that Sam, together with some of the other characters in the fictitious world of the series, may have believed this; but only in the context of wish-fulfillment.

4. Transcribed from the DVD of the episode "Internal Displacement" (7/11).
5. Note the difference in attitude here to CJ's passionately humanitarian stance in the earlier episode "The Women of Qumar" (3/9).
6. As Leonard Cohen would put it in his song "Democracy," America was the cradle of the best and the worst. America is for example, the only nation to have put a man on the moon; but also the only nation to have used nuclear weapons.
7. This neglect of narrative continuity was prevalent throughout *The West Wing*. See Chapter 21 for a fuller discussion of this aspect to the series.
8. Cass 2007, 33.
9. Cass 2007, 33.
10. Stokes 2003.
11. Sontag 2009.
12. Fanon 2001.
13. For example, in the episode "Stirred" (3/18), Bartlet's staff met with the clear and serious consideration of dropping Hoynes from the ticket, with the cynically motivated reasoning: "Texas was no longer on the table." In other words, as Hoynes could no longer win his home state, another vice president might be able to win his or her state.
14. Herr 2000, 83.

Chapter 11

1. Stephen Hawking *A Brief History of Time: From the Big Bang to Black Holes* (London: Bantam 2011), p. 1.
2. Whether the other cynical, intelligent and worldly-wise characters in the series had such devout and literal beliefs is open to speculation. Toby Ziegler attended synagogue, but there were few other discernible examples of characters possessing a religious faith.
3. Grahame Greene *Brighton Rock* (London, Vintage Books, 2010), p. 268.
4. Cited in "Extracts from a Manuscript Notebook," in *The Collected Essays, Journalism and Letters of George Orwell*, Vol. 4 (1968).
5. For example, Sigmund Freud perceived religion as "a universal neurosis"—with the implied conclusion that much of the world was made up of individuals with delusional personalities.
6. Corkery 2014, 83.
7. In other words, from a British rather than an American point-of-view.
8. Cited in Fahy 2005, 135.
9. Parry-Giles and Parry-Giles 2006, 27. The authors went on to note: "This religiosity works on several levels, as it enhances the president's intellect, tempers his liberalism, and elevates his moral character" (Parry-Giles and Parry-Giles 2006, 41). However, a counter-argument might suggest religious belief accomplishes the opposite—it may temper liberalism, but it would seem more likely to reduce the intellect, or at least reduce the capacity for rational thought.
10. Philpott and Mutimer 2006, 345.
11. Crawley 2006, 157.
12. As Alexis de Tocqueville put it: "In America puritanism was almost as much a political theory as a religious doctrine" (de Tocqueville 1998, 17).
13. Crawley 2006, 158.
14. Eagleton 2004, 100.
15. Eagleton 2004, 100.
16. However, it might be noted Bernard Law was briefly mentioned, in the episode "And It's Surely to Their Credit" (2/5). Bartlet made a passing reference to Law, then the archbishop of Boston. Law would resign from his position in 2002, amid accusations that he had had extensive knowledge of Catholic priests committing multiple acts of sexual abuse on children.
17. Eagleton 2004, 203. Eagleton slightly underestimated the death toll, while *The West Wing* (albeit in a fictitious discourse) appeared to overestimate the number of deaths, citing seventeen schoolgirls dying. From authoritative accounts of the incident, it would seem that the number of schoolgirls who died in the fire was fifteen.
18. This would paraphrase Terry Eagleton: "The grandest narrative of all [was] eschatology" (Eagleton 2004, 99).
19. Paraphrased from Watson 2000. In his book Watson went on to develop the argument that fundamentalist religious belief (acting to curtail freedom of thought) has led to the backwardness of Islamic societies.
20. Eagleton 2004, 203.
21. To take an example from the Book of Isaiah in the Bible, this is a polemical textual body, one that would cause most discerning readers more than a degree of moral consternation. As Terry Eagleton commented: "The Book of Isaiah is strong stuff for these post-revolutionary days. It is only left in hotel rooms because no one bothers to read it" (Eagleton 2004, 178).
22. Paraphrased from Watson 2000.
23. Cited in Robert Willoughby Corrigan, *Classical Tragedy, Greek and Roman* (New York: Applause Theatre Books, 1990), p. 352.
24. Cited in Theodore Roszak, *Where the Wasteland Ends: Politics and Transcendence in*

Postindustrial Society. (New York: Doubleday, 1972).

25. Terry Eagleton has ridiculed the nativity story: "It would be hard to think up a more ludicrous way of registering the population of the entire Roman empire than to have them all return to their birthplaces" (Eagleton 2004, 205).

26. In terms of this aspect of Christian doctrine, Christopher Hitchens often quoted the Scottish philosopher, David Hume, who famously asked: "Which is more likely, that the whole natural order is suspended, or that a Jewish minx should tell a lie?"

27. Paraphrased from Watson 2000. The oft-expressed metaphor of a whirlwind passing through a scrap-yard and assembling a jumbo jet offers a tangible way of understanding this; such an event is possible, but hardly likely.

28. There is also the issue of theodicy: Why would an all-loving, all-caring God permit so much evil to exist? As Stendhal famously put it: "The only excuse for God is that he does not exist."

29. Watson 2000.

30. Watson 2000.

31. This would be to disregard the show's only catchphrase, "What's next?"—a phrase that could be read as one of the most existentialist of questions.

32. Stokes 2003.

33. Cited in Stokes 2003, 155.

34. There is also Christopher Hitchens's well-known argument that might be paraphrased as follows: Why would an all-powerful, all-knowing God leave human beings without a manifest savior for tens of thousands of years? In other words, as human beings have prevailed for at least 100,000 years (this was Hitchens's estimate, it is probably much more), why wait 98,000 years to redeem them?

35. Eagleton 2004, 194.

36. Hawking 2011, 209–210.

Chapter 12

1. At least until the presidency of Barack Obama, which post-dated *The West Wing*.

2. Parry-Giles and Parry-Giles 2002, 222.

3. Challen 2001, 74. See also Donnalyn Pompper: "The NAACP charged that *The West Wing*... lacked diversity... Sorkin apologized in *Newsweek*, saying, 'I genuinely appreciate the tap on the shoulder from the NAACP, and they're quite right in being upset'" (Cited in Rollins and O'Connor 2003, 30–31).

4. For Leslie Fiedler this would have been of some interest, inasmuch as his book *Love and Death in the American Novel* posited the idea that the basic pattern of the classic American novel involved a homoerotic relationship between a white man and a "colored" boy (See Fiedler 1997, vi). Richard Schiff, on *The West Wing Weekly* podcast for the "Talking Points" (5/19) episode, stated: "Butt boy, that's what the Clinton White House called [the equivalent of] Charlie Young." This was a comment Fiedler may well have appreciated, at least in the context of this argument. Fiedler died in 2003 and therefore may have viewed the early seasons of the show—but any comment he may have made cannot be found on record.

5. As Trevor and Shawn J. Parry-Giles put it: "Just as Leo's questions about Charlie's race are cosmetic, so, too, are concerns about network casting" (Parry-Giles and Parry-Giles 2006, 95).

6. The last word uttered by Fitzwallace would be "dodo"—whether this had some degree of satiric inference was open to question.

7. As Simon Philpott and David Mutimer commented: "The absence of a father and the violent death of his mother ... make Charlie a 'typical black'" (Philpott and Mutimer 2006, 345).

8. Transcribed from the DVD of the episode "Lord John Marbury" (1/11).

9. Philpott and Mutimer 2006, 346.

10. Morrison 1993, 49–50. Trevor and Shawn J. Parry-Giles remark on some of the subtleties herein:

> From its very constitutional beginning, race and citizenship were contested issues for the United States. In Article 1, section 2 of the Constitution, significantly, the measure of taxation was calculated 'by adding the whole Number of free Persons, including those bound to Service for a Term of Years, and excluding Indians not taxed, three fifths of all other Persons.' Indeed, the authors of many of the nation's founding documents wrestled with the persistent conundrum of slavery." (Parry-Giles and Parry-Giles 2006, 87)

See the episode "Mr. Willis of Ohio" (1/6) for a discussion of this issue and for *The West Wing*'s trepidation in offering too clear a delineation of an inconvenient truth.

11. Fiedler 1997.

12. Morrison 1993, 9. Morrison added: "What was distinctive in the New World was, first of all, its claim to freedom and, second,

the presence of the unfree within the heart of the democratic experiment" (Morrison 1993, 48).

13. Those episodes were "Mr. Willis of Ohio" (1/6), "Six Meetings Before Lunch" (1/18), "The Two Bartlets" (3/13), "Night Five" (3/14), "Dead Irish Writers" (3/16), "Han" (5/4), "The Supremes" (5/17) and "The Debate" (7/7).

14. Cited in Parry-Giles and Parry-Giles 2006, 113. In fact, the figure was higher—620,000, with some sources suggesting as many as 850,000—but whether they were all white is open to question. Forty thousand black Union soldiers are thought to have died in the Civil War, and even on the Confederate side—black slaves acted as hand-servants and manual laborers—large numbers died during the conflict.

15. As Joshua Malina put it, on *The West Wing Weekly* podcast for the episode "The Two Bartlets," slavery was "an enormous, grotesque injustice of an entire country whose economy and economic prosperity was built on the back of slaves." Perhaps only a satirical discourse was able to approach the issue. For example, Frank Pembleton, as portrayed by Andre Braugher in the television drama *Homicide: Life on the Streets*, the precursor to *The Wire*, put the case well: "Everyone was an immigrant at some point in this country—some even by choice."

16. See Fahy 2005, 147–177. Of course, we are dealing here with linguistic niceties and with different models of political correctness; nonetheless, if Mr. Bambang could use the correct nomenclature why could the main characters in the show not do the same?

17. However, the use of language was arguably more offensive elsewhere. "The Redskins suck," said Josh in the episode, "The State Dinner" (1/7). It was an offhand comment, a reference to a poor result by the Washington Redskins, the local NFL team, but the comment could also have been read as a reference to their racist name. In other words, it was not so much that the football team was playing poorly, but that their non-PC nomenclature "sucked."

18. It has been said that Columbus may have thought he had sailed around the world and had landed in the Indies, and that the first indigenous people he encountered had painted their skins red—this may be an apocryphal story—but the term "Red Indian" remains both disparaging and offensive.

19. Topping 2002, 294.
20. Parry-Giles and Parry-Giles 2006, 112.
21. Cass 2007, 36.
22. Transcribed from the DVD of the episode "Dead Irish Writers" (3/16).
23. Khoday 2009, 42–43.
24. To allude to merely a small number of other instances: in the "Pilot" (1/1) episode, it was clear in the brief scene of Leo at home that he was being served by a black maid; at the end of the episode "Two Cathedrals" (2/22), it was a black janitor who found the discarded cigarette Bartlet had disposed of in the cathedral; and in the episode "Impact Winter" (6/9), after Donna (white, attractive, slim, sweet-tempered) had resigned, her replacement was presented as black, plain, obese, and ill-tempered.
25. Coates 2014.
26. Parry-Giles and Parry-Giles 2002, 222
27. Parry-Giles and Parry-Giles 2006, 93.
28. Parry-Giles and Parry-Giles 2006, 111.
29. Fiedler 1997, 404.

Chapter 13

1. Similarly, in the episode "Galileo" (2/9), when Donna made use of the word "philately," Josh told her: "Be careful how you say that word."

2. James 2016, 67. The contrast between President Clinton's libido and Bartlet's lack of one has been much commented on in the literature on the show. For example, Bartlet was "a Clinton without vices" (Engelstad 2008, 313); Bartlet's administration was "an idealized Clinton White House" (Gans-Boriskin and Tisinger 2005, 103); Bartlet was "a bimbo-less Bill Clinton" (Biswas 2008, 19); and in essence, *The West Wing* was "the ultimate Hollywood fantasy: the Clinton White House without Clinton" (Rollins and O'Connor 2003, 223).

3. There were rare exceptions, one occurring in the episode "Night Five" (3/14), wherein Donna and Josh made some unusually salacious comments. Donna remarked: "I'm going to sell my farm-girl ass for a carton of Lucky's." Josh said: "I hate these people.... I'm going to personally screw them with their pants on!"

4. Wolff 2000.
5. Jackson 2000.
6. McCabe 2013, 47.
7. As Paul Ruditis and Ian Jackman noted: "If it's a choice between her job and Danny, there is no choice" (Ruditis and Jackman 2002, 104). Also, CJ's relationship with the secret service agent Simon Donovan would come to nothing, with Donovan being shot and killed just as a relationship with CJ seemed about to begin.

8. McCabe 2013, 48.
9. However, note that in the episode "17 People" (2/18), there was a subtle indication that Sam and Ainsley were sexually involved with each other.
10. Parry-Giles and Parry-Giles 2006, 68.
11. See Parry-Giles and Parry-Giles 2006, 31, and Fahy 2005, 121, for a further analysis of this unusual scenario.
12. Cited in Rollins and O'Connor 2003, 72.
13. This was particularly apposite, as Amy was one of the few characters in the series to exude a genuine sense of sexual chemistry.
14. See Philpott and Mutimer 2006, 348, who went on to note how the scene acted as "an epiphany for Josh who suddenly realizes the narrowness of his thinking on gay issues."
15. In such a sense, it was perhaps of significance that the issue under discussion was "gay marriage." This issue was to recur throughout the run of the series: from Roberto Mendoza ruling in its favor in the episode "The Short List" (1/9), to the discussion in the episode "Faith Based Initiative " (6/10). In this latter episode what was significant was the disclosure that Bartlet, himself, did not agree with same-sex marriage; he agreed to civil union of same-sex couples, but not to marriage, most probably because of his religious faith.
16. Anindita Biswas was perceptive in summing up this issue: "How do we interpret the fact that a show of this calibre does not make much effort to address concerns like sexual preference [while] claiming to be liberal and progressive at the same time?" (Biswas 2008, 1).
17. The three main "gay" characters in *The Wire* were Kima Greggs, Omar Little and William Rawls—see Chapter 15 for a more detailed discussion of this issue.
18. Siann 1994, 15.
19. Furthermore, when individuals do indulge in heterosexual coitus, there is commonly a much greater concern about *avoiding* conception than achieving it.
20. Nelson and Longfellow 1994. As intimated in Chapter 5, in terms of New Testament teachings, especially the teachings of St. Paul, these might more accurately be interpreted as a reaction against the sexual mores in the Greco-Roman world of the time, sexual relations between boys and adult men. This was somewhat different from the condemnation today of same-sex couples in consenting relationships.
21. Horrocks 1997, 183.
22. Horrocks 1997, 119.
23. Horrocks 1997, 120.
24. Horrocks 1997, 120. Horrocks went on to comment that Carl Jung saw this as "the source of the God image found in many cultures. To put it crudely, sex can make us feel god-like. Perhaps it is not surprising then that Christianity has been so suspicious about sex."
25. Eagleton 1996, 196.
26. Gallop 1992, 275.
27. However, Leo would appear not to know, as this derogatory comment from the episode "Faith Based Initiative" (6/10) would seem to suggest: "So are the queers gonna destroy marriage as we know it, or what?"
28. Cited in Quinn 2007, 279.
29. Spargo 1999, 12.
30. Siann 1994.
31. Garber 1995, 14.
32. Garber 1995, 249.
33. Barry 1995.
34. Butler 1990, 8.
35. As Mark Simpson noted: "By dressing up as a man, he [a gay man] threatens to reveal that all soldiers are, in fact, dressing up as men and that being a soldier—the most manly of all occupations—might just be another kind of performance" (Simpson 1996, 7). In this context, it might be noted that Josh, in the episode "Ways and Means" (3/4), revealed—for no apparent reason—that when he was four he wanted to be a ballerina. Judith Butler noted the drag artist's mockery of masculinity, and that this, along with other examples of cross-dressing such as pantomime, fancy dress, and so on, had the virtue of showing that gender was imitative in structure. In other words, being male or female entails a performance that requires certain cultural signals, which perhaps goes some way to explain Josh's eccentric confession. On the topic of cross-dressing, note also CJ's laconic comment in the episode "The Fall's Gonna Kill You" (2/20) that 1 in 40 men wore women's clothes and that there had been more than 40 presidents.
36. Bristow 1997, 205.
37. Bristow 1997, 205.
38. It has been suggested that Shakespeare may have deliberately presented this "odd couple" in order to present an ambiguous echo of Hamlet's own ambiguous sexuality.
39. In *The West Wing Weekly* podcast for the episode "Bartlet for America" (3/10), Alison Janney described the relationship between Bartlet and Leo as "the most beautiful love story between two men … it's purely that, it's one human being having love and respect for another human being … it's not a sexual love story, it's not a romantic love

story, but it's a pure kind of love and devotion and respect."

40. Melissa Crawley's description of Sam was perhaps relevant here: "Sam is the most sensitive and politically naive of the principal characters ... Sorkin often feminizes his masculinity" (Crawley 2006, 94).

41. Fiedler 1997, 31.

42. Charles B. Harris in his 1997 introduction to *Love and Death in the American Novel*, cited in Fiedler 1997, x.

43. Fiedler 1997, 350–351.

44. Charles B. Harris in his 1997 introduction to *Love and Death in the American Novel*, cited in Fiedler 1997, vi.

45. To clarify, Joey (albeit with a masculinized name) was a hearing-impaired woman speaking through a male interpreter.

46. A viewing of the episode in question, "Post Hoc, Ergo Propter Hoc" (1/2), with such an idea in mind allows one to observe this potential relationship in this particular way.

47. Garber 1995.

Chapter 14

1. What was relevant here was that Joey's deafness was never a significant issue; Joey was a character who had a significant hearing impairment, but this was never a part of the plotlines she inhabited. Joey had an interpreter and her spoken speech—when used—was noticeably that of a hearing-impaired person, but a viewing of each episode in which she appeared demonstrated her disability was wholly irrelevant.

2. Aside from her spelling difficulties, most likely caused by a combination of impaired working memory and slow processing speed, Carol was also left-handed. It has been noted that individuals with dyslexia have a slightly higher incidence of left-handedness than the population as a whole.

3. There were numerous other examples of CJ's clumsiness. For example, in the episode "Drought Conditions" (6/16), CJ spilled coffee over her suit; this may have seemed like an ordinary accident, but when Margaret looked in CJ's wardrobe for a replacement outfit, her other outfits were also stained, one with "penne and red sauce," one with "vodka and cranberry."

4. Bradley Whitford on *The West Wing Weekly* podcast for the episode "In the Shadow of Two Gunmen Part 2." In terms of the choice of disability, it is not wholly implausible that it was selected insomuch as MS echoed Martin Sheen's initials, even if this was an unconscious decision on the part of Aaron Sorkin and the other writers on the show.

5. In fact, the actor playing the role, Robert David Hall, had had both of his legs amputated as a result of a traffic accident in 1978; nonetheless, the character, as played in the episode, still retained some degree of resemblance to the appearance of an individual with MS, especially as the chronology of the episode was so close to the plotline in which Bartlet's own MS was revealed.

6. See Topping 2002, 28.

7. Topping 2002, 29.

8. Altman 2001.

9. Beavers 2002, 215.

10. In addition, one might note that President Nixon was prone to phlebitis, a condition that threatened his life in the midst of the Watergate scandal. There were also numerous questions about President Reagan's mental capacity; Vice President Dick Cheney attempted to hide his heart condition while in office—and so on. Thus Bartlet was not alone in attempting to disguise his medical problems.

11. As Matthew David Barber put it: "Just as Kennedy had the Bay of Pigs, Nixon had Watergate, Reagan had Iran-Contra and Clinton had Lewinsky, Bartlet had MS" (Barber 2009, 218).

12. Zoller and Worrell 2006, 70.

13. Zoller and Worrell 2006, 72.

14. Zoller and Worrell 2006, 74.

15. Zoller and Worrell 2006, 74.

16. This is the most common form of the disease—with some 85 percent of people with MS being initially diagnosed with this form of the condition.

17. The acting between Martin Sheen and Stockard Channing in this scene was arguably as convincing as acting anywhere in the series. This was perhaps due to the quality of the script, written by Deborah Cahn. Her writing here arguably was as good as any of the much-vaunted scripts by Aaron Sorkin.

18. In the imagined future C.J. was married to Danny and had a young child; Toby was working at Columbia University; Kate had written a successful memoir; Will was a congressman; Charlie was studying law; Donna, however, was not present, by which it might be inferred she may or may not have married Josh. At the end of the scene Josh appeared to announce that the president was on his way; although it was not explicitly stated, it was clear that Josh was the then president's chief of staff—hence somewhat undermining any sense of dramatic tension,

in the next seventeen episodes, as to who was to win the election.

19. The IMDb website lists a number of other films with MS as a central narrative device. These include the following:

Duet for One (1986) Andrei Konchalovsky
In Sickness and in Health (1992 TV Movie) Jeff Becker
Go Now (1995) Michael Winterbottom
Eden (1996) Howard Goldberg
Freak City (1999 TV Movie) Lynne Littman
Guru (2007) Mani Ratnam

20. It might be noted that although Bartlet was in office for two terms and was generally perceived as being a liberal-leaning president, there was little evidence of his administration attempting to improve healthcare as—for example—Barack Obama at least attempted to do in the real world of U.S. politics.

Chapter 15

1. David Simon was the primary creator of the series; however, it should be noted that Ed Burns, a former Baltimore police detective, was also a significant contributor.

2. Baltimore, although only 40 miles from Washington, D.C. and hence within the boundaries of the northern United States, has nonetheless been seen as part of the South and as being redolent of the racism of the south. As David Simon put it: "That line about the most northern southern city or most southern northern city is one known to all Baltimoreans" (cited in Hornby 2007).

3. Transcribed from an interview included in the special features of the DVD of The Wire, Season 4. In a further interview, Simon expanded on this idea: "Instead of the usual good guys chasing bad guys framework, questions would be raised about the very labels of good and bad, and, indeed, whether such distinctly moral notions were really the point" (Hornby 2007, 9/31).

4. Sorkin cited in Fahy 2005, 14.
5. Crawley 2006, 81.
6. Jameson 2010, 359.
7. Jameson 2010, 370.
8. Jameson 2010, 370.
9. Transcribed from the DVD of the episode "Five Votes Down" (1/4). Illicit drug use was seldom a matter of concern in The West Wing. Other than Leo's addiction to prescription drugs and Jean-Paul's use of recreational drugs, it rarely contributed to the narrative discourse of the drama. An exception concerned a scene in the episode "Mandatory Minimums" (1/20). Here the personal aides of a number of high-ranking politicians were asked to justify the light sentences for drug offences some of the close relations of the politicians had received. Leo and Toby acted as interrogators. Leo noted: "Dick, your boss's son was arrested for carrying 25 grams of cocaine. That's a crime that usually carries— what Toby?" Toby: "Eight to fifteen years." Leo: "And what did the Congressman's son get?" Toby: "Six months house arrest." Leo then went on to cite a number of other examples. Unfortunately, a year after the episode was broadcast, Aaron Sorkin was arrested at Burbank Airport for possession of crack cocaine—he subsequently pleaded guilty to two felony charges, but was only sentenced to a short term of probation. As with the cases cited in the episode above, had Sorkin been black and poor he would have likely served a significant prison sentence. Jasbir K. Puar and Amit Rai, in their 2002 article "Monster, Terrorist, Fag: The War on Terrorism and the Production of Docile Patriots," alluded to this scene, noting Sorkin's high moral stance in the "Isaac and Ishmael" episode, and commenting on Sorkin's arrest for possession of illicit drugs, concluding that "this would seem to have some bearing on his status as moral arbiter for the nation" (Puar and Rai 2002, 133–134).

10. Slajov Žižek, "The Clash of Civilisations in One Country," 2012, https://www.youtube.com/watch?v=Fsf4rAGlR5s. (Accessed February 25, 2016) One aspect of such a "high case of realism" might be seen in the sense of television itself; for example, it is often said that the one thing people in soap operas do not do is to watch soap operas. In The West Wing, the protagonists seldom watched television for entertainment. Televisions were seen on The West Wing, but they were there predominantly for access to breaking news. However, in the case of The Wire, with its realist sense of verisimilitude, there were numerous scenes of characters watching television.

11. David Simon was to comment how The Wire was not interested in fulfilling conventional audience expectations: "I think what you sense in The Wire is that it is violating a good many of the conventions and tropes of episodic television. It isn't really structured as episodic television and it instead pursues the form of the modern, multi-POV novel" (Hornby 2007, 3/31).

12. Cited in Fahy 2005, 168.
13. It should be admitted that such polit-

ical maneuvering in *the Wire* was also, at times, almost impenetrable. There was a sense that much that was being said for much of the time was not the literal truth, as if most of the characters in play were dissembling most of the time.

14. Jameson 2010, 359.
15. Jameson 2010, 360.
16. Žižek 2012. As Simon put it: "The show [was] about untethered capitalism run amok, about how power and money actually route themselves in a postmodern American city" (Hornby 2007, 9/31).
17. Hornby 2007, 9/31.
18. Hornby 2007, 9/31.
19. Hornby 2007, 5/31.
20. Hornby 2007, 6/31.
21. Transcribed from the DVD of the episode "Dead Soldiers" (3/3).
22. Jameson 2010, 359–360. A comparison to Dickens has been noted by other commentators such as, Chris Roberts, who made the point that although the show has "often [been] compared to 'an epic novel,' *The Wire* avoided any Dickensian moralising, refusing to serve up catharsis or 'just' resolutions" (Roberts 2014, 99).
23. Žižek 2012. In addition, it should perhaps be noted that the sixth episode of the fifth and final season of *The Wire* was entitled "The Dickensian Aspect."
24. Note that with the exception of the opening and closing titles of each episode—together with one rare exception in the series finale, wherein an emotive montage was enhanced with a musical backing—non-diegetic music was not employed in *The Wire*.
25. Note that apart from one brief flashback scene in the opening episode of Season 1 (an insert apparently placed within the episode at the behest of HBO) *The Wire* did not otherwise make use of such easily manipulative techniques to tell its story.
26. *The West Wing* told its story by using many of the techniques open to conventional television dramas, for example, the use of voice-over narration and also the use of numerous flashbacks. There were examples of analepsis in at least thirteen episodes, together with one example of prolepsis: a flash forward three years into the future in the episode "The Ticket" (7/1).
27. This was exemplified in the famous scene between McNulty and Bunk Moreland in "Old Cases," the fourth episode of Season 1. This was the so-called "fuck" scene—as Žižek named it. For several minutes McNulty and Bunk, re-investigating the scene of an old homicide case, used only one four-letter

word to describe their incredulity as they put together the actual way in which the murder in question had been committed.

28. In the United Kingdom this was not the case. Channel 4, a network channel, showed *The West Wing*, while BBC2, another network channel, showed *The Wire* uncut, albeit usually after 11:00 p.m. and with warnings of explicit content.
29. McCabe 2013, 14.
30. McCabe 2013, 17. Sorkin would subsequently write a series for HBO, *The Newsroom* (2012–2014); there was some greater flexibility in the use of language, but otherwise the series occupied a discursive space similar in many ways to that of *The West Wing*.
31. Both shows have been seen as *zeitgeist* dramas on numerous occasions. For example, *The West Wing* was to become, in the words of *George* magazine, "a *zeitgeist* show, a reflection of the tenor of our times" (cited in Parry-Giles and Parry-Giles 2002, 210).
32. "In Excelsis Deo" (1/10) was the first of a number of Christmas episodes in *The West Wing*, the others being "Noel" (2/10), "Bartlet for America" (3/10), "Holy Night" (4/11), "Abu el Banat" (5/9) and "Impact Winter" (6/9). Note that *The Wire*, in its five seasons, contained only one episode set at Christmas, the holiday being evidenced only remotely (and wholly without festive cheer) at the end of Season 4.
33. There were other examples: Benjamin Busch, who played Anthony Colicchio, a police officer, in *The Wire*, had a small role as a police sergeant in "In the Shadow of Two Gunmen Part 2" (2/2); Delaney Williams, who played the regular role of Sergeant Jay Landsman in *The Wire*, had a small role as a reporter in "Inauguration Part 2: Over There" (4/15); likewise, Thomas McCarthy, who played the reporter Scott Templeton in *The Wire*, had a small role as Senator Thomas in "Ways and Means" (3/4). Finally, Clark Johnson, who had major roles in both *Homicide: Life on the Streets* and *The Wire*, directed one episode of *The West Wing*: "Six Meetings Before Lunch" (1/18).
34. Hornby 2007, 26/31.
35. One reason for the show's critical acclaim may have derived from the fact that David Simon was much less willing to lessen the level of realism in order to placate the average viewer's expectations. In Simon's words: "My standard for verisimilitude is simple, and I came to it when I started to write prose narrative: fuck the average reader" (Hornby 2007, 23/31).
36. This description is Slajov Žižek's. See Žižek 2012.

Chapter 16

1. In addition, there is also the point that *The West Wing* spanned the periods just before and just after the events of 9/11, this being significant insomuch as the events of this date have been seen as marking the end of the postmodern era. In his book *After Theory*, Terry Eagleton perceived the end of postmodernism: "With the launch of a new global narrative of capitalism, along with the so-called war on terror, it may well be that the style of thinking known as postmodernism is now approaching an end" (Eagleton 2004, 221).
2. To put this more succinctly, in David Lyon's words, postmodernity was "a multi-layered concept that alerts us to a variety of major social and cultural changes taking place in the late 20th century within many advanced societies" (Lyon 1995, vii).
3. Lyon 1995, 16.
4. Cass 2007, 32.
5. An apt example comes from the world of popular music: the concept of the tribute band, the deliberate copying of a previously manufactured entity. In fact, the situation becomes still more perverse, insomuch as there are now even tribute bands of tribute bands. It has been said that Abba's main tribute band, Bjorn Again (in itself a playful, postmodernist joke), now has a tribute band of its own.
6. As Peter Barry argued, postmodernism positions many aspects of theory as an abandonment of principles of rational objectivity—and truth "in any given situation can only be a matter of the values and beliefs that happen to prevail among members of some existing 'interpretative community'" (Barry 2009, 282–283).
7. In this sense, it might be noted how *The West Wing* appeared to deliberately undermine history—creating an alternative history of the world that was similar to but nonetheless different from our own. Hence, albeit in a somewhat simplistic way, this was indicative of the idea of a hyper-real narrative.
8. See Hanson 2005, who makes use of the term "Disney-fication."
9. Lyon 1995, 29.
10. For example, it has been estimated that over 60 million people were killed in World War II, some 3% of the world population at the time.
11. Cited in William Peter Blatty's novel *Legion* (Glasgow: William Collins, 1983). Hence we are forced to prevail with the knowledge that nature is "red in tooth and claw," and are thus left (if we believe in a God) with the difficulty of envisaging a so-called benevolent creator deliberately designing such a gruesome form of creation. One thinks here of Woody Allen who, when told that nature reveals the glory of God, replied that he only saw a giant restaurant.
12. Paraphrased from remarks by Frederic Jameson cited in Lewis 2008, 194–195.
13. In other words, postmodernism offered a culture of quotations; a culture of the already said, as Umberto Eco would put it; a culture of duplicitous signs, meanings within meanings, fictions within fictions; a culture concerned with the signifier rather than the signified; in other words, a culture merely consisting of "the perpetual circulation of signs and other signs" (Storey 2001, 160).
14. Parry-Giles and Parry-Giles 2002, 210.
15. Young Hoon Kim has also alluded to this. Without explicitly drawing upon postmodern theory he questioned whether the line "We're gonna raise the level of public debate in this country" could be seen as a self-referential statement (Kim 2009).
16. There were deliberate differences in lighting and shooting: a more immediate and less considered *mise-en-scène*; an arbitrary use of black and white against color; the use of video stock as against film stock; deliberately out-of-focus shots; erratic camera movements and so on.
17. Note the deliberate mixing of the factual and fictional—archival images of Kennedy, Johnson and Nixon were shown on archival footage and factual press secretaries Ron Ziegler and Pierre Salinger mixed with fictional press secretaries and with CJ herself.
18. Russo 2009.
19. The episode was also of interest in the way it offered little by way of an explanation of changes to the usual programming format; the episode came toward the end of Season 5 of the drama, flanked on either side by conventional episodes continuing with the previously established narratives—but there was no explanation for this narrative aberration.
20. Krauss 2012, 147–148.
21. Lyon 1995, 67.

Chapter 17

1. Gans-Boriskin and Tisinger 2005, 109. The authors also comment upon "a situation where it is open season on leaders of foreign countries." One notes here the potential perils of pursuing such a strategy. For example, President Kennedy's alleged attempts to have Fidel Castro assassinated would seem to have

broken the informal code of world leaders; as a reporter says in the episode "Jefferson Lives" (5/3): "The most practical reason for not engaging in the assassination of foreign leaders is that our own officials and their families are vulnerable to retaliation." Shareef was not a world leader, but Bartlet's decision to have him killed may have given him pause for thought.

2. Transcribed from the DVD of the episode "Posse Comitatus" (3/22). Note the potential sexual subtext in Bartlet's final remark, his order to have Abdul Shareef murdered. Given the repeated trope in the series comparing masculine violence to masculine prowess, this was a potential reading of the comment: "Take him!" Here there was the suggestion of a sense of the joy of killing being akin to the joy of sex—the sense of dominance of the alpha male, which Bartlet certainly aspired to be.

3. Kim 2009, 6/16.
4. Parry-Giles and Parry-Giles 2006, 146.
5. Crawley 2006, 179.
6. Parry-Giles and Parry-Giles 2006, 143.
7. To speculate further would be to go beyond narrative convention and the confines of the story being told. However, there is always the issue that any story refrains from offering full and total information. This is the iceberg principle, the idea that there is always a disproportionate amount of narrative information withheld from the reader or, in this case, the viewer.

8. Transcribed from the DVD of the episode "College Kids" (4/3).
9. Note also Bartlet's cynicism in his personal dealings with Shareef; for example, in the way Bartlet welcomes Shareef to the Oval Office with supposed hospitality—but refuses to shake hands (to offer human contact) because of a spurious skin complaint. In addition, Bartlet's goodwill gift of a pen to Shareef actually contained a monitoring device designed to assist in confirming Shareef's killing. The fact that Bartlet was aware of this, but nonetheless would give the order to kill the man in front of him, all suggests a man very different in moral stature than the man Bartlet was often held up to be.

10. Transcribed from the DVD of the episode "We Killed Yamamoto" (3/21).
11. Note, for example, the Amiriyah shelter bombing of February 13, 1991. This occurred when two F117 stealth bombers each dropped a 2,000-pound laser guided bomb on Public Shelter 25; 408 civilians were killed. Most of the dead—including women and children—were incinerated by the intense heat of the fire.

12. Parry-Giles and Parry-Giles 2006, 142.
13. This comment was made by Nixon in the fifth of the five television interviews with David Frost originally broadcast in 1977, cited here from its publication in the *New York Times*, May 20, 1977.
14. As Melissa Crawley put it: "Intelligence and moral purpose are the two most important attributes we ought to expect from our political leaders" (Crawley 2006, 190).
15. This discussion is derived from material cited in Watson 2000.
16. This derives from the idea that political and legal systems are so inherently corrupt that this "truth" must be kept from the public; that for order to be maintained the public must be prevented from understanding the actual truth—this being the role of princes and politicians.
17. Parry-Giles and Parry-Giles 2006, 148.
18. One might recall here the famous quotation by Stanley Kubrick: "The great nations have always acted like gangsters, and the small nations like prostitutes." Originally cited in *The Guardian* June 5, 1963.
19. Crawley 2006, 179.
20. Gans-Boriskin and Tisinger 2005, 111.
21. Robert Harris's novel *The Ghost* (and the subsequent film, *The Ghost Writer*, directed by Roman Polanski in 2010) was a thinly veiled depiction of a figure clearly modeled on Tony Blair. The plot of both novel and film centered around the risk of the Blair-esque ex-prime minister, Adam Lang, being made to answer to potential war crimes.
22. In English: "*The West Wing*: Does the U.S. president care about international law when deciding upon military intervention?" The paper was published in French, although the abstract is available in English translation.
23. Corten went on to comment that in contrast, "a comprehensive viewing of its 155 episodes reveals a more subtle representation of international law, particularly as far as the UN Charter rules are concerned." Corten's essay also argued that "self-defense is broadly conceived as an action that appears necessary in order to counter terrorist groups of states that support them ... international law has no prohibition against any government, superpower or otherwise, targeting terrorist command control centers" (Corten 2014).
24. Corten 2014, 1.
25. In Kathryn Bigelow's film *Zero Dark Thirty* (2013), the use of "enhanced interrogation techniques," torture by any logical definition, seemed to be taken almost for granted. In one scene President Obama was shown on television stating that the use of torture would

not be tolerated; however, the CIA interrogators did not even seem to trouble to acknowledge this, ignoring the broadcast as if it were part of another reality. Note that Obama had prohibited the use of torture on his second day in office, but how long this took to take effect remains open to speculation.

26. Of course, the argument as to whether Bush did "win" the 2000 election remains a contentious issue. It is clear that the majority of voters voted for Gore. Gore received 48.4 percent of the popular vote, as against 47.9 percent for Bush; over half a million more Americans voted for Gore than Bush; however, Bush received 271 electoral votes as against Gore's 266 and hence "won" the election. In the case of Bartlet's fictional election to the presidency, on the presumed date of November 3, 1998, this was not dealt with in any detail in the series, but we were made aware that he was elected with only 48% of the popular vote and yet achieved 303 electoral votes. The only way to explain this would be to extrapolate that there was a third candidate; Bartlet's Republican opponent could hardly have lost the electoral college by this margin against an opponent with such a low popular vote.

27. It is highly unlikely, but an imagined future sequel of the show might envisage an ageing Bartlet—being visited by his equally ageing staff—not on his farm in New Hampshire, but in a prison cell in The Hague.

28. The charge of hypocrisy would seem difficult to evade, insomuch as America has refused to recognize the jurisdiction of the International Criminal Court (ICC), while at the same time expecting the rest of the world to submit to its legal authority. In the episode "Running Mates" (7/10), Leo argued this was the case "because the U.S. regularly takes the leading role in military interventions overseas, [and therefore] it leaves itself especially vulnerable to potentially illegitimate legal claims motivated solely by ideological or political animas with no countervailing checks and balances." However, there is still the sense that Americans are answerable to no one but their own government and their own laws simply because they have the power to avoid other constraints.

Chapter 18

1. For more details of this subject area, see Niamh Thecla, "These Women: Is *The West Wing* Sexist?" Available at: https://leigh anoisgocuramach.wordpress.com/2012/06/ 26/these-women-is-the-west-wing-sexist (Accessed July 1, 2017)

2. Paraphrased from Selden and Widdowson 1993, 203.
3. Segal 1994, xiii.
4. Amy Gardner was perhaps the one character in the series with a clear feminist viewpoint, and the only character to have a genuinely militant attitude toward the equality of the genders.
5. Melissa Crawley, in a perceptive appraisal of CJ's character, noted: "While C.J. is depicted as independent, assertive and a strong member of the Bartlet family, the character is also frequently portrayed as a victim of her emotions" (Crawley 2006, 87).
6. Biswas 2008, 55.
7. It should perhaps be noted that although the "teleplay" of the episode was credited to a man, Aaron Sorkin, the "story" was credited to three women: Felicia Willson, Laura Glasser and Julia Dahl.
8. Laura K. Garrett made a similar point: "By casting women in supportive roles as staff secretaries and assistants, Sorkin creates a common gender dynamic found in Washington politics of male superiors and female aides" (cited in Fahy 2005, 188–189).
9. Parry-Giles and Parry-Giles 2002, 221.
10. Philpott and Mutimer 2006, 349–350.
11. Chambers and Finn 2001, 3.
12. Challen 2001, 24.
13. The episode was broadcast in 2001, ten years after the release of the song; however, in an anachronism befitting the series, to CJ it appeared as if she had only just heard it. See Parry-Giles and Parry-Giles 2002, 221.
14. Clive James used this term in his article "Winged Words in *The West Wing.*" James was referring to Janel Moloney, but the term perhaps applied more accurately to Alison Janney (James 2003).
15. Laurie was never described as a sex worker—the politically correct nomenclature. From the extant transcripts of the show (125 of the 155 episodes are available in generally accurate transcriptions at www.westwingtranscripts.com) there were eight examples of the word "prostitute," ten examples of the word "call-girl" and only one use of the term "sex worker"—this latter usage not referencing Laurie.
16. Challen 2001, 3.
17. Philpott and Mutimer 2006, 348.
18. Shepherd 2013, 57.
19. Parry-Giles and Parry-Giles 2006, 17.
20. Parry-Giles and Parry-Giles 2006, 17.
21. The word "gazed" chimes here with Laura Mulvey's coining of the term in her 1970s

essay "Visual Pleasure in Narrative Cinema," a work that became a core feminist text in terms of the representation of women on screen.

22. See, for example, Laura K. Garrett's comment of this scene: "The traits make C.J. sound like a lovable pet, not a professional woman" (Fahy 2005, 187).

23. "Let Bartlet Be Bartlet" (1/19).

24. "18th and Potomac" (2/21).

25. Fahy 2005, 180.

26. First cited on *The West Wing Weekly* podcast for "The U.S. Poet Laureate" (3/17).

27. Cass 2007, 40.

28. James 2003.

29. In this context one might note Bartlet's comment in the episode "20 Hours in America Part 2" (4/2) that Josh and Toby had 300 IQ points between them. He did not mention Donna—who had also been on the impromptu road trip with Josh and Toby, and who, in fact, had been the most proficient in getting them back to Washington.

30. Such sexist nomenclature persisted throughout the series; for example, in the episode "The Lame Duck Congress" (2/6), the assistant to the inebriated Ukraine politician Vassily Kononov was described as being a "possible hooker." This was in addition to other instances of sexist banter. For example, in the episode "Jefferson Lives" (5/3), Josh, was able to refer to "cute girls in shorts"—while in the episode "17 People" (2/18), Josh asked whether Donna had her "old Catholic school uniform on." There was also the ambiguous relationship between Toby and Marina as portrayed in Season 5 from the episode "Shutdown" (5/8) to the episode "The Supremes" (5/17). Marina was an ambivalent character. She was not given a surname, and when asked about her first name, she merely replied: "I was born on a boat." There was a sexualization of her body throughout her scenes, so much so that Toby would describe her as "a walking lawsuit." The ambiguity lay in why Toby should have been wary of a "walking lawsuit" in the first place. At around the same time it was mentioned that Toby's third research assistant had "quit her post." Hence the question might be posed: Where had all Toby's interns gone—and why was he so suspicious of Marina? Was there an untold story of sexual abuse in the deep background of the narrative?

31. Given recent events regarding sexual harassment in the entertainment industry, such behavior might now seem to be even more inappropriate. In many of today's workplaces such conduct would not be tolerated; and it is likely that Sam would have been reprimanded or even dismissed for his actions. However, as the episode was first broadcast in February 2002, some account of its historical provenance must be accepted.

32. Incidentally, the underlying intent of Sam's phrase could be seen as entailing a further sexist affront. The "good dog" breaking his leash would presumably have been intent on chasing a "bitch"—hence this could be seen as being a further derogatory reference toward Ainsley.

Chapter 19

1. This statistic may have been true in the past, but the actual figure would now seem to suggest that 38 percent of Americans are passport holders.

2. Said's book would prove to be highly influential, to the extent of being described as one of the most important works of scholarship of the twentieth century.

3. The term "Eurocentric," as used here, would also apply to nation states and cultures that have derived from European origins, the United States being one example.

4. Barry 1995.

5. The show was shown around the world, and, according to one (possibly apocryphal) story, when the series was shown in Japan the title was changed to *Some Aspects of Western Culture*.

6. Barry 1995.

7. See Song 2015, section 3.2.1, who offers a similar postcolonialist approach to this scene.

8. Barry 1995.

9. Barry 1995.

10. The fact that Bartlet somewhat miraculously appeared to succeed in this peace accord was arguably one of the least believable of his many political successes in the drama.

11. For example, Yasser Arafat (who had actually been alluded to by name earlier in the series) was clearly the model for the fictitious Palestinian leader Chairman Farad.

12. Cass 2007, 42.

13. Incidentally, it was Edward Said, in the fifth of his six Reith Lectures on BBC Radio in 1993, who is thought to have first used the phrase "speaking truth to power"—a phrase alluded to several times in the course of *The West Wing*.

14. Cited in McCabe 2013, 99.

15. Spigel 2004, 244–245.

16. Parry-Giles and Parry-Giles 2006, 156–157.

17. For example, one might consider the number of Nobel Prize winners from the Judaic world—compared to Nobel Prize winners from the Islamic world. It is said that nearly 25 percent of all Nobel Prize winners have been Jewish, although less than 0.2 percent of the world population are of Jewish descent; in contrast, while adherents of Islam number 1.8 billion—approximately 24 percent of the world population—there have only been twelve Muslim Nobel laureates, of which seven received the Nobel Peace Prize—this representing only 1.4 percent of Nobel Prize winners.

18. Watson 2000.
19. Thompson 2008, 131.
20. Language in itself, especially the English language, might be seen as an oppressive force, language perhaps being the lasting remnant of imperialism, the final residue of empire. The fact that large parts of the Middle East do not predominantly speak English (or Spanish, or French or other European languages) perhaps says something as to the strength of Islam as a cultural and linguistic force.
21. The portrayal of the United States in the show rarely admitted to such flaws; there was little sense of how young and how immature America might be conceived of as a nation state: as a bullying teenager with a limited and adolescent grasp of mental facility. This is a game that can be played with other nation states and their supposed mental health issues. For example: the United Kingdom has a superiority complex, France a still greater one; Northern Ireland (as Britain's last colony) has an inferiority complex; Israel has Post-Traumatic Stress Disorder (from the effects of the Holocaust); Sweden is manic depressive; Germany has Obsessive Compulsive Disorder; North Korea is paranoid schizophrenic—and so on.

Chapter 20

1. Spigel 2004, 242.
2. Hanson 2005, 2/9.
3. Russo 2009, 2/21.
4. Dumlao 2005.
5. Richardson 2006, 66.
6. Philpott and Mutimer 2006, 337.
7. Rollins and O'Connor 2003, 19.
8. Beavers 2002, 214.
9. Cited in Gillan 2006, 16.
10. Baker 2011.
11. Cass 2007, 37.
12. Gans-Boriskin and Tisinger 2005, 104.
13. Spigel 2004, 245.

14. Parry-Giles and Parry-Giles 2006, 162.
15. Holland 2010, 7, 17.
16. However, from other perspectives the show has been seen as ultimately failing in its attempt to educate its public. For example, Yair Rosenberg wrote: "While *The West Wing* may be some of the best American television ever produced, it is not a particularly accurate or insightful guide to the actual workings of American democracy. In fact, the very artistic and narrative choices that make it a superb drama make it a very poor representation of politics. Rather than depicting how our government actually functions, *The West Wing* reflects many popular misunderstandings of it" (Rosenberg 2012).

17. Rosenberg 2012.
18. The congressman's ignorance hence suggested that the N.E.A.—the National Endowment for the Arts—*was* needed.
19. Incidentally, the vernal equinox in question was most probably that of Friday March 21, 2003. By coincidence March 21, 2003 was the day that America's "shock and awe" bombing campaign of Iraq began, not that this existed within the alternate and much happier universe of *The West Wing*.
20. For example, see Beavers 2002, Holbert et al. 2003 and Journell 2013.
21. Sims 2016.
22. James 2016, 72.
23. Cited in Ruditis and Jackman 2002, 46.
24. Davis 2015.

Chapter 21

1. de Jonge 2001.
2. This was in contrast to the actors playing Bartlet's staff; for example, it would seem that Rob Lowe—as a more famous actor—was paid significantly more than the regular cast. Lowe would eventually leave in Season 4, partly over disagreements about pay differences.
3. Cited in Rollins and O'Connor 2003, 224. Myron A. Levine made a similar point: "Ambition and staff politics are recurrent features of the White House that curiously have little place in the stories of *The West Wing*" (cited in Rollins and O'Connor 2003, 45).
4. Cited in Rollins and O'Connor 2003, 167.
5. John Podhoretz in Rollins and O'Connor 2003, 223.
6. Pamela Ezell in Rollins and O'Connor 2003, 160.
7. Trevor and Shawn J. Parry-Giles in Parry-Giles and Parry-Giles 2006, 153.

8. Myron A. Levine in Rollins and O'Connor 2003, 48.
9. Cited in Fahy 2005, 148, 157.
10. McCabe 2013, 69.
11. For example, the way in which Sam and CJ were recruited to serve in the Bartlet administration might be noted. In Amar Khoday's words, they were "highly accomplished and educated individuals who have foregone higher salaries in the private sector to dedicate themselves to public service" (Khoday 2009, 14).
12. de Jonge, 2001.
13. Fahy 2005, 130.
14. Khoday 2009, 14.
15. Rosenberg 2012.
16. As Matthew David Barber put it: "The average White House staffer leaves after about 18 months because the burnout rate is so high" (Barber 2009, 248). Toward the end of the series there were some staff changes: CJ replaced Leo as chief of staff, Toby was dismissed for "whistle-blowing" and Josh left to run the Santos campaign. However, for most of the show the staff remained in the same roles.
17. Crawley 2006, 103.
18. Gans-Boriskin and Tisinger 2005, 109.
19. Cited in Fahy 2005, 143.
20. Cited in Fahy 2005, 171.
21. Rosenberg 2012.
22. Cited in Rollins and O'Connor 2003, 195.
23. Cited in Rollins and O'Connor 2003, 29.
24. Parry-Giles and Parry-Giles 2006, 25.
25. "To go where" and to "do what," journalist Laura Lippman noted, "that apparently falls under Mr. Sorkin's Don't Ask, Don't Tell policy. When the hour is up, the hour is up, allowing Bartlet to avoid real-life consequences for his Hardy Boy policy solutions" (Lippman cited in Challen 2001, 32).
26. Also in Season 5, Toby seems to have believed he had found a way to save Social Security; and, in the fairytale world of the show, it seems he may have done so by the end of the episode—see "Slow News Day" (5/12).
27. This has often been commented on in the literature on the show. For example, Nathan A. Paxton commented: "The parallels between the campaigns of Bartlet's competitor and the George W. Bush campaign of 2000 are not subtle, and they do not seem to be designed as such" (cited in Fahy 2005, 175n).
28. Barber 2009, 230. Barber offers an astute analysis of Richie as a cipher for George W. Bush: "Ritchie is presented as a plain speaking, apparently uncomplicated man contrasting with Bartlet's polymath intellectualism and complex moral integrity.... As a character, Ritchie does not develop beyond being a cipher of Republicanism, unilateralism and plain speaking.... The problem with Ritchie as a character is that he is a cipher and that his only function is to be denigrated by Bartlet and his staff" (Barber 2009, 232, 233).
29. One cast member, Richard Schiff, suggested a radical solution: "I pitched an idea to both of them [Aaron Sorkin and Thomas Schlamme] 'You know what would be amazing? If we lost [the election]. Just imagine. No one would be expecting it. We would lose and we're gone. That's the end of it'" (cited in Lacey, O'Connell and Bernardin 2014).
30. Sorkin 2003b, 226.
31. The title of the episode referred to CJ's father and the onset of Alzheimer's Disease. Although presented in an earnest and well-meaning way, the episode was something of a cliché. In addition, Matthew Modine—in a cameo role as a past high-school friend of CJ—seemed somewhat redundant, and the idea of him and CJ getting a hotel room and having a brief erotic tryst seemed as unlikely as it was unnecessary.
32. Engelstad 2008, 310, 314. See also Myron A. Levine, who argued how the show would often shift "from the logic of politics ... to the logic of romanticism" (cited in Rollins and O'Connor 2003, 43).
33. Quinn 2004, 198.
34. Zoey's kidnapping and subsequent rescue was perhaps one of the least credible aspects of the show; the happy ending of her being found safe and well was unconvincing. In another context, it has been suggested by some conspiracy theorists that certain individuals vulnerable to kidnapping, such as the president's daughter, would be "biologically tagged." The prospect of such an idea was raised when the actress who played Zoey, Elizabeth Moss, subsequently appeared in the role of Offred in the television adaptation of Margaret Atwood's dystopian novel *The Handmaid's Tale* (2017–). In the drama, Offred *did* have a telemetry implant; and, after escaping from Gilead, she was forced to remove it—a small tracking device—from behind one of her ears in order to prevent recapture. It was a gruesome and bloody scene, far worse than anything found in Atwood's original novel, but whether this clarified the speculation around Zoey Bartlet's kidnapping remains open to question.
35. Cited in Challen 2001, 62.
36. Cass 2007, 33.
37. Topping 2002, 198.

38. Gans-Boriskin and Tisinger 2005, 102. There were numerous other criticisms relating to the show's sense of a beguiling unreality. For example, see Peter de Jonge, who described it as a "glittering lie" (de Jonge 2001), while Erica Harmon observed: "*The West Wing* is an American fairy tale" (cited in Handscombe 2016, 22).

Chapter 22

1. Eagleton 2004, 79.
2. Stokes 2003, 139.
3. Garber 1995, 184.
4. In other words, they have become "true" because sufficient numbers of people believe they may be true; in this way psychoanalysis resembles a concept somewhat akin to a religion—and of course the beginnings of psychoanalysis did have some semblance of a religious faith, albeit a secular religious faith.
5. Eagleton 2004, 138.
6. Watson 2000.
7. Barry 1995.
8. Only one example has been detected, in Heather Richardson Hayton's essay entitled "The King's Two Bodies: Identity and Office in Sorkin's *West Wing*." "In the Lacanian sense, C.J.'s mirroring allows Bartlet to recognize his own identity and the limits of the kings' 'bodies'" (cited in Rollins and O'Connor 2003, 68n). In fact, Freudian readings of *The West Wing* are sparse in the literature on the show, one exception being Patrick Finn, who commented that the location of Ainsley Hayes's office in the White House "cries out for Freudian analysis." Ainsley, the "blonde Republican sex kitten," inhabited a room deep in the basement of the White House, "the heat exchange room" (cited in Rollins and O'Connor 2003, 118).
9. See Chapter 14 for a discussion of the actual cause of Bartlet's lameness in the opening episode of the series.
10. Crawley 2006, 156. See also, Matthew David Barber: "Bartlet as the father of his children with President Bartlet as the father of the country is repeated throughout the series" (Barber 2009, 208).
11. Crawley 2006, 113.
12. As Joshua Malina would often intone on *The West Wing Weekly*: "He gave him the knife!"
13. As Trevor and Shawn J. Parry-Giles put it: "Even though Jed Bartlet's biological mother is seemingly alive in *TWW*'s narrative, she receives no character development and is noticeably absent from the story's plotlines" (Parry-Giles and Parry-Giles 2006, 64, 99).
14. Eagleton 1983.
15. Transcribed from the DVD of the episode "Post Hoc, Ergo Propter Hoc" (1/2).
16. A number of other fathers, other than the father who never liked Bartlet, were mentioned in the episode: CJ was shown talking to her father on the phone; Duchamp was referred to as the father of Dadaism—to allow the joke, the dada of Dada; Toby commented that his father had benefitted from the GI bill; and Bob, the character who believed Fort Knox housed aliens, told Sam his father had died three months ago.
17. Crawley 2006, 184.
18. Toby was Jewish, as was Freud and nearly all the early followers of psychoanalysis. The Brooklyn shrink comment therefore seeming to add a deliberately anti-Jewish note to Bartlet's discourse. Two episodes later, in "Hartfield's Landing" (3/15), some kind of rapprochement seems to have taken place between the two men, with Bartlet sending Toby a note: "Sigmund, come play chess"—a not so nuanced indicator of Bartlet's view of the psychoanalytical approach. Freud himself was seldom mentioned by name in the series; and in the only two instances it was Toby who made the reference. Toby spoke of a "Freudian fratricidal mania" in the episode "Undecideds" (7/8); similarly, Toby asked CJ, "You think this is a Freudian temper tantrum?" in the episode "Institutional Memory" (7/21).
19. One of the main areas of disagreement between Bartlet and his father would appear to have been religion. The young Bartlet had followed his mother's religion of Roman Catholicism—of which his father seemed to disapprove—this being the reason for the older Bartlet striking his son in "Two Cathedrals." Here perhaps was the crucial moment: had the younger Bartlet hit his father back, then all might have been different—he might never have been driven to become president.
20. It is perhaps significant to note, however, how Bartlet often became diminished from this role. For example, in the episode "7A WF 83429" (5/1), Bartlet was said to "look small"—this in contrast to the much more powerful frame of the temporary president, Glen Allen Walken. In the episode, "Impact Winter" (6/9), Bartlet seemed to be infantilized, being carried off Air Force One by his new bodyman, Curtis, Bartlet suffering temporary paralysis due to MS—both instances suggesting a lack of phallic authority.
21. In the case of the taboo on incest,

Bartlet's almost lurid interest in the sex life of Zoey, his youngest daughter, was of relevance. There was comedic quality to this facet of the drama, but there was also a serious point to be made in Bartlet's attitude to his daughter's sexuality.

22. As Staci Beavers put it, these scenes were "frequently shot so that the Washington Monument, signifying the strength and power of the presidency, is clearly evident" (Beavers 2002, 216).

23. Paraphrased from Barry 1995.

24. It should be noted that, as feminist theorists have pointed out, "the phallus is not a biological attribute, but a discursive position which constitutes women in terms of lack and men in terms of the threat of a lack" (Segal 1994, 131–132). See also Susan Bordo: "I certainly agree with Lacan that the phallus belongs to the realm of ideas, it's a symbol not a body part" (Bordo 1999, 94).

Chapter 23

1. The IMDb website lists some 96 composer credits for Walden, a range of television series, mini-series and television movies dating from 1987 to the present day. However, it is perhaps significant to note Walden has no credits in feature films—he has worked consistently within the world of television drama.

2. Lambert 2000. *Sports Night* was the show created and written by Sorkin just prior to *The West Wing*. The show ran for 45 episodes from 1998–2000.

3. Lambert 2000.

4. Sorkin's writing in such speeches seemed to strive toward a discourse of exordium, an exordium being the use of a highly rhetorical term at the start of a speech, one that aimed to attract the audience's attention. Lincoln's use of the phrase "four score" at the start of the Gettysburg Address is an apt example; however, Bartlet's speeches in *The West Wing* seldom seemed to achieve this.

5. Topping 2002, 57.

6. The next line in the scene came from Bruno Gianelli, who asked Sam: "When did you write that last part?" "In the car," said Sam. "Freak" said Bruno. But in fact neither Sam nor Sorkin behind him actually wrote this part of the scene. The line "the streets of heaven are too crowded with angels" derived from the acceptance speech Tom Hanks delivered at the Academy Award ceremony in 1993, in which Hanks won the Oscar for best actor in the film *Philadelphia* (1993).

7. McCabe 2013, 99.

8. To this one might add the use of a rendition of the song "My Country 'Tis of Thee" in the episode, "An Khe" (5/14). In the episode, Bartlet mentions that Crosby, Stills and Nash "came by" to receive a National Medal of the Arts award and left him a tape of the song. The song (actually performed by Crosby and Nash) reached new levels of maudlin sentimentality. Bartlet's secretary, Deborah Fiderer, perhaps acknowledging such maudlin sentimentality, commented: "I've always been more of a Crazy Horse gal, Mr. President." In other words, there was to be no sign of Neil Young—who may have raised objections—having been included in an off-screen visit to a fictional White House.

9. Haven's performance was a stirring rendition of a stirring song—but it was hardly a song to accompany the victory of a sitting president. It was a song of youthful rebellion, a song telling senators and congressmen to get out of the way—to stop blocking the halls.

10. Cited in Goldwag 2007, 335.

11. It is perhaps possible to argue that such a sense of sentimentality lessened after Sorkin's departure at the end of the fourth season, and that the final three seasons of the show were not so encumbered with unearned emotion.

12. McCabe 2013, 25.

13. Philpott and Mutimer 2006, 352.

14. Biswas 2008, 12.

15. Kim 2009, 12/16.

16. Dumlao 2005.

17. Malina made this remark a number of times during the course of the podcast *The West Wing Weekly*.

18. The only viewers who would seem to have inadvertently succeeded in so doing could be said to be those viewers with a hearing impairment, who would have followed the drama via the closed captions and lip reading—with little awareness of Walden's music. In a sense, it would be of interest to know how such viewers responded to the show; for example, it would be interesting to speculate what opinions Marlee Martin, who played Joey Lucas in the show, might have had.

19. Bicker 2007, 22.

Chapter 24

1. All quotations in the first two paragraphs of this chapter derive from "Foucault TV," *Flow*, https://www.flowjournal.org/2006/06/foucault-tv/?print=print, accessed, May 3, 2018).

2. The term discourse, as used here, was

Foucault's way of describing how systems work within culture, ideology and language, discourse being the unstable sum of countless elements of information constantly at play within such systems.

3. Terry Eagleton makes a similar argument: "There was no single determinable truth to any particular narrative or event, just a conflict of interpretations whose outcome was finally determined by power rather than truth" (Eagleton 2008, 197).

4. Watson 2000.

5. Watson 2000.

6. Derrida went further, claiming that there was no fixed conceptual order between signifiers: the relationship between the signifier and the signified was not only arbitrary but volatile as well. As Terry Eagleton would put it: "Poststructuralism goes a step further: it divides the signifier from the signified" (Eagleton 1983, 128).

7. Barry 1995.

8. Watson 2000.

9. Such a charge would be highlighted via the Paul de Man scandal of the 1990s; de Man, one of the key figures within the poststructuralist school of thought, would be revealed as being a Nazi sympathizer, having written some 200 articles for a collaborationist newspaper in his native Belgium during the early years of World War II. David Lehman's book *Signs of the Times: Deconstruction and the Fall of Paul de Man* offers an incisive discussion of de Man's fall from grace. In his book, Lehman pointed out one of the potential flaws in poststructuralist theory, its disavowal of any kind of ultimate truth: "There were no truths. They had all become texts, duplicitous texts, fictions within fictions within fictions" (Lehman 1991, 155).

10. Barry 1995.

11. Quinn 2007, 254.

12. There is space for continual debate around this question, both for and against the phenomenological position. Arthur Goldwag commented: "The proverbial tree in the forest has a being, an identity in and of itself, whether or not someone is looking at it or thinking about it" (Goldwag 2007, 122). Or as comedian Steven Wright put it: "If you tell a joke in the forest but nobody laughs, is it still a joke?"

13. Watson 2000, 31.

14. Watson 2000.

15. Culler 1975, 230.

16. The general argument here is drawn from Toolan 1988, 91.

17. Barry 1995.

18. Chambers and Finn 2001, 3.

19. How Toby managed to buy such an expensive property in what was presumably an exclusive neighborhood of Washington, D.C. was never fully explained. A cynical answer might be to say it was helped by the $125,000 Toby made on the stock market in the episode "Five Votes Down" (1/4); this incident was treated in a humorous way, but there was a potential interpretation that perhaps Toby *was* aware he was involved in insider trading. In this context one might note Toby's beginnings at the start of the episode, "Holy Night" (4/11). In a flashback sequence to December 23, 1954, in Brooklyn Heights, we learned this was the night of Toby's birth; his father, however, was a member of Murder Incorporated. In the present day, Toby's father was played by Jerry Adler. He was aptly cast, as Adler was simultaneously playing the recurrent character of Hesh Rabkin in *The Sopranos*; in other words, another role with "mob" connections.

Conclusion

1. Cited in Biswas 2008, 12.

2. John Nein made a similar argument: "At one point in the first season, Jed Bartlet gives a speech in front of a banner that reads 'Practical Idealism.' It's amusing because on the one hand, the phrase is so laughably vacant. But on the other hand, is there a more apt description of Sorkin's invented White House?" (cited in Fahy 2005, 208).

3. Some critics have contested the charge of naivety. As Ann C. Hall put it: "We may be able to see *The West Wing*'s weakness in a more positive light. That is, it is not naïve or idealized, but, rather, a successful piece of postmodern propaganda whose goal is to create greater faith in the American political processes" (cited in Fahy 2005, 118).

4. Philpott and Mutimer 2006, 353.

5. Kim 2009, 13/16.

6. McCabe 2013, 117–118.

7. Cited in Fahy 2005, 127.

8. In an attempt to mitigate this potential difficulty, a synopsis of each of the seven seasons of the show, together with a list of every episode, is included in the Appendices of this book.

9. Incidentally, it might be noted that Eagleton's book, in its different editions, has now sold close to one million copies; a unique occurrence for a book looking at critical theory.

10. Eagleton 2008, vii.

11. Eagleton 2008, ix. Eagleton also made

the point that theory's "very distance from the everyday allows it to act ... as a powerful critique of the everyday ... [theory does not want to know what a text means, but rather queries] our common-sense notions of what it is to 'mean' in the first place" (Eagleton 2008, viii).

12. Culler 1997, 4.
13. Culler 1997, 16.
14. Lehman 1991, 41.
15. Lehman 1991, 41.
16. This would certainly seem to be the case in terms of *The West Wing*. As intimated previously, few of the main characters died in the series—only Mrs. Landingham and Leo. The latter death was forced upon the narrative insomuch as the actor playing the character, John Spencer, died while in the process of performing the role.
17. Culler 1997, 121.
18. Culler 1997, 122.
19. Eagleton 2004, 86.
20. Crawley 2006, 191.
21. One verification of this claim might be seen in the success of *The West Wing Weekly*; this was an American podcast presented by Hrishikesh Hirway and Joshua Malina that has been running since March 2016. The podcast has attracted both a wide audience and a wide range of guests, up to and including Aaron Sorkin, and has become one of the most successful podcasts of its kind.
22. For example, it is difficult to forget the closing scene of "The Midterms" (2/3)—arguably the base nadir of the show—a scene in which few other dramas could have recovered. As intimated at the beginning of this book, this was the famous (some would say infamous) scene in which CJ, Josh, Toby and Sam sat on a "stoop" and intoned with little or no sense of irony: "God bless America."

Bibliography

Altman, Lawrence K. October 9, 2001. "The Doctor's World: Very Real Questions for Fictional President." *New York Times*.
Anderson, Karrin Vasby. Spring 2007. "The Prime-Time Presidency: *The West Wing* and U.S. Nationalism." *Rhetoric and Public Affairs* Vol. 10, Issue 1, pp. 134–137.
Armstrong, Mark K. July 24, 2002. "*West Wing*: Low Pay Sparks Lowe Exit." *E! Online*. Available at: https://www.eonline.com/news/43631/west-wing-low-pay-sparks-lowe-exit (accessed March 12, 2015).
Baker, Cory. September 2011. "#TVFail Entry 9: *The West Wing*, 'Isaac and Ishmael.'" Available at: http://tvsurveillance.com/2011/09/08/tvfail-entry-9-the-west-wing-isaac-and-ishmael/ (accessed February 28, 2015).
Baker, William F., and Beth A. Fitzpatrick. October 2010. "The Never-ending Story: Palestine, Israel and *The West Wing*." *Fordham Law Review* Vol. 79, No. 1, pp. 835–839.
Barber, Matthew David. September 2009. "Shooting the President: The Depiction of the American Presidency on Film and Television from John F. Kennedy to Josiah Bartlet." Unpublished Doctoral Thesis, University of Exeter.
Barry, Peter. 1995. *Beginning Theory*. Manchester, UK: Manchester University Press.
Barry, Peter. 2009. *Beginning Theory* (Third Edition). Manchester, UK: Manchester University Press.
Barthes, Roland. 1992. "The Death of the Author." In Lodge, David. *Modern Criticism and Theory: A Reader*. Harlow, UK: Longman, pp. 167–172.
Barthes, Roland. 2009. *The Grain of the Voice: Interviews 1962–1980*. Evanston, IL: Northwestern University Press.
Baudrillard, Jean. 1999. *America*. London: Verso.
Baudrillard, Jean. 2009. *Simulations*. New York: Semiotext(e).
Beavers, Staci L. June 2002. "*The West Wing* as a Pedagogical Tool." *PS Online* Vol. 35, No. 2, pp. 213–216. Available at: www.apsanet.org (accessed March 3, 2015).
Belek, Cassandra. May 2010. "Congress in the Mass Media: How *The West Wing* and Traditional Journalism Frame Congressional Power." Unpublished Master's Thesis, University of Missouri.
Bettelheim, Bruno. 1976. *The Uses of Enchantment*. New York: Alfred A. Knopf.
Bicker, Stewart P. 1985. *Friends and Other Strangers*. Novaprint.
Biswas, Anindita. December 2008. "Unwrapping the Wings of the Television Show *The West Wing*." Unpublished Master's Arts Thesis, Wake Forest University.
Bordo, Susan. 1999. *The Male Body: A New Look at Men in Public and Private*. New York: Farrar, Straus and Giroux.
Bore, Inger-Lise Kalviknes, and Jonathan Hickman. September 2013. "Studying Fan Activities on Twitter: Reflections on Methodological Issues Emerging from a Case Study on *The West Wing* Fandom." *First Monday* Vol. 18, No. 9.
Bristow, Joseph. 1997. *Sexuality*. London: Routledge.

Bush, Harold K. Easter 2009. "Symbol Drain and *The West Wing*." *Cresset: A Review of Literature, the Arts, and Public Affairs* Vol. 72, No. 4, pp. 60–65.
Butler, Judith. 1990. *Gender Trouble: Feminism and the Subversion of Identity*. London: Routledge.
Cass, Philip. 2007. "The Never-ending Story: Palestine, Israel and *The West Wing*." *Journal of Arab and Muslim Media Research* Vol. 1, No. 1, pp. 31–46.
Cavendish, Sarah E. 2002. "*The West Wing*: President as Symbol." Unpublished Master's Thesis, Marshall University.
Challen, Paul. 2001. *Inside the West Wing: An Unauthorized Look at Television's Smartest Show*. Toronto: ECW Press.
Chambers, Samuel A. December 2001. "Language and Politics: Agnostic Discourse in *The West Wing*." *CTheory*. Available at: http://ctheory.net/ctheory_wp/language-and-politics-agonistic-discourse-in-the-west-wing/ (accessed March 3, 2015).
Chambers, Samuel A. 2003. "Dialogue, Deliberation, and Discourse: The Far-Reaching Politics of *The West Wing*." In Rollins, Peter C., and John E. O'Connor (eds.). The West Wing: *The American Presidency as Television Drama*. Syracuse, NY: Syracuse University Press, pp. 83–100.
Chambers, Samuel A., and Patrick Finn. November 2001. "*The West Wing* Digital Democracy: When Culture Becomes News." *CTheory*. Available at: https://journals.uvic.ca/index.php/ctheory/article/view/14589/5434 (accessed March 3, 2015).
Clarke, Myles B. 2011. "Book Review." *International Journal of Communication* 5, pp. 644–650.
Coates, Ta-Nehisi. June 2014. "The Case for Reparations." *Atlantic*. Available at: https://www.theatlantic.com/magazine/archive/2014/06/the-case-for-reparations/361631/ (accessed March 8, 2017).
Corkery, Diane. 2014. "Religion, Education and *The West Wing*." *REA: A Journal of Religion, Education and the Arts* 9, pp. 78–95.
Corten, Olivier. September 2014. "'A la maison blanche': le président des Etats-Unis se soucie-t-il du droit international lorsqu'il décide d'une intervention militaire?" *European Society of International Law*, Conference Paper No. 15/2014.
Crawley, Melissa. 2006. *Mr. Sorkin Goes to Washington: Shaping the President on Television's The West Wing*. Jefferson, NC: McFarland.
Cuddon, J.A. 1992. *The Penguin Dictionary of Literary Terms and Literary Theory*. Harmondsworth, UK: Penguin.
Culler, Jonathan. 1975. *Structuralist Poetics*. Ithaca, NY: Cornell University Press.
Culler, Jonathan. 1997. *Literary Theory: A Very Short Introduction*. Oxford: Oxford University Press.
Davis, Peter. January 15, 2015. "Beyond Josh Lyman Politics: How *The West Wing* Miseducated My Political Generation." *Front Porch Republic*. Available at: http://www.frontporchrepublic.com/2015/01/beyond-josh-lyman-politics-west-wing-miseducated-political-generation/ (accessed January 25, 2015).
Davison, Andrew. 2010. "The 'Soft' Power of Hollywood Militainment: The Case of *The West Wing*'s Attack on Antalya, Turkey." *New Political Science* Vol 28, No. 4, pp. 467–487.
de Jonge, Peter. October 28, 2001. "Aaron Sorkin Works His Way through the Crisis." *New York Times*. Available at: http://www.nytimes.com/2001/10/28/magazine/28SORKIN.html?pagewanted=all (accessed October 15, 2015).
de Tocqueville, Alexis. 1998. *Democracy in America*. Ware, UK: Wordsworth.
Douglas, Susan J. March 29, 2002. "The West Wing's Workaholics." *In These Times*. Available at: http://inthesetimes.com/article/1441/the_west_wings_workaholics (accessed December 31, 2016).
Downing, Spencer. 2005. "Handling the Truth: Sorkin's Liberal Vision." In Fahy, Thomas (ed.). *Considering Aaron Sorkin: Essays on the Politics, Poetics and Sleight of Hand in the Films and Television Series*. Jefferson, NC: McFarland, pp. 127–145.
Dumlao, Michael. Spring 2005. "*The West Wing* Legacy: Rescuing Democracy and Civic Engagement." *Critical Approaches to TV*. Available at: http://www.michaeldumlao.com/PDFs/West%20Wing%20Legacy.pdf (accessed March 6, 2015).
Eagleton, Terry. 1983. *Literary Theory: An Introduction*. Oxford: Blackwell.
Eagleton, Terry. 1996. *Literary Theory: An Introduction*. (Second Edition). Oxford: Blackwell.

Eagleton, Terry. 2004. *After Theory*. London: Penguin.
Eagleton, Terry. 2008. *Literary Theory: An Introduction*. (Anniversary Edition). Oxford: Blackwell.
Easthope, Anthony. 1986. *What a Man's Gotta Do: The Masculine Myth in Popular Culture*. Boston: Unwin Hyman.
Economist. July 4, 2002. "Unreality TV: Irreverent Television is Good for Politicians."
Engelstad, Audun. 2008. "Watching Politics: The Representation of Politics in Primetime Television Drama." *Nordicom Review* Vol. 29, No. 2, pp. 309–324.
Ezell, Pamela. 2003. "The Sincere Sorkin White House, or, the Importance of Seeming Earnest." In Rollins, Peter C., and John E. O'Connor (eds.). *The West Wing: The American Presidency as Television Drama*. Syracuse, NY: Syracuse University Press, pp. 159–174.
Fahy, Thomas. 2005. "Athletes, Grammar Geeks, and Porn Stars: The Liberal Education of *Sports Night*." In Fahy, Thomas (ed.). *Considering Aaron Sorkin: Essays on the Politics, Poetics and Sleight of Hand in the Films and Television Series*. Jefferson, NC: McFarland, pp. 61–76.
Fanon, Frantz. 2001. *The Wretched of the Earth*. Harmondsworth, UK: Penguin.
Fiedler, Leslie. 1997. *Love and Death in the American Novel*. Normal, IL: Dalkey Archive Press.
Finn, Patrick. November 2001. "Remediating Democracy: The Public, Intellectual Hyper Text and *The West Wing*." *CTheory*. Available at: http://ctheory.net/ctheory_wp/remediating-democracy-the-public-intellectual-hypertext-and-the-west-wing/ (accessed March 3, 2015).
Finn, Patrick. 2003. "*The West Wing*'s Textual President: American Constitutional Stability and the New Public Intellectual in the Age of Information." In Rollins, Peter C., and John E. O'Connor (eds.). *The West Wing: The American Presidency as Television Drama*. Syracuse, NY: Syracuse University Press, pp. 101–124.
Fortier, John C. September 24, 2003. "*The West Wing* and Presidential Succession." Washington, D.C.: American Enterprise Institute. Available at: http://www.aei.org/publication/the-west-wing-and-presidential-succession/ (accessed March 3, 2015).
Foucault, Michel. 1978. *The History of Sexuality*, Vol. 1. New York: Random House.
Foucault, Michel. 2003. *"Society Must Be Defended": Lectures at the Collége de France, 1975–76*. New York: Picador.
Fuchs, John Andreas. Fall 2010. "Showing Faith: Catholicism in American TV Series." *Moravian Journal of Literature and Film* Vol. 2, No. 1, pp. 79–98.
Fujiwara, Chris (ed.). 2007. *The Little Black Book: Movies*. London: Cassell.
Gallop, Jane. 1992. *Around 1981: Academic Feminist Literary Theory*. New York: Routledge.
Gans-Boriskin, Rachel, and Russ Tisinger. March 2005. "The Bushlet Administration: Terrorism and War on *The West Wing*." *Journal of American Culture* Vol. 28, No. 1, pp. 100–113.
Garber, Marjorie. 1995. *Vice-Versa: Bisexuality and the Eroticism of Everyday Life*. Harmondsworth, UK: Penguin.
Garrett, Laura K. 2005. "Women of *The West Wing*: Gender Stereotypes in Political Fiction." In Fahy, Thomas (ed.). *Considering Aaron Sorkin: Essays on the Politics, Poetics and Sleight of Hand in the Films and Television Series*. Jefferson, NC: McFarland, pp. 179–192.
Gillan, Thomas J. October 2006. "*The West Wing*'s 'Isaac and Ishamel' [sic] as a Captivity Narrative and American Jeremiad." *University of Central Florida Undergraduate Research Journal* Vol. 2, pp. 15–19.
Goldwag, Arthur. 2007. *Isms and Ologies: 453 Difficult Doctrines You've Always Pretended to Understand*. London: Quercus.
Green, Keith, and Jill Le Bihan. 1996. *Critical Theory and Practice: A Coursebook*. London: Routledge.
Hall, Ann C. 2005. "Giving Propaganda a Good Name: *The West Wing*." In Fahy, Thomas (ed.). *Considering Aaron Sorkin: Essays on the Politics, Poetics and Sleight of Hand in the Films and Television Series*. Jefferson, NC: McFarland, pp. 115–126.
Handscombe, Claire (ed.). 2016. *Walk with Us: How The West Wing Changed Our Lives*. n.p.: CH Books.
Hanegraaff, Hank. 2001. "President Bartlet's Fallacious Diatribe." *Christian Research Journal* Vol. 23, No. 3.

Hanson, Trudy L. April 2005. "*The West Wing*—A Hyperreal, Not a Reality Show." *Flow*. Available at: http://flowtv.org/2005/04/the-west-wing-a-hyperreal-not-a-reality-show/ (accessed February 27, 2015).

Hayton, Heather Richardson. 2003. "The King's Two Bodies: Identity and Office in Sorkin's *The West Wing*." In Rollins, Peter C., and John E. O'Connor (eds.). The West Wing: *The American Presidency as Television Drama*. Syracuse, NY: Syracuse University Press, pp. 63–79.

Henderson, Jennifer Jacobs. 2007. "What *The West Wing* Tells Us." *Journal of Mass Media Ethics: Exploring Questions of Media Morality* Vol. 22, Nos. 2–3, pp. 229–231.

Herr, Michael. 2000. *Kubrick*. London: Picador.

Hocquenghem, Guy. 1993. *Homosexual Desire*. Durham, NC: Duke University Press.

Holbert, Lance R., et al. September 2003. "*The West Wing* as Endorsement of the U.S. Presidency: Expanding the Bound of Priming in Political Communication." *Journal of Communication* Vol. 53, No. 3, pp. 427–443.

Holland, Jack. September 2011. "When You Think of the Taliban, Think of the Nazis: Teaching Americans 9/11 in NBC's *The West Wing*." *Millennium: Journal of International Studies* Vol. 40, No. 1, pp. 85–106.

Hornby, Nick. August 2007. "David Simon: Creator-Writer-Producer of HBO's *The Wire*." *Believer*. Available at: http://www.believermay.com/issues/200708/?read=interview_simon (accessed March 29, 2016).

Horrocks, Roger. 1997. *An Introduction to the Study of Sexuality*. London: Macmillan.

Jackson, Chris. February 2000. "Picturing the President: *The West Wing*." Available at: http://usf.usfca.edu/pj//westwing.htm (accessed May 8, 2015).

James, Clive. April 4, 2003. "Winged Words in *The West Wing*." *Times Literary Supplement*. Available at: http://www.clivejames.com/articles/clive/west-wing (accessed January 20, 2015).

James, Clive. 2016. *Play All: A Bingewatcher's Notebook*. New Haven, CT: Yale University Press.

Jameson, Frederic. 1990. *Postmodernism or, the Cultural Logic of Late Capitalism*. Durham, NC: Duke University Press.

Jameson, Frederic. Summer/Fall 2010. "Realism and Utopia in *The Wire*." *Criticism* Vol. 52, Nos. 3–4, pp. 359–372.

Jenkin, Andrew. 2012. "To What Extent Is *The Wire* a Marxist Television Drama?" Available at: https://andrewjenkin.wordpress.com/2012/05/26/to-what-extent-is-the-wire-a-marxist-television-drama/ (accessed January 12, 2017).

Jones, Robert, and George N. Dionisopoulos. 2004. "Scripting a Tragedy: The Isaac and Ishmael episode of *The West Wing* as Parable." *International Journal of Culture and Media* Vol. 2, No. 1, pp. 21–40.

Journell, Wayne. 2013. "Making Every Year a Presidential Election Year: Using *The West Wing's* Santos/Vinick Race to Simulate Election Politics." *Ohio Social Studies Review* Vol. 50, No. 1, pp. 6–16.

Journell, Wayne, and Lisa Brown Buchanan. 2013. "Fostering Political Understanding Using *The West Wing*: Analyzing the Pedagogical Benefits of Film in High School Civics Classrooms." *Journal of Social Studies Research* Vol. 37, No. 2, pp. 67–83.

Katz, Jonathan Ned. 1995. *The Invention of Heterosexuality*. New York: Dutton.

Khoday, Amar. 2009. "Prime-Time Saviors: *The West Wing* and the Cultivation of a Unilateral American Responsibility to Protect." *Southern California Interdisciplinary Law Journal* Vol. 19, No. 1.

Kim, Young Hoon. 2009. "The Justice of Melodrama: *The West Wing's* Coping Strategies in a World of Violence and Terror." *Americana: The Journal of American Popular Culture 1900 to Present* Vol. 8, Issue 2.

Kirkham, Pat (ed.). 1996. *The Gendered Object*. Manchester, UK: Manchester University Press.

Kooijman, Jaap. 2008. *Fabricating the Absolute Fake: America in Contemporary Pop Culture*. Amsterdam: Amsterdam University Press.

Krauss, Lawrence M. 2012. *A Universe from Nothing: Why There Is Something Rather Than Nothing*. London: Simon & Schuster.

Kristeva, Julia. 1980. *Desire in Language: A Semiotic Approach to Literature and Art*. New York: Columbia University Press.

La Berge, Leigh Claire. 2010. "Capitalist Realism and Serial Form: The Fifth Season of *The Wire*." *Criticism* Vol. 52, Nos. 3–4, pp. 547–567.
Lacey, Rose, O'Connell, Michael, and Marc Bernardin. May 23, 2014. "*West Wing* Uncensored: Aaron Sorkin, Rob Lowe, More Look Back on Early Fears, Long Hours, Contract Battles and the Real Reason for Those Departures." *Hollywood Reporter*.
Lambert, Mel. December 2000. "Interview with W.G. Snuffy Walden: Composing Scores for *The West Wing* and Other Shows." *Insight*. Available at: http://www.mediaandmarketing.com/13Writer/Interviews/MIX.Snuffy_Walden.html (accessed June 9, 2016).
Lambton, Sophie. April 30, 2013. "Change and Decline in US TV Drama: *The West Wing*." *Oxford Student*. Available at: https://www.oxfordstudent.com/2013/04/30/change-and-decline-in-us-tv-drama-the-west-wing/ (accessed January 18, 2016).
Lane, Christina. 2003. "The White House Culture of Gender and Race in *The West Wing*." In Rollins, Peter C., and John E. O'Connor (eds.). *The West Wing: The American Presidency as Television Drama*. Syracuse, NY: Syracuse University Press, pp. 32–41.
Lehman, David. 1991. *Signs of the Times: Deconstruction and the Fall of Paul de Man*. London: Andre Deutsch.
Lehmann, Chris. 2003. "The Feel-Good Presidency: The Pseudo-Politics of *The West Wing*." In Rollins, Peter C., and John E. O'Connor (eds.). *The West Wing: The American Presidency as Television Drama*. Syracuse, NY: Syracuse University Press, pp. 213–221.
Levine, Myron A. 2003. "The Transformed Presidency: People and Power in the Real *West Wing*." In Rollins, Peter C., and John E. O'Connor (eds.). *The West Wing: The American Presidency as Television Drama*. Syracuse, NY: Syracuse University Press, pp. 235–258.
Levine, Myron A. 2003. "*The West Wing* (NBC) and the West Wing (D.C.): Myth and Reality in Television's Portrayal of the White House." In Rollins, Peter C., and John E. O'Connor (eds.). *The West Wing: The American Presidency as Television Drama*. Syracuse, NY: Syracuse University Press, pp. 42–62.
Lewis, Jeff. 2008. *Cultural Studies: The Basics*. London: Sage.
Lyon, David. 1995. *Postmodernity*. Buckingham, UK: Open University Press.
Lyotard, Jean-François. 1984. *The Postmodern Condition: A Report on Knowledge*. Manchester, UK: Manchester University Press.
McCabe, Janet. 2013. *The West Wing: TV Milestones Series*. Detroit: Wayne State University Press.
Melcher, Ralph. March 2001. "The Virtual President." *CTheory*. Available at: http://www.media-ecology.org/list/mediaecology/2001-05.txt (accessed January 1, 2019).
Middleton, Peter. 1992. *The Inward Gaze: Masculinity and Subjectivity in Modern Culture*. London: Routledge.
Miles, Rosalind. 1991. *The Rites of Man: Life and Death in the Making of the Male*. London: Grafton.
Miller, Eric. October 2001. "The Children of Light: Good Writing and Acting Cover a Multitude of Biases on *The West Wing*." *Christianity Today*.
Mitchell, Juliet. 1975. *Psychoanalysis and Feminism*. Harmondsworth, UK: Penguin.
Mittell, Jason. Fall 2016. "Narrative Complexity in Contemporary American Television." *Velvet Light Trap* No. 58, pp. 29–40.
Mobley, Kayce, and Sarah Fisher. 2015. "A Field Guide to Teaching Agency and Ethics: *The West Wing* and American Foreign Policy." *Dialogue: The Interdisciplinary Journal of Modern Culture and Pedagogy* Vol. 2, No. 1, pp. 101–111.
Moi, Toril (ed.). 1987. *French Feminist Thought: A Reader*. Oxford: Blackwell.
Morrison, Toni. 1993. *Playing in the Dark: Whiteness and the Literary Imagination*. London: Picador.
Moulton, Michelle. 2003. "Victorian Parliamentary Novels, *The West Wing* and Professionalism." In Rollins, Peter C., and John E. O'Connor (eds.). *The West Wing: The American Presidency as Television Drama*. Syracuse, NY: Syracuse University Press, pp. 187–199.
Nein, John. 2005. "The Republic of Sorkin: A View from the Cheap Seats." In Fahy, Thomas (ed.). *Considering Aaron Sorkin: Essays on the Politics, Poetics and Sleight of Hand in the Films and Television Series*. Jefferson, NC: McFarland, pp. 193–209.
Nelson, James B., and Sandra P. Longfellow (eds.) 1994. *Sexuality and the Sacred: Sources for Theological Reflection*. London: John Knox.

Oppenheimer, Jean. 2000. "The Halls of Power." *American Cinematographer* 81, No. 10, pp. 74–80.
Paglia, Camille. 1990. *Sexual Personae*. New Haven, CT: Yale University Press.
Park, James (ed.). 1991. *Cultural Icons: Cultural Figures Who Made the 20th Century What It Is*. London: Bloomsbury.
Parrinder, Patrick. 1987. *The Failure of Theory: Essays on Criticism and Contemporary Fiction*. Brighton, UK: Harvester.
Parry-Giles, Trevor, and Shawn J. Parry-Giles. May 2002. "*The West Wing*'s Prime-Time Presidentiality: Mimesis and Catharsis in a Postmodern Romance." *Quarterly Journal of Speech* Vol. 88, No. 2, pp. 209–227.
Parry-Giles, Trevor, and Shawn J. Parry-Giles. 2006. *The Prime-Time Presidency: The West Wing and U.S. Nationalism*. Urbana: University of Illinois Press.
Paxton, Nathan A. 2005. "Virtue from Vice: Duty, Power, and *The West Wing*." In Fahy, Thomas (ed.). *Considering Aaron Sorkin: Essays on the Politics, Poetics and Sleight of Hand in the Films and Television Series*. Jefferson, NC: McFarland, pp. 147–177.
Philpott, Simon, and David Mutimer. 2006. "Inscribing the American Body Politic: Martin Sheen and Two American Decades." *Geopolitics* Vol. 10, No. 2, pp. 335–355.
Podhoretz, John. 2003. "The Liberal Imagination." In Rollins, Peter C., and John E. O'Connor (eds.). *The West Wing: The American Presidency as Television Drama*. Syracuse, NY: Syracuse University Press, pp. 222–231.
Polan, Dana. June 16, 2006. "Spoofing the Simpsons." *Foucault TV*. Available at: https://www.flowjournal.org/2006/06/foucault-tv/?print=print (accessed December 1, 2017).
Pompper, Donnalyn. 2003. "*The West Wing*: White House Narratives That Journalism Cannot Tell." In Rollins, Peter C., and John E. O'Connor (eds.). *The West Wing: The American Presidency as Television Drama*. Syracuse, NY: Syracuse University Press, pp. 17–31.
Poniewozik, James. October 2001. "*West Wing*: Terrorism 101." *Time*.
Puar, Jasbir K., and Amit S. Rai. Fall 2002. "Monster, Terrorist, Fag: The War on Terrorism and the Production of Docile Patriots." *Social Text* Vol. 20, No. 3, pp. 117–148.
Quinn, Edward. 2004. *Collins Dictionary of Literary Terms*. Glasgow, UK: HarperCollins.
Rainbow, Paul (ed.). 1991. *The Foucauldian Reader*. Harmondsworth, UK: Penguin.
Richardson, Kay. 2006. "The Dark Arts of Good People: How Popular Culture Negotiates 'Spin' in NBC's *The West Wing*." *Journal of Sociolinguistics* Vol. 10, No. 1, pp. 52–69.
Riegert, Kristina. 2007. "The Ideology of *The West Wing*: The Television Show That Wants to Be Real." In Riegert, Kristina (ed.). *Politicotainment: Television's Take on the Real*. New York: Peter Lang, pp. 213–236.
Ringelberg, Kirstin. 2005. "His Girl Friday (and Every Day): Brilliant Women Put to Poor Use." In Fahy, Thomas (ed.). *Considering Aaron Sorkin: Essays on the Politics, Poetics and Sleight of Hand in the Films and Television Series*. Jefferson, NC: McFarland, pp. 91–100.
Roberts, Chris. 2014. *The Ultimate Box Set Guide*. London: Carlton.
Roedecker [pseud.]. October 15, 2005. Comment on http://www.alternatehistory.com/forum/threads/the-west-wing-presidential-election-timeline.22516/ (accessed June 3, 2016).
Rollins, Peter. 2003. "The Future of *The West Wing*: Discussion on H-PCAACA Listserv." *Film & History: An Interdisciplinary Journal of Film and Television Studies* Vol. 33, No. 1, pp. 55–63.
Rollins, Peter C., and John E. O'Connor (eds.) 2003. *The West Wing: The American Presidency as Television Drama*. New York: Syracuse University Press.
Rosenberg, Yair. October 1, 2012. "Why *The West Wing* Is a Terrible Guide to American Democracy." *Atlantic*.
Rosenzweig, Jane. December 2000. "All the President's Men." *American Prospect* Vol. 11 Issue 25, p. 36.
Rowley, Keith A., and William S. Boyd. 2009. "Is There a Lawyer in the (White) House? Portraying Lawyers in *The West Wing*." University of Nevada.
Ruditis, Paul, and Ian Jackman. 2002. *The West Wing: The Official Companion*. London: Channel 4 Books.
Russo, Julie Levin. 2009. "Inside the Box: Accessing Self-Reflexive Television." *E-Media Studies* Vol. 2, No. 1.

Ruthven, K.K. 1984. *Feminist Literary Studies*. Cambridge: Cambridge University Press.
Said, Edward. 1995. *Orientalism*. London: Penguin.
Schwenger, Peter. 1984. *Phallic Critiques: Masculinity and Twentieth-Century Literature*. London: Routledge.
Sedgwick, Eve Kosofsky. 1985. *Between Men: English Literature and Male Homosocial Desire*. New York: Columbia University Press.
Segal, Lynne. 1994. *Straight Sex*. London: Virago.
Selden, Rama, and Peter Widdowson. 1993. *A Reader's Guide to Contemporary Literary Theory*. Hemel Hempstead, UK: Harvester Wheatsheaf.
Semmler, Shane M., et al. June 2013. "Gendered Depictions in *Commander in Chief* versus *The West Wing*." *Atlantic Journal of Communication* Vol. 21, No. 5, pp. 247–262.
Shepherd, Laura. 2013. *Gender, Violence and Popular Culture: Telling Stories*. New York: Routledge.
Siann, Gerda. 1994. *Gender, Sex and Sexuality: Contemporary Perspectives*. London: Taylor & Francis.
Simpson, Mark. 1996. *It's a Queer World*. London: Vintage.
Sims, David. May 10, 2016. "Bartlet for America, Forever," *Atlantic*.
Skewes, Elizabeth A. 2009. "Presidential Candidates and the Press on *The West Wing* and in the Rest of the World." *Quarterly Review of Film and Video* Vol. 26, No. 2, pp. 131–142.
Skewes, Elizabeth A. 2010. "*The Prime-Time Presidency:* The West Wing *and U.S. Nationalism*." Book review. *Journal of Broadcasting and Electronic Media* Vol. 51, No. 4, pp. 688–689.
Smith, Greg M. 2003. "The Left Takes Back the Flag: The Steadicam, the Snippet, and the Song in *The West Wing*'s 'In Excelsis Deo.'" In Rollins, Peter C., and John E. O'Connor (eds.). *The West Wing: The American Presidency as Television Drama*. Syracuse, NY: Syracuse University Press, pp. 125–135.
Smudde, Peter M., and John R. Luecke. 2005. "Using *The West Wing* for Problem-Based Learning in Public Relations Courses." *Communication Teacher* Vol. 19, No. 4, pp. 107–110.
Song, Angeline M.G. 2015. *A Postcolonial Woman's Encounter with Moses and Miriam*. New York: Palgrave Macmillan.
Sontag, Susan. [1966] 2001. *Against Interpretation and Other Essays*. New York: Picador.
Sontag, Susan. 2009. *Styles of Radical Will*. London: Penguin.
Sorkin, Aaron. 2003a. *The West Wing Script Book*. London: Channel 4 Books.
Sorkin, Aaron. 2003b. *The West Wing Seasons 3 and 4: The Shooting Scripts*. New York: Newmarket.
Spargo, Tamsin. 1999. *Foucault and Queer Theory*. Cambridge: Icon.
Spigel, Lynn. June 2004. "Entertainment Wars: Television Culture after 9/11." *American Quarterly* Vol. 56, No. 2, pp. 235–270.
Stokes, Philip. 2003. *Philosophy: 100 Essential Thinkers*. London: Arcturus.
Storey, John. 2001. *Cultural Theory and Popular Culture: An Introduction*. Harlow, UK: Pearson.
Stuttaford, Andrew. March 24, 2003. "The President of the Left." *National Review*.
Sutin, L. Anthony. 2001. "The Presidential Powers of Josiah Bartlet." *Northern Kentucky Law Review* Vol. 28, pp. 560–572.
Thompson, Damian. 2008. *Counterknowledge*. London: Atlantic.
Tiffin, George. 2013. *All the Best Lines: An Informal History of the Movies in Quotes, Notes and Anecdotes*. London: Head of Zeus.
"Tom Del Ruth, ASC Lends an Idealistic Ambience to NBC's Critically Acclaimed Presidential Drama *The West Wing*." n.d. Available at: https://www.theasc.com/magazine/oct00/power/pg3.htm (accessed June 3, 2015).
Toolan, Michael J. 1988. *Narrative: A Critical Linguistic Introduction*. London: Routledge.
Topping, Keith. 2002. *Inside Bartlet's White House: An Unofficial and Unauthorised Guide to* The West Wing. London: Virgin.
Trombley, Stephen. 2012. *Fifty Thinkers Who Shaped the Modern World*. London: Atlantic.
TV Tropes. n.d. "Series: *The West Wing*." Available at: http://tvtropes.org/pmwiki/pmwiki.php/Series/TheWestWing (accessed January 21, 2015).
Vest, Jason P. 2003. "From *The American President* to *The West Wing*: A Scriptwriter's Perspective." In Rollins, Peter C., and John E. O'Connor (eds.). *The West Wing: The*

American Presidency as Television Drama. Syracuse, NY: Syracuse University Press, pp. 136–156.

Watson, Peter. 2000. *A Terrible Beauty: A History of the People and Ideas That Shaped the Modern Mind.* London: Weidenfeld & Nicholson.

Waxman, Sharon. 2003. "Inside *The West Wing*'s New World." In Rollins, Peter C., and John E. O'Connor (eds.). The West Wing: *The American Presidency as Television Drama.* Syracuse, NY: Syracuse University Press, pp. 203–212.

Webster, Roger. 1990. *Studying Literary Theory: An Introduction.* London: Edward Arnold.

Williams, Rebecca. 2011a. "This Is the Night TV Died: Television Post-Object Fandom and the Demise of *The West Wing*." *Popular Communication: The International Journal of Media and Culture* Vol. 9, No. 4, pp. 266–279.

Williams, Rebecca. 2011b. "Wandering Off into Soap Land: Fandom, Genre and 'Shipping' *The West Wing.*" *Participations: Journal of Audience and Reception Studies* Vol. 8, No. 1, pp. 271–295.

Wodak, Ruth. 2010. "The Glocalization of Politics in Television: Fiction or Reality?" *European Journal of Cultural Studies* Vol. 13 No. 1, pp. 43–62.

Wolff, Michael A. December 4, 2000. "Our Remote-Control President." *New York Magazine.* Available at: http://nymag.com/nymetro/news/media/features/4134/ (accessed May 13, 2015).

Zoller, Heather A., and Tracy Worrell. 2009. "Television Illness Depictions, Identity, and Social Experience: Responses to Multiple Sclerosis on *The West Wing* among People with MS." *Health Communication* Vol. 20, No. 1, pp. 69–79.

Index

Abner, Allison 235*n*
"Abu el Banat" (5/9) 20, 52, 106, 125, 161, 232*n*, 234*n*, 250*n*
Abu Ghraib 150
academic response to the series 2, 3, 31, 68, 69, 104, 152, 173, 227*n*, 228*n*, 241*n*
"Access" (5/18) 27, 144, 213, 235*n*, 239*n*, 251*n*
Adler, Jerry 259*n*
After Theory (Terry Eagleton) 3, 251*n*
Agnew, Spiro 23, 232*n*
"The Al Smith Dinner" (7/6) 44, 160
Albert, Carl 23, 232*n*, 233*n*
alcohol and alcoholism 7, 10, 55–56
Alda, Alan 96, 228*n*, 229*n*
Ali, Raqim 75, 76, 242*n*
Alice Through the Looking Glass 16
All the President's Men (Alan J. Pakula) 7
Allen, Woody 242*n*, 251*n*
alternate universe in the narrative of the series 13, 23, 25, 27, 30, 70, 209, 255*n*
Althusser, Louis 80
Altman, Lawrence K. 124
Altman, Robert 15
Amadeus (Milos Forman) 194
Ambassador Hotel, Los Angeles 50
The American President 13, 230*n*
American Tabloid 29
Amiriyah shelter bombing 252*n*
Amos, John 100, 229*n*
Amos, Tori 194
"An Khe" (4/14) 213, 229*n*, 232*n*, 258*n*
"And It's Surely to Their Credit" (2/5) 64, 109, 159, 244*n*
Annie Hall (Woody Allen) 242*n*
Antichrist (Lars von Trier) 194
Aoun, Steve 165
Arafat, Yasser 26, 233*n*, 254*n*
Arnold, Matthew 124
Ashland, Roy 59
Attie, Eli 32, 235*n*
Atwood, Margaret 256*n*
auteur theory 36, 236*n*

autism 121
Ayres, Colin 60

Babish, Oliver 26, 59, 60, 146
"Bad Moon Rising" (2/19) 18, 26, 60, 146, 170, 243*n*
Bailey, Will 15, 26, 107, 160, 204, 229*n*, 240*n*
Baker, Cory 170
Balzac, Honoré de 81
Barber, David 7, 31, 35, 69,180, 228*n*, 232*n*, 238*n*, 241*n*, 248*n*, 256*n*, 257*n*
Barker, Corey 68, 170
Barry, Peter 251*n*
Barthes, Roland 30, 36–37, 54, 55, 57, 59,198, 203, 228*n*, 230*n*, 236*n*, 239*n*
Bartlet, Abigail (Abbey) 9, 17, 20, 21, 57, 64, 76, 109, 110, 120, 123, 125, 126, 153, 157, 161, 180, 214, 229*n*, 230, 232*n*, 237*n*
Bartlet, Elizabeth (Westin) 20, 161, 232*n*
Bartlet, Ellie 10, 20, 120, 188
Bartlet, Josiah (Jed) 6, 8, 9, 10, 11, 14, 16, 19, 22, 24, 25, 26, 28, 29, 40, 41, 42, 46, 50, 58, 61, 64, 71, 78, 81,87, 90, 101, 129, 144, 179, 185–189, 192, 198, 204, 209, 229*n*, 230*n*, 237*n*, 239*n*, 246*n*, 248*n*, 249*n*, 252*n*, 253*n*, 257*n*, 258*n*, 259*n*; abortion, views on 44, 153, 160, 237*n*–238*n*; abusive language 237*n*; biblical knowledge 41–44; bicycle accident, actual cause 56; bullying character 47; censure for not disclosing MS 124, 229*n*; cowardice of 11, 112; death penalty, attitude to 9, 229*n*–230*n*, 237*n*; duplicity 252*n*; feminization of 64; first election result 179–180, 253*n*; an ideal president 8; as intellectual 7, 128–149, 256*n*; Latin, use of 8, 20, 55, 61–62, 212, 240*n*; as a moral leader 7, 8, 11, 42, 124, 146, 148–149, 151, 161, 212, 230*n*, 244*n*, 252*n*, 256*n*; name, derivation of 57; Nobel Prize winner 8, 15, 78, 93, 187 ; phallic pretentions 47; Roman Catholicism of 6, 8, 56, 92, 93, 94, 96, 97, 99, 149, 230*n*, 237*n*, 244*n*, 257*n* ; same-sex

269

marriage, against 247n; sexual reticence 64, 109–110, 112, 116; shortcomings of 9–11; as surrogate father to his staff 110–111, 185–186, 257n; war criminal 146–151, 162, 209, 253n; women, attitude to 47, 152–153, 156, 161; as a wounded king 56,123, 185
Bartlet, Zoey 19, 20, 59, 60, 90, 101, 106, 110, 181, 194, 212, 213, 229n, 231n, 232n, 256n, 258n
"Bartlet for America" (3/10) 19, 27, 34, 122, 161, 234n, 247n, 250n
"Bartlet's Third State of the Union" (2/13) 117, 229n
Baudrillard, Jean 53, 137, 138, 139, 144, 239n
Beavers, Staci 124, 170, 258n
Beckett, Samuel 136
Beckman, Ronna 58, 118, 158, 239n-240n
Belek, Cassandra 31
"The Benign Prerogative" (5/11) 240n
Benning, Annette 14
Berryhill, Lewis 25, 231n
The Best Man 14, 231n
The Big Lebowski (The Coen Brothers) 17, 231n
Bigelow, Kathryn 252n
bin Laden, Osama 71, 150, 241n
"The Birnam Wood" (6/2) 16, 60, 213
Biswas, Aninidita 243n, 246n, 247n
"The Black Vera Wang" (3/20) 27
Blair, Tony 150, 252n
Blake, Angela 17, 133
Blatty, William Peter 251n
Blind Ambition 230n
Bob Roberts (Tim Robbins) 17, 144
Bond, James 16
Bon Jovi, Jon 158, 233n
Bonnie (no given surname) 58
Bordo, Susan 258n
Bound for Glory (Hal Ashby) 238n
Braugher, Andre 246n
Breckenridge, Jeff 103
A Brief History of Time (Stephen Hawkins) 92, 99
Britten, Benjamin 62, 240n
Broom, Maria 133
Buber, Martin 243n
Buckley, Jeff 194
Buckley, William F., Jr. 230n
budget of the series 1, 227n, 236n, 238n
Buffalo Springfield 194
Burchill, Julie 104
Burns, Ed 249n
Burton, Richard 28
Busch, Benjamin 250n
Bush, George W. 6–7, 12, 74, 86, 88, 150, 151, 173, 179, 180, 209, 228n, 229n, 232n, 233n, 253n, 256n
Bush, Harold K. 47
Butch Cassidy and the Sundance Kid (George Roy Hill) 16

Butler, Judith 115, 120, 247n
Butterfield, Alexander 234n
Butterfield, Ron 234n

Cabot Harrison, Peyton III 89
Caddell, Patrick H. 235n
Cahill, Karen 117
Cahn, Deborah 235n. 236n, 243n, 248n
Caldwell, Al 44
"The California 47th" (4/16) 160
Camelot 27–28, 59, 234n
Camelot (musical) 28, 234n, 240n
Campbell, Karis 118, 239n-240n
Camus, Albert 98
Capra, Frank 16, 138, 181
Carter, Jimmy 6, 90, 232n, 233n
Cash, Johnny 104
Cass, Philip 25, 38, 69,72, 73, 87, 88, 138, 157, 165, 170, 241n
casting of the series 5–12
Castro, Fidel 26, 213, 233n, 251n
"Celestial Navigation" (1/15) 123, 240n
Challen, Paul 2, 31, 101, 155, 227n, 228n, 235n
Chambers, Samuel 155, 204, 241n
"A Change Is Gonna Come" (6/7) 27, 125, 133, 194, 213
Channing, Stockard 69, 70, 229n, 248n
Chase, David 235n
Chastain, Jessica 231n
Cheney, Dick 248n
Chigorin, Pyotr 18
Chomsky, Noam 73–74
Churchill, Winston 79, 240n
Citizen Kane (Orson Welles) 134
Civilisation 163, 254n
Clarke, Arthur C. 241n
Clarke, Kenneth 163
Cleveland, Rick 33
Clinton, Bill 6, 24, 25, 88, 109, 111, 168, 173, 209, 230n, 232n, 233n, 245n, 246n
Coates, Ta-Nehisi 107
Coen Brothers 17
Cohen, Leonard 194, 244n
"The Cold" (7/13) 158
"College Kids" (4/3) 252n
Commander in Chief 15
"Commencement" (4/22) 34, 204
commercial success of the series 1, 53, 134, 227n
Concannon, Danny 65, 87, 110, 204, 246n, 248n
"Constituency of One" (5/5) 19, 111
Cooke, Sam 194
Copernicus, Nicolaus 183
Corten, Olivier 150, 252n
Costner, Kevin 15
"The Crackpots and These Women" (1/5) 8, 154, 156, 185, 192, 211, 229n
Crash (Paul Haggis) 107

Index

Cravenly, Bertram 59
Crawley, Melissa 20, 27, 31, 32, 69, 82, 87, 93, 94, 129, 149, 178, 185, 209, 227n, 248n, 252n, 253n
Cregg, CJ 6, 10, 17, 18, 19, 23, 24, 30, 52, 58, 60, 64, 65, 67, 81, 87, 88, 95, 105, 106, 110, 111, 112, 118, 119, 120, 121, 122, 126, 139, 144, 153, 154, 155, 156, 157, 163, 169, 172, 179, 188, 194, 204, 211, 212, 213, 227n, 228n, 233n, 234n, 237n, 239n, 242n, 243n, 244n, 246n, 247n, 248n, 251n, 253n, 256n, 257, 260n
Cregg, Hogan 58
Crouch, Joseph 10–11, 211, 230n
Cruise, Tom 47, 231n, 238n
Culler, Jonathan 203, 207, 208
cultural theory 3, 38, 153, 162, 183, 203, 207, 208

Dahl, Julia 253n
Daniels, Jeff 86
Darfur genocide 87–88
Darwin, Charles 141, 183
Davis, Pete 175
Davison, Andrew 233n
"Dead Irish Writers" (3/16) 17, 246n
The Dead Zone (David Cronenberg) 231n
Dean, John 26, 230n
"The Death of the Author" (Barthes) 31, 36–38, 198, 228n, 230n, 236n
"The Debate" (7/7) 213, 246n
"Debate Camp" (4/5) 243n
Declaration of Independence 88, 102
de Jonge, Peter 32, 33, 176, 232n, 240n, 257n
de Man, Paul 259n
De Palma, Brian 149
Del Ruth, Thomas 2, 49, 51, 238n
dementia 106, 121, 122, 212, 256n
Dern, Laura 65, 231n
Derrida, Jacques 199, 200, 203, 259n
Descartes, Rene 202
Designated Survivor 15, 16
de Tocqueville, Alexis 244n
Devane, William 231n
Dickens, Charles 59, 131, 188, 250n
Dionisopoulos, George 69, 241n, 242n
Dire Straits 194
disabilities in the series 121–127, 248n; social model of disability 127
"Disaster Relief" (5/6) 158, 171
divergence of history in the series 15, 22–26
"The Dogs of War" (5/2) 16, 17, 25, 64, 233n, 235n
Donaldson, Roger 15
Donovan, Simon 130, 188, 246n
Don't Look Back (D.A. Pennebaker) 17
Douglas, Michael 14
Douglas, Susan J. 83
"The Dover Test" (6/6) 194
Downing, Spencer 93, 178, 206

"Drought Conditions" (6/16) 19, 248n
Duchamp, Marcel 257n
Dumlao, Michael 50, 170, 195
du Prez, Jacqueline 126
Dylan, Bob 17, 194, 231n, 241–242n; *Blonde on Blonde* 231n; "Clothesline Saga" 17; *Highway 61 Revisited* 231n; "Highway 61 Revisited" 17; "Leopard-Skin Pill-Box Hat" 17; "The Times They Are a-Changin'" 194, 258n; "Union Sundown" 241n-242n
dyspraxia, implied condition of CJ Cregg 121, 122, 248n

Eagleton, Terry, 3, 54, 81, 82, 94, 95, 96, 99, 113, 181, 183, 184, 207, 208, 244n, 245n, 251n, 259n, 260n
Eco, Umberto 2, 251n
Ed and Larry (no given surnames) 115, 116
education in the series 169–175, 255n; as a silver bullet 169, 174, 175
Ehrlichman, John 14
"18th and Potomac" (2/21) 27
Einstein, Albert 141
Eisenhower, Dwight D. 26, 232n, 234n
"Election Day Part 1" (7/16) 118
"Election Night" (4/7) 194
"Ellie" (2/15) 20, 109, 188
Ellroy, James 29
"Enemies" (1/8) 10, 35, 50, 116, 230n, 234n
"Enemies Foreign and Domestic" (3/19) 30, 94, 168, 234n
Engels, Friedrich 84
Engelstad, Audun 180, 246n
"Eppur Si Muove" (5/16) 133, 213, 232n
Euripides 97
"Evidence of Things Not Seen" (4/20) 18, 172
existentialist discourse 4, 16, 98, 99, 113
Ezell, Pamela 33, 176

Fahy, Thomas 31, 33, 227n, 241n, 247n
Faison, Vic 10
"Faith Based Initiative" (6/10) 118, 172, 247n
Fallow, Dr. John 163, 164
Falls, Kevin 32, 35, 232n, 234n
"The Fall's Gonna Kill You" (2/20) 9, 16, 110, 172, 188, 247n
Fanon, Frantz 89
Farad, Nizar 233n, 254n
Farragut, Mark 59
feminist reading of the series 3, 47, 52, 57, 113, 119, 152–161, 207, 253n, 254n, 258n; definition of feminism 152; sexist nomenclature 254n; significant female characters in the series 153
A Few Good Men (Rob Reiner) 47
fictitious countries 25, 167; Kundu 25, 36, 107, 158, 167, 168, 179, 233n; Qumar 9, 25, 35, 60, 146, 153, 154, 162, 167, 168, 179, 194, 212, 233n, 244n

Fiderer, Deborah 258*n*
Fiedler, Leslie 102, 107, 116–117, 245*n*
Finkelstein, Joanne 63
Finn, Patrick 155, 204, 241*n*, 257*n*
Fitzwallace, Admiral Percy 18, 69,100, 101, 121, 130, 148, 162, 213, 229*n*, 234*n*, 245*n*
"Five Votes Down" (1/4) 49, 110, 123, 205, 233*n*, 249*n*, 259*n*
Fonda, Henry 14
Ford, Gerald 24, 232*n*, 233*n*
Fortis, Tabitha 59, 65
Foucault, Michel 78, 113, 114, 131, 165, 197, 198, 199, 258*n*, 259*n*; *Society Must Be Defended* 197–198
"Freedonia" (6/15) 18, 243*n*
Freud, Sigmund 63, 114, 120, 139, 141, 182, 183, 184, 185, 186, 188, 189, 244*n*, 257*n*; religion as a "universal neurosis" 141, 244*n*
Frost, David 148, 252*n*
"Full Disclosure" (5/15) 106, 234*n*

al-Gaddafi, Muammar 26, 229*n*, 233*n*
Gail (CJ's goldfish) 65
"Galileo" (2/9) 157, 234*n*, 246*n*
Gallop, Jane 113
"Game On" (4/6) 63, 122, 180, 240*n*
Gans-Boriskin, Rachel 69, 74, 146, 170, 178, 233*n*, 241*n*, 242*n*, 246*n*, 251*n*, 252*n*, 257*n*
Garber, Marjorie 114, 120, 183
Gardner Amy 14, 19, 110, 111, 153, 154, 155, 204, 237*n*, 247*n*, 253*n*
Garrett, Laura K. 157, 253*n*, 254*n*
Gault, Samuel 84
Gayle, Lesley 181
"Gaza" (5/21) 17, 35, 50, 51, 157, 162, 213
Gender Trouble (Judith Butler) 115
Germinal (Emile Zola) 79
Gerrard, Lisa 194
Gettysburg Address 258*n*; as example of an exordium 258*n*
The Ghost (Robert Harris) 252*n*
Gianelli, Bruno 9, 169, 174, 234*n*, 258*n*
Gillan, Thomas J. 72, 241*n*, 242*n*
Ginger (no given surname) 58, 156
Glasser, Laura 232*n* 253*n*
The Godfather (Francis Ford Coppola) 18–19, 149
The Godfather Part 2 (Francis Ford Coppola) 18–19
The Godfather Part 3 (Francis Ford Coppola) 18–19
Goldman, Akiva 236*n*-237*n*
Goldwag, Arthur 259*n*
"Gone Quiet" (3/7) 155
"A Good Day" (6/17) 71
Goodman, John 17
Gore, Al 7, 150, 179, 228*n*, 253*n*
Gramsci, Antonio 80
The Grapes of Wrath (John Steinbeck) 79

Graves, Alex 36, 144, 236*n*
The Great Escape (John Sturges) 16
the greatest country in the world 71–72, 86–91, 209, 241*n*
Greenwood, Bruce 15
Griffith, Millicent 20
Groundhog Day (Harold Ramis) 17
Grunwald, Mandy 6
Guantanamo Bay 150
Gulf War 1991 88, 148
Gulf War 2003 74, 88, 148, 150, 255*n*
gun control 13, 50, 178
"Guns Not Butter" (4/12) 240*n*, 243*n*

"H. Con-172" (3/11) 19, 110, 116, 229*n*, 234*n*
Haggis, Paul 107
Halderman, H.R. 14, 26
Hall, Ann C. 259*n*
Hall, Robert David 248*n*
Halloween episode (unmade) 67
Hamlet 16, 116, 247*n*
Hampton, Mandy 6, 26, 50, 58, 116, 117, 119, 120, 153, 154, 155, 156, 193, 211, 229*n*, 234*n*, 236*n*
"Han" (5/4) 9, 35, 232*n*
Handel, George Frederic 194
The Handmaid's Tale (Margaret Atwood) 256*n*
Hanegraaff, Hank 41–47, 238*n*
Hanks, Tom 258*n*
Hanson, Trudy L. 169, 251*n*
Harmon, Erica 257*n*
Harper, Kate 118, 248*n*
Harris, Robert 252*n*
"Hartsfield's Landing" (3/15) 16, 169
Hasselhoff, David 24
Havens, Richie 194, 258*n*
Hawking, Stephen 92, 99
Hayes, Ainsley 57, 58, 110, 121, 154, 155, 157, 159, 160, 247*n*, 254*n*, 257*n*
"He Shall from Time to Time" (1/12) 16, 18, 123, 171, 189
Hedren, Tippi 160
Hemingway, Ernest 7
"Here Today" (7/5) 10, 18, 120, 238*n*
Herr, Michael 91
Hilary and Jackie (Anand Tucker) 126
Hill, Dulé 69, 70, 100, 229*n*
Hirsch, Judd 228*n*
Hirway, Hrishikesh 260
Hitchens, Christopher 245*n*
Hitler, Adolf 148–149
Holland, Cathy 133
Holland, Jack 72, 74, 171, 242*n*
Hollis, Frank 179
the Holocaust 138, 140, 142, 200, 255*n*
"Holy Night" (4/11) 34, 212, 250*n*, 259*n*
Homeland 150
Homicide: Life on the Streets 246*n*, 250*n*

Index 273

homosociality 65, 115, 116, 240n, 247n-248n
Hooper, Margaret 154, 156, 157
Horrocks, Roger 113, 247n
Hotchkiss, Jamie 60
House of Cards 15, 16
Hoynes, John 10, 26, 55, 89, 90, 171, 176, 229n, 233n, 244n
HUAAC investigations 84
"The Hubbert Peak" (6/5) 63, 118
Huddleston, David 231n
Huke, Professor Donald 163, 164
Hume, David 245n
Humphrey, Hubert 23
Husserl, Edmund 202
Hyatt, Michael 133

"Impact Winter" (6/9) 18, 158, 246n, 250n, 257n
"In Excelsis Deo" (1/10) 8, 30, 33, 112, 133, 232n, 250n
"In God We Trust" (6/20) 44, 96
"In the Room" (6/8) 213, 233n
"In the Shadow of Two Gunmen Part 1" (2/1) 33, 71, 181
"In the Shadow of Two Gunmen Part 2" (2/2) 34, 122, 248n, 250n
"In This White House" (2/4) 25, 159, 193
"Inauguration Part 1: Over There" (4/14) 59, 107, 158
"Inauguration Part 2: Over There" (4/15) 17
"The Indians in the Lobby" (3/8) 9, 59, 81, 104, 212, 230n
"Institutional Memory" (7/21) 19, 179, 257n
intelligence of characters in the series 86, 93, 97, 119, 157, 171, 172, 177, 252n
"Internal Displacement" (7/11) 60, 87
intertextuality in the series 4, 13-21, 28, 30, 37, 55, 62, 131, 143, 149, 207, 231n-232n
"Isaac and Ishmael" (3/1) 17, 24, 34, 67, 68, 69, 70, 71, 74, 75, 94, 106, 133, 158, 162, 166, 194, 201, 209, 212, 235n, 238n, 242n, 249n; critical attention received by the episode 68; story-telling aberration 70
Isaacs, Jason 60
Isaiah, Book of 244n
Iser, Wolfgang 38

Jackman, Ian 246n
Jackson, Shirley 17
Jacobs, Dr. Jenna 10, 40-44, 46-47, 230n, 237n, 238n
James, Clive 109, 157, 173, 231n, 235n, 240n, 253n
James, Henry 62
Jameson, Frederic 129, 130, 131, 137, 139, 144
Janney, Allison 5, 6, 52, 69, 70, 155, 228n, 247n, 253n
Jauss, Hans Robert 236n
"Jefferson Lives" (3/22) 252n, 254n

JFK (Oliver Stone) 29
Johnson, Blind Willie 194
Johnson, Clark 250n
Johnson, Lyndon B. 23, 232n, 233n, 234n, 251n
Jones, Robert 69, 241n, 242n
Joyce, James 137, 195, 206
Julius Caesar 16
Jung, Carl 113, 247n

Kelly, Moira 6, 119
Kendall, Jordon 19, 58
Kennedy (television drama) 231n
Kennedy, Jacqueline 28
Kennedy, John F. 6, 15, 23, 27, 30, 59, 90, 93, 124, 192, 231n, 232n, 234n, 248n, 251n; assassination of 28-29, 88, 235n; as a constant presence in the series 27-29
Kennedy, Robert 50, 230n; assassination of 50
Kessler, Donald J. 173; Kessler Effect 173
Keyworth, Stanley 10, 59, 100, 186
Khoday, Amar 256n
Kierkgaard, Soren 98
Kim, Young Hoon 146, 206, 241n, 251n
"King Corn" (6/13)
King George III 102
King Lear 16, 19-21, 232n
Kinsey, Alfred 120
Kooijman, Jaap 76, 240n-241n
Kostroff, Michael 133
Krauss, Lawrence M. 145
Kristeva, Julia 13
Kubrick, Stanley 17-18, 50, 194, 196, 228n, 236n, 238n, 252n; *A Clockwork Orange* 18; *Dr. Strangelove: Or How I Learned to Stop Worrying and Love the Bomb* 17-18; *Eyes Wide Shut* 17, 231n; *The Shining* 18, 50, 238n; *Spartacus* 18

Lacan, Jacques 61, 182, 184, 185, 186, 188, 189, 199, 257n, 258n; mirror stage 185; Name of the Father 182, 185, 186, 187, 188, 257n
"The Lame Duck Congress" (2/6) 89, 254n
Landingham, Delores 20, 55, 58, 61, 64, 109, 130, 154, 156, 157, 178, 182, 186, 187, 188, 189, 212, 239n, 260n; surrogate mother to Bartlet 186, 188
Lane, Christina 82
Lassiter, Owen 24, 233n
"The Last Hurrah" (7/20) 133, 158
Laussen, Steve 87
Law, Cardinal Bernard Francis 94, 244n
"The Leadership Breakfast" (2/11) 19, 117
Lehman, David 208, 259n
Leno, Jay 24
Lerner, Alan Jay 28
"Let Bartlet be Bartler" (1/19) 111, 143, 157, 189

Index

Levi-Strauss, Claude 54, 55, 57
Levine, Myron A. 255n, 256n
Levy, Eugene 228n
"Lies, Damn Lies and Statistics" (1/21) 23, 231n, 243n
limerence 38, 236n
Lippman, Laura 256n
literature review 2–3, 228n
Lobell, Max 231n
Lone Feather, Jack 105
"The Long Goodbye" (4/13) 35, 122, 180, 212
"Lord John Marbury" (1/11) 18
"The Lottery" (Shirley Jackson) 17
Love and Death in the American Novel (Leslie Fiedler) 117–118
Lovejoy, Deirdre 133
Lowe, Frederick 28
Lowe, Rob 5, 69, 70, 87, 236n, 255n
Lucas, Joey 58, 117, 121, 153, 154, 155, 248n, 258n
Lydell, Lowell 112
Lyman, Josh 6, 9, 16, 18, 19, 26, 27, 50, 55, 57, 58, 60, 63, 64, 65, 67, 71, 72, 73, 75, 76, 81, 89, 93, 100, 102, 103, 104, 110, 111, 115, 116, 117, 118, 119, 121, 123, 139, 154, 156, 157, 158, 159, 166, 170, 186, 204, 211, 213, 227n, 228n, 231n, 233n, 235, 239n, 240n, 242n, 246n, 247n, 248n, 254n, 256n, 260n
Lyon, David 53, 137, 139, 251n
Lyotard, Jean François 137

Ma, Yo Yo 194
Macbeth 16
"Mad Cow Disease" 179
Madam Secretary 231n
Magruder, Jeb 234n
Malden, Karl 230n
Malina, Joshua 14, 15, 192, 195, 229n, 246n, 257n, 260n
"Manchester Part 1" (3/3) 237n
"Manchester Part 2" (3/3) 60, 106, 174
"Mandatory Minimums" (1/20) 19, 28, 111, 119, 157, 249n
Marathon Man (John Schlesinger) 238n
Marbury, Lord John 106, 243n
Marcus, Ted 18, 111
Marina (no given surname) 243n, 254n
Martin, Marlee 121, 258n
Marx, Karl 78, 79, 80, 82, 83, 84, 141
Marx Brothers 243n
Marxist reading of the series 3, 78–85. 131, 139, 141, 207, 243n; alienation 82; class issue within the series 63, 78, 79, 80, 82, 83, 113, 116, 131, 200, 205, 243n; *Critique of Hegel's Philosophy of Right* 83; as grandest of grand narratives 84, 95, 244n; religion, Marxist views on 83–84, 141
Massive Attack 194
Matheson, Tim 229n

Matlin, Marlee 121, 258n
Mayers, Michael 2, 227n, 238n
McAvoy, Will 86
McCabe, Janet 50, 132, 177, 193, 195, 206, 227n, 229n, 230n, 238n, 239n
McCarthy, Joseph 78, 84
McCarthy, Thomas 250n
McCormack, John 23
McGarry, Leo 5, 7, 15, 17, 18, 19, 25, 26, 41, 44, 49, 55, 57, 58, 60, 67, 75, 76, 80, 81, 101, 104, 110, 112, 116, 118, 121, 129, 130, 139, 143, 144, 146, 147, 149, 154, 156, 167, 171, 172, 178, 180, 181, 188, 211, 213, 214, 228n, 229n, 231n, 232n, 233n, 234n, 235n, 236n, 237n, 238n, 240n, 242n, 244n, 245n, 246n, 247n, 249n, 253n, 256n, 260n
McGovern, George 6
McLuhan, Marshall 242n
McNally, Nancy 59, 71, 100, 153, 154
McQueen, Steve 16
Mecca Girl Intermediate School tragedy 95; fictionalized depiction in the series 95
"Memorial Day (5/22) 35, 213
Mendoza, Roberto 11, 193, 230n, 237n, 247n
Mercator, Geradus 163, 164
"Message of the Week" (7/3) 234n, 238n
"The Midterms" (2/3) 10, 40, 52, 211, 260n
Miller, Steve 194
mise en scène of the series 49–53; average shot length (ASL) 52; camera movement 51; cinematic quality of the series 49; conventional mood of expression 51; lighting 49, 50–51; montage, use of 52; picture definition 51; set design 49; steadicam, use of 49, 50, 213, 238n; voice-over 52; "walk and talk" scenes 14, 49
Misiano, Christopher 36, 236n
The Missiles of October (television drama) 230n
"Mr. Frost" (7/4) 194, 234n
Mr. Smith Goes to Washington (Frank Capra) 16, 181
"Mr. Willis of Ohio" (1/6) 16, 17, 117, 170, 231n, 245n, 246n
modernism 53, 136, 142
Modine, Matthew 256n
Moloney, Janel 52, 69, 158, 231n, 253n
"The Mommy Problem" (7/2) 52, 194
Monod, Jacques 96
Moore, Kevin Roosevelt 195
Morningstar Charles, Maggie 105
Morrison, Toni 102, 245n–246n
Moss, Donna 16, 27, 52, 58, 60, 63, 67, 110, 117, 118, 154, 156, 157, 158, 160, 162, 170, 172, 173, 180, 204, 231n, 243n, 246n, 248n, 254n
Moss, Elizabeth 229n, 256n
Mouton, Michelle 20, 179, 229n
Mozart, Wolfgang Amadeus 194
Muffley, Merkin 18, 228n

multiple sclerosis 9, 56, 70, 90, 121, 122, 123, 124, 125, 126, 127, 144, 146, 161, 175, 193, 212, 213, 229n, 231n, 238n, 248n, 249n, 257n; films with MS as a central narrative device 249n
Mulvey, Laura 253n-254n
Mutimer, David 93, 154, 156, 205, 241n, 245n, 247n
Myers, Dee Dee 6, 32
Mythologies (Roland Barthes) 30, 239n

Naidu, Ajay 75
National Review 11, 230n
Native Americans 88, 104, 105, 212
Nein, John 259n
Nelson, Kirsten 186
Newman, D. Wire 24, 233n
The Newsroom 86, 250n
Nicholson, Jack 231n
"Night Five" (3/14) 10, 100, 159, 168, 186, 242n, 246n
"Ninety Miles Away" (6/19) 27, 213, 233n, 240n
Nixon, Richard 6, 14, 22, 23, 24, 26, 57, 148, 228n, 232n, 233n, 234n, 248n, 251n, 252n
"No Exit" (5/20) 16
No Exit (Satre play) 16
"Noël" (2/10) 194, 211, 217, 250n
Nosebleed (unmade Jackie Chan film) 241n

"O Superman" (Laurie Anderson) 241n
Obama, Barack 150, 173, 209, 228n, 245n, 249n, 252n, 253n
O'Brien, Mallory 28, 58, 59, 110, 169, 174, 231n; derivation of name 240n
Occam's Razor 97
O'Connor, John E. 32, 227n
O'Connor, Molly 59, 130
O'Donnell, Lawrence 182, 235n
O'Leary, Deborah 240n
"On the Day Before" (3/5) 26, 193
"100,000 Airplanes" (3/12) 27, 71, 115, 237n
"Opposition Research" (6/11) 52, 213
Orientalism (Edward Said) 162, 166

Paine, Thomas 89
"La Palabra" 232n
Parry-Giles, Shawn J. and Trevor 32, 38, 69, 93, 100, 105,107, 110, 143, 146, 147, 148, 149, 154, 156, 166, 171, 179, 227n, 241n, 245n, 257n
Paxton, Nathan 104, 130, 177, 178, 229n, 256n
Penn and Teller 213, 233n
Pennebaker, D.A. 17, 144
Philadelphia (Jonathan Demme) 258n
Phillips, Adam 243n
Philpott, Simon 93, 154, 156, 205, 241n, 245n, 247n
Pierce, Ryan 243n

"Pilot" (1/1) 5, 17, 33, 44, 49, 59, 63, 117, 122, 123, 185, 193, 211, 229n, 233n, 236n, 237n, 238n, 239n, 246n
Plato 149; "noble fable" 179, 252n
Podhoretz, John 176
Poitier, Sidney 228n
Polanski, Roman 252n
Pompper, Donnalyn 179, 245n
"The Portland Trip" (2/7) 111
"Posse Comitatus" (3/22) 34, 194. 212, 232n, 252n
"Post Hoc, Ergo Propter Hoc" (1/2) 9, 117, 232n, 248n
post traumatic stress disorder 121, 211, 255n
postcolonialism 3, 89, 162-168, 207, 254n
The Postmodern Condition (Jean François Lyotard) 137
postmodernism 3, 53, 70, 131, 135-145, 183, 207, 208, 250n, 251n, 259n; the cultural logic of late capitalism 139-140; grand narratives 137-138; hyper-reality 138-139
poststructuralism 13, 36, 37, 114, 197-204, 207, 239n, 259n
Pounder CCH 228n, 240n
Primary Colors (Mike Nichols) 155
"Privateers" (4/18) 60, 237n
"Process Stories" (4/8) 169
"A Proportional Response" (1/3) 27, 33, 101, 117, 189, 211
Pryor, Nicholas 234n
psychoanalytical reading of the series 3, 61, 182-190, 207, 257n; castration symbolism 64; Freudian symbols 63-64, 65, 188, 189, 258n; oedipal relationships 185, 186, 188
Puar, Jasbir 75, 242n, 249n

Queen Elizabeth II 26, 233n
Quinn, Edward 201
Qumar 9, 25, 35, 60, 146, 153, 154, 162, 167, 168, 179, 194, 212, 233n, 244n

racist issues in the series 3, 4, 6, 57, 59, 75. 76, 100-108, 129, 205, 207, 211, 212, 228n, 242n, 245n, 246n; the British, clichéd attitude towards 104, 106; Charlie as "bodyman" 100, 101; Charlie as stereotyped black character 101; CJ, racist views 105-106; the French, clichéd attitude towards 60-61, 104, 106, 198; lynching 101, 103; Native Americans, racist attitudes to 104-105, 246n; token black characters 101, 129, 229n; violence and race 29, 89, 101; in *The Wire* 129-130
Rafferty, Ricky 58
Rai, Amit 75, 242n, 249n
reader response theories 30, 36, 37-38, 123, 199, 203, 207, 208, 236n, 244n, 250n, 252n
Reagan, Ronald 24, 230n, 232n, 233n, 248n
"Red Haven's on Fire" (4/17) 36, 160

"The Red Mass" (4/4) 60, 167
Reddick, Lance 133
Redford, Paul 235n
Rees, Roger 243n
Reese, Daisy 119
Reid, Taylor 239n
Reiner, Rob 13, 47
religion in the series 3, 4, 48, 57, 72, 76, 83–84, 92–99, 112, 113, 114, 120, 136, 139, 141, 142, 166, 167, 189, 209, 211, 238n, 242n, 243n, 244n, 247n, 257n; the Bible 26, 41, 42, 44, 45, 47, 94, 96, 244n; Christianity, attitudes to 41, 43, 43, 44, 47, 55, 56, 62, 73, 95, 96, 97, 112–113, 237n, 243n, 245n, 247n; eschatological discourse 95; Islam, attitudes to 73, 94, 95, 96, 104, 106, 113, 142n, 162, 165, 166, 168, 170, 212, 241n, 244n, 255n; Judaism, attitudes to 42, 43, 73, 95, 96, 165, 242n, 245n, 255n, 257n; Puritanism, impact on religion in USA 94, 112, 244n; the Quran 96, 242n; "sacred" texts 37, 96
Rendezvous with Rama (Arthur C. Clarke) 241n
"Requiem" (7/18) 7
Revere, Paul 186
Richardson, Kay 170
Richardson, Mark 129
Richardson Hayton, Heather 111, 257n
Richie, Robert 6, 7, 63, 122, 179, 180, 229n, 256n
Robards, Jason 14, 228n
Robbins, Tim 17, 144
Roberts, Chris 250n
Robertson, Cliff 14
Rocky (John G. Avildsen) 238n
Roedecker 23, 24, 232n
Rollins, Clement 234n
Rollins, Laurie 5, 58, 155, 156, 241n, 253n
Rollins, Peter C. 32, 155, 227n
roman à clef 6
Roosevelt, Franklin D. 124
Rosenberg, Yair 178, 255n
Rosencrantz and Guildenstern 116
Roszak, Theodore 97
Ruditis, Paul 246n
"Running Mates" (7/10) 7, 27, 214, 234n, 240n, 253n
Russell, Bertrand 92, 98
Russell, Lloyd 117
Russell, Robert ("Bongo Bob") 171, 172, 213n
Russell, William 14
Russo, Julie Levin 170

Said, Edward 162, 164, 165, 254n
Salieri, Antonio 194
Salinger, Pierre 27, 251n
Santos, Helen 18, 27, 65, 133, 158, 174
Santos, Matt 18, 19, 27, 65, 116, 119, 133, 158, 174, 213, 214, 229n, 229n, 238n, 256n

Sartre, Jean Paul 16, 98
Sayles, Dr. Cynthia 163
Scandal 15
Schaffner, Franklin F. 14
Schiff, Richard 5, 6, 7, 35, 69, 70, 228n, 245n, 256n
Schlamme, Thomas 34, 36, 236n, 256n
Schlessinger, Laura 40, 46, 237n
Schmidt, Lauren 144
Schott, Annabeth 63
Seaborn, Sam 5, 6, 19, 28, 55, 58, 66, 67, 72, 73, 84, 87, 89, 93, 101, 110, 111, 116, 117, 118, 139, 154, 155, 156, 157, 159, 160, 167, 169, 178, 211, 227n, 229n, 236n, 239n, 240n, 243n, 247n, 248n, 254n, 256n, 257n, 258n, 260n; sexual harassment 159–160, 254n
Sedgwick, Eve Kosofsky 115
Segal, Lynne 153, 258n
semiotic approach 54, 55, 63, 64, 65, 207
sentimentalized discourse in the series 1, 4, 10, 94, 98, 99, 108, 126, 128, 139, 145, 151, 180, 192, 193, 194, 195, 196, 209, 227n, 258n
"Separation of Powers" (5/7) 232n
September 11, 2001 24, 67–77, 94, 133, 150, 151, 158, 168, 171, 240n, 241n, 242n, 251n
"7A WF 83429" (5/1) 26, 64, 194, 234n, 257n
"17 People" (2/18) 16, 18, 26, 34, 211, 228n, 247n, 254n
Sexual Behaviour in the Human Male (Alfred Kinsey) 120
sexual relationships, paucity of 109, 110–111
sexuality 3, 4, 45, 46, 109–120. 153, 155, 159, 183, 184, 198, 242n, 247n, 258n; bisexuality 114, 119, 183; cross-dressing 247n; "gay marriage" 247n; heterosexuality 46, 56, 57, 111, 112, 114, 115, 116, 117, 118, 120, 184, 238n, 247n; homophobia 40, 46, 112, 113, 115, 116, 117; homosexuality 40, 41, 42, 43, 45, 46, 62, 111, 112, 113, 115, 117, 118, 120, 132, 153, 239n–240n, 245n, 247n, 252n; queer theory 113–116, 120; theoretical perspectives 113–115
Shakespeare, William 16, 19, 20, 21, 63, 143, 247n
Shales, Tom 68
Shareef, Abdul 9, 146; assassination of 9, 25, 147, 148, 149, 150, 162, 168, 204, 212, 252n
Sheen, Martin 5, 6, 7, 8, 11–12, 14, 15, 17, 61, 69, 99, 214, 228n, 229n, 230n, 248n
Shepard, Matthew 112
Shepherd, Andrew 230n
"Shibboleth" (2/8) 16, 179, 186, 189, 211, 232n
"The Short List" (1/9) 10, 89, 193, 211, 237n, 247n
"Shutdown" (5/8) 52, 180, 213, 254n
Simon, David 128, 131, 134, 235n, 249n, 250n
Simpson, Mark 247n
Sims, David 173

Index   277

"Six Meetings Before Lunch" (1/18) 16, 26, 103, 119, 169, 211, 246n, 250n
Skinner, Matt 111
slavery in the series 41, 42, 59, 81, 88, 100, 102, 103, 106, 107, 211, 243n, 245n, 246n
"Slow News Day" (5/12) 213, 256n
Smits, Jimmy 229n
"Somebody's Going to Emergency, Somebody's Going to Jail" (2/16) 84, 116, 163
Song, Angeline M.G. 254n
Sons and Lovers (D.H. Lawrence) 79
Sontag, Susan 3, 89
The Sopranos 181, 235n, 259n
Sorkin, Aaron 1, 2, 4, 5, 7, 13, 14, 15, 25, 30, 42, 44, 47, 52, 59, 62, 80, 86, 87, 90, 93, 101, 122, 129, 132, 144, 166, 176, 178, 180, 181, 185, 191, 192, 195, 205, 209, 212, 227n, 229n, 231n, 232n, 234n, 236n, 237n, 245n, 248n, 250n, 253n, 256n, 258n, 259n, 260n; authorship of the series 31–39, 228n, 235n, 236n; choice of published scripts 34; departure from the series 35, 236n; drug use 249n, 250n; educational approach 170, 174, 175; "Isaac and Ishmael" episode, writing of 67–68, 240n, 241n, 242n; meter of dialogue 35; misogynist approaches 152, 155, 159; plagiarism, charges of 40, 44–45
Spargo, Tasmin 114
Spencer, John 5, 7, 69, 70, 214, 228n, 229n, 231; death of 7, 260n
Spigel, Lynn 165, 169, 170, 241n
Sports Night 191, 258n
Stackhouse, Howard 14, 121
"The Stackhouse Filibuster" (2/17) 110, 116, 237n, 239n
Stark, Ann 59
"The State Dinner" (1/7) 27, 104, 116, 123, 179, 193, 246n
Stendhal 245n
Stephanopoulos, George 6, 241n
"Stirred" (3/18) 16, 244n
Stone, Oliver 29, 229n
"The Stormy Present" (5/10) 35
Straight Sex (Lynn Segal) 153
structuralist readings of the series 3, 54–66, 114, 198, 199, 200, 203, 207, 239n; binary oppositions 55, 56–57; character driven quality of the series 6; gender ambivalent female names 58; phallic semiotics of the necktie 55, 63–65; profane language 59–62, 109, 132, 182, 237n, 246n, 250n; proper names 55, 57–59; scatological nomenclature 59–60
Sturgeon, Theodore 52, 140, 239n
Stuttaford, Andrew 11–12, 230n
Suffragettes 242n
Superman (comic book) 70
"The Supremes" (5/17) 133, 237n, 243n, 246n, 254n

Sutherland, Kiefer 16
Sutin, L. Anthony 230n
"Swiss Diplomacy" (4/9) 35, 59

"Take Out the Trash Day" (1/13) 109, 110, 112, 156, 188, 234n
"Take the Sabbath Day" (1/14) 9, 51, 110, 211, 237n
"Talking Points" (5/19) 245n
Tanner '88 15, 231n
Teamsters Union 179
A Terrible Beauty (Peter Watson) 166
Thatch, Bernard 59, 106
Thecla, Niamh 253n
"Things Fall Apart" (6/21) 116, 231n
"Third Day Story" (6/3) 116, 180, 237n
Third Watch (television drama) 241n
Thirteen Days 15, 231n
Thompson, Damian 166
Thornton, Lou 58
Thuman, Kenny
"The Ticket" (7/1) 125, 240n, 250n
Tisinger, Russ 69, 74, 146, 170, 178, 233n, 241n, 242n, 246n, 251n, 252n, 257n
Tolliver, Michael 101, 187, 230n
"Tomorrow" (7/22) 20, 27, 38, 59, 65, 158, 185, 194, 197, 235n, 239n, 240n
Topping, Keith 2, 68, 73, 105, 192, 232n, 234n, 235
Travolta, John 155
Tribbey, Roger 16
Triplehorn, Wendell 59
Truman, Harry 11
Tucker, Anand 126
The Turn of the Screw (novel) 62
The Turn of the Screw (opera) 62
25th Amendment 15, 23, 232n
"Twenty-Five" (4/23) 23, 34, 193, 212, 236n
"20 Hours in America" (4/1/2) 18, 27, 34, 192, 194, 212, 254n
"20 Hours in L.A." (1/16) 18, 24, 111
"The Two Bartlets" (3/13) 102, 105, 187, 237n, 246n
"Two Cathedrals" (2/22) 16, 20, 34, 55, 61, 92, 144, 186, 187, 194, 212, 246n; use of Latin in 20, 55, 61, 62, 212, 240n
"2162 Votes" (6/22) 51, 52

Ulysses (James Joyce) 206
Uncertainty Principle, Heisenberg's 201
"Undecideds" (7/8) 257n
Underwood, Frank 15, 231n
Underworld (Don Delillo) 231n
United 93 passengers 71, 74 , 75; as suicide bombers 74–75
The Untouchables 149
"The U.S. Poet Laureate" (3/17) 65, 231n, 254n
usury 44

Index

Vaughn, Robert 14, 231n
Veep 231n
Vest, Jason P. 32, 52
Vicomte de Bourbon, Jean-Paul 60, 106, 249n
Vidal, Gore 14, 231n
Vietnam War 7, 75, 88, 104, 148, 156, 213, 232n, 234n
viewing figures 68, 227n, 236n, 241n
Vinick, Arnold 57, 96, 121, 160, 213, 214, 228n, 229n, 234n, 238n
Von Trier, Lars 194

W (Oliver Stone) 229
"The Wake-Up Call" (6/14) 235n
Walden, W.G. Snuffy 2, 191–196, 258n; soundtrack music to the series 2, 36, 69, 132, 191, 192, 193, 194, 195, 196, 209, 250n, 258n; source music, use of in the series 194–195
Walken, Glen Allen 17, 26, 64, 212, 235n, 257n
Walton, Celia 159, 160
"The War at Home" (2/14) 125, 193, 233n, 234n
"War Crimes" (3/6) 10
"The Warfare of Genghis Khan" (5/1) 35, 194
Washington, George 22, 231n, 234n
Washington Behind Closed Doors 14, 234n
Washington Redskins 41, 43, 246n
Watergate 26, 88, 124, 212, 232n, 234n, 248n
Watson, Peter 98, 166, 202, 244n, 245n, 252n
"Ways and Means" 234n, 247n, 250n
"We Killed Yamamoto" (3/21) 122, 146, 147
websites, most useful on the series, 23, 228n
"The Wedding" (7/9) 118, 194
Wegland, Doug 174
"Welcome to Wherever You Are" (7/15) 17, 233n
Wells, John 31, 68, 228n, 237n
The West Wing Weekly (podcast) 192, 228n, 243n, 245n, 246n, 247n, 248n, 254n, 257n, 258n, 260n
Westin, Doug 87, 161
"What Kind of Day Has It Been" (1/22) 102, 119
White, Theodore 28
White House 13, 15, 18, 25, 28, 30, 36, 38, 40, 49, 51, 52, 55, 59, 64, 65, 66, 67, 68, 71, 75, 87, 100, 101, 109, 110, 112, 117, 144, 146, 153, 157, 158, 161, 174, 176, 180, 185, 206, 210, 231n, 234n, 237n, 239n, 255n, 256n, 257n, 258n, 259n
"The White House Pro-Am" (1/17) 157
Whitford, Bradley 5, 6, 69, 70. 76, 228n, 248n
Williams, Delaney 250n
Williams, Rebecca 38
Williams, William Carlos 136
Willson, Felicia 253n
Wilson, Woodrow 124, 230n
Winnicott, Donald 38
The Wire 59, 79, 81, 111, 128–134, 174, 181, 233n, 235n, 243n, 246n, 247n, 249n, 250n; as Dickensian novel 131; as Greek tragedy 131
Wodak, Ruth 30, 70
Wolfe, Lisa 133
Wolff, Michael A. 35
"The Women of Qumar" (3/9) 60, 153, 179, 212, 244n
Woodward, Bob 234n
Woolf, Virginia 136
work ethic in the series 6, 41, 66, 76, 80, 82, 83, 110, 139, 154, 156, 157, 177, 206, 242n
Worrell, Tracy 124, 125
Wyatt, Andy 58, 59, 110, 204

Yarlett, Claire 47
Young, Charlie 59, 60, 61, 64, 65, 81, 100, 101, 109, 110, 117, 133, 139, 186, 193, 229n, 245n, 248n
Young, Neil 258n

Zedong, Mao 72, 241n
Zero Dark Thirty (Kathryn Bigelow) 150, 252n
Ziegler, Ronald 57, 251n
Ziegler, Toby 6, 7, 16, 57, 58, 59, 60, 63, 65, 67, 73, 81, 89, 102, 104, 106, 110, 111, 117, 139, 156, 159, 168, 169, 171, 173, 187, 193, 204, 211, 212, 213, 227n, 228n, 229n, 230n, 231n, 239n, 240n, 242n, 243n, 244n, 248n, 249n, 254n, 256n, 257n, 259n, 260n; insider trading 259n; moral conscience of the series 8, 10, 26, 168, 229n, 242n; sexual misconduct 254n
Žižek, Slajov 130, 131, 250n
Zoller, Heather A. 124, 125

www.ingramcontent.com/pod-product-compliance
Lightning Source LLC
Chambersburg PA
CBHW021349300426
44114CB00012B/1147